Mark Simpson • Tony Hawkins

The Primacy of Regime Survival

State Fragility and Economic Destruction in Zimbabwe

palgrave
macmillan

Mark Simpson
University of London
London, UK

Tony Hawkins
University of Zimbabwe
Harare, Zimbabwe

ISBN 978-3-030-10219-7 ISBN 978-3-319-72520-8 (eBook)
https://doi.org/10.1007/978-3-319-72520-8

Cover illustration: Image Source / Alamy Stock Photo

Printed on acid-free paper

This Palgrave Macmillan imprint is published by the registered company Springer International Publishing AG part of Springer Nature.
The registered company address is: Gewerbestrasse 11, 6330 Cham, Switzerland

The Primacy of Regime Survival

"The destruction of Zimbabwe's economy and institutions over the last four decades has been nothing short of spectacular. This carefully researched book shows that the cause of this carnage is the attempts of Robert Mugabe's regime to survive by polarizing society, rewarding the regime's cronies and weakening the economy. A must-read for anybody interested in learning from Zimbabwe's mistakes so that we can better defend against other autocrats doing the same."

—Daron Acemoglu, *Elizabeth and James Killian Professor of Economics at MIT, and co-author of Why Nations Fail - The Origins of Power, Prosperity and Poverty*

"If you want an authoritative, dispassionate and forensic analysis of Zimbabwe's catastrophic economic decline, set in political context, go straight for this definitive work by Hawkins and Simpson. Their exposure of the way the country's ruling Zanu-PF party turned a once-thriving economy into a milch cow for an elite, whilst systematically subjugating dissent and enforcing an increasingly despotic regime, makes for an engrossing read. The authors pose some awkward questions about the performance of the IMF and the World Bank: should they have done more to expose Mugabe's venal regime? And above all, are they in danger of making the same mistake when dealing with the new regime of President Emmerson Mnangagwa?"

—Michael Holman, *former Africa editor of the* Financial Times

"The book describes the economic and political history of post-independence Zimbabwe. It focuses on the causes of the country's economic collapse, and details the policies and processes that drove it. It is the only volume I've seen of its kind that covers the entire post-independence period. The referencing is outstanding and it shows genuine scholarship. It is a book that an interested layman would find fascinating and I'd see the international diplomatic and economic community being genuinely interested. It is also well referenced, bringing in both general theory and local documents. Both authors have impeccable credentials."

—Tony Leiman, *School of Economics, University of Cape Town*

"At a time of momentous change in Harare and across Southern Africa, this timely study is a must read for anyone who wants to know if economic prospects are set to take a turn for the better."

—Ed Balls, *Senior Research Fellow, Kennedy School of Government, Harvard and former UK Shadow Chancellor of the Exchequer (2011–2015)*

Administrative map of Zimbabwe

To Natalie Inês and Nicholas Tiago who were also there, and above all to Allison who shared the space at the coalface.
M.S.
To Glynne who shares the frustrations and disappointments of life in a fragile state, as well as the hope of better days to come.
T.H.

"As usurpation is the exercise of power, which another has a right to; so tyranny is the exercise of power beyond right, which nobody can have a right to. And this is making use of the power any one has in his hands, not for the good of those who are under it, but for his own private advantage. When the governor, however intitled, makes not the law, but his will the rule; and his commands and actions are not directed to the preservation of the properties of his people, but the satisfaction of his own ambition, revenge, covetousness, or another other irregular passion"

—John Locke, *Two Treatises on Government (1689)*

Preface

The military coup of November 2017, which eventually forced the resignation of Robert Mugabe and led to the evisceration of the ZANU-PF faction associated with his wife's political ambitions, was the logical conclusion of the creeping militarization of the Zimbabwean state, a dominant aspect of the country's political, social and economic regression. The new President's reimbursement for the long-standing support of the military and War Veterans – essential props in the maintenance of the extractive political and economic institutions that had long determined the country's trajectory and enabled his move into State House – was both immediate and generous.

The Commander of the Zimbabwe Defence Forces was rewarded with the post of Vice-President, the Major-General who had acted as spokesperson for the military during the November events took over the Foreign Ministry, and the Commander of the Air Force became the Minister of Agriculture and Land Affairs. The leader of the War Veterans, who had helped orchestrate demonstrations of support for Mnangagwa during the bitter succession struggle between the latter and the President's wife which eventually triggered the putsch, took on the role of Special Advisor to the President. Hopes were quickly dashed that ZANU-PF's new leader would reach out to the opposition parties and form a coalition government to oversee the necessary reforms to pave the way for free and fair elections scheduled for later this year. In addition to the dominant presence of securocrats in the new Cabinet, all other posts were distributed to old ZANU-PF notables linked to the Mnangagwa faction.

Retribution was also swift, with the full prosecutorial powers of the state deployed to settle scores with opponents within the ruling party. While Mugabe and his immediate family were allowed to remain in the country, and granted a series of privileges and immunities, a number of senior ranking officials from the former administration were not so favoured. Former Ministers and their minions who had not slipped out of the country have been targeted by the country's anti-corruption agency, and those who did manage to escape have had their assets seized. The highly selective singling out of individuals on charges of corruption and abuse of office – which many in the new dispensation would be hard-pressed to mount a credible defence against should the net be widened – has also provided further and extraordinary insights into the extent of the plundering under Mugabe.

Photos of police charge sheets listing hundreds of properties accumulated by insiders from the Mugabe era, reports of stashes of foreign currency found in the homes of those who had gone to ground, and footage of the palatial mansions of beneficiaries of the former patronage networks (including a 54 room mansion that allegedly belonged to the former Minister in charge of Indigenisation), circulated widely within the country. They have shocked even those Zimbabweans who had seemingly become inured to the venality of their leaders.

Notwithstanding such highly visible, and widely trumpeted, demonstrations of good intent by the new administration, a huge leap of faith is required to buy into the government's narrative that the military coup heralds a 'New Dispensation' and 'New Economic Order'. Two elements stand out in the post-coup economic narrative – that only one man, Robert Mugabe, and only a small handful of his close associates, are responsible for the country's protracted economic decline, and that 'bold reforms' promised by the Mnangagwa administration will turn the economy around overnight.

While there is an apparent consensus amongst many domestic and foreign observers that the Mnangagwa administration is more likely to implement economic reforms than its predecessor, with the ruling party in electoral mode expectations are being stoked with scant regard to the economic and social reality on the ground. An extreme example was Mnangagwa's recent claim that $3 billion in foreign investment had been secured in just seven weeks to February 2018. In this heady atmosphere, the new administration is planting the seeds of another future crisis of expectations, not least because it portrays the post-coup mantra of 're-engagement with the international community' as all gain and no pain.

That the economy will benefit from the removal of the obdurately anti-reform Mugabe and some of those around him is undeniable, but the state and party architecture, and the dirigiste mind-set within which it operates, will continue to determine any reform trajectory. The extension and expansion of the 'command agriculture' programme referenced in this book, a pet project of the new President, carried out with the extensive involvement of the military when he was Mugabe's deputy, and now backed up by the former Major-General in charge of the portfolio, is a clear sign of the strong elements of continuity at work.

This is also obvious already in the rejection of political reform, most notably foot dragging in terms of granting the significant (and potentially decisive) number of Diaspora Zimbabweans an opportunity to exercise their right to vote in their current countries of residence. There is virtually no new blood at political level, while the bureaucracy was untouched by the putsch. As a result, it is hardly surprising that after the initial public euphoria that accompanied Mugabe's relinquishing of office, many now view the November 2017 coup as a domestic spat, with septuagenarians replacing a nonagenarian, all being hewn from the same wood.

In espousing what he calls the 'China model' of economic development, Mnangagwa hopes that Zimbabwe will emulate the bad-politics, good-economics strategies that have proved so attractive to many African leaders. Some foreign investors, IFI staff and bilateral donors are only too willing to accept this 'good enough governance' stance for Zimbabweans, their justification being that a bad solution is better than none, a replay of the myopia of their earlier efforts during the 1980s and 1990s at promoting reform.

To the very limited extent that it has been articulated, the economic reform menu is essentially similar to that of the unsuccessful Economic Structural Adjustment Programme, and other reform programmes of the past. Then as now, the authorities have committed themselves to public sector reform, including privatisation, fiscal deficit reduction, trade, investment and monetary liberalization and a reduction of the civil service payroll. In its 38 years in office, not one of these policies has been adopted on a sustained basis, posing the question why the post-coup future should be any different.

The gain-without-pain scenario promoted assiduously by the government and its state media publicity arm assumes, for example, that a massive international bailout, including as much as $8 billion for farm compensation, itself a hugely unrealistic number, will be forthcoming. The Structural Adjustment package of 1991 was less than $1 billion a year for 5 years, but current estimates are that Zimbabwe will need $30 to $40 billion over ten years.

Policymakers are similarly reluctant to discuss the economics of job creation, taking refuge in grandiose and meaningless promises to generate a million jobs a year, equivalent to jobs growth of 15 percent of formal employment each year. Over the long haul in Zimbabwe employment has grown at half the rate of output, which means that GDP would have to increase by 30 percent annually. Since this is not going to happen, the realistic conclusion is that millions of the 200,000 well-educated school and university leavers each year who fail to get formal jobs will continue to have to choose between the informal sector and joining the Diaspora.

Politicians have long been content to sweep such long-term problems under the carpet of an exploding informal sector and deepening rural poverty, especially in communal farming areas. But two immediate challenges that cannot be hidden from public scrutiny are the unsustainable debt burden and the currency regime.

At the end of 2016, foreign debt was $9.4 billion or 57 percent of GDP. This has since increased by at least $2 billion, mostly through new offshore borrowings (another strong element of continuity in terms of economic management) from Zimbabwe's new lender of last resort, the Cairo-based Afreximbank, and which the Reserve Bank of Zimbabwe claims is partly being used to back the continued printing of bond notes in its efforts to solve the country's liquidity problems. Simultaneously, domestic debt – denominated in US dollars, which means it cannot be inflated away as happened with Zimbabwe dollar debt during hyperinflation – has burgeoned to over $6 billion. This debt will likely exceed $8 billion by the end of 2018, by which time the debt-to-GDP ratio will likely exceed 100 percent.

These numbers underline the necessity for the immediate tightening of fiscal and monetary policy. But that is not feasible politically during an election year, which helps explain why Mnangagwa has made it clear that he wants the polls to be held as soon as possible.

The same logic applies to the government's exchange rate dilemma. It is common cause that the currency is overvalued to the tune of 40 to 50 percent and that a switch to a different currency anchor, such as the South African rand, makes no sense unless it is part of a devaluation strategy. The new President has ruled out the rand option, but has promised to launch a new Zimbabwe currency backed either by gold or a currency board arrangement.

Inflation and currency depreciation, driven by excessive government spending, borrowing and money printing, has bedevilled the country since independence, with all the market-destroying and state fragility effects described in this book. Repeatedly over the 38 years since 1980 when ministers have had to choose between economic stabilisation via austerity on the one hand, and populism (and opportunities for elite enrichment) on the other, the latter has always won. The military acknowledges the populist nature of its coup, leaving little room for doubt over its stance when forced to choose, as it will be in the years ahead, between on the one hand the pain of political and economic reforms and potential challenges to the ruling party's monopoly on national political and economic life which might thereby emerge, and on the other regime survival which will remain the priority.

University of London
London, UK
University of Zimbabwe
Harare, Zimbabwe
February 2018

Mark Simpson

Tony Hawkins

Acknowledgements

Both authors were privileged to have been members of a group of eminent Zimbabwean economists, brought together between 2007–2010 under the aegis of the United Nations Development Program (UNDP) and tasked with analysing and reporting on the state of the economy, the wider social consequences of the country's economic travails, and providing policy advice in terms of recovery options. In addition to the present authors, what came to be known as the UNDP 'Recovery Team' included Dr. Godfrey Kanyenze, Professor Daniel Makina, Dr. Daniel Ndlela and Dr. Dale Doré, all exceptionally talented professionals who in uniquely challenging circumstances were able to probe, dissect and explore the drivers of Zimbabwe's economic meltdown during the crisis period of the late 1990s and 2000s, and its historical roots. Their willingness to work as a team, and the fact they were all amenable to being challenged by evidence, ensured that work produced was of the highest quality. We remain deeply indebted to this earlier collective effort, and hope the present book reflects the quality of those earlier influences.

We are also indebted to Dr. Agostinho Zacarias, Mr. Lare Sisay and Ms. Bettina Kittel of UNDP Zimbabwe. They recognised the potential of the policy-relevant research being carried out by the aforementioned team of economists in a context in which many international development agencies had either left Zimbabwe, downgraded their operations, or were focused on the country's humanitarian crisis, and provided the team with a 'long leash' and generous administrative and financial support to engage in the challenging exercise of understanding and reporting on what turned out to be a unique case of economic regression. At the time, Pauline Brine in Harare helped wrestle 'economese' into intelligible language.

Mark Simpson takes this opportunity to thank Professor Philip Murphy, Director of the Institute of Commonwealth Studies in the School of Advanced Study of the University of London, for having welcomed him as a Visiting Research Fellowship at the institute which he heads, a uniquely conducive environment for reflective work of this kind. Rachel Sangster, Head of Economics and Finance at Palgrave Macmillan, was everything the authors could have wished for in terms of providing advice and support, and patiently held our hands throughout the editorial and production processes.

Mark Simpson and Tony Hawkins

Contents

Abbreviations

AAPPG	Africa All Party Parliamentary Group
ACP	Africa Caribbean and Pacific
AfDB	African Development Bank
AIPPA	Access to Information and Protection of Privacy Act
AU	African Union
BIPPA	Bilateral Investment Promotion and Protection Agreement
BWI	Bretton Woods Institution
CAAZ	Civil Aviation Authority of Zimbabwe
CC	Constitutional Commission
CES	Community Empowerment Scheme
CFU	Commercial Farmers Union
CIO	Central Intelligence Organisation
CISOMM	Civil Society Monitoring Mechanism
COPAC	Constitutional Parliamentary Select Committee
CPIA	Country Policy and Institutional Assessment
CRF	Consolidated Revenue Fund
CRISE	Centre for Research on Inequality, Human Security and Ethnicity
CSO	Civil Society Organisation
CSRC	Crisis States Research Centre
CZI	Confederation of Zimbabwe Industries
DAC	Development Assistance Committee
DANIDA	Danish International Development Agency

DC	Delimitation Commission
DFID	Department for International Development
DRC	Democratic Republic of Congo
EES	Employers Empowerment Scheme
EMA	Environmental Management Agency
ESAP	Economic Structural Adjustment Programme
ETF	Education Trust Fund
EU	European Union
FAO	Food and Agriculture Organization
FDI	Foreign Direct Investment
FPL	Food Poverty Line
FTLRP	Fast Track Land Reform Programme
GAPWUZ	General Agricultural and Plantation Workers Union of Zimbabwe
GDI	Gross Domestic Income
GDP	Gross Domestic Product
GFATM	Global Fund to fight Aids, Tuberculosis and Malaria
GMB	Grain Marketing Board
GOZ	Government of Zimbabwe
GPA	Global Political Agreement
GRA	General Resource Account
HDI	Human Development Index
HIPC	Highly Indebted Poor Country
HIV and AIDS	Human Immuno-Deficiency Virus and Acquired Immuno-Deficiency Syndrome
HTF	Health Transition Fund
HWRS	Health Workers Retention Scheme
ICG	International Crisis Group
IDA	International Development Association
IDP	Internally-Displaced Persons
IFI	International Financial Institution
IG	Inclusive Government
ILO	International Labour Organization
IMF	International Monetary Fund
JOC	Joint Operations Command
JOMIC	Joint Monitoring and Implementation Committee
LICUS	Low-Income Countries Under Stress
MDC	Movement for Democratic Change
MDC-M	Movement for Democratic Change – Mutambara

MDC-N	Movement for Democratic Change – Ncube
MDC-T	Movement for Democratic Change – Tsvangirai
MDGs	Millennium Development Goals
MDRI	Multilateral Debt Relief Initiative
MMCZ	Minerals Marketing Corporation of Zimbabwe
MPLA	People's Movement for the Liberation of Angola
MPOI	Mass Public Opinion Institute
NCA	National Constitutional Assembly
NEPAD	New Partnership for Africa's Development
NGO	Non-Governmental Organisation
NHS	National Health Strategy
NIEBB	National Indigenisation and Economic Empowerment Board
NPRC	National Peace and Reconciliation Commission
NRZ	National Railways of Zimbabwe
NSC	National Security Council
ODA	Official Development Assistance
OECD	Organization for Economic Co-operation and Development
OECD-DAC	Organization for Economic Co-operation and Development-Development Assistance Committee
ONHRI	Organ on National Healing, Reconciliation and Integration
PASS	Poverty Assessment Study Survey
PE	Public Enterprise
PF	Patriotic Front
PIN	Public Information Notice
POSA	Public Order and Security Act
PRC	People's Republic of China
PRGF	Poverty Reduction and Growth Facility
PRSP	Poverty Reduction Strategy Paper
PVT	Parallel Voting Tabulation
RBZ	Reserve Bank of Zimbabwe
RENAMO	Mozambique National Resistance
SADC	Southern African Development Community
SAM	Severe Acute Malnutrition
SDR	Special Drawing Right
SME	Small and Medium Enterprise
SMP	Staff Monitored Programme
SSA	Sub-Saharan Africa
STERP	Short-Term Emergency Recovery Programme

TCPL	Total Consumption Poverty Line
TNDP	Transitional National Development Plan
UN	United Nations
UNCDF	United Nations Capital Development Fund
UNCTAD	United Nations Conference on Trade and Development
UNDESA	United Nations Department of Economic and Social Affairs
UNDP	United Nations Development Programme
UNICEF	United Nations Children's Fund
UN-OCHA	United Nations Office for the Coordination of Humanitarian Affairs
USAID	United States Agency for International Development
WFP	World Food Programme
WJP	World Justice Project
ZAADDS	Zimbabwe Accelerated Arrears clearance, Debt and Development Strategy
ZANLA	Zimbabwe African National Liberation Army
ZANU	Zimbabwe African National Union
ZANU-PF	Zimbabwe African National Union-Patriotic Front
ZAPU	Zimbabwe African People's Union
ZASMC	Zimbabwe Artisanal and Small-Scale Mining Council
ZBC	Zimbabwe Broadcasting Corporation
ZCTU	Zimbabwe Congress of Trade Unions
ZEC	Zimbabwe Electoral Commission
ZESA	Zimbabwe Electricity Supply Authority
ZESN	Zimbabwe Elections Support Network
ZIDERA	Zimbabwe Democracy and Economic Recovery Act
Zim Asset	Zimbabwe Agenda for Sustainable Socio-Economic Transformation
ZIMCORD	Zimbabwe Conference on Reconstruction and Development
ZIMPREST	Zimbabwe Programme for Economic and Social Transformation
ZIMRA	Zimbabwe Revenue Authority
ZimVAC	Zimbabwe Vulnerability Assessment Committee
ZINARA	Zimbabwe National Roads Administration
ZIPRA	Zimbabwe People's Revolutionary Army
ZLHR	Zimbabwe Lawyers for Human Rights
ZMDC	Zimbabwe Mining Development Corporation
ZNA	Zimbabwe National Army
ZRP	Zimbabwe Republic Police

1

Introduction

Notwithstanding damage to the economy, loss of life, large numbers of refugees forced to leave the country, and tense inter-racial relations resulting from the bitterly fought liberation war which brought an end to white minority rule, at Independence in April 1980 Zimbabwe was widely feted as a country that had the potential to be an African success story. Although it was just emerging from 15 years under United Nations comprehensive mandatory economic sanctions against the white-minority government, as well as from a decade of debilitating guerrilla and counter-insurgency warfare, Zimbabwe was widely seen as being better placed than many, perhaps most, African countries to deliver prosperity to its citizens.

The Lancaster House Agreement of 1979 between the government in Salisbury and the two liberation movements – the Zimbabwe African National Union (ZANU) led by Robert Mugabe and the Zimbabwe African People's Union (ZAPU) led by his rival Joshua Nkomo which came together as the Patriotic Front (PF) for the Independence negotiations hosted by London – resulted in a constitutional arrangement which entrenched the fundamental principles of the separation of powers, an independent judiciary, democratic multi-party elections, and a justiciable Declaration of Rights. Within the senior echelons of both liberation

M. Simpson, T. Hawkins, *The Primacy of Regime Survival*,
https://doi.org/10.1007/978-3-319-72520-8_1

movements, a willingness to compromise prevailed during the Lancaster House negotiations. The Patriotic Front delegates had also been under pressure from a number of neighbouring African states interested in bringing the Rhodesian conflict to an end as quickly as possible given the negative spill-over effects on their own peoples and economies, and accepted a number of constitutional provisions which they undoubtedly saw as contentious in order to bring the talks to a successful conclusion.

Foremost amongst these was the establishment of a separate white voters roll for the elections of 20 white lower House of Assembly representatives out of a total of 100, and 10 white senators out of a total of 40. This arrangement was to all intents and purposes frozen for a period of seven years, since amendments were only allowed subject to an unlikely unanimous vote in favour of changes in the House of Assembly. In addition, the Patriotic Front accepted provisions embedded in the constitution's Declaration of Rights which severely circumscribed the scope for compulsory acquisition by the new state of private property, and which could only be altered after a period of ten years, again subject to an unlikely unanimous vote in the House of Assembly. In those exceptional cases in which compulsory acquisition was permitted (on the grounds of national defence, public order and safety, public health and town and country planning considerations), there was to be prompt payment of adequate compensation, with owners to be granted access to the High Court to contest both the acquisition order, as well as the amount of compensation to be paid. The provisions also covered land, despite the fact that the need to address the highly inequitable distribution of this asset between whites and blacks had been a key rallying cry of both liberation movements. Both ZANU and ZAPU had to accept that these provisions hindered their ability, at least for the first ten years of independence, to trigger a process of land reform that was not based on the willing buyer, willing seller market-driven principle entrenched at Lancaster House.

In the run-up to Independence President Samora Machel of Mozambique, who had granted ZANU's armed forces bases along its extensive border with Rhodesia, famously advised future Prime Minister Robert Mugabe to tone down revolutionary Marxist rhetoric in order not to trigger an exodus of whites as had happened in Mozambique in 1974–75 with dire economic consequences (*Zimbabwe Today* 2017). Mugabe went on to surprise many observers with his conciliatory speeches in the run-up to Independence, calling upon the new country's white citizens to remain in order to help build a new country on the basis of "a common interest that knows no race, colour or creed" (Ministry of Information, Immigration and Tourism 1980, 3). In addition, during the years of sanctions and the liberation war, many of those making up Zimbabwe's first Cabinet had lived in failing neighbouring economies, particularly Mozambique and Zambia. When they took office, they were able to bring to their deliberations direct experience of the consequences of highly *dirigiste* economic policies, and how important it was to maintain the institutional fabric and physical infrastructure they were inheriting.

Unlike many of its African peers, Zimbabwe was never a mono-economy heavily dependent on a single export product. Instead it boasted a diversified economy driven primarily by large-scale commercial agriculture, underpinned by Sub-Saharan Africa's third largest manufacturing sector – after South Africa and Nigeria – a small, but diverse and profitable mining industry, and the region's second most sophisticated financial and banking sector after South Africa. There was immense potential in tourism, and the country had an exceptionally strong human capital base by Sub-Saharan African standards, with more skilled and trained people than any other African country at Independence. Although it was to lose thousands of skilled, experienced, white citizens in the late 1970s and early 1980s,[1] this outflow was offset by the return of many thousands of highly-educated and trained black Zimbabweans. After South Africa it also had the most developed and best maintained physical infrastructure in Sub-Saharan Africa, while health and education facilities, although historically heavily skewed in favour of the privileged white minority, were years ahead of those available elsewhere on the continent, again with the exception of South Africa.

Moreover, Zimbabwe enjoyed the benefits of being a late-comer. It was one of the last African states to achieve independence, and had plenty of experiences in terms of Africa's post-independence trajectory, both negative and positive, which it could draw upon as it set about devising its political governance systems and economic development strategies. The new government that took office in April 1980 also enjoyed tremendous international goodwill, and the donor/international lender community also had 20 years of history and experience in Africa that it could tap into when devising development and lending strategies for the new country.

In theory then, in 1980 Zimbabwe was well placed to learn from the lessons of economic failure elsewhere in Africa. Unlike many – indeed most – of its African peers, the country was not starting from scratch, but from the sturdy platform of a well-diversified economy richly endowed with skills and expertise and with the goodwill of most of its neighbours – with the vitally important exception of apartheid South Africa – and of the international community.

Understandably – and with the advantage of hindsight perhaps even inevitably – Zimbabwe's strengths and potential were exaggerated, especially by Western governments and a donor community avidly in search of an African economic success story. The West needed Zimbabwe to showcase how an African country could thrive as a non-racial society in the hope that this would smooth the path to majority rule in Namibia, and especially South Africa. A failure in Zimbabwe would only serve to bolster intransigence in South Africa, strengthening the hand of the white die-hards in that country. For this reason, as international pressure mounted on apartheid South Africa, Robert Mugabe's government attained a strategic importance in the eyes of the West well beyond its punching weight, and notwithstanding Mugabe's and ZANU's declared adherence to Marxism-Leninism.

Accordingly, it was in a better-the-devil-you-know spirit that even conservative Western governments – the Reagan Administration in the US and the Thatcher government in Britain – threw their weight behind the new government. Western diplomats insisted that Zimbabwe was 'in play' in the sense that during its formative years the new government would be open to advice and technical assistance that would help the West achieve its goals of showcasing Zimbabwe as a non-racial African success story, while simultaneously, and in the context of the Cold War, detaching Mugabe from the Eastern bloc and Chinese backers that had supported his party and its armed forces during the liberation war. In these endeavours the West was enthusiastically backed by the IMF and World Bank, especially the latter, anxious to demonstrate that their advice could produce African economic success stories.

Yet the long-term outcome could not have been more disappointing. From a situation of great promise and high popular expectations at Independence, by 2008 Zimbabwe had regressed to the point where daily life for the majority was characterised by completely empty supermarket shelves and a relentless search for basic goods as people lugged around wads of worthless currency. In addition, should they fell sick they were forced to sleep and await treatment in the corridors of hospitals that had neither staff, equipment nor medicines, while many children sat in classrooms devoid of electricity, furniture, text-books and increasingly teachers. Many were so desperate to flee the country they joined a mass exodus, sneaking under barbed wire fences and crossing over into South Africa and other neighbouring countries in search of refuge. Many of those who remained inside the country became increasingly reliant on emergency food aid distributed by international organisations and local charities, while if they openly opposed the government they ran the risk of joining the growing ranks of the victims of state-sponsored violence and torture, photographs of the disturbing results of this circulating widely on the internet to be viewed only by those with strong stomachs.

Economists and political scientists will long ponder the reasons for Zimbabwe's initially disappointing, and subsequently catastrophic, post-independence political governance and economic performance. How and why did one of Sub-Saharan Africa's best-endowed economies – in terms of physical infrastructure, human capital and diversified production – fail to exploit the potential it inherited? Why did successive governments fail to trigger economic growth rates that attracted foreign investment, and improve the welfare of its citizens through increased employment opportunities and rising real incomes on a long-term and sustainable basis? How was initial and significant progress during the 1980s in terms of improved public services and social indicators reversed so quickly during the 'crisis decade' between 1998 and 2008, and from which the country is still trying to recover? How did national economic policies result in a disastrously weakened and fragile state that presided over a dramatically impoverished, cowed and alienated population, and which at the peak of the crisis had turned Zimbabweans into arguably the unhappiest people in the world?

The most plausible explanation for this spectacular, if not historically unprecedented, socio-economic collapse and growing fragility of the Zimbabwean state, is the combination of the primacy given to the retention of political power at all costs, and consequential and inevitable deteriorating political and economic governance. The two go together because in the pursuit of monopoly political power and permanent control, parties ignore the tenets of good governance on both the political and economic fronts.

As a party that had come to power through an armed struggle with the support of other single-party regimes in Eastern Europe, Asia and Africa, ZANU-PF believed – and still does – that because it had liberated the country it had earned the right to rule the country in perpetuity. Furthermore, the economy was simply seen as an asset to be used to ensure its continued monopoly on political power. This in turn often translated into the radical circumscribing of the operation of free markets and independent economic agents over which the ruling party had limited control, as the latter might become alternative centres of political power and undermine the centrality in national life of ZANU-PF as the sole source of all riches which it could distribute as it saw fit.

Zimbabwe's post-independence path provides strong evidence in support of the work of Acemoglu and Robinson on the interactions between economic and political institutions, and their varying degrees of inclusiveness, as key explanations for why some countries prosper and others seem to be trapped in poverty and decline. More specifically, Zimbabwe's track record lends credence to their central thesis regarding the primacy of political institutions in explaining the economic history of countries, and the role of elites in controlling and shaping these to their advantage. As they have argued:

> Economic institutions shape economic incentives: the incentives to become educated, to save and invest, to innovate and adopt new technologies, and so on. It is the political process that determines what economic institutions people live under…it is the political institutions…that determine the ability of citizens to control politicians and influence how they behave. This in turn determines whether politicians are agents of the citizens…or are able to abuse the power entrusted to them, or that they have usurped, to amass their own fortunes and to pursue their own agendas, ones detrimental to those of the citizens. (Acemoglu and Robinson 2013, 24)

As this book shows, the imperative of regime survival – defined in terms of ZANU-PF's monopoly of state power and until 2017 the maintenance of Mugabe as the country's leader – and the political and economic institutions that were moulded to support regime maintenance, eventually trumped all developmental considerations. This was particularly evident during the 'crisis decade' which saw both record breaking regression in terms of development indicators, as well as unprecedented popular contestation of the dominant roles that both Mugabe and his party had enjoyed since Independence.

Between 1998 and 2008, Zimbabwe underwent what, in global historical terms, was an unparalleled decline for a country not suffering from armed conflict, such that by the end of this period it ranked amongst the very worst performers in terms of the UN's Human Development Index (HDI).[2] Those were years characterised by political regression in the form of the increasing centralisation of power in the Presidency, undermining of the rule of law and independence of the judiciary, growing constraints on the operations of the independent media, widespread human rights violations, a growing militarisation of national life and an increasing recourse to state-sponsored violence against opponents. In parallel, the state apparatus was used by the ruling party to extend its control over the economy and, central to the regime's survival strategy, to support an extensive patronage network based on the distribution of largesse extracted through both legal and illegal means from the public and private sectors.

The increasing fragility of the Zimbabwean state was both a cause and consequence of the wider economic malaise. As the economy contracted, the financial resource base of the public sector was eroded and human capital drained away. This, in turn, led to diminished state capacity to plan and finance economic growth and ensure the provision of basic public goods.

Gross and protracted economic mismanagement meant that by 2008 Zimbabwe was undergoing a rapid economic meltdown. This was manifested in vertiginous inflation rates, an unserviceable foreign debt burden, a catastrophic collapse in levels of output and employment, decrepit productive and social infrastructure, the destruction of markets and livelihoods with disastrous consequences for poverty levels as millions were driven below the poverty line, growing dependence on international humanitarian assistance, and hundreds of thousands of Zimbabweans fleeing the country every year in search of a better life elsewhere.

As the popular support base of ZANU-PF and its leader shrank during the 'crisis decade' due to the disastrous performance of the economy, so the ruling party came to rely as an essential prop on the naked power and intimidation capacity provided by its close allies in the national defence and security apparatus. By 2008, as the initial election results of that year demonstrated, the majority of the Zimbabwean people had come to see the regime and state in which they had deposited such high hopes at Independence as purely extractive, predatory, and operating to the benefit of a small elite. And in stark contrast to its promising status at Independence, Zimbabwe featured regularly in lists of 'fragile' states devised by international think tanks, with some analysts arguing by 2008 that to all intents and purposes it had become a 'failed' state.

This book explores the catastrophic political, social and economic decline of Zimbabwe under the rule of ZANU-PF. While the primary focus is on the period 1998–2008, years which saw a concentrated and dizzying deterioration in all aspects of national life, the authors have also pushed the story backwards in time, analysing the seeds of this collapse sown in the period between Independence in 1980 and 1997. In addition, the country's trajectory is brought up to date with an examination of the difficulties faced by the country's opposition forces when they gained limited access to the reins of power between 2009 and 2013, and analysis of the problems the country continues to face given the extent of the damage inflicted on the country's institutional and economic fabric in the preceding years, and severe constraints thereby imposed on its recovery prospects since the end of the 2008 power-sharing arrangement, ZANU-PF's victory in the 2013 elections, and the end of Robert Mugabe's presidency in late 2017.

Chapter 2 situates Zimbabwe's experience within the wider phenomenon of fragile/failed states. While most research on fragile states has tended to focus on those cases of state fragility and failure characterised by prolonged civil unrest, open armed conflict and the severe weakening if not complete disappearance of central authority that usually characterise such situations, less attention has been paid to other contexts in which gross economic mismanagement has led to equally catastrophic developmental consequences even in the absence of war and institutional rupture. The chapter reviews international evidence on the strong positive links between economic growth and poverty reduction, helping to throw light on Zimbabwe's experience where economic destruction rather than growth, and poverty production rather than reduction, seemed to be the overriding objectives of national economic policy.

The authors review global evidence on the positive links between state effectiveness, state legitimacy, economic growth and poverty reduction which provides essential insights into the causes and nature of Zimbabwe's uniquely negative experience. Particular attention is paid to the role of effective state bureaucracies in triggering both economic growth and development through nurturing of markets, the removal of obstacles to the participation of the poor in the economy, upholding the rule of law, building social and fiscal contracts, and ensuring the credibility and predictability of state policies which in turn impact positively on investor decisions and capital formation, all features that were increasingly conspicuous by their absence in Zimbabwe.

Chapter 3 surveys the first decade of Zimbabwe's independence from 1980 to 1990. While robust early post-independence economic growth rates seemed to augur well for the future, these soon dropped to more moderate levels, setting the pattern for subsequent years with the economy continually failing to create enough jobs for a growing population. As the chapter shows, while there were significant, rapid and laudable gains in areas such as health and education, lower growth rates meant persistent budget deficits and a growing domestic and foreign debt. There were also clear and early signs of ruling party mistrust of markets and private sector-led growth, as the number of state enterprises inherited from the pre-independence period increased and the economy was subjected to growing interventionism.

More ominously, the decade was also characterised by slow progress in the area of land reform, storing up trouble for the future. There were also significant slippages on the political governance front, as steps were taken to transform the country into a *de facto* one-party state. Soon after Independence, ZAPU as a rival political party was crushed through the employment of military force and eventually absorbed into an enlarged

ZANU-PF. Simultaneously, a number of constitutional amendments were introduced which, amongst other changes, resulted in the abolition of the post of prime minister and the granting of increased powers to an Executive President.

These trends were to continue during the period from 1990 to 1997/98. When in the early 1990s the ruling party was eventually compelled to adopt an economic structural adjustment programme as a result of growing economic difficulties, it did so reluctantly, and as subsequent developments were to prove half-heartedly. As shown in Chap. 4, the results of economic liberalisation were sub-optimal due to a combination of both exogenous factors and poor design and implementation. The latter reflected opposition within the ruling party to both any weakening of state control over the economy which improvements in the conditions for private enterprise necessarily required, as well as reductions in the scope for patronage which was its corollary. By 1997, and notwithstanding the launch of a successor economic reform programme, opposition to market-led reform within ZANU-PF triumphed, leading to further declines in the country's fiscal, domestic and foreign debt positions, falling output and real wages, and rising unemployment.

Faced with the rise of a new organised political opposition in the form of the Movement for Democratic Change (MDC), these developments meant not only that market-driven reform would eventually be completely abandoned, but also that ZANU-PF would go on to adopt even more comprehensive and interventionist policies that were informed by its own short-term survival considerations. The popular rejection in 2000 of a new constitution, the drafting of which was seen by many as having been manipulated by ZANU-PF and which would have resulted in an even greater concentration of powers in the hands of the President and legalised the seizure of white-owned commercial farms, led the ruling party to opt for a course of action that would profoundly radicalise Zimbabwe's political economy in an effort to intimidate its opponents and rebuild its support base.

Chapter 5 focuses on the watershed development which more than any other was to catapult Zimbabwe down the path of economic destruction and deepening state fragility, namely the Fast Track Land Reform Programme (FTLRP) launched in 2000. It is argued that contrary to

ZANU-PF attempts to portray the FTLRP as solely an attempt to correct a historical social injustice, the initiative should be understood primarily in terms of regime survival imperatives.

The situation in which the ruling party found itself facing by the end of the 1990s was one characterised by a pressing need to revive its support amongst the country's rural population which had been strained as a result of the deteriorating economy and slow pace of land reform. In addition there were signs of increased factionalism within the ruling party itself, and so pressure grew to secure a new and major source of patronage to strengthen cohesion within the senior ranks of the party and the country's security apparatus, and ensure continued loyalty to Mugabe. By destroying the white commercial farming sector, the FTLRP also had the benefit of severely weakening an important source of financial support for the MDC opposition which had come to constitute a serious threat to ZANU-PF rule.

The authors dissect the manner in which the FTLRP was carried out, characterised by the extensive employment of violence and the introduction of both draconian legislation and constitutional amendments in order to buttress the programme and stifle dissent. The devastating collateral damage wrought by the FTLRP on Zimbabwe's economy with the collapse of commercial agricultural production negatively affected other sectors of the economy, and was to contribute to falling overall output levels, rising unemployment, shrinking export receipts, and growing budget deficits.

As economic activity contracted, the Government adopted increasingly profligate monetary and fiscal policies in a forlorn effort to arrest the decline. The authors argue that the continued pursuit of such policies, notwithstanding growing and compelling evidence of their failure, is best understood in terms of the opportunities for further elite enrichment that arose from the extensive distortions such policies created, the speculative activities which thereby flourished, and which would eventually result in the 'economic meltdown' of 2008.

Chapters 6 and 7 detail some of the human costs of the crisis decade, linking regime preservation considerations, elite enrichment and hollowing out of state capacity to the calamitous decline in the welfare of the vast majority of the Zimbabwean population. Chapter 6 focuses on the collapse in formal employment which resulted in a swelling of the ranks of those forced to seek their livelihoods in the informal sector. By 2005, this growing urban informal sector had become a significant support base for the MDC, and thus a threat to ZANU-PF's continued rule. It had also become a potential source of spoils that could be distributed to lower-ranking elements of the regime's support structures, and the full force of the state was eventually used to eliminate it in one of the African continent's most notorious urban clean-up operations. This impacted negatively on the lives of hundreds of thousands of Zimbabweans, compounding their poverty and as detailed in Chap. 7 forcing them to join the growing exodus of Zimbabweans whose remitted earnings became vital to the survival of poor households left behind. In the face of worsening working conditions, large numbers of public sector workers also fled the country, and as capacity drained out of the public sector so the quality of planning and service delivery deteriorated, impacting directly on a range of public goods. The formal private sector was not able to shield itself from the increasingly unpredictable monetary and fiscal policies pursued by Government, and was also crippled by the mass migration of skilled and semi-skilled workers.

As detailed in Chap. 8, as the economic meltdown gathered pace, and political repression was ramped up, so Zimbabwe found itself increasingly isolated from its traditional Western development partners who sought to pressure Harare to reverse course in terms of its domestic policies. There were also growing concerns in the West regarding Zimbabwe's military involvement in the Democratic Republic of Congo (DRC) in support of the Kabila government which was fighting rebels, with the intervention providing another opportunity for members of the regime to accumulate wealth. The economic downturn severely affected the country's ability to service its growing foreign debt, and would eventually lead the Bretton Woods Institutions (BWIs) to adopt restrictive measures, cutting Zimbabwe off from new loans, grants and technical assistance. In addition, in response to Zimbabwe's deteriorating political governance, Western capitals introduced targeted sanctions against the ruling elite, and Western donor agencies terminated their development assistance programmes while also increasing their provision of emergency humanitarian assistance to a growing population of vulnerable Zimbabweans.

Faced with such Western hostility, Harare countered by depicting Zimbabwe as a country under siege from Western powers intent on 'regime change', a reversal of its land reform, and control of its natural resources. The ruling party also sought to build alliances with a range of developing countries, most particularly China with which it came to enjoy close economic, political and military ties, as an alternative to Western assistance.

Chapter 9 tracks Zimbabwe's trajectory as it reached the nadir of its post-independence fortunes in 2008, amidst apparent disinterest on the part of the regime to the long-term consequences for the country and its people of the quickening pace of decline over which it was presiding. The economy descended into hyperinflation, output and employment levels reached new lows, and the final stages of the hollowing out of state capacity were played out, most damagingly in the areas of health and education where the state's inability to deliver even the most basic public goods led to the effective collapse of those sectors. Popular discontent continued to be dealt with harshly by the security forces, while the political opposition, human rights groups and independent media all reeled under intense and heavy-handed persecution.

The chapter recounts how the 2008 Presidential and legislative elections were held in an atmosphere of massive intimidation and vote-rigging by the ruling party. When the results led to the need for a Presidential run-off between Mugabe and the leader of the opposition MDC-T, Morgan Tsvangirai, and the regime was confronted with clear evidence of the extent of popular disillusionment with the ruling party, the full force of state repression was unleashed against the MDC-T and its supporters, forcing Tsvangirai to withdraw from the run-off and thus paving the way for Mugabe's re-election.

Regional efforts to break the impasse created by the 2008 elections were to eventually lead to a power-sharing arrangement between ZANU-PF and the MDC-T (Movement for Democratic Change – Tsvangirai) and the smaller breakaway MDC-M (Movement for Democratic Change – Mutambara).[3] As the authors note, the overall outcome was a compromise that meant a meaningful transition was arrested. ZANU-PF was able to retain control of key ministries, and thereby stymie any efforts to rebuild the economy and institutional fabric that might impinge on its core interests and survival prospects.

Chapter 10 highlights the difficulties faced by the Opposition in terms of putting the country back onto a path of sustainable development and reverse state fragility during the cohabitation years of the Inclusive Government (IG) between 2009 and 2013. The period allowed the full extent of the socio-economic regression to be brought out into the open, as the new partners in government found the state coffers had been left empty by ZANU-PF, hospitals and health clinics were bereft of medical supplies, schools were left without textbooks, most frontline health and education workers had been compelled out of necessity to abandon their posts to either emigrate or eke out a living in the informal sector, and water, sanitation and electricity generation and distribution were all severely debilitated.

Some early and not insignificant gains did result from the fact that certain ministries were allocated to the MDC factions, particularly in terms of the Health and Education portfolios, as Western donors poured substantial funds into the rebuilding of delivery systems, and health and education workers returned to their posts. MDC-T's control of the Ministry of Finance also helped ensure that macroeconomic stability was restored as the new MDC-T Minister maintained a tight grip on public spending, while the establishment of a dollarized economy brought an end to the country's hyperinflation, and the Minister successfully pushed back against attempts by ZANU-PF to restore the Zimbabwe currency following its demise in late 2008.

Yet as Chap. 10 shows, ZANU-PF's red lines soon made themselves felt and blocked progress on other fronts, most notably a solution to Zimbabwe's unsustainable foreign debt which would have implied a level of intrusion and oversight of the country's finances and decision-making processes by the IFIs judged unacceptable by Mugabe and his lieutenants. ZANU-PF also consistently obstructed MDC efforts to repeal a battery of repressive legislation enacted to help ensure maintenance of its monopoly on power. In addition, the chapter draws attention to signs of the 'zanufication' of certain members of the Opposition, by which is meant that once in power the latter came to internalise attitudes, and show patterns of predatory behaviour, strongly reminiscent of ZANU-PF norms.

Chapters 11 and 12 detail ZANU-PF's efforts during the IG to maintain control over the complex extractive political and economic institutions it had built up since Independence which had helped ensure regime survival. On the political front, once a constitutional revision process was launched and some concessions made to the MDCs in the area of constitutional and electoral reform, minimal progress was made in terms of transitional justice and overhaul of the security sector. Chapter 11 highlights the significance of the Opposition's failure to reform the country's defence, police and intelligence forces given the veto power over political change the former enjoyed, and the symbiotic relationship that had developed between senior securocrats and the leadership of ZANU-PF, evidenced by the undisguised pro-ZANU-PF partisanship of senior commanders. ZANU-PF was also able to ensure that there would be little change in terms of circumscribing the powers of the Executive Presidency, and that the new constitution contained provisions allowing Mugabe additional terms of office should he win future elections.

Chapter 12 throws light on the parallel economic systems that ZANU-PF successfully kept beyond the control of its partners in the IG, allowing it both access to its own sources of revenue and the means to continue feeding its patronage networks. The country's diamond wealth provided ZANU-PF with the primary means of ensuring independence from the national Treasury under the control of the MDC-T Minister of Finance, while the close links established between ZANU-PF, the security forces and certain mining companies helped maintain high levels of secrecy in regards to the operations of this sector, an aspect of mineral wealth management strongly associated with the 'resource curse', with Zimbabwe rapidly became a prime example of the syndrome at work.

As Chap. 12 also shows, ZANU-PF attempts to access new resources to oil its patronage machinery and strengthen its support base went beyond diamonds. In the post-FTLRP era, this meant that a new form of asset stripping had to be found, the quest for which would eventually lead to the development of the country's Indigenisation and Economic Empowerment policy. The latter was widely seen as responsible for the low levels of both domestic and foreign investment which afflicted the economy, but also as an essential means for ZANU-PF to attract support on the basis of promises of future largesse.

Chapter 13 outlines how ZANU-PF, following the shock it had suffered in the first round of the 2008 elections, was to single-mindedly and successfully focus on regrouping, rebuilding and strengthening its support base, and also took advantage of serious shortcomings within the ranks of the Opposition to ensure that in the 2013 elections there would not be a repeat of its dismal performance of 2008. Concerned with, and focused solely on, regaining its monopoly on political power, ZANU-PF was to capitalise on the MDC-T's inability to make major inroads into the complex networks of influence and mutual dependence built up between ZANU-PF and a range of old and new social and economic forces, interests and institutions. The MDC-T's failure to successfully advance its own reform programme was partly a result of its gradual accommodation to ZANU-PF governance practices during the IG, but also an indication of just how difficult it is to displace deeply entrenched extractive political and economic systems which had gone uncontested over decades, and around which all aspects of national life had come to be structured.

In the aftermath of the 2013 elections, with ZANU-PF firmly again in power and the Opposition imploding, things appeared to have come full circle, with the IG likely consigned to a footnote in ZANU-PF's official historiography. Chapter 14 shows how in the aftermath of ZANU-PF's 2013 victory, economic growth rates which had picked up during the IG once again began to falter, unemployment rose as companies in the non-farming sector began again to close, agricultural output remained anaemic, and electricity and water cuts as well as epidemics of contagious diseases reappeared as they had during the crisis decade. The ruling party, once in control of monetary and fiscal policy, used these instruments to engage again in deficit financing, ignored the effects of its growing external debt problem, and focused on ensuring that its patronage systems were replenished with the necessary resources. Corruption was soon on the rise again, the securocrats were being rewarded with posts in already bankrupt state enterprises and parastatals from which they would be able to extract their last ounce of flesh from the carcasses over which they presided, and Zimbabweans were once again emigrating both legally and illegally in increasing numbers. Leaving aside the short interregnum of the IG, as of 2018 and notwithstanding the military coup of November 2017 which saw Mugabe's removal from power, Zimbabwe seems never to have left the downward path towards economic destruction, poverty production and growing state fragility which had begun two decades earlier.

Notes

1. Notwithstanding Mugabe's efforts to allay the concerns of the white population of Zimbabwe, by the early 1980s this was estimated at 140,000 – approximately half the peak of around 275,000 in the mid-1970s.
2. The HDI is a composite index developed by the United Nations Development Program (UNDP). It brings together life expectancy at birth, education (expected and mean years of schooling) and gross national income per capita indicators, with countries grouped into four human development categories based on their index, namely Very High, High, Medium and Low.
3. The MDC was to split into two factions in 2005, putatively on the issue of whether the party should participate in senate elections that year. The split would eventually result in a much larger MDC-T led by its original founder Morgan Tsvangirai who had favoured a boycott of the elections and overruled the decision of the party's National Council to participate in the polls, and what would eventually become the significantly smaller MDC-M led by Arthur Mutambara. At the time there were complaints from dissidents within the MDC that Tsvangirai was demonstrating disturbing signs of authoritarianism, and that his grassroots supporters had employed violence against them.

References

Acemoglu, Daron, and James A. Robinson. 2013. *Why Nations Fail—The Origins of Power, Prosperity and Poverty*. London: Profile Books.

Ministry of Information, Immigration and Tourism. 1980. *Address to the Nation by the Prime Minister Elect—4th March 1980*. Harare.

Zimbabwe Today. 2017. Samora Machel 1980 Warning to Mugabe: Chasing White Rhodesians Will Ruin Zimbabwe, February 6. https://zimbabwe-today.com/samora-machel-warning-mugabe-chasing-white-rhodesians-will-ruin-zimbabwe/.

2

The Economics of State Fragility

Since the end of the Cold War, a growing theoretical and policy-relevant literature has focused on a group of states in the developing world that are seen to be 'fragile' as measured by their susceptibility to breakdown. The label has been applied to those states judged to be in crisis – usually characterised by prolonged political deadlocks, declining legitimacy of state institutions, low-level civil unrest, and deteriorating economic and social indicators – and who are therefore moving towards complete collapse. At worse they may already be considered as 'failed states', with high levels of open armed conflict, the disappearance of state authority at both central and local levels, as well as complete non-performance of a range of core functions such as the provision of public safety and health and education services.

This body of work reflects international concern with the phenomenon of fragile and failed states, the apparent increase in their number, and most particularly their impact on global security in a post-9/11 world given the scope for transnational criminal and terrorist organisations to occupy the vacuum caused by the collapse of national authority in such situations, the phenomenon of 'ungoverned spaces' being seen as a key characteristic of such failed states. At the same time, the international development and humanitarian communities have also been seized of the

M. Simpson, T. Hawkins, *The Primacy of Regime Survival*,
https://doi.org/10.1007/978-3-319-72520-8_2

problem given that such states are characterised by severe socio-economic and political regression, often combining high and worsening levels of poverty, low economic growth rates and poor health and education outcomes, as well as severe deficits in terms of human rights and governance indicators. Additional international concerns revolve around the destabilising regional spill-over effects of state fragility, such as forced migration and the burden this imposes on host countries, the flows of weapons and intrusion of armed groups into neighbouring states, and the disruption to established regional trade patterns caused by rising levels of insecurity.

For reasons related to the immediacy of the security threats and humanitarian disasters that arise from such situations, the focus of much research has tended to be on those states seen as being at an advanced stage of the downward trajectory, or as having already collapsed, though the distinction between the two phases is often difficult to determine and open to a degree of subjectivity. Under these scenarios, and often as a result of armed conflict between central governments and dissident groups, the political centre has lost effective control over large parts of its national territory and its external borders, with the administrative writ of the state often reduced to a few kilometres outside the capital city.

Another feature of such extreme situations, namely the disappearance of public services, contributes to the decline of state legitimacy and rise of popular discontent, which can in turn feed armed contestation of existing power structures. Economic activity in the productive formal sector is severely circumscribed, and often accompanied by a proliferation of illegal activities such as arms and human trafficking, illegal mining and poaching, or maritime piracy. The majority of the population is reduced either to survivalist coping strategies for those who remain inside the country, or compelled to seek refuge beyond national borders.

Examples abound of states which meet such criteria; both before the end of the Cold War, and as a result of protracted civil wars, states such as Afghanistan, Cambodia, Mozambique and Angola displayed many of these features, while in the post-Cold War and post-9/11 world their ranks were swelled by the addition of states such as Bosnia, Yemen, Rwanda, Liberia, Sierra Leone, Ivory Coast, Sudan, the Central African Republic and the DRC. More recently, they have been joined by South

Sudan, Libya and Syria. *In extremis* there was the paradigmatic case of Somalia, a 'stateless state' in which all semblance of *de facto* national authority had disappeared.

However, there is also another group of states that has come to the attention of fragile states analysts. While displaying signs of being profoundly dysfunctional in political and economic terms over extended periods of time, this has not translated into open, prolonged, widespread and violent armed conflict between central government and rebel movements. In such cases the increase in state fragility has been more gradual, incremental and protracted, though the consequences in terms of the welfare of their populations have been no less damaging. In this category one might include countries such as Haiti, Equatorial Guinea, Guinea-Bissau, or recently Venezuela, and the subject of this book, Zimbabwe.

One consequence of the growing international concern with fragile and failed states is that it has also triggered research that seeks to identify the early warning signs and trends associated with such processes of deterioration, and prescribed remedial actions.[1] The growth in the post-conflict and post-crisis reconstruction industry since the end of the Cold War and post-9/11, evidenced by the multiplication of research institutes and operational agencies working in this area, is an indication of both the growing number of states requiring assistance, and the increased international attention paid to their plight.

Yet the international community has tended to be subjective in terms of which qualifying criteria to adopt and emphasise, and therefore which states are deemed to fall into the net and those which escape the triage. Lists of fragile states have expanded or contracted on the basis of shifting indicators, and the relative weight given to each of these and thresholds applied. This is partly a reflection of the varied expertise of those brought in to devise such frameworks (economists, sociologists, social sector specialists, political scientists or security experts), and the shifting foreign policy agendas of Western states and extent to which any particular case of state fragility impacts on their specific national interests.

There is currently no hard and fast set of rules that one can apply to cases of state fragility. Some definitions and indices prioritise the presence or absence of conflict (be this defined as low levels of civil unrest or open armed conflict between clearly defined groups), while others anchored in crisis-prevention considerations focus on the potential for such conflict to erupt, the need to clarify the fault lines within those societies, the multiple forces and complex processes at work, and the mitigation measures that might be applied. Some frameworks stress the importance of poor social and economic indicators, the quality of state policies and institutions and their performance along various dimensions such as service delivery, economic growth, transparency, corruption levels, public financial management, human rights, the quality of elections and progress on poverty reduction. Others focus on measuring national cohesiveness, such as the extent of horizontal inequalities expressed in terms of cleavages along ethno-regional and confessional lines and concomitant rise of group grievances.

The Search for Definitional Clarity

Notwithstanding the large number of variables under consideration, some composite definitions of state fragility have been developed and gained purchase, and these seek to capture the multi-dimensionality of the phenomenon. The Organization for Economic Co-operation and Development (OECD), for example, in a landmark definition of state fragility and upon which it subsequently went on to build a set of operational guidelines for OECD bilateral donor development agencies working in such difficult operational environments, argued that:

> States are fragile when governments and state structures lack capacity – or in some cases, political will – to deliver public safety, good governance and poverty reduction to their citizens…the capability of states to fulfil their core functions is essential in order to reduce poverty. Priority functions include: ensuring security and justice; establishing an enabling environment for basic service delivery, strong economic performance and employment generation. (OECD-DAC 2005, 2)

It is significant that the above definition is based on a recognition of the connections between the political, economic, security and social aspects of fragility, with shortcomings in one area seen as necessarily compromising progress in the others. It is also noteworthy that a key distinction is drawn between the capacity and the political will of governments in terms of enabling state structures to perform their core functions, since depending on the diagnosis of these critical variables different remedial measures are required. This distinction serves as a useful corrective to a widespread tendency within the field of development studies to take as a given the political willingness of developing country governments to use their states to deliver public goods and improve the welfare of their citizens, and therefore to attribute poor state performance solely to capacity constraints susceptible to purely technical and financial solutions. As this book shows by drawing upon the experience of Zimbabwe, such a fallacy, based on a misreading of the political economy of the incentive structures operating within the governing elites of any given fragile state, lies at the root of the failure of many external efforts to reverse fragility.

Another pioneering effort to deepen understandings of the phenomenon of state fragility was that of the World Bank. In 2002 it developed the concept of Low-Income Countries Under Stress (LICUS) to highlight the challenges such unstable entities presented to the international development community, capture the main features of fragility, and develop a metric which would permit an evaluation of the degree of fragility of specific states.[2]

At the time the concept was first developed, LICUS countries were those with per capita incomes less than US$825, the latter being the threshold for access to the World Bank's International Development Association (IDA) concessional resources. In addition to low-income status, they suffered from a combination of weak governance, poor policies and debilitated institutions, ranking amongst the lowest (bottom two quintiles) in the World Bank's Country Policy and Institutional Assessment (CPIA).[3] Also central to the notion of a LICUS was that such the combination of negative fragility indicators was not episodic, i.e. the result of short-term stress factors, but rather had persisted over an extended period of time thereby indicating deeper structural problems.

Differential human development outcomes served to underscore the critical importance of the quality of state policies and institutions as an explanatory variable for the poor performance of such states when compared to their non-LICUS low-income peers. The World Bank noted that LICUS countries had average infant mortality rates one-third higher, maternal mortality rates around 20 percent higher, and life expectancy 12 years lower, than those of other low-income countries (World Bank 2006, 4).

Efforts by international organisations such as the OECD and World Bank to improve definitional clarity led to growing recognition of the importance of the non-security-related dimensions of state performance (often subsumed under the rubric of 'good governance') in terms of their impact on human development, and so helped to further elucidate the complex pathologies afflicting fragile states. One result was recognition of the need to ascribe fragility not only to states which had yet to descend into open armed conflict but nevertheless displayed high levels of instability and occasional violent contestations of the status quo due to failures to accommodate political dissent, but also to extend the label to cover both pre- and post-conflict situations where severe and persistent deficiencies in key areas of state performance were evident.

These new variables of state performance included service delivery, economic growth and poverty reduction metrics, as well as legitimacy defined in terms of the extent to which the state in its executive, legislative and judicial roles was willingly accepted as the provider of a range of functions in exchange for societal compliance with state demands. Significant shortcomings in terms of state capacity/willingness to support economic growth, employment creation, service provisioning and poverty reduction, coupled with weak legitimacy in the eyes of their populations, were seen to increase the likelihood of eventual violent contestation of the status quo.

One substantive criticism of these frameworks is that such broad and multi-dimensional definitions of state fragility have tended to become excessively broad, catch-all concepts. State fragility is conflated with the more ubiquitous problems of low growth rates, stagnant human development indicators, lack of progress in terms of democratisation and weak state legitimacy which characterise many developing countries, if not all of those in the low-income category, with the application of the concept of state fragility thereby losing its focus, analytical value and policy-relevance.

This happens because definitions such as those of the OECD and World Bank fail to distinguish between, on the one hand, the large numbers of states in the developing world that fall short of meeting standards such as those contained in the OECD's aforementioned three pillars (capacity to perform core functions, legitimacy and accountability, and the establishment of an environment conducive for economic growth), but which nevertheless and over a protracted period of time demonstrate a high degree of apparent resilience and do not lapse into a process of state failure and collapse, and on the other hand those states that do suffer from such degenerative processes. The key point is that notwithstanding lack of progress in terms of improved functionality in social provisioning, and lacklustre performance in the sustaining of economic growth rates that translate into significant reductions in poverty levels, many states in the developing world seem nevertheless to enjoy stability over extended periods of time, do not suffer from open conflict, and so it is argued should not be classified as fragile.

Attempts to limit the use of the fragility label have thus sought to restrict its application to cases where there are significant shortcomings in a more restricted set of core state functions. So, for example, one approach would strictly limit the application of the term to those states that fail to exercise a monopoly over the legitimate use of force, or fall short in terms of basic bureaucratic capacity as defined by a monopoly over taxation powers, or are unable to ensure their institutions or rules achieve supremacy over rival domestic sets of rules and centres of political power, or that suffer from a significant deficit in terms of control over their national territories (Putzell 2010, 2–3).

In turn, however, one problem arising from the use of such a restricted set of criteria is that apparent resilience, defined in terms of possession of a reduced set of key attributes, may in fact mask serious underlying dysfunctionalities in other aspects of state performance, obscuring deepening fault lines and growing popular grievances within society which eventually lead to violent contestations of the legitimacy of existing state arrangements. While, for example, a state may well enjoy a monopoly over the means of coercion, and is able to protect its citizens from large-scale violence from third parties, any state must be seen to be suffering from serious shortcomings, and risks undermining its legitimacy over the longer-term, if it regularly uses those same means against its own population to ensure compliance with its diktats. Likewise, the manner in which the state achieves a monopoly of taxation (whether through extortion, or a consensual state-citizenry fiscal contract), as well as how it uses the revenues thereby collected (to the advantage of an elite, or the wider public good), will also be key to enhancing or weakening its legitimacy.

This in no way detracts from the important role that coercive capabilities and administrative reach play in enabling states to ensure peace within their national borders. However, excessive reliance on these tools of statecraft, and a neglect of other dimensions of state responsibility such as improvements in citizen welfare, means that states that rely primarily on the former, and neglect the latter are sowing the seeds of eventual contestation of their legitimacy. Zimbabwe's experience, in particular during its crisis years, is once again highly instructive in this regard, as the period saw a widening gap between the state's growing coercive capacities and its declining commitment to the welfare of large segments of its population.

The Sovereignty Gap and State Effort

One notable effort to expand definitions of state responsibilities that goes beyond the security and authority related criteria discussed above is the work of Ashraf Ghani and Clare Lockhart.[4] Adopting an expansive definition of state fragility, their key argument is that notwithstanding apparent resilience, a large number of contemporary states are in fact in the active process of failing. This is happening because such states are consistently unable, or unwilling, to deliver on a set of basic domestic responsibilities ranging from the provision of public goods such as security and social services to the strengthening of a broader social contract between citizens and the state. The result is deepening estrangement between national authorities and their populations. Such states may not yet have lapsed into open and violent conflict, and there may still be a recognisable central government with the necessary associated institutions (even if only *pro forma* in terms of substantive performance), and they may still retain a monopoly over the means of coercion, but such states are nevertheless seen as being on a downward trajectory.

Closer to the definitions of fragility utilised by the OECD and the World Bank, the Ghani and Lockhart framework highlights the existence of 'sovereignty gaps'. They detect a growing chasm in many states between, on the one hand, definitions of sovereignty derived from international law, i.e. the external aspect of the *de jure* sovereign equality of all states, and on the other hand the fact that many states are failing in terms of what they see as the key attributes of an inward looking *de facto* sovereignty.

In addition to standard criteria such as a monopoly of the means of coercion and administrative control of national territory, Ghani and Lockhart identify *de facto* sovereignty with the ability of a state to meet a series of additional domestic obligations. These include the upholding of the rule of law, provision of infrastructure, sound management of public finances and public assets, effective public borrowing, market formation, investment in human capital, and the development of a mutually accepted set of rights and obligations binding citizens and the state.

There is thus a greater emphasis in the Ghani and Lockhart framework on what the state actually does with its monopoly over the means of coercion, territorial control, administrative capacity and rules and institutions, and also whether it is strengthening its own legitimacy by triggering and sustaining a development process that encompasses both economic and governance aspects. As they put it, the approach is one based on a "new framework for state functionality based not just on state theory but more importantly on state practice" (Ghani and Lockhart 2008, 223).

Such a distinction between *de facto* and *de jure* sovereignty is particularly apposite in the case of Zimbabwe. As this book shows, the regime in Harare increasingly relied on a political discourse centred on the need for the population to rally around the ruling party to counter perceived threats to its *de jure* sovereignty from Western powers (in particular the UK) in their purported efforts to recolonise Zimbabwe, while simultaneously neglecting its responsibilities in terms of *de facto* sovereignty.

Notwithstanding the utility of such a performance-oriented definition of fragility, there still remains the problem of identifying empirically the direction of travel of any one given state, in other words how to avoid the tautological trap referenced above of automatically associating poverty, and the general challenges of development facing many countries, with high levels of state fragility. Notable amongst efforts to address this problem is the work of Stewart and Brown (Stewart and Brown 2010). One particularly useful aspect of their research is the focus on the service delivery variable as a way of assessing what might be termed 'state effort'. Given that service delivery – defined in terms of basic health provision (with infant mortality as an indicator), education services (measured by primary school enrolment rates) and the provision of clean water (percentage of the population which had access to this public good) – is sub-optimal in all developing economies, they argue that it would be unwise to automatically attribute this solely to shortcomings in terms of government capacity.

However, they go on to argue that where performance in terms of these indicators is significantly below that of the average of countries with similar GDP levels, it would be reasonable to attribute such shortfalls to failures in terms of government agency (the question as to whether this was due to simply a lack of interest at the political centre in improving social welfare indicators, or failure to develop the necessary design and delivery capacity, is left open). As a result, where such sub-optimal performance is present this could be judged a failure on the part of the states in question. It is not the case that the laggard states in question are unable to deliver, but rather that they have not granted the necessary priority to the delivery of such services, and as such are failing to meet their basic domestic obligations (Stewart and Brown 2010, 14–15).

Such insights again speak powerfully to Zimbabwe's experience, particularly from 1998 to 2008, as the country saw a dramatic decline in its population's access to basic sanitation, healthcare, education and employment, as well as declining economic growth rates and income levels. It is significant that such regression took place notwithstanding the state's proven capacity to successfully deliver significant improvements in terms of human development indicators, as was evident during the early post-independence period.

Economic Management, Poverty Reduction and State Fragility

Central to the Ghani and Lockhart framework in terms of fragility reduction is the importance attached to the design and implementation of sound national economic policies, and which is borne out by international data. Based on extensive cross-national evidence, not only does good performance along this dimension result in enhanced prospects for sustained growth defined in terms of aggregates such as GDP, but also translates into improved rates of poverty reduction. Zimbabwe's experience during the crisis years and beyond again provides strong additional proof of the robust link between sound economic management and rates of poverty reduction on the one hand, and in its absence increasing state fragility.

Evidence from one seminal study, based on a large sample of 92 countries, showed that, assuming a constant income distribution, overall economic growth rates led to a proportionate rise in the income of a country's poorest quintile (Dollar and Kraay 2001). In other words, in the context of growth, the average incomes of the poorest quintile moved almost on a one-to-one basis with overall average national income, and therefore the faster and longer such growth was sustained the greater the positive impact on poverty levels.

This strong positive correlation between growth rates and poverty reduction becomes even more compelling in terms of its policy implications when, in addition to a focus on achieving robust and sustained growth which itself has a positive impact on poverty, countries are able to design targeted programmes that ensure that the rate of poverty reduction is even higher than the GDP growth rate. Such programmes recognise the importance of ensuring growth in those sectors in which the poor are concentrated and from which they derive their livelihoods, or alternatively ensure that the structural transformation of an economy made possible under conditions of high growth is accompanied by the necessary employment opportunities in new sectors from which the poor are able to take advantage.[5] They are also usually complemented by targeted social provisioning, aimed at the removal of obstacles to the participation of the poor in growth processes and enhancing their capacity to integrate into the workforce and markets.

One key feature of such targeted approaches to poverty reduction, though often not explicitly formulated in such terms, is that they aim at not only reducing the absolute number of those falling below a given national poverty line, but also seek to ensure that the share of the poor in national income increases, and by implication that inequality levels are reduced. Such an explicitly 'pro-poor' approach to economic development is based on the understanding that similar growth rates can translate into highly differentiated impacts on poverty levels.[6]

One important implication of such findings for states suffering from fragility is that not only do states characterised by high levels of income inequality experience higher levels of political and social instability, but that such economies also experience lower overall growth rates. The reverse also holds true, namely that there appears to be a positive causal effect of low inequality on economic growth rates.[7]

The transmission channels through which such economic growth and poverty reduction impact on state fragility are both varied and complex, but nevertheless worth outlining in schematic form given that they speak powerfully to Zimbabwe's experience. Firstly, and most obviously, growth in average national per capita income, and a drop in the absolute numbers of those living below any given national poverty line (even assuming income distribution only remains constant), reduces levels of deprivation, mitigates feelings of alienation from public authority and of exclusion from national life, and therefore reasons for contestation of the status quo. The second transmission channel linking economic growth, poverty reduction and levels of state fragility variables operates through a set of derived benefits from robust and sustained economic growth rates. In a situation in which the national economic product is growing, and assuming sound tax collection and public expenditure systems, the state is able to both collect and invest more revenue in social and productive infrastructure. Amongst the positive spin-offs are enhanced competitiveness of the economy through the provision and maintenance of public infrastructure such as roads, railways, bridges, power generation and transmission networks, as well as the integration of the entire national territory into a single market which such investments facilitate. This, in and of itself, may help strengthen national unity and counter popular feelings of alienation, neglect and resentment.

Under conditions of economic growth, the increase in resources available for public investment in human capital through expanded education and health programmes also translates into enhanced capacity of the economically active population to integrate into national economic processes, to assimilate new technologies and increase their productivity as workers. The relationship between education, health and economic growth is one of 'cumulative causation', whereby investments in these areas contribute to growth by improving the productivity of a country's human resources, generating wealth which in turn permits both states and individual households to invest more in human capital.

The employment opportunities produced by economic growth, the increased ability of people to take advantage of these, and the improvements in both income and non-income metrics of wellbeing that result from private and public investments, may also assist in enhancing the legitimacy of the state through a 'fiscal contract'. In best case scenarios, the latter is characterised by broad compliance with the revenue demands of the state through taxation in exchange for the delivery of high-quality public goods and services, mediated by sound, transparent and accountable public institutions and financial management systems. The importance of this form of interaction between any given state and its citizens should not be underestimated as an explanatory variable in determining levels of state fragility, as the fiscal relationship is an essential means whereby citizens are able to hold those who control the state to account. And the more dependent governing elites are upon their citizens for the wherewithal to finance the operations of the state, the more likely they are to build the capacity of the state apparatus to develop and deliver policies that meet the needs of the taxpaying citizenry.

However, in many if not all fragile states, the fiscal relationship between states and citizens is characterised by either widespread coercive, corrupt and *ad hoc* taxation practices, or the non-existent delivery of public services, and more commonly a mixture of both. The resentment felt by a citizenry in regard to revenue demands placed upon it by a public authority which at best is seen as incompetent, and at worse as predatory, illegitimate and to be resisted, is widespread in many developing countries. Nowhere is this more so than in fragile states, where state revenue demands are often purely extractive without any element of reciprocity in terms of the delivery of public goods, a phenomenon that became increasingly evident in the case of Zimbabwe.

One significant example of the impact of weak fiscal contracts on fragility concerns states suffering from a 'resource curse', i.e. states that have access to significant subsoil natural resources, and whose budgets rely to a large extent on rents derived from the exploitation of this wealth. In such cases fiscal contracts are often non-existent. There is little reliance upon a tax-paying citizenry for revenue, with resources flowing to state coffers (often subject to substantial 'leakages') from the payment of taxes on profits and royalties by companies. That being the case, state service delivery also tends to be deficient, and public investments in infrastructure such as transport systems, power generation and transmission and communications are often geographically restricted to those areas in which the activities of extractive industries are concentrated, reinforcing the enclave nature of such industries and their lack of linkages with the rest of the economy.

The economies of such states are also characterised by low levels of diversification, extreme export concentration, and therefore highly susceptible to external shocks and rapid and steep downturns in growth rates and export receipts. They tend to experience higher levels of corruption given the ease with which revenues and expenditures may be hidden from public scrutiny when the bulk of state revenues are derived from a small number of sources. Given the 'autonomy' of the state in fiscal terms, there are also few incentives for the state to actively encourage growth in other than its minerals, diamonds or oil sectors, let alone embark on a programme of poverty reduction. As noted by one analyst of the resource curse afflicting many oil rich countries in the developing world:

> The state apparatus, and the people who control it, have a "guaranteed" source of income that makes them independent of their citizens (potential taxpayers). Why listen to citizens or give them any kind of democratic influence over the state? Why use scarce administrative resources to promote broad economic development when the state can feed itself from mineral resources, or from using those revenues to establish "mega-projects" under state control? (Moore 2004, 306)

However, the existence of mineral wealth need not automatically result in high levels of poverty and corruption, or low levels of state effectiveness and poor delivery of public goods and services. This can be seen in the distinct experiences of two mineral resource-rich Sub-Sahara African economies, namely Botswana and the DRC. Botswana over the period 1960–2002 was able to achieve both an average annual growth rate of 7.5 percent, while from 1975 to 2005 it improved the welfare of its population as measured by the UN's Human Development Index (HDI) by 28 percent. In stark contrast, the DRC achieved an average growth rate of

0.2 percent, and its HDI remained largely stagnant over the same period, with the country also falling victim to protracted internal armed conflict as disparate groups fought for control over these resources (Hawkins 2009, 22).

Such contrasts, as well as Zimbabwe's poor track record in this domain following the discovery of rich diamond deposits during the crisis decade, constitute compelling evidence of the importance of sound management of such natural resources for national development purposes. More specifically, they also highlight the role of technically competent overall macroeconomic management, as well as committed political leadership, in determining the extent to which mining activities contribute to improvements in a country's long-term growth prospects and welfare indicators, and reduce rather than compound a state's fragility.

Fragility and Bureaucratic Capacity

Another transmission channel linking state performance in terms of key development indicators and levels of state fragility also operates through the benefits derived from robust and sustained growth rates. It does so through the impact of growth on the effectiveness of national institutions, most particularly, but not only, those responsible for economic affairs such as treasuries, central banks, revenue collection agencies, and planning and finance ministries.

Assuming economic growth is triggered and sustained by competent national economic institutions, a virtuous cycle then becomes possible. An expanding revenue base allows national authorities to embark on processes of public sector reform and ongoing capacity-building aimed at improving state efficiency and effectiveness, most particularly the quality of planning, implementation, and the monitoring and evaluation of performance. Over time these will in turn impact positively on the prospects for additional economic growth, expanding the scope for additional future revenue collection and further improvements in state effectiveness.

In addition, increased revenues that become available through the taxation of enterprises and citizens in the context of a growing economy enable those states to tackle one of the most common sources of estrangement between themselves and their citizens, namely the widespread problem of predatory behaviour by public sector workers in many developing countries, who due to their poor conditions of service are often forced to supplement low wages through corrupt practices. The ability of a state under conditions of robust economic growth to offer competitive conditions of service, and to recruit the best national talent available, is in turn central to the building of effective national bureaucracies.

A technically competent, properly remunerated and motivated public sector workforce (in particular those civil servants operating at the apex of the state) is a precondition for avoiding state fragility. It can drive both the design and successful implementation of a range of national policies in areas such as market formation and expansion, the formalisation of often large informal sectors, economic diversification and improved competitiveness aimed at reducing vulnerability to external shocks, effective investments in productive and social infrastructure, and targeted programmes of poverty reduction aimed at raising both income levels and other human development indicators such as health and education.

Where a civil service is gradually undermined – as was the case in Zimbabwe particularly during the crisis decade due to deteriorating conditions of service and the increasing requirement to demonstrate loyalty to a specific political party in order to secure professional advancement – the result is a decline both in the professionalism of those who remain and the effectiveness of public policy. The negative impact of this on state fragility is both significant, and tremendously challenging to reverse, given the extended timeframes required to rebuild the necessary human capital.

One pioneering attempt to analyse the link in the development process between the quality of bureaucracies and growth rates was that of Evans and Rauch. Drawing on the work of Max Weber who argued that effective bureaucracies constituted an essential component of market-based growth, they examined the relationship in a range of both developed and developing countries between, on the one hand, the efficiency of core economic agencies as measured by a composite indicator of 'Weberianness', and on the other hand their GDP growth rates.[8]

After controlling for variables such as initial levels of human capital and GDP per capita, their findings were significant. The four East Asian economies in their sample (Hong Kong, Taiwan, Singapore and Korea) scored high on both the Weberianness scale and GDP per capita growth over the period 1970–1990, while the four Sub-Sahara African economies (Ivory Coast, Zaire, Nigeria and Kenya) ranked low on the scale, and also had negative cumulative GDP per capita growth over the same period (Evans and Rauch 1999).[9]

Additional benefits flowing from credible and technically competent state bureaucracies – again starkly illustrated by the negative example of Zimbabwe's experience – include the predictability of state policies and rules, reductions in discretionary powers, and their use of long-term planning horizons which both domestic and foreign economic actors can base decisions on. There is greater certainty for economic agents concerning existing and future market conditions which can impact positively on growth rates due to an increased willingness on the part of entrepreneurs to undertake long-term investments in plant, equipment, workforces, and to expand production.

In regard to the latter consideration, Ghani and Lockhart have highlighted the devastating impact of the unpredictability of state policy on a country's economic growth and development prospects:

> Unpredictable rules – often idiosyncratically interpreted or corruptly applied – can generate a climate of distrust and contribute to a crisis in state legitimacy. Pervasive corruption not only undermines confidence but also deters investment…Today the bulk of direct foreign investment goes to only ten countries in the developing world, leaving the bulk of other countries outside the flows of the system. (Ghani and Lockhart 2008, 133)

The resource curse also has a particularly strongly impact on the effectiveness of state bureaucracies; nowhere are the difficulties of building efficient bureaucracies more keenly felt than in the case of countries suffering from the resource curse, where the pathology of ineffective public sectors is most manifest, and the incentives for a reversal of the situation so weak. As argued by Moore, the explanation for this lies in the fact that in a situation of high dependence on oil and mineral extraction and revenue flowing from a small number of production facilities:

> The task of raising revenue from the mineral facilities requires few specialists, and these may be imported to make them more easily controllable. It is not necessary to establish the kind of meritocratic public bureaucracy that is required to manage a complex tax system or to establish the control mechanisms and public-service values needed to protect against the worst abuses in tax collection. (Moore 2004, 308)

As detailed in Chap. 12, Zimbabwe's rapid manifestation of symptoms of the resource curse following the discovery of significant diamond deposits in 2006, and the control that the ruling party quickly established over this revenue source which it was to use for regime preservation, contributed significantly to the hollowing out of bureaucratic capacity and the increasing unpredictability of overall public policy.

Market Strengthening, Poverty Reduction and State Legitimacy

One characteristic of national economic life shared by low-income fragile states is the weakness of their markets, which takes a number of forms. Firstly, it is reflected both in the limited presence and restricted size of markets for labour, finance, and land. Secondly, they are highly susceptible to various forms of market failure, such as pervasive information asymmetries and monopolies.[10]

In all low-income fragile states, a large percentage of households are engaged in subsistence activities, consuming most if not all of their output, and therefore do not possess a surplus to sell or exchange for other goods and services. While low factor productivity is a common if not defining feature of developing countries, the prevalence of subsistence economies is markedly higher in fragile states given that incentives for surplus production and exchange are weaker than normal. This is partly attributable to the unpredictability of economic life under authoritarian and predatory states, with household assets and surpluses regularly being appropriated, and markets destroyed or driven underground at the whim of state functionaries and their political masters. This was yet another strong and recurrent feature of life in Zimbabwe during its crisis decade, and remains so to the present day.

Such weak incentives to produce also reflect the impact of poor national economic policies, in particular in the areas of fiscal and monetary policy. Fiscal policy may be poorly designed and targeted. It may prioritise expenditure on non-productive areas such as defence and internal security, as opposed to public investments in directly productive infrastructure, or health and education. In the worst case scenario of states controlled by kleptocratic elites, fiscal policy may reflect no imperative other than that of elite enrichment.

Monetary policy may also obey the same logic, and be used to feed profligate fiscal policy. One consequence is high levels of inflation, leading to reduced savings and investment, thus trapping an economy in a low-level equilibrium. Poor monetary policy that drives inflation not only corrodes the real value of assets and the incentive to save and invest, but under conditions of hyperinflation leads to a collapse of the mechanism of price signals and the allocative role this plays, the growing irrelevance of money as a medium of exchange, and *in extremis* the extensive bartering of goods and services. All the former are features common to the economies of many low-income fragile states, and were particularly prominent in Zimbabwe in the mid-2000s, with the country enjoying the dubious distinction of having the world's highest inflation rate as a result of the ruling party's profligate fiscal and monetary policies.

Under such conditions there is little scope for financial services markets to develop, and deficient financial intermediation acts as a further brake on increases in levels of savings, investment and output, with particularly damaging effects on the access of the poor to working capital. Efforts by development experts engaged in building 'inclusive financial markets' – part and parcel of a wider effort to understand the micro-level constraints to the participation of the poor in economic activity – have played a critical role in bringing to light the various shortcomings that characterise financial systems in developing economies.[11] Once again, the Zimbabwean experience provides a powerful example of additional negative consequences of defective monetary and fiscal policies, as during the crisis years policy decisions severely weakened the country's financial system, with the majority of the population – and not only the poor – excluded from an increasingly stressed formal financial system.

The problem of the thinness of markets in fragile states is compounded by low (or non-existent) investments in public infrastructure. The poor condition of roads and bridges which have not been maintained can substantially increase the time required to transport inputs and finished goods, and impose additional costs on producers, buyers and sellers. Where power generation and transmission has been neglected, power supplies become erratic forcing enterprises to regularly interrupt production, lay off workers, or rely on costly alternatives such as generators. Zimbabwe once again vividly illustrates the impact of deteriorating infrastructure on economic performance, as physical assets underwent a process of deterioration more usually associated with situations of open armed conflict.

Given degraded or non-existent transport and communications infrastructure, as well as severe deficits in terms of electricity and water provisioning, an additional feature of fragile state markets is that they are also highly fragmented, i.e. physically isolated from each other as a result of obstacles to the transportation of goods and services beyond their immediate point of production. The phenomenon of rural economies that are disconnected from urban markets is a pervasive one. Such fragmented markets fail to produce goods even though there is both domestic demand, and the costs of production are lower than the prices consumers would be willing to pay, because of bottlenecks in terms of roads, bridges, rail and fluvial transport, and telecommunications.

Not only might government policy be remiss in terms of the provision of such public goods and therefore fail to assist the process of market formation and strengthening, but it may also perversely and actively reduce the incentives for economic agents to engage in production and exchange. In extreme cases such as Zimbabwe, governments can engage in market destruction to ensure a state monopoly for any given product or service, in turn reflecting the imperatives of political patronage and the increased scope for rent-seeking which elite control of such monopolies permits. The driving of production and markets underground due to a heavy state-imposed regulatory burden and the high costs of compliance, the excessive tax demands placed on enterprises, and the attendant high levels of informality that constitute a reaction to such burdens, are also ubiquitous features of the economies of fragile states.

Additional state functions essential to the operation of markets, such as legal systems that ensure security of property and the enforcement of contracts, also tend to be highly deficient. As this book demonstrates,

Zimbabwe again constitutes a paradigmatic example of what happens once such support systems are actively undermined, contributing to the unpredictability of state policies and the unwillingness of private sector actors to undertake investments.

The consequences of state failure in this area of market formation and strengthening are forcefully highlighted by Ghani and Lockhart:

> When weak states cannot enable the market to function or when they actively subvert its functioning, they block development and prosperity and fail to generate institutional linkages. This freezes capital, which cannot flow through an economy. Inadequate regulation leads to the informalization of transactions, and if property security is tenuous and arbitration unpredictable, then capital is not attracted to a state but flees it instead. (Ghani and Lockhart 2008, 153)

Equally importantly, and on a more foundational level, such weaknesses in markets contribute directly to the restriction of a fundamental freedom seen by some economic theorists such as Amartya Sen as integral to both development as an objective, as well as a basic liberty that humans value, namely the freedom to participate as economic agents in markets. As Sen has argued:

> a denial of opportunities of transaction, through arbitrary controls, can be seen as a source of unfreedom in itself. People are then prevented from doing what can then be taken to be – in the absence of compelling reasons to the contrary – something that is within their right to do. This point does not depend on the efficiency of the market mechanism or any extensive analysis of the consequences of having or not having a market system; it turns simply on the importance of freedom of exchange without let or hindrance. (Sen 2000, 25–26)

As this book details, restrictions of this nature played a central role in the drama of Zimbabwe's political and economic regression, as an increasing number of rules and regulations were introduced which severely curtailed, and in some cases destroyed, both markets and economic freedoms, and compounded the processes of pauperisation of the vast majority of Zimbabweans and the state's growing fragility.

Notes

1. So, for example, the work of the International Crisis Group (ICG), an international NGO founded in 1995 in the aftermath of the conflicts in Rwanda, Somalia and Bosnia. It keeps a watching brief on countries undergoing or prone to conflict, and through its publications provides advice on conflict prevention and resolution.
2. The term LICUS was used by the World Bank until 2006, when it adopted the more widely-used term 'fragile states' in common with other international development actors.
3. The CPIA is a composite index of 16 indicators grouped into four broad clusters, namely economic management, structural policies (these include the extent of openness to trade, the state of the financial sector in terms of variables such as stability and access, and the business regulatory environment in terms of whether it supports or hinders private enterprise), policies on social inclusion and equity, and public sector management and institutions. The CPIA is used by the World Bank, amongst other things, to determine eligibility of countries to access International Development Association (IDA) resources, the highly concessional soft loan window of the World Bank. The notion of 'quality' of any given country's policy and institutional framework is defined as how conducive that framework is for fostering poverty reduction, sustainable growth and effective use of Official Development Assistance (ODA).
4. Based at the Institute of State Effectiveness in Washington, DC, Ghani and Lockhart played a key role in highlighting the problem that fragile and failed states present to the international community, and have carried out seminal work in terms of designing toolkits for practitioners working in the area of building effective states in the developing world.
5. The concept of economic structural transformation is based on the key observation, derived from global evidence, that as growth occurs there is a reallocation of economic activity away from agriculture in terms of output (contribution to GDP) and employment towards urban-based manufacturing and service sector activities. This is accompanied by a migration of workers from rural to urban areas. This process is an ongoing one, and its features are present even in advanced industrial economies.
6. The study showing the beneficial effects of such explicitly pro-poor programmes was conducted by Martin Ravallion. Based on a sample of 47

developing countries, he demonstrated that where there was both growth and rising income inequality, the average annual rate of poverty reduction as measured by the percentage of the population living below the US$1/day metric averaged 1.3 percent per annum (interestingly, the latter figure being close to the rate of poverty reduction in the Dollar and Kraay study). This contrasted sharply with those countries that combined rising average incomes with falling inequality, and which achieved average annual rates of poverty reduction closer to 10 percent per annum. Even more significant as an explanation of what happened in Zimbabwe during its 'deep crisis' years in the mid-2000s – which saw a rapidly contracting GDP, a rise in income inequality, as well as a vertiginous increase in both the number of Zimbabweans falling below the national poverty line and in the depth of their poverty – is the robust correlation between these variables established by Ravallion in the 47 developing countries sampled: "Amongst contracting economies it also mattered greatly what was happening to inequality: on average, when inequality was rising and average incomes were falling the poverty rate was rising by a dramatic 14 percent per year" (Ravallion 2001, 17).

7. On this point, and based on the experience of East Asian economies, see Birdsall et al. 1995.
8. Amongst the variables examined by Evans and Rauch were meritocratic recruitment (seen as translating into a greater likelihood of civil servants meeting minimum standards of technical competence), the existence of clearly defined long-term and rewarding career paths which led to an increased scope for experience to be accumulated, greater corporate coherence, reduced temptations to engage in corrupt practices given performance-based reward systems, as well as the adoption of longer-term planning horizons. They posited that bureaucracies that possessed such characteristics would help to trigger and sustain growth through a number of causal paths. The possibility of adopting longer-term planning horizons, for example, increased the likelihood that civil servants would be advocates for increased public sector infrastructure investment rather than consumption, with long-term benefits for growth.
9. It is worth recalling that the legitimacy of the state in many East Asian countries such as South Korea and Taiwan during the period of their economic miracles was based on their ability to both plan and implement programmes leading to high economic growth rates that were sustained over extended periods of time and which resulted in the structural

transformation of those economies. As with a later generation of East and South East Asian countries such as Singapore, Malaysia, Thailand, Vietnam, Indonesia and China, which have enjoyed rapid economic growth, undergone structural transformation, and overseen significant improvements in the welfare of their citizens, the legitimacy of the state in all these successful Asian economies (arguably irrespective of the degree of openness of their political systems) derived precisely from the fact that they are seen as 'plan rational', i.e. the *raison d'être* of the state was conceived in terms of its ability to oversee rapid economic development and ensure significant improvements in living standards, which in some cases took place over the course of a single generation.

10. One common feature of such markets is that producers, buyers and sellers have differentiated access to information in such areas as prices and potential markets, allowing some to exploit the ignorance of others. The most common example given of such information asymmetries is that of small-scale agricultural producers, who are often exploited by middlemen given their inability to access information regarding market prices of both inputs as well as the prices their produce will fetch in destination markets. In such 'thin' markets, a few producers and traders may also achieve a monopoly position, and through such market power charge higher prices by restricting supply which in turn further restricts the growth of markets.
11. Significant efforts have been made by the United Nations Department of Economic and Social Affairs (UNDESA) and the United Nations Capital Development Fund (UNCDF) to analyse the various constraints operating on financial markets in developing economies, the extent to which the poor are excluded from these, and to propose remedial measures that would enhance access of the poor to financial services. For an example of this work see UNDESA and UNCDF 2006.

References

Birdsall, Nancy, David Ross, and Richard Sabot. 1995. Inequality and Growth Reconsidered: Lessons from East Asia. *World Bank Economic Review* 9 (3, September 1): 477–508.

Dollar, David, and Aart Kraay. 2001. *Growth Is Good for the Poor*, Policy Research Working Paper No. 2587, April. Washington, DC: World Bank Development Research Group.

Evans, Peter, and James E. Rauch. 1999. Weberian Bureaucracy and Economic Growth: A Cross-National Analysis of the Effects of "Weberian" State Structures on Economic Growth. *American Sociological Review* 64 (5, October): 748–765.

Ghani, Ashraf, and Clare Lockhart. 2008. *Fixing Failed States—A Framework for Rebuilding a Fractured World.* New York: Oxford University Press.

Hawkins, Tony. 2009. *The Mining Sector in Zimbabwe and Its Potential Contribution to Recovery*, Comprehensive Economic Recovery in Zimbabwe Working Paper Series, No. 1. Harare: United Nations Development Programme.

Moore, Mick. 2004. Revenues, State Formation and the Quality of Governance in Developing Countries. *International Political Science Review* 25 (3): 297–319.

OECD-DAC. 2005. *Piloting the Principles for Good International Engagement in Fragile States and Situations*, April. Paris.

Putzell, James. 2010. *Why Development Actors Need a Better Definition of "State Fragility"*, Policy Direction Series, September. CSRC, London School of Economics.

Ravallion, Martin. 2001. *Growth, Inequality and Poverty—Looking Beyond Averages*, Policy Research Working Paper No. 2558, February. World Bank Development Research Group.

Sen, Amartya. 2000. *Development as Freedom.* New York: Anchor Books.

Stewart, Francis, and Graham K. Brown. 2010. *Fragile States: CRISE Overview 3.* Oxford: Centre for Research on Inequality, Human Security and Ethnicity (CRISE).

UNDESA and UNCDF. 2006. *Building Inclusive Financial Sectors for Development.* New York: United Nations.

World Bank. 2006. *Engaging with Fragile States: An IEG Review of World Bank Support to Low-Income Countries Under Stress.* Washington, DC: World Bank Independent Evaluation Group.

3

Zimbabwe's First Decade: Building the One-Party State and Controlling the Economy

The Revolutionary Vision

While Zimbabwe's next generation of political leaders were busy directing the guerrilla armies in the 1970s campaign against the Rhodesian white minority government, Zimbabwean intellectuals and economists focused on their plans for rebuilding, and especially transforming, the economy. Many of their ideas were subsequently set out in a two-volume economic and social survey, 'Zimbabwe: Towards a New Order', published by the United Nations Conference on Trade and Development (UNCTAD 1980).

The flavour of the document is captured in its characterisation of the country as the "under-development of African areas and the over-development of European areas" (Ibid., vol. II, 66). The vision of the future Zimbabwe was wholly autarkic. Development must be reliant on the "fullest exploitation of domestic materials", while foreign aid and investment should be considered "a bonus, excluded from state economic planning. Foreigners may help or hinder but their impact… is marginal" (Ibid., vol. II, 66–67). The document set out the case against foreign investment, arguing that in the medium and long-term Zimbabwe's

M. Simpson, T. Hawkins, *The Primacy of Regime Survival*,
https://doi.org/10.1007/978-3-319-72520-8_3

"productive forces" must be in Zimbabwean hands, reminiscent of policies revived during the crisis decade and still currently in play. Foreign firms should be forced to cooperate in their own demise, maintaining output and investment during an interim period while local managers and workers were trained to take over (Ibid., vol. I, 413–541).

The key challenge was that of ending "one of the worst colonial and racial-class structures and restructuring an extremely dependent economy" (Ibid., vol. II, 103). Centralised decision-making was endorsed to impose "national control over a largely externally-controlled and oriented economy" (Ibid., vol. II, 135).

The document's sections on land reform spelled out what was to come, though only many years later:

> The objective solution is the confiscation of all land and distribution to those without land. No compensation should be paid to those who have stolen land. These methods were used in all socialist countries of Asia and Europe with encouraging results, particularly in China, Albania and Korea. The correct application of a Marxist-Leninist ideology based on the concrete conditions in Zimbabwe is essential. (Ibid., vol. I, 17)

In terms of manufacturing industry, a socialist development model was considered essential "to eliminate poverty, unemployment, social insecurity and misery which are the results of the development of the present peripheral-capitalist mode of production". To achieve this a "superstructural institution" would be needed. "The socialist state can only create a socialist mode of production by establishing social ownership of the means of production through nationalisation" (Ibid., vol. I, 91).

In the event, however, the incoming government in 1980 initially turned out to be more cautious in its pursuit of these revolutionary goals (though twenty years later, the ideals, threats, hopes and promises contained in the 1980 document had mutated into the FTLRP of the early 2000s and the Indigenisation and Economic Empowerment Act signed into law by Mugabe in 2008). While the language of Marxism-Leninism continued to figure prominently in early post-independence party documents, and Leninist principles continued to strongly influence the ruling party – its organisational makeup was similar to that of Marxist-Leninist parties around the world as seen in its Central Committee and Politburo and women's, youth and labour wings – official planning documents were more circumspect.

In February 1981, the government's first economic policy statement in the form of a White Paper – 'Growth with Equity' – seemed to partially de-emphasise the revolutionary thrust on immediate redistribution, and to grant greater importance to the need for rapid growth in order to create the wealth necessary for subsequent distribution. Given the at times conflicting content, the final version was clearly the product of a compromise between economic pragmatists and a more revolutionary wing within the party.

> The government is determined to undertake a vigorous programme for the development of the country, and within it to pursue and implement policies based on socialist, egalitarian and democratic principles, in conditions of rapid growth, full employment, price stability, dynamic efficiency in resource allocation and an equitable distribution of the ensuing benefits. (GOZ 1981a, 2)

In other sections of the document, however, the revolutionary rhetoric did come forcefully to the fore, such as the declared intention to grant the state a central role in national life, with promises to "end imperialist exploitation, achieve a more equitable pattern of resource ownership, including land, and promote participation in, and ownership of, a significant portion of the economy by nationals and by the state" (Ibid., 2).

In an early indication of what came to represent planning throughout the post-independence period, the brief – 18 pages – policy White Paper contained rafts of ambitious targets, but little detail. It admitted that "rapid industrialization" could not be expected to solve the unemployment crisis, suggesting that rural development would have to play the major role in job creation for the fast-growing population. The government promised to liberate the informal sector, removing all "unjustifiable, legal, social and economic discrimination against this sector" while regulating it in order to raise product standards and persuading all those who could not find formal sector jobs to "return to the land and participate in rural development" (Ibid., 10).

Social policy included the promulgation of a national minimum wage, with free primary schooling for all and free health services for the rural and urban poor, and the establishment of a National Pension and Social Security Scheme. It also promised to set up a National Development Fund to mobilise domestic and external finance. The White Paper described the fiscal system as "a major instrument for achieving the objectives of growth, equity and full employment" (Ibid., 15). New state-owned entities to be established included the Zimbabwe Development Bank, the Zimbabwe Development Corporation, Mining Development Corporation, National Tourism Corporation, State Trading Corporation and the National Science and Technology Foundation.

Some of the government's ambitious developmental objectives were fleshed out in the subsequent report for the Zimbabwe Conference on Reconstruction and Development (ZIMCORD) in March 1981, a roundtable aimed at garnering international donor support. The ZIMCORD document stated that "Government's priority objective is to transform and develop the rural peasant sector where the overwhelming majority of the population live and to integrate that sector with the commercial primary and industrial/urban sectors" (GOZ 1981b, 3). The main thrust of ZIMCORD was not nationalisation of manufacturing or mining operations, but "justice and equity in the ownership of land".

> Government is determined to ensure that the resettlement programme will not be a transfer or extension of subsistence farming practices to new areas. Government will provide extension services, infrastructure and the other services needed to assure higher productivity and a better standard of living for the settler families. Simultaneously with the resettlement of families on new lands, work is being done in traditional areas to improve their infrastructure and develop them into integral and productive sectors of the economy. (Ibid., 3)

As events were later to show, the vision for land reform set out in the ZIMCORD report could hardly have been more different from the subsequent FTLRP after 2000, which saw not only the large-scale transfer of subsistence farming methods to former commercial farmland, but also the collapse of the necessary infrastructure and agricultural support services. Significantly, the ZIMCORD report also promised that: "Land in commercial areas that is being farmed productively will not be diverted from its present use and ownership", adding that "land required for resettlement will be paid for in cash, long-term bonds or a combination of these measures" (Ibid., 37).

The extent to which national realities were refracted by the ruling party through the prism of Marxist-Leninist analytical categories was most evident in the subsequent Transitional National Development Plan (TNDP). In sharp contrast to ZIMCORD, the authors of the TNDP – who did not have to play to a primarily external Western donor audience – made little effort to disguise their impatience with the pace of progress towards Marxist-Socialist transformation. Writing in late 1982, just two-and-a-half years after Independence, they noted that property relations had remained basically unchanged, bemoaning the fact that almost the entire mining and financial sectors were in the hands of foreign multinationals and vested interests: "A considerable stock of capital and the technical knowledge that goes with it, come from, and are under, foreign control. Our Independence and political power should now transform into an instrument for establishing an equitable socio-economic order" (GOZ 1982, 18).

As long as ownership and control of the means of production lay in the hands of "privileged groups in society", the bulk of the people would remain "mere wage earners, to be exploited and manipulated at will by the bourgeoisie". Seventy percent of the people, it said, were peasants living in communal areas. The TNDP's main thrust "was to correct the existing imbalance between the depressed rural communal sector and the developed sectors of the economy", in part by organising the peasants into Peasant Associations to stimulate their "collective spirit" (Ibid., 18).

A second category of Zimbabwean beneficiaries was made up of workers who had suffered years of exploitation in the form of meagre wages and harsh working conditions. This class would grow as the country industrialised and eventually comprise the largest class and, as the national proletariat, wield greater economic power. The "middle bourgeoisie" and the capitalists would be "regulated and coordinated" by the state, while the petty bourgeoisie would be assisted to set up cooperatives "so that they can expand their services to the people in a socialised way" (Ibid., 19). The government's role would be to provide the institutional environment necessary for the establishment of popular mass organisations, including party-affiliated trade unions, and youth and women's wings.

Significantly, the TNDP also set out the framework for what was to eventually become, decades later, the government's Indigenisation and Economic Empowerment programme. Participation in and ownership of a significant proportion of the economy by nationals and the state would imply collective participation of Zimbabweans in the ownership and management of private enterprise alongside state control of some enterprises for both economic and political security reasons. By the end of 1982 the new Zimbabwe government had set out its stall – how it planned to transform the economy (though precise timings were left unspecified), and the role the state would play as planner, coordinator, implementer, and where necessary enforcer.

Economic Performance and Social Gains

When viewed against the backdrop of Sub-Saharan Africa as a whole, the 1980s in Zimbabwe were a moderately successful decade in terms of economic growth, and certainly so when compared to the country's later performance. While growth did slow from the levels reached during the Unilateral Declaration of Independence (UDI) period (1965–1980), this could be explained by the deterioration in the global economic situation, a bad drought in 1982–83, notably weaker global commodity prices and relatively slow growth of world trade, as well as tensions in Southern Africa as Western nations tightened sanctions against the regional economic superpower, South Africa.

Zimbabwe's GDP growth of around 4.0 percent a year, during what might be termed the 'command economy' years from 1980 to 1990, was slower than the UDI period (1965–1980) during which output had risen by an average annual rate of 4.7 percent a year. This was, however, still substantially higher than the Sub-Saharan average of 2.4 percent. Consequently, Zimbabwe was one of a minority of Sub-Saharan economies in which per capita incomes actually increased during the 1980s given that for Sub-Saharan Africa as a whole (excluding South Africa), income per head fell from an average of US$572 during the 1975–1984 period to an average of US$503 between 1985 and 1989. However, while the average nominal wage increased 14 percent a year during the 1980s, consumer prices rose more than 13 percent a year, and as a result average real wages increased only marginally at around one percent annually (ZIMSTAT. various).

The decade from 1980 to 1990 did, however, see significant improvements in terms of social indicators. Infant mortality per 1,000 live births fell from 86 in 1980 to 49 in 1990, against a Sub-Saharan African average of 103. Life expectancy rose between 1980 and 1990 from 56 years to 62 years, against a Sub-Saharan average of 52. Immunisation coverage rose from 25 percent to 80 percent. In education, primary school enrolments rose from 1.2 million children in 1980 to 2.2 million ten years later, while the increase in secondary school enrolments was even more dramatic – from 74,000 to 675,000 (World Bank 1995). But because these undoubted successes in terms of human development were not matched by economic growth and rising per capita incomes which would have sustained a growing government revenue base, the cost of government spending programmes was to eventually translate into a growing fiscal deficit.

Formal sector employment data for the decade was particularly alarming. A mere 182,000 formal sector jobs were created during the whole of the 1980s. By the end of the 1980s the population growth rate had been revised upwards to 3.4 percent a year, while the labour force was estimated to be growing at 3.7 percent annually. By 1990, the number of new school leavers entering the labour market each year had increased nearly sevenfold to 200,000. The rapid expansion in school enrolment at both primary and secondary levels after Independence had the effect of postponing labour market entry until the latter part of the 1980s for the majority of new entrants to the workforce, in an economy that was simply not growing fast enough to absorb them.

Early Warning Signs of Macroeconomic Mismanagement

By the end of the first decade of independence, it was abundantly clear the economic policy stance was not sustainable. Firstly, there was the growing fiscal deficit, a product of unsustainably high levels of spending against the backdrop of weak GDP and government revenue growth rates, increasing subsidies to an expanding list of loss-making parastatals,[1] a worsening domestic debt profile, and rising interest payments. While during the 1980s government revenue averaged 27 percent of GDP, public expenditure averaged 34 percent, and as a result annual interest payments rose tenfold to reach 4.8 percent of GDP by 1990, early signs of what would become Zimbabwe's intractable fiscal problem, though its magnitude was subsequently dwarfed by what was to come.

Secondly there was the growing balance-of-payments deficit, financed increasingly by offshore borrowing in the form of short-term official loans. Lacklustre export performance – between 1980 and 1990 export volumes fell 15 percent while export prices declined 10 percent – is attributable both to weakness in global commodity prices in the 1980s, but also to an inherent anti-export bias in the country's economic policy framework in the form of an overvalued exchange rate, with exports growing at less than 2 percent a year over the decade.

Thirdly there was a growing external debt burden. During the 1980s private capital inflows – both Foreign Direct Investment (FDI) and bank lending – was negative to the tune of US$230 million. At the same time the International Financial Institutions (IFIs) and bilateral lenders disbursed US$1.95 billion over the decade, as a result of which Zimbabwe's external debt more than doubled, rising from US$1.07 billion (19.6 percent of GDP) in 1980 to US$2.5 billion (56 percent of GDP) ten years later.

Finally there was an investment drought, which translated directly into slow growth and rising unemployment. During the 1980s investment fell sharply to average only 13 percent of GDP (in comparison, between 1968 and 1976, during the period of mandatory UN sanctions prior to Independence, investment had averaged 23 percent of GDP). Factors included the risk perceptions associated with undertaking investments in Zimbabwe held by foreign firms, the costs of doing business in a highly regulated environment, as well as constraints in terms of foreign exchange availability which inhibited domestic private sector investment.

While both domestic and foreign investors were initially reassured by Mugabe's promises of reconciliation and non-racialism, and the fact that much of the radicalism of the aforementioned pre-independence report on the economy that had been prepared by Mugabe's advisers seemed to have been quietly shelved, they remained concerned by the new government's early insistence on Marxist-Socialist transformation, even if this was often attributed to the need for Mugabe to play to the gallery. With a small number of exceptions, major foreign investors largely stayed on the sidelines, watching and waiting for Mugabe to publicly reject the command economy model.

Exogenous variables also had an impact. While in the 1970s Zimbabwe's geographical proximity to South Africa was the key factor enabling the white minority Smith government to circumvent mandatory UN sanctions, in the 1980s the boot was on the other foot. The international sanctions campaign against South Africa heightened regional instability, with adverse knock-on effects on investment and foreign trade given that South Africa was the main market for exports of Zimbabwean manufactured goods. This was initially compounded by South Africa's destabilisation strategy in the region, which included the suspension of a 1964 trade agreement with Zimbabwe that was vital to the country's manufactured exports.[2] Investment prospects suffered not just from Zimbabwe's fraught relationship with South Africa, and the disadvantage of being located next door to the continent's largest industrial power, but also civil wars in Mozambique and Angola which led to heightened risk perceptions of the region as a whole.

But while such exogenous influences – exogenous in the sense that they were externally driven – were a drag on economic performance, this should not be allowed to obscure the contribution of domestic economic policies, allied with weak economic policy implementation and poor economic governance. A pattern was gradually established during the first decade of independence – and which would reach its full fruition during the crisis decade – whereby public expenditure dominance was the order of the day. The state became a serial over spender, and the government was forced to borrow both at home and abroad to finance its budget deficit as a result of which domestic and foreign debt escalated alarmingly. In addition, the state was increasingly borrowing to finance recurrent outlays and not only its capital budget. Consequently, by the late 1980s, Zimbabwe was already slipping into a debt-trap whereby it needed to raise new loans to pay interest on its existing borrowings.

Slippages on the Political Governance Front

If the pace of progress towards Marxist-Socialist transformation of the economy during the first decade of independence was more muted than early declared policy positions might have suggested, moves on the political front towards the establishment of a *de facto* one-party state were less disguised. Soon after Independence ZANU's willingness to use force to crush dissent quickly became apparent, establishing a pattern of behaviour which has continued to the present day.

In the course of the armed struggle, tensions had become apparent between the armed wings of ZANU and ZAPU, respectively the Zimbabwe African National Liberation Army (ZANLA) and the Zimbabwe People's Revolutionary Army (ZIPRA). These reflected both ethno-regional factors, with ZIPRA recruiting primarily amongst Ndebele speakers in the Matabeleland provinces, while ZANLA was dominated by Shona-speakers, as well as the fact that ZANLA operated from bases in Mozambique and ZIPRA from Zambia, with limited coordination between the two in terms of joint military operations against the white minority government. On those occasions when their operational zones overlapped, there were reports of clashes between ZANLA and ZIPRA guerrillas. In the context of the Sino-Soviet split, additional fault lines between the two liberation movements and their armies mirrored the ideological disputes between their respective international backers, with ZANLA being supported by Beijing and ZIPRA by Moscow.[3]

Such mistrust led to heightened tensions following the Lancaster House Agreement in the run-up to Independence, with violent incidents between ZIPRA and ZANLA soldiers quartered in assembly points awaiting their integration into a new, unified, national army. This led eventually to small groups of ZIPRA soldiers abandoning their assembly points and returning to the bush. When arms caches were discovered in Matabeleland in 1982, the ZANU leadership openly accused ZAPU of planning an armed revolt aimed at overturning the results of the 1980 general elections in which ZAPU had been defeated. ZAPU and ZIPRA leaders were arrested and a number of former ZIPRA guerrillas abandoned their posts in the new army.

Between 1981 and 1982, ZAPU members increasingly expressed their opposition to what they saw as Shona/ZANU dominance of state institutions. Violent clashes between former ZIPRA guerrillas who had returned to the bush and the new Zimbabwean Defence Forces (ZDF) eventually led to the ruling party's decision to launch Operation *Gukurahundi*, a Shona term for the 'rains which wash away the chaff'.

Soon after Independence, Harare had entered into an agreement with North Korea for the training and equipping of a brigade in the new army. In January 1983, this Fifth Brigade was deployed to Matabeleland to crush the dissent. Extensive and well-documented brutality was inflicted on both the armed dissidents and the civilian population, with the latter subjected to torture, rape, and the destruction of crops, livestock and homesteads. The final figures of the number of civilian deaths during *Gukurahundi* range from 3,000 to as high as 20,000 (Catholic Commission 1997).

In an interesting preview of what would to happen in the aftermath of the 2008 general elections when the Movement for Democratic Change (MDC) was pummelled into submission and forced into a power-sharing arrangement with ZANU as junior partner, ZAPU's Joshua Nkomo was eventually compelled to enter into a Unity Accord with ZANU in 1987. ZAPU was dissolved, and its members absorbed into the new ruling party which was designated ZANU-PF (Patriotic Front).

Following the Unity Accord, intense debates began to take place within ZANU-PF on the need to move towards a *de jure* one party state in line with its Marxist-Leninist principles, with Mugabe increasingly arguing at party congresses in favour of the necessary enabling legislation to be passed by Parliament. The arguments presented often harkened back to an earlier generation of African Socialist leaders, with the one-party state being put forward as the best instrument for the twin tasks of nation-building and development, both of which would be facilitated by a putative, innate, African collectivism. The 1989 ZANU-PF Party Congress passed a resolution supporting the proposal, and with the expiry of the Lancaster House Agreement the last legal impediment to the establishment of a *de jure* one party state was removed.

In the event, however, the necessary steps were not taken. At the time, some within the ruling party argued that given ZANU-PF's overwhelming dominance of the legislature and increasing control of the state apparatus such a move was simply unnecessary. It might also lead to tensions with Western countries upon which Zimbabwe then relied heavily in terms of foreign investment, markets and development assistance, particularly at a time when Western capitals were openly supportive of the winds of multi-party democratisation sweeping the continent in the early 1990s following the collapse of Eastern bloc communism.

In addition, unease was expressed within ruling circles that such a decision would lead to fractures within the party. Such concerns were given credence when Edgar Tekere – a veteran of the liberation struggle, founding member of ZANU and its former Secretary-General – broke ranks and founded the short-lived Zimbabwe Unity Movement (ZUM) in the late 1980s in response to Mugabe's increasingly strident statements in favour of a one-party state which Tekere strongly opposed. While a *de jure* one-party state was not established, there were nevertheless moves towards increasingly authoritarian *de facto* single party rule. This was achieved through incremental amendments to the constitution, the net effect of which was to entrench ZANU-PF power and that of the Presidency, and to silence dissent.

So, for example, Constitutional Amendment No.4 of 1984 reconstituted the country's Judicial Services Commission in order to give the President greater control over its operations and in the appointment of members of the Bench. Foremost amongst the amendments during the 1980s which gave constitutional backing to this drift towards authoritarian rule was Amendment No.7 of 1987. This abolished the post of prime minister and replaced the post of non-Executive President with that of an Executive President with significantly expanded powers. Some provisions of the Amendment placed the President above both Parliament and the judiciary, with the latter denied the right to question the President on the substance of policies or the processes through which decisions were arrived at. Furthermore, through the provisions granting extended powers to the head of state under the 'Temporary Measures' clauses, the President was granted significant rule-making powers that rivalled those of Parliament.

Amendment No.9 of 1989 restructured the legislature, abolishing the Senate, expanding the lower House of Assembly from 120 to 150 representatives, of whom 20 members were appointed by the new Executive President in the form of 8 provincial governors and 12 special Presidential appointees. The net result was to further weaken checks and balances within the country's political governance system.

Events at the time also highlighted a pattern of behaviour that would become commonplace in subsequent years, namely Mugabe's use of his prerogative to grant Presidential Amnesties and Clemency Orders. In the aftermath of *Gukurahundi*, pardons were granted to both ZIPRA dissidents and members of the security forces, though the latter were the major beneficiaries for actions committed in the 'bona fide' execution of their mandates.[4] Such pardons were not limited to the perpetrators of human rights violations. They were also increasingly granted to corrupt politicians and officials, amidst growing popular perceptions that the revolutionary frugality apparent during the armed struggle had been quickly overtaken in the post-independence period by personal greed.

While the ruling party introduced a strict Leadership Code which proscribed party members from extensive ownership of private businesses, this quickly proved to have limited impact given the increasingly common use of privileged access by state and party functionaries to controlled goods for personal gain. The growing scope for the latter was underpinned by a cosy alliance between ZANU-PF politicians and businessmen, with the latter owing their existence to the operating and foreign-exchange licenses granted by ruling party appointees. State-awarded contracts became increasingly opaque in terms of the procurement processes followed, and state-owned enterprises were increasingly led by executives appointed by ZANU-PF based on their party affiliation.

Most notorious amongst the corruption scandals of the 1980s – though dwarfed in terms of scale by the far larger kleptocratic undertakings in the new millennium – was the Willowgate scandal involving government ministers, provincial governors and senior civil servants.[5] Though a commission of inquiry into Willowgate was instituted, the findings made public and five ministers eventually resigned, Mugabe was subsequently to grant them pardons. As two Zimbabwe analysts were to note, similar scandals and lack of accountability constituted "an early signal that the rule of law would be sacrificed to predation" (Bratton and Masunungure 2011, iv).

By the end of the first decade of independence, it was already clear to more attentive observers that the die had been cast in terms of how Zimbabwe was to be ruled. ZANU-PF, and its associated elites in the private sector and the security forces, had already come to manifest the key features of predatory leadership, namely a willingness and capacity to "accumulate and deploy a high degree of concentrated political power and economic discretion and…both gain and keep power through a combination of ruthless coercion and material inducement" (Bavister-Gould 2011, 2).

However, if ruling party preferences were clearly towards the establishment of single-party rule and increasing state control of the economy, seismic changes at a global level were to interfere with such plans. Coupled with the increasingly poor performance of the economy, such developments were to compel ZANU-PF to undertake a rethink, even if subsequent developments were to show that the changes adopted were no more than tactical retreats.

Notes

1. As the Government's subsequent economic reform programme in 1991 was to note: "not only do public enterprises absorb a large proportion of recurrent budgetary expenditure in direct subsidies, grants and advances from government, but as a group they produce very small returns, if any, on capital invested" (GOZ 1991: Annex 1, 1).
2. The agreement, part of Pretoria's strategy of strengthening the economies of neighbouring, minority-ruled states, gave manufacturers in Southern Rhodesia preferential access to the South African market. When both Zambia and Malawi imposed sanctions against Southern Rhodesia after its UDI in November 1965, Rhodesian firms switched their exports to South Africa with the clothing, textile and furniture industries being the main beneficiaries. By the time of the 1979 Lancaster House Conference, an estimated 75 percent of Rhodesia's manufactured exports were being sold to South Africa. After independence, South Africa remained Zimbabwe's top trading partner, but with the deterioration in relations between the two countries Zimbabwe firms began to lose their preferential treatment in the South African market.

3. In the aftermath of Independence, in line with the path taken by other liberation movements and despite its earlier Maoist leanings, ZANU was to nurture closer ties with Moscow as China proved unable to match the USSR's ability to provide the economic, military, diplomatic, and technical assistance required to consolidate it rule.
4. The regular granting of such pardons in the context of state-sponsored violence throughout Zimbabwe's post-independence history has not, however, allayed the fears of perpetrators that with a change in regime they might be brought to trial for human rights violations, either by domestic courts or by the increasingly long reach of international courts. Such fears help to explain both the deep reluctance of ZANU-PF and its supporters in the security forces to contemplate change, as well as their willingness to support Mugabe who often projected himself as a bulwark against the reach of international criminal tribunals.
5. Named after the state-owned car assembly plant in Harare, investigative journalists revealed that in the course of 1988–1989 party notables had used their privileged access to buy vehicles cheaply at a time when imports were tightly controlled, and sold them on at considerable mark-ups to private dealers.

References

Bavister-Gould, Alex. 2011. *Predatory Leadership, Predatory Rule and Predatory States*, Developmental Partnership Program Concept Paper, No. 1, September. University of York, UK.

Bratton, M., and E. Masunungure. 2011. *The Anatomy of Political Predation: Leaders, Elites and Coalitions in Zimbabwe, 1980–2010.* Developmental Leadership Program Research Paper, No. 9, January. University of Birmingham, UK.

Catholic Commission for Justice and Peace in Zimbabwe. 1997. *Report on the 1980s Disturbances in Matabeleland and the Midlands.* Harare.

GOZ. 1981a. *Growth with Equity: An Economic Policy Statement.* Harare.

———. 1981b. *Zimbabwe Conference on Reconstruction and Development. Report on Conference Proceedings.* Harare: Zimbabwe Ministry of Economic Planning and Development.

———. 1982. *Transitional National Development Plan 1982/1985.* Harare.

———. 1991. *Framework for Economic Reform 1991–1995.* Harare.

UNCTAD. 1980. *Zimbabwe: Towards a New Order. An Economic and Social Survey* (n.p. UNDP/UNCTAD Project-PAF/78/010).
World Bank. 1995. *Zimbabwe Achieving Shared Growth*. Country Economic Memorandum, April 21. Report No. 13540-ZIM, Vol. 2.
ZIMSTAT. *National Accounts (Various) and ZIMSTAT Database*. Harare.

4

Regime Interests and the Failure of Economic Reform in the 1990s

The evolution of economic policy in Zimbabwe from Independence in 1980 until the present has always been dominated by a single, central theme – the search for an economic system that would entrench the ruling party in power indefinitely. The liberation party believed in 1980, as indeed it still does, that it derived its legitimacy through the barrel of a gun. In dislodging the white minority regime, ZANU-PF earned the right not just to monopoly power, but to perpetual power. However, in common with a number of African liberation movements that subsequently took office as political parties, ZANU-PF recognised that 'liberation legitimacy' could not be relied upon indefinitely, and that economic success was an essential element in the power retention equation.

However, the real test of economic success was not whether it delivered impressive growth figures that translated into long-term and sustainable improvements in the conditions of the country's population, but whether it helped to win elections. For ZANU-PF, management of the economy was a means to an end. It is now clear with the advantage of hindsight that Marxist-Socialist transformation – the ZANU-PF rallying call of the 1980s – was a convenient transmission mechanism for siphoning income and wealth from the private sector to the public sector, and then back

M. Simpson, T. Hawkins, *The Primacy of Regime Survival*,
https://doi.org/10.1007/978-3-319-72520-8_4

into the hands of a select few. Although in part this reflected and built on an early and apparently widespread popular rejection of white colonial capitalism, in intent it was mostly about the transfer of economic assets to the state from the private sector which could then be used in such a way as to ensure victory at election time.

It is worth highlighting that ZANU-PF has never been simply either a liberation movement or a political party. The building of what have appropriately been designated 'party-business empires' was common to all Southern African National Liberation Movements, and reflected their need to ensure greater reliability and control over financial resources to support party machineries than that provided by national legislation on party funding by the state, the misappropriation of state resources, or through pressuring private sector operators for 'donations'. Their requirements were thus to be ensured by "their own companies…and investments designed to ensure a constant flow of income" (Southall 2013, 284).

In the case of ZANU-PF, the process of building such interests began soon after Independence, with one of its main holding companies, ZIDCO, having equity interests in enterprises engaged in activities ranging from the production of school textbooks to property development, and at one stage claiming to employ 10,000 people (Dawson and Kelsall 2012, 57). Needless to say, links between party and state functionaries and company employees were kept under wraps, though the list of companies that subsequently found themselves on Western sanctions lists provided a clue as to the extent of the party's business interests. It is common knowledge that any large independent business operator in Zimbabwe is forced to reach an 'understanding' with such holding companies if it wants to continue to operate, while preferential treatment for these companies in the context of operating licenses, state tender processes, government contracts and party procurement helps to grease the wheels of these commercial empires.[1]

Because the state was subservient to the party – the most powerful institutions were the ZANU-PF politburo and central committee, not the cabinet or a parliament dominated by the ruling party which increasingly took on a rubber-stamping role – the ultimate aim was to transfer power to a party which over time evolved into the hub of a nation-wide patronage system. Mugabe and his closest advisers framed policy not on the basis of what was good for the people of Zimbabwe as a whole, but what would most benefit ZANU-PF in the short-term and ensure regime survival in the long-term. The national interest and the ruling party's core interests were seen as identical, and all policy decisions, whether they pertained to economic, social, constitutional or foreign affairs, were refracted through the prism of regime preservation. Moreover, the President himself was instinctively anti-Western as well as hostile to private enterprise and market forces, partly for ideological reasons but mostly because they fell outside ZANU-PF's control, and therefore threatened the ruling party's monopoly on the patronage networks which fed its support base.

However, and despite all the hyperbole, Zimbabwe never remotely approached Marxist-Socialist status. The intended transformation did not occur during the first decade of independence. Structurally, by the end of the 'command economy' decade (1980–1990), the economy was little different from that inherited in 1980. Commercial agriculture, closely integrated with manufacturing, remained the driver of the economy, and was still dominated by some 5,000–6,000 white farmers. Land reform and resettlement had also virtually disappeared from the radar screen of political debate, though it was occasionally dusted off and expounded upon at party congresses and national day speeches. Employment growth lagged far behind the increase in the labour force. While real wages increased very modestly, the growth in labour incomes also fell well short of the promised redistribution of income from rich to poor contained in early post-independence documents.

By the end of the 1980s, both international developments and mounting economic pressures domestically forced the hand of the ruling party to engage in reforms. On the international front, the political shock waves from the collapse of communism in Eastern Europe in 1989/90 resulted in the almost overnight abandonment by Moscow and other Eastern European regimes of their former 'client states' in the developing world. A significant part of Harare's external alliance system rapidly unravelled, as the new Soviet leadership under Gorbachev made it clear that there was going to be a retraction of Soviet support to its allies in order to focus resources on domestic problems.

By the early 1990s such developments were to exert pressures on ZANU-PF's regional ideological and former liberation movement allies such as FRELIMO in Mozambique and the MPLA in Angola, compelling them to reach peace agreements with their respective rebel movements and adopt multi-party constitutions and market-friendly economic reforms. Democratisation also spread in other parts of Africa, as single-party political systems and statist economic policies were widely rejected, a process fed by a rampant Western triumphalism that increasingly tied development assistance to reforms in political and economic governance in the developing world. In regards to economic reform, the prescriptions were encapsulated in a package which would eventually come to be known as the Washington Consensus.[2]

For ZANU-PF, growing domestic economic difficulties in the form of low growth rates, rising unemployment, and growing external debt and fiscal deficit, eventually forced the ruling party to experiment with market-driven reform in the form of the Economic Structural Adjustment Programme (ESAP). In return for implementing market reforms, Mugabe believed that Zimbabwe would benefit from substantially increased aid flows, including additional funding – without strings – for the stalled land resettlement programme which was the cornerstone of his long-run strategy, as well as increased private sector investment. Subsequent developments were to show that such ZANU-PF concessions were only tactical, and made only as long as they did not compromise ZANU-PF's political monopoly and patronage system.

ESAP (1991–95) and Its Shortcomings

Significantly, the ESAP contained in the 'Zimbabwe: Framework for Economic Reform 1991–95' published in January 1991 (GOZ 1991) carried no imprint from the government, nor from its main authors in the World Bank. Although it was debated by parliament, the fact that the document itself was not an official Zimbabwe government publication attracted little comment at the time, though later in the 1990s, as President Mugabe and cabinet ministers distanced themselves from it, this omission came to be seen as deliberate.

In an effort to characterise it as a continuation of past government policy and not a fresh initiative, the authors of the ESAP report highlighted a number of pre-ESAP reforms. These included the 8 percent real depreciation of the Zimbabwe dollar in 1989 and a further 12 percent in 1990, a reduction in the budget deficit from 13.1 percent of GDP in 1986 to 10.6 percent in 1990/91, the establishment of the Zimbabwe Investment Centre, and a relaxation of repatriation regulations for new foreign investment.

The main objective of economic reform in Zimbabwe as set out in the ESAP was to "improve living conditions, especially for the poorest groups, by increasing real incomes and lowering unemployment by generating higher economic growth". Transformation of the economy entailed "moving away from a highly regulated economy to one where market forces were allowed to play a more decisive role, while concurrently taking steps to alleviate any transitional social hardships which may arise from this transition" (Ibid., 4).

GDP was targeted to grow 5 percent annually by 1995, with the manufacturing sector driving growth with expansion of 5.8 percent a year, while the service sector was projected to grow 5 percent a year and agriculture 3.2 percent. Investment would need to rise to 25 percent of GDP, with both exports and imports increasing their shares of GDP, and economic growth would make it possible to sustain social programmes while overall government expenditure as a share of GDP would fall.

Loss-making public enterprises were projected to generate profits by the mid-1990s, with ESAP promising 'comprehensive programmes' for improved efficiency in the parastatal sector, including the outright sale of shares and assets, commercialisation and management contracts. Promised financial sector reform targets included reducing inflation to 10 percent by 1995, abolishing administered interest rates which discouraged savings, while the banking sector was to be opened up to new banks. Trade liberalisation would be phased in over a 5-year period so that by 1996 all sectors of the economy would face competition from imports. Other measures to liberalise the economy included the phasing out of price controls, the deregulation of agricultural pricing and marketing, and the relaxation of labour regulations.

On land resettlement, the document stated that a further 110,000 families would be settled in addition to the 52,000 relocated during the 1980s (see Chap. 5). Significantly, and in sharp contrast to the policy later pursued by the Government, the extent and speed of resettlement would be determined by the availability of finance as well as by the pace at which 'properly-trained' small-scale farmers could be identified. There would be a tax on underutilised farm land to encourage large-scale commercial farmers to sell their land. In addition, ESAP targeted infrastructure investment in rural areas, public services for smallholder agriculture, and access to credit and finance.

ESAP's subsequent failure to deliver the goods was part bad luck, especially the 1991/92 drought (then the worst in living memory), part poor design and sequencing, but mostly the toxic combination of inappropriate timing and serious shortcomings in implementation. The timing was inappropriate because it subsequently became clear there was no political consensus for the fiscal belt-tightening and other sweeping reforms implicit in structural adjustment. At the same time the donor community, then basking in the glow of Western triumphalism at the end of the Cold War, was in no mood to listen to those who counselled caution in their hurry to find an African structural adjustment success story and prove the worth of the Washington Consensus.[3]

The blame for poor design lay largely with the World Bank whose officials crafted the programme, notwithstanding repeated claims by both the Zimbabwe government and the BWI officials that the programme was 'homegrown'. On the other hand, the blame for the failure to implement fully agreed reforms lay mostly with the Zimbabwe government, reflecting the combination of civil service inertia, and more importantly political opposition within the Cabinet and the ruling party.

The reformers in the government were also undermined both from within and without. Within the administration there were many voices, including that of Mugabe himself, questioning the pace and direction of reform and stalling change when it was obviously at odds with ZANU-PF dogma, as was frequently the case. Public sector reform – a central plank of ESAP – was one of Mugabe's many 'red lines', and opposition to civil service rationalisation and privatization was to become a permanent feature of government policy. There was no way that he was going to allow so-called 'strategic sectors' to be taken over by private enterprise, and especially not foreign-owned private firms, less on the grounds that they might fail to deliver the expected economic benefits and more because this would have necessarily resulted in a weakening of state control, reducing the scope for patronage that such control permitted.

Outside government the main opposition to ESAP came from the trade unions, including at that time the Secretary-General of the Zimbabwe Congress of Trade Unions (ZCTU), Morgan Tsvangirai, later to become leader of the opposition Movement for Democratic Change (MDC). The labour movement feared that public sector reform would mean job losses, higher taxes and reduced government spending. It was implacably opposed to privatisation, sceptical of foreign direct investment and favoured price controls and industrial protectionism. Indeed, its economic policy stance at the time was little different from that of the ruling party, though it could hardly have foreseen the extreme forms that statism would subsequently take on in the 2000s, and the damage that would be done to the economy, the wellbeing of its own rank and file membership, and the Zimbabwean people in general. It was ironic that a decade later the identical coalition of forces outside the government that opposed ESAP – the labour unions, NGOs, civil society, academia and many in the media – coalesced to establish the MDC, one of whose election platforms was market-driven economic reforms.

Perhaps the greatest irony was the degree to which implementation was also undermined by those driving the programme – bilateral donor and BWI officials – who often seemed to bend over backwards to explain away missed targets and implementation delays, claiming repeatedly that the programme was 'on track' when it was manifestly obvious that it was not. In so doing they damaged their own cause and that of reform-minded groups within Zimbabwe, becoming apologists for what was often a glacial pace of reform. Accumulating evidence that ESAP-driven reform was not working was stoutly denied by Western diplomats and the BWIs. Just how wrong that assessment was became clear towards the end of the 1990s, but it reflected what the donors seemed to want to hear and wanted to believe.

Because at that time Mugabe's image in the West was still largely unblemished notwithstanding *Gukurahundi* and other indications of the country's deteriorating political and economic governance, and because the BWIs with years of previous structural adjustment failure across Africa during the 1980s under their belts were desperate for a success story, serious economic, political and social analysis was abandoned in favour of wishful thinking. Indeed, in the early to mid-1990s, representatives of both the World Bank and the IMF took the fight to the perceived enemies of reform, often decrying the Zimbabwean critics of ESAP in business, politics, the media and academia. Seemingly fearful of alienating Mugabe, the Western donor community clung to their mantra that the reform programme was going according to plan.

The fact was that virtually all ESAP targets were missed – the sole exceptions being exports and imports, both of which exceeded target and, perhaps surprisingly, the civil service wage bill as a percentage of GDP, with the civil service establishment, excluding uniformed forces, declining by over 20,000 which was broadly in line with the programme. Annual GDP growth targeted at 4.6 percent had an actual outturn of 3.4 percent, while the GDP per capita growth rate set at 1.9 percent in fact fell by 1.9 percent. Inflation at the end of the ESAP period had risen to 25.8 percent against the target of 10 percent. Savings as a percentage of GDP stood at 11.9 percent, significantly below the target of 25.3 percent. Government debt as a percentage of GDP reached 84 percent against the target of 64.4 percent. The budget deficit target was missed by a very wide margin. Over the ESAP period revenue declined by 7.3 percentage points of GDP but expenditure fell only 4.6 points so that the deficit widened to over 11 percent of GDP from 8.5 percent (ZIMSTAT National Accounts (Various Editions); IMF 1997).

Accordingly, the common criticism levelled by the Government that the BWIs had imposed savage cuts, especially in respect of social spending, was misplaced. The real underlying problem was slow revenue growth that mirrored the poor performance of the economy on the one hand, and the steep increase in interest payments on the other. The latter was the consequence not of ESAP but of the post-independence borrow-and-spend strategy. While the share of health and education spending in the total budget declined from 26.8 percent at the start of the period to 22.8 percent in the 1995/96 fiscal year, this had little to do with IMF-imposed cuts in overall spending as was subsequently frequently suggested, and more to do with the near-doubling of interest payments on debt from 5.8 percent of GDP to 10.5 percent.

ESAP's central plank, which turned out to be its Achilles heel, was public sector reform. Those who at the time warned that the Zimbabwe authorities would not implement the measures to which they had committed themselves were eventually proved right. If the core of the programme – restoring fiscal balance – could not be achieved, peripheral improvements would fall far short of what was needed. That indeed was the record of ESAP – a number of reforms in the fields of monetary policy, financial liberalisation, exchange-rate strategy, industrial protection and trade facilitation were carried out, but far from shrinking and become more efficient the public sector became an even greater fiscal drag on the overall economy.

So, for example, the red line drawn through proposals to embark on a comprehensive programme of privatisation and commercialisation envisaged in ESAP meant that these reforms never got off the starting line, and were a forlorn hope as ZANU-PF used, and continues to use, positions in the parastatals to reward loyal supporters and ensure continued state control of key sectors of the economy. It was not until 1994 that an interministerial policy paper on parastatals was produced, a sure indication of the extent to which the issue had been put on the backburner. By 1997–98, public enterprise losses had come to represent 8.6 percent of GDP. A large part of the explanation for the dismal performance of these entities is attributable to the lack of skills and know-how of those appointed to act as their managers, and the use of such posts to reward politically loyal deadwood. As noted by one eminent Zimbabwean labour economist:

> The boards and managers of these institutions are appointed predominantly on partisan lines, without due regard to the necessary skills required. Performance-management does not exist, as political allegiance is the key to retaining one's position. (Kanyenze 2009b, 38)

The missed targets for GDP growth can be readily explained by the severe 1991/92 drought as a result of which GDP plummeted 6.8 percent in 1992 when agricultural production fell by a quarter. However, there was a 48 percent rebound in the subsequent year so that the impact of the drought was short lived. Indeed, real GDP grew 9.7 percent in 1993 and 1994 before growth turned negative in 1995, again as a result of a poor farming season when agricultural production declined 12 percent.

While the poor growth performance could be explained away by adverse climatic conditions, the underlying structural deterioration in unemployment and deindustrialisation of the economy could not. By the mid-1990s, GDP per capita (in US dollars) at $616 was lower than in 1990 (US$690) and 1980 (US$740). Annual employment growth between 1986 and 1996 had fallen from 2.5 percent to 1.2 percent, and this at a time when the workforce was increasing at close to double that rate (Kanyenze 2009a, 4). Simultaneously manufacturing, which according to ESAP was supposed to drive growth during structural adjustment, fell sharply. The volume of manufacturing production growth as measured by value-added declined from an average of 3.4 percent per annum between 1980 and 1989 to 2.1 percent between 1990 and 1996 (Hawkins 2010, 10).

The economic reforms, initially implemented with apparent enthusiasm, were subsequently allowed to wither on the vine. Public sector reform, without which there could be no private sector response, was carefully left on the back burner. Military spending and parastatal subsidies were maintained at still unsustainable levels. Yet throughout the IMF and the World Bank insisted the programme was on track.

After ESAP

The BWIs response to the failure of ESAP was two-pronged. The first line of defence was to insist that ESAP had not failed at all, and that there had been major gains in terms of trade liberalisation and broad structural reform. They admitted that "persistently large budget deficits presented a serious impediment to growth" and that the reform of public enterprises had proceeded "rather slowly". Nonetheless, the ESAP targets in the field of monetary policy had been achieved and "most" public enterprises were beginning to operate more efficiently (IMF 1997, 10–11).

Given the fact that virtually all the macroeconomic targets were missed, employment had stagnated, inflation accelerated and poverty worsened, so threadbare was this explanation that both the World Bank and IMF soon fell back to their second line of defence. This was that the programme had been too ambitious as well as poorly sequenced – an explanation that by the late 1990s had become generic for most, if not all, structural adjustment programmes in Sub-Saharan Africa.

While both BWIs resorted to often arcane explanations for the outcome of ESAP, the Zimbabwe government, by then thoroughly disillusioned with structural adjustment as promoted by BWIs, initiated the first of a series of programmes that would gradually add up to a complete rejection of market-driven reform. The first, published in February 1996, was the Zimbabwe Programme for Economic and Social Transformation 1996–2000 (ZIMPREST), which by the time of its publication had already been overtaken by events. The economy, it argued was poised for growth due to investments in health, education and infrastructure. It admitted that after a decade of state-led development in the 1980s it had become clear that the economy had failed to generate adequate growth in incomes and employment, which explained why the government had turned to ESAP in 1990.

ZIMPREST's assessment of ESAP differed sharply, however, from that of the IMF. While the IMF claimed that by the end of the period Public Enterprises (PEs) were operating more efficiently, ZIMPREST stated that overall PE performance had "deteriorated significantly during the reform period" (ZIMPREST 1996, 4). In a blunt rejection of the BWIs claim that ESAP was broadly successful, ZIMPREST noted: "The unfavourable conditions which prevailed at the end of ESAP cannot be allowed to continue" (Ibid., 6). Laying the blame for the parlous state of the country's public finances squarely on ESAP, it said the reforms had brought the country to the brink of a debt trap where the surplus of revenue over spending was insufficient to pay the interest in debt accumulated from past budget deficits.

ZIMPREST's approach was essentially hybrid, and founded on the belief that ESAP had failed because it was too narrowly economic and had not taken sufficient account of social and political considerations. In other words, no more Washington Consensus-dictated reforms and, in a foretaste of what was to come the programme stressed that socio-political as well as economic aspirations must be addressed.

The plan prioritised poverty reduction, noting that 62 percent of the population was living in poverty with a much higher proportion in rural areas (72 percent) compared to urban areas (46 percent). Demographic realities demanded "a quantum change" in the rate of job creation which in turn depended upon a rise in the level of investment. The economy needed to grow at rates of between 8 percent and 10 percent annually in non-drought years to restore per capita incomes to pre-ESAP levels. It set a growth target of 6 percent annually for the 1996–2000 period. On the assumption that the country could expect to experience at least one drought during the period, growth would need to reach 10 percent in 1999 and 9.5 percent in 2000.

In addition to the ambitious target of a minimum 6 percent annual growth in GDP, ZIMPREST targeted 42,400 new jobs a year, which while a vast improvement on the ESAP performance was still way below the 183,000 new jobs required annually to absorb all new entrants to the labour force. It projected per capita income growth of 3.4 percent annually and consumption growth of 4.4 percent. Achieving these targets would mean halving the budget deficit to 5 percent of GDP which was the original ESAP goal, increasing domestic savings so that investment averaged 23 percent of GDP, expanding exports by at least 9 percent a year and maximising employment growth through a number of policy initiatives which included active indigenisation measures, the promotion of Small and Medium Enterprises (SMEs) and other (unspecified) steps to ensure that as many jobs as possible were created.

The ZIMPREST strategy was based on two pillars – reduce the budget deficit to escape a looming debt-trap while simultaneously fostering 'economic empowerment' and private sector expansion to accelerate growth. Reducing public sector spending and restoring macroeconomic stability was the main prerequisite for the resumption of steady economic growth. The core of ZIMPREST was therefore, "the restructuring of government" to be achieved by fiscal rationalisation and the "reorientation" of government. This was to extend well beyond civil service reform to include the parastatals as well as decentralisation of some government functions to local government.

In the event, however, and as with ESAP, almost all targets were missed. GDP growth over the period 1996–2000, targeted at 6.0 percent, in fact fell to −2.5 percent per annum. Annual income per capita growth shrank by 2.0 percent against a targeted increase of 3.5 percent. By 2000, inflation had reached 56 percent per annum against a target of 8 percent. Formal sector employment, which was to have increased to 1.46 million jobs, stagnated at 1.23 million (ZIMPREST 1996; ZIMSTAT 2002; IMF 2003).

Two conclusions arise from the failure of both the ESAP and ZIMPREST reform programmes – the first externally designed and the latter homegrown. Firstly, implementation was poor, but secondly and more importantly the designers of both programmes misread and misunderstood the political environment within which they were operating. In both instances the policy advisers assumed the politicians, or at least the key decision-makers, were genuinely committed to reform. By the completion of the ESAP timetable in 1996, it should have been clear to those designing ZIMPREST that without a change in policy direction at Presidential and Ministerial level, their strategy was unlikely to succeed.

Misjudgements in Harare, Washington and many Western capitals grew out of the conviction that the economic case for reform was so overwhelming that the Mugabe government would – albeit reluctantly as in 1990 – go along with it. But as subsequent events – right up until the present – demonstrated, it was politics and the need to maintain ZANU-PF's monopoly on power, and not economics and development imperatives, that dominated government decision-making. Indeed, at the very moment that the World Bank was publishing reports advocating further reforms, the Zimbabwe government was going back to its roots. By 1997, when President Mugabe abandoned all pretence of fiscal consolidation with the announcement of an unbudgeted payout of Z$420 million to war veterans (see below) and his plans for accelerated land resettlement, it was obvious in Harare, though not in Western capitals or to the BWIs, that reform was dead.

It was only after Zimbabwe's entry into the civil war in the DRC in 1998 when Mugabe sent Zimbabwean forces to support his ally President Laurent Kabila, and two more IMF loans, that the donor community reluctantly accepted this reality. And it would not be until 1999, i.e. 17 years after *Gukurahundi*, that the British government with some other Western countries insisted that the BWIs could no longer finance a government which by then was, in effect, using donor money to indirectly bank its intervention in the civil war in the DRC.[4] In October 1999, the major Western shareholders of the IMF managed to convince the lender, which had protested that it did not extend loans to countries involved in conflicts, that in fact loans extended under its Poverty Reduction and Growth Facility (PRGF) to Zimbabwe were being used not for poverty reduction and growth as both Zimbabwean government officials and its own representatives in Harare claimed, but because of the fungibility of aid monies were helping finance Zimbabwe's military operations in the DRC.[5]

Playing the Aid Game

The gap between Western perceptions as mirrored in World Bank and IMF lending, and what was actually happening on the ground in Zimbabwe, cannot be readily explained. There appeared to be a stubborn refusal on the part of outsiders to acknowledge that far from being ready for more reforms – as claimed by the World Bank in two subsequent reports, 'Achieving Shared Growth' in 1995 and 'Consolidating Trade Liberalisation' in 1996 (World Bank 1995, 1996) – the ruling party had a distinctly different agenda.

By the end of the 1990s, however, the data showed the full extent of the failure of programmes, whether World Bank and IMF-designed or homegrown, during the decade of economic reforms. Real GDP increased a mere 5 percent, while per capita incomes declined 12 percent. Employment growth was negligible when population growth is taken into account such that unemployment had risen from 13 percent to 30 percent, and inflation of 31.5 percent a year was well above the Sub-Saharan African average. External debt had increased by 23.7 percent over the decade to the point where the country had begun to accumulate arrears, while domestic debt as a percentage of GDP had increased from 31 percent to 53 percent.

Quite why this was not publicly acknowledged until 1999 can only be guessed at. Undoubtedly part of the explanation already referred to was the 'culture of optimism' in the donor community. Part of the story too was donor miscalculation – a mistaken confidence in their own capacity to influence opinions and mould developments at the political level.

Analysts, including diplomats, simply could not fathom the opaque, not to say, byzantine nature of ZANU-PF political relationships, many of them founded on extended family ties or regional and ethnic associations. The President was a past master at manipulating these in order to pre-empt challenges to his own position within the party through extensive recourse to patronage backed up by the threat or actual use of violence to dispose of challengers, and notwithstanding the fact that such patronage compounded institutional decay, economic regression and state fragility.

It was no surprise then that donors, whose focus was the economy rather than politics of reform, misread the dynamics. They helped to keep the taps open in terms of flows of Official Development Assistance (ODA) over the first two decades of independence. In line with the problem referenced in Chap. 2, there was a widespread inability throughout the donor community to distinguish between perceived shortcomings in state capacity on the one hand, and the willingness of the political elite controlling the state to deliver on the other. The proliferation of capacity-building initiatives, pushed for and funded by development agencies in areas ranging from health and education to public financial management, reflected the operational assumption that the constraints were rooted in technical capacity gaps rather than the willingness of Zimbabwe's political masters to implement reforms.

As a result, between 1980 and 1990, ODA flows totalled US$1.835 billion, and then doubled to US$3.86 billion over the period 1990–1999. Significantly, such inflows dwarfed FDI which totalled US$305 million between 1980 and 1999 (World Bank (various issues) and IMF World Economic Outlook database). In a clear sign of growing economic fragility, this was the reverse of what would have been expected if sound management of the economy had triggered robust growth. It certainly stood in stark contrast to the pattern observed in the successful Asian economies of the same period, which saw an exponential growth in FDI (and domestic investment), accompanied by a reduction in the weight of ODA in both absolute and relative terms in their economies.

Just as in 1990 when the convergence of the global collapse of communism and domestic economic underperformance in terms of investment, growth and jobs convinced a reluctant Mugabe to implement

ESAP, albeit half-heartedly, so towards the end of the decade the shifting sands of donor strategies, growing Western disillusionment with the President, and the first significant domestic political stirrings, came together to force ZANU-PF into its second policy U-turn. The result was a return to the undisguised *dirigiste* policies which continue to the present day.

Initiated by the 1997 unbudgeted payout to the war veterans following threatening public protests by this well-organised group which claimed to have been ignored by Harare after Independence, the U-turn continued in January 1999 with a managed exchange-rate policy of 'voluntary restraint' whereby the Reserve Bank of Zimbabwe (RBZ), and foreign-exchange dealers agreed to an exchange-rate ceiling of Z$40 to the US dollar. Few bankers believed that voluntary restraint could succeed, but went along with the central bank in the hope that this might avoid a return to the previous pegged exchange-rate system.

In August 1999, the IMF bizarrely came to Zimbabwe's rescue yet again, with an enlarged standby facility of US$193 million, a clear indication of the triumph of hope over experience and/or the pressures to lend versus its due diligence obligations. This was contingent upon across-the board cuts in government spending (excluding education and health), strict monitoring of defence expenditure, higher interest rates and the phasing out of the managed exchange-rate system. Donors and lenders committed, in total, to provide US$780 million over three years, including US$140 million from the World Bank which was to be used to retire some of the government's short-term borrowings.

Following the announcement of the package, the RBZ effectively went ahead and pegged the exchange rate at Z$38 to the US dollar, and the IMF standby agreement collapsed faster than even the most pessimistic analysts had expected. Only one disbursement – for US$35 million – was made before Western members of the IMF Executive Board finally decided in October 1999 that they could no longer turn a blind eye to the use of IMF money to finance Mugabe's military intervention in the DRC war. Funding from the IMF, World Bank, EU and the African Development Bank was frozen, donors began to phase out their support, and the government was left with a choice between its political agenda of intervention in the DRC, a huge increase in government spending to buy votes in the upcoming 2000 legislative elections, direct controls to try and hold down inflation and accelerated land resettlement on the one hand, and an IMF imposed economic agenda on the other.

The Watershed

The late 1990s were the watershed. All the while unemployment continued to mount, and public spending on health and education was cut. In the first ten years after Independence in 1980, while GDP had grown enough to ensure modest – though still inadequate – per capita income growth of over 1 percent a year, this was reversed in the 1990s, especially in the first half of the decade and then again in 1999/2000, to leave the country with per capita incomes in 2000 (in constant Zimbabwe dollars) that were some 15 percent lower than at Independence.

No explanation of Zimbabwe's crisis of expectations is complete without further analysis of wages and employment in the formal economy. Although nominal wages continued to increase during the early 1990s, they fell well behind the pace of accelerating inflation, as a result of which by 1994 the average real wage had declined by a third. Data show that less than a quarter of a million jobs were created between 1980 and the peak year of 1998. The percentage of the total population employed in the formal sector fell from 14.2 percent in 1980 to 11.5 percent in 1998 (ZIMSTAT 2006; UNDP 2008, 103).

Poverty deepened, and a classic crisis of unfulfilled expectations developed. The fledgling opposition MDC – a coalition of disillusioned trade unionists, human rights activists, professionals and some business people (and mostly erstwhile members of ZANU-PF and Mugabe supporters), was taking shape amid calls from all sides, including from within the ruling party itself, for a new political dispensation in the form of a new constitution.

It is now clear that the late 1990s marked a turning point both for Mugabe and Zimbabwe. The government that had run out of ideas and was visibly losing support had to reinvent itself. Although few realised it at the time, Mugabe was slowly coming to the conclusion that his flirtations with non-racialism, diluted socialist economics and cooperation with the West and international institutions like the IMF and World Bank, had passed their sell-by date. It is likely that he reasoned there was a simple choice between what would 'please' Western governments, donor agencies and the BWIs, international investors and corporations and the country's few remaining whites, and what was needed to reassure his own political constituency and bolster his party's diminishing popularity. The moderates in his party could no longer convince him that – if given a chance – free, or at least freer, market economics might pay dividends. Hard-line advisers were warning that his popularity was waning and that a new strategy was essential.

Reform was abandoned not just because – donor protestations to the contrary – it had failed economically and especially socially, but because reform threatened ZANU-PF's political monopoly and threatened to undermine its support base. The unbudgeted payout to the war veterans who had fought in the ranks of ZANLA and ZIPRA is illustrative of the trumping of economic logic by narrow party-political interests.[6] The Z$420 million pension package, which had not been included in the annual budget announced only weeks earlier, pushed the budget deficit up to 12.5 percent of GDP.

Ironically, only weeks before the war veterans payout, the World Bank had praised the 'turnaround' in Zimbabwe's public finances when it announced a US$62 million balance-of-payments support loan, carefully ignoring the fact that the budget – without the war veterans payment – had increased the deficit to 8.9 percent of GDP from 7 percent previously. However, following the announcement of the war veterans' payment, the World Bank said it was withholding disbursement pending details of the cost of the pension package, and how it was to be funded.

Despite damning evidence to the contrary, there was no shortage of apologists for the Mugabe government claiming that while virtually all economic targets had consistently been missed, there had been very real gains in terms of structural reforms – the abolition of price controls, the liberalisation of the financial sector and the exchange-rate system, the privatisation of one bank and two agricultural marketing parastatals, and the partial reform of the tariff system. Apologists also argued that over time structural adjustment would be seen to have worked. This, however, overlooks one uncomfortable truth – that the true test of reform is irreversibility. If reforms are swiftly reversed – as happened in Zimbabwe after 1997 – structural adjustment had failed.

Zimbabwe's economic reform experience epitomised the old adage that if something cannot work, it won't work. Reform could not work in Zimbabwe because of a hostile political environment and the primacy of short-term regime survival considerations over long-term growth and development imperatives. It was the reluctance, failure or refusal of the reform lobby at home and abroad to recognise that, in the absence of political will on the part of the government and a conducive institutional environment, wrenching reforms as envisaged first under ESAP, and subsequently under ZIMPREST, could not work.

The Crisis of Unfulfilled Expectations and the Rise of the Movement for Democratic Change

Following the crushing of ZAPU in the 1980s and signing of the National Unity Agreement in 1987 uniting the two liberation parties in ZANU-PF, there was no serious challenger to Mugabe's leadership. But towards the end of a second disappointing decade of independence during which almost all economic targets had been missed while promises of land redistribution and housing for all remained unfulfilled and most social indicators had deteriorated,[7] the electorate was becoming increasingly restive. The launch of a private daily newspaper, the *Daily News*, in 1999 gave political critics and civil society both a voice and a fast-growing audience.[8]

Occupying centre-stage in the litany of popular grievances was the country's rising unemployment rate. Coupled with falling real wages, urban voters were the ones most likely to turn against the government. However, unlike South Africa and Zambia, Zimbabwe did not have a long history of trade union involvement in politics, with the notable exception of the founder of ZAPU and eventual Senior Vice-President, Joshua Nkomo, who had cut his political teeth as a union activist working for the Rhodesia Railways in the 1950s.[9] In Zimbabwe not only was the trade union movement weak, but there were no widely-known, popular, labour leaders. As part of its methodical progress towards the one-party state, ZANU-PF had sidelined the unions or turned them into one of the many 'mass organisations' of the ruling party, in the process co-opting the leadership of the ZCTU.

But trade union tolerance of the Mugabe government ran out progressively from the mid-1990s as unemployment worsened, social service provision deteriorated, and real wages plunged. In 1997 the ZCTU called a series of strikes demanding increased wages, tax reductions and more open government, and two years later in September 1999 it finally broke ranks with the ruling party to establish the Movement for Democratic Change (MDC) led by Tsvangirai.

The MDC's platform was a better deal for workers, greater transparency in government, a new democratic constitution and an immediate end to Zimbabwe's involvement in the war in the DRC. Its first political campaign led it to join up with a civil rights group, the National Constitutional Assembly (NCA), in boycotting the government's Constitutional Commission (CC) established to draft a new constitution to replace the one negotiated at Lancaster House in London in 1979.

The omens for this nascent political opposition were not promising given that just weeks before the launch of the MDC, ZANU-PF had swept the board in local government elections that were characterised by high levels of voter apathy. Mugabe, acutely aware that his party was losing political support, announced plans to increase public sector wages despite growing budget deficits, along with compensation for victims of his government's *Gukurahundi* campaign in Matabeleland in the early 1980s in an effort to gain some support in that region, though the latter promise was to remain unfulfilled.

Resorting to constitutional amendments to secure the position of his ruling party and that of his Presidency, Mugabe launched a constitutional revision process in 1999. The revised constitution was to be drawn up after an extensive consultative process led by a government-appointed CC of 400 members.

In the event the CC was a farce. The submissions of the Commissioners, after meetings with men and women from all walks of life around the country, were massaged, amended or wholly rewritten to satisfy the ruling party. As noted by one analyst:

> the credibility of the CC exercise was thrown into serious doubt when its draft omitted and misrepresented some of the citizens' views on what the new constitution should contain. For instance, consistent sentiments had been expressed in public hearings as well as in other submissions that the extensive powers of the President should be reduced considerably, that the size of the Cabinet should be significantly reduced to about 15 posts, and that an independent electoral commission should be appointed...To complicate matters, the President unilaterally inserted certain provisions including those on land reform. (Sachikonye 2011, 11)

In February 2000, the draft constitution – opposed by the MDC and a range of civil society organisations – and which bore little resemblance to the advice of Commissioners, was rejected when it was put to the electorate in a referendum.

The referendum brought home to the ruling party, yet again, the extent to which its popular support had waned. Within days of the President's conciliatory TV address in which he said he accepted the electorate's verdict, his followers were taking matters into their own hands. By mid-March 2000, some 500 white-owned farms had experienced what were initially termed 'walk-ons' by 'war veterans', many of whom were men and women far too young to have participated in the Liberation War that had ended 20 years earlier.

The die was cast. Deciding that ZANU-PF was not going to win parliamentary elections scheduled for later in 2000, and amidst mounting foreign investor and donor disillusionment with Zimbabwe which meant that Mugabe had nothing to lose from breaking with the West, ZANU-PF changed the rules of the game, adopting extra-constitutional means to get its way.

While Mugabe's August 1997 radio announcement on the payment to the war veterans had contained references to plans to launch an 'accelerated land reform programme', few at the time had taken it seriously. While some economists and businessmen expressed alarm over the budgetary – and inflationary – consequences of the unbudgeted war veterans payout, extracted from Mugabe under some duress, little attention was paid to the President's comments about the land situation.

At diplomatic receptions and business lunches, commercial farmers, bankers, businessmen, journalists and diplomats agreed that nothing had changed. On innumerable occasions the President and his ministers had expressed similar sentiments but land redistribution – which was at the forefront of the Liberation War objectives of both ZANU and ZAPU, a highly controversial topic issue at the Lancaster House talks in late 1979, and at the heart of the new government's first economic development programmes in the early 1980s – had been on the back-burner for more than a decade, with the result that references to it in the August 1997 radio announcement had been largely ignored.

So inured were Zimbabwe's 5,000 to 6,000 white commercial farmers to such warnings and threats of the loss of their land – even when by the end of 1997 the Government produced a list of commercial farms for compulsory acquisition – that they casually shrugged off these remarks with much bravado on the grounds the government knew how essential they were to the economy. Similar assessments were made by the business and Western diplomatic communities. In their book Mugabe was a shrewd politician, skilled in saying one thing while doing something completely different, noting that he had refrained from adopting the sweeping programme of nationalisations that many had initially feared at Independence.

But 2000 was different, though only with hindsight did that become obvious. After twenty years in power, initially as prime minister and subsequently as President, in what was to all intents and purposes a *de facto*, though not a *de jure*, one party state, Mugabe and the ruling ZANU-PF party felt cornered. Frequently repeated promises of land, jobs, housing for all and better transport facilities were being increasingly questioned, while the undoubted improvements in terms of health and education achieved in the immediate post-independence years were rapidly being eroded.

For Mugabe the popular rejection of the draft constitution in February 2000 was a moment of truth. For the first time in twenty years he and ZANU-PF faced a serious political challenge at the polls in the form of the MDC. He concluded that his best – perhaps his only – card was land reform. His Information adviser – subsequently minister – Jonathan Moyo, coined the party's election slogan: 'Land is the economy – the economy is land'. A line in the sand had been crossed and Zimbabwe would never be the same again.

Notes

1. On infighting around control of these holding companies and issues of mismanagement see *Zimbabwe Independent* 2017.
2. The Washington Consensus was the West's development orthodoxy from the late 1980s to the mid-1990s, its component parts shared by economists within many Western bilateral donor agencies, the World Bank and the IMF. Originally devised as a response to Latin America's debt crisis of the 1980s and poor growth rates, it constituted a set of policy reforms intended to reverse decades of statist development policies, and included fiscal discipline, liberalisation of trade, interest and exchange rates, deregulation and privatisation, and the reordering of public expenditures. In sum, the policy prescriptions sought to reduce the role of the state in the development process and give markets free rein in the allocation of resources. With minor modifications, the Washington Consensus was subsequently to be exported from Latin America to Africa.
3. It would only be a decade later that international development agencies would come to develop the necessary tools and approaches that would help them move beyond the assumption that the existence of technically sound policy advice sufficed, in and of itself, to induce reform in the governments of developing countries. These efforts have led to a recognition of the need to better understand the role of incentive structures, institutional inertia and resistance, and for external agencies to deepen their analysis of local political dynamics and identify drivers of change, reform champions and anti-reformers in the context of risk assessments of their programmes.
4. Given an already strained fiscal situation, Zimbabwe could not afford such military activism even if, as repeatedly claimed, the Kabila government was footing the bill. The actual financial arrangements under which Zimbabwe supported the Kabila family – first Laurent and subsequently his son, Joseph, who succeeded him as President of the DRC – have never been revealed. However, it subsequently became clear that a number of senior ZANU-PF party officials and ministers benefited from a variety of commercial contracts. But the government accounts show no inflow of revenue to the Ministry of Finance, implying that a substantial – if unknown – part of the financial burden of the DRC war was carried by the Zimbabwe taxpayer and partially if indirectly funded by donor inflows, including the loans made by the IMF.

5. That Harare was able to use BWI and bilateral donor loans and grants to indirectly finance military expenditures was due to the well-known and intractable problem of the fungible nature of aid flows. By cutting down on budgetary allocations for health and education, for example, and using aid flows to make up shortfalls in those sectors, a recipient government can then simply redirect domestically generated resources thus freed up in accordance with its own preferences. The fact that aid may not be used for its original intended purpose is one aspect of the fiduciary risk associated with aid transfers. The problem is compounded in the case of countries such as Zimbabwe when, as was increasingly noted by the BWIs during the second half of the 1990s and during the crisis years, budgets and accounts of expenditure become increasingly opaque and difficult to analyse.
6. In addition to their protests at the slow pace of land reform and deterioration in living conditions under ESAP, the war veterans complained about the manipulation of the War Victims Compensation Fund set up for their benefit after Independence. Reports suggested that the Fund was being looted by members of the ruling party and government who were awarding themselves large and unjustified compensation packages, while many rank and file members of the war veterans association were forced to wait for many years on their claims submitted soon after Independence.
7. According to the UNDP, life expectancy at birth had fallen from 63 years in 1990 to 50.9 years by 1998. The infant mortality rate had increased from 46 per 1,000 live births to 73 per 1,000 live births over the same period. While the deterioration in the latter indicators is partly explained by the HIV and AIDS epidemic then ravaging the Southern African region, others are not. The primary school enrolment rate which had peaked at 128 percent in 1990 dropped to 93 percent by 1998. In overall terms, Zimbabwe's Human Development Index fell from 0.284 in 1990 to 0.232 in 1998 (UNDP 2010).
8. Prior to the launch of the Daily News, ZANU-PF had a virtual media monopoly – radio, television, as well as all the daily and Sunday newspapers. Only the two financial weeklies – the *Financial Gazette* and the *Zimbabwe Independent* – and a handful of monthly publications, expressed highly tempered criticism of government and the ruling party. For a brief period until its banning in September 2003, the *Daily News* had given the emerging political opposition an increasingly powerful voice.

9. In South Africa labour unions were arguably the driving force for political change in the 1980s and early 1990s, while in Zambia it was the leader of the miners' union on the Copperbelt, Mr Frederick Chiluba, who led a political coalition in 1991 that defeated President Kenneth Kaunda who had held office since Independence in 1964.

References

Dawson, Martin, and Tim Kelsall. 2012. Anti-developmental Patrimonialism in Zimbabwe. *Journal of Contemporary African Studies* 30 (1): 49–66.

GOZ. 1991. *Zimbabwe: A Framework for Economic Reform 1991–1995*. Harare.

Hawkins, Tony. 2010. *Manufacturing Industry, Economic Recovery and Poverty Reduction*, Comprehensive Economic Recovery in Zimbabwe Working Paper Series, No. 10. Harare: United Nations Development Programme.

IMF. 1997. *Zimbabwe: Recent Economic Developments*, Country Report 97/59, July 25. Washington, DC.

———. 2003. *Article IV Consultation – Staff Report*, July 25. Washington, DC.

———. World Economic Outlook Database.

Kanyenze, Godfrey. 2009a. *Labour Markets and the Rebuilding of Human Capital*, Comprehensive Economic Recovery in Zimbabwe Working Paper Series, No. 8. Harare: United Nations Development Programme.

———. 2009b. *Restructuring Public Enterprises and the Rehabilitation of Infrastructure in Zimbabwe*, Comprehensive Economic Recovery in Zimbabwe Working Paper Series, No. 8. Harare: United Nations Development Programme.

Sachikonye, Lloyd. 2011. *Zimbabwe's Constitution-Making and Electoral Reform Processes: Challenges and Opportunities*. Paper Presented at Conference on 'Legitimacy of Power – Possibilities of Opposition', Department of Political Science and Public Administration. Makerere University and Chr. Michelsen Institute (CMI). May 30–June 1.

Southall, Roger. 2013. *Liberation Movements in Power: Party and State in Southern Africa*. London: James Currey.

UNDP. 2008. *Comprehensive Economic Recovery in Zimbabwe: A Discussion Document*. Harare: United Nations Development Programme.

———. 2010. *Human Development Report 2010 – The Real Wealth of Nations: Pathways to Human Development*. New York: United Nations Development Programme.

World Bank. 1995. *Zimbabwe Achieving Shared Growth*. Country Economic Memorandum (13540-ZIM), Vol. 2.

———. 1996. *Consolidating Trade Liberalisation*. Washington, DC: World Bank.

———. *Global Development Finance Reports (Various Issues)*. Washington, DC: World Bank.

Zimbabwe Independent. 2017. Zanu PF Bigwigs Renew Fight Over Companies, July7. https://www.theindependent.co.zw/2017/07/07/zanu-pf-bigwigs-renew-fights-companies.

ZIMPREST. 1996. *Zimbabwe Programme for Economic and Social Transformation (1996–2000)*. Harare.

ZIMSTAT. 2002. *National Accounts 2002*.

———. 2006. *Labour Force Survey 2004*. Harare.

ZIMSTAT. *National Accounts* (Various Editions).

5

Regime Survival and the Fast Track Land Reform Programme

Twenty years after Independence the transformation of the Zimbabwe economy – and the economic benefits which would thereby accrue to the Zimbabwean population as promised by ZANU in 1980 – had barely begun. While the state had gradually increased its share of GDP and its interventions in day-to-day decision-making by the private sector, the same private corporations still dominated mining, manufacturing, and financial services. In the course of the new millennium, however, this promise of transformation was to be fulfilled in a manner, and with consequences that not even the worst pessimists could have predicted.

The first signs of the new approach to be taken were – not surprisingly given historic sensitivities and grievances around the issue of land – in the area of agriculture. The ruling party's approach to the land question served to trigger a process of rapid economic regression, and perfectly embodied its increasingly hard line and dismissive attitude to sound principles of political and economic governance and the rule of law. It also brought to the surface the expanding role of the country's security forces in national decision-making processes.

The land question, and the demand for the correction of historical injustices, had been the driving force of the liberation struggle. These were

M. Simpson, T. Hawkins, *The Primacy of Regime Survival*,
https://doi.org/10.1007/978-3-319-72520-8_5

now to be revived by the ruling party during what it chose to characterise as the 'Third Chimurenga'[1] in a manner that caught both external observers, as well as most of the Zimbabwean population, by surprise.

The Land Question at Lancaster House

It is worth recalling that the Lancaster House Agreement, brokered by the British government and which led to Zimbabwe's independence, had been plagued by contention over the issue of how the profound inequalities in terms of land distribution the new country would inherit were to be addressed, and more specifically the issue of compensation for land acquisition and who should foot the bill. Going into the conference, the position of both ZANU and ZAPU was that a newly independent Zimbabwe had the right to exercise its sovereignty to compulsorily acquire land in the public interest, while compensation would be payable at the discretion of the state.

Under pressure from its African allies, in particular states such Mozambique which was suffering significantly from the spill-over effects of the war in Rhodesia and therefore interested in a speedy resolution of the conflict, the ZANU-ZAPU Patriotic Front alliance negotiating team had been compelled to accept a series of compromises put forward by the UK government concerning the land question. The first of these was the entrenchment of the willing buyer, willing seller principle for ten years, i.e. there would be a free market in commercial agricultural land. The second was that during that period any land compulsorily acquired by the state would be limited to underutilised land or in restricted cases on grounds of defence, public safety, order and health, and subject to prompt and adequate compensation. The third was that access to the courts would be guaranteed for commercial farmers to resolve disputes arising out of such compulsory land acquisitions.

Given the initial lukewarm reception of the nationalists to these proposals, the UK government offered to provide financial assistance for land acquisition as a sweetener.[2] Coupled with Mozambican and Zambian pressure on the liberation movements they individually supported to accept the deal on the table, this enabled the talks to reach a successful conclusion. However, understandings as to what precise commitments had been entered into on the land question – particularly on the issue of funding for the compulsory acquisition of land – differed sharply, and would become a festering sore and poison future relations between Harare and the West.[3]

A Divided Agricultural Sector and Resettlement Efforts from 1980 to 2000

At Independence, production of most crops – the chief exceptions being maize and cotton – was dominated by some 5,000–6,000 large-scale commercial farms, mostly owned and managed by white farmers, and a smattering of corporate-owned agricultural estates specialising in sugar, coffee, tea, cattle ranching and forestry. These commercial farmers had access to some 15.5 million hectares of land. In stark contrast, an estimated 800,000 black smallholders subsisted on 16.4 million hectares. Such a skewed pattern of land distribution reflected the dispossession of indigenous land dating back to the bloody colonial pacification of the Shona and Ndebele people in the 1890s, and subsequent establishment of Native Reserves in the 1930s. The process had been accompanied by the expulsion of whole communities from areas now designated as 'European' and forced movement into Native Reserves, subsequently renamed Tribal Trust Lands in the 1960s, and then communal areas after Independence.

The most productive land in the country's Agro-Ecological Regions 1–3, with superior soils and climatic conditions, was largely owned by white farmers. They had also been extensively supported by the colonial state and the successor UDI government in terms of subsidies, infrastructure, marketing and agricultural support services. Most of the poorer communal farming areas were in Natural Regions 4 and 5, where agricultural potential was limited given poor soils and rainfall patterns.

At Independence, the average size of a commercial farm was over 1,000 hectares, compared to communal area smallholdings which averaged less than 10 hectares. Population growth in the communal areas had also led to a decrease in farm size through continual subdivisions, accompanied by a move of households to ever more marginal land. Communal production was characterised by slash and burn agriculture, the unsustainable use of natural resources such as grazing land, water and woodlands, while smallholders had historically been starved of both official support and resources during the colonial and UDI periods.

Another important distinction between the commercial and communal agriculture related to tenure arrangements. While commercial farmers enjoyed freehold title to their land, smallholders in communal lands were subject to customary law, with chiefs being the trustee of lands within their chiefdoms and allocating land to the male heads of households. The picture in the communal areas became more complex (and confused) in the early post-independence period once the 1982 Communal Land Act was passed, which transferred land allocation powers to district councils, though the evidence points to both the state and chief-based systems coexisting in large parts of the country. Nevertheless, the fundamental distinction still held, namely that commercial farmers enjoying freehold title could use their title to sell land on the open market, as well as use it as collateral for loans, while under the system of customary law this was not possible. The overall picture, therefore, was one of an extreme inherited and patently unfair pattern of land distribution and economic dualism in the agricultural sector, with "large and fecund white commercial farms lay alongside pools of communal poverty, where thousands of black smallholders had to subsist on tiny holdings" (UNDP 2008, 149).

The key aim of post-independence land policy was to redress this imbalance by relieving the pressure of population and livestock in the overcrowded communal areas. At the 1981 ZIMCORD donor conference, the stated objective had been the transformation and development of the rural peasant sector. Decongestion of the communal areas was to be achieved by resettling communal farmers on former commercial farms, while simultaneously encouraging non-farm families to migrate to urban centres where it was assumed jobs would be created as part and parcel of the structural transformation of the economy.

In 1982, the TNDP had targeted the resettlement of 162,000 families on 9 million hectares (58 percent) of commercial farm land deemed to be underutilised. The aim was to reduce the number of households in the communal areas to their estimated 'carrying capacity' of 325,000 families. This meant that some 235,000 families would be relocated either on commercial farm land, or move to urban centres.

The government's first efforts at land redistribution in the 1980s fell short of expectations. Nevertheless, progress was not insignificant when viewed against the backdrop of the country's recent independence, and the fact that a number of state institutions established to support the programme were still finding their feet. Around 2.3 million hectares were acquired between 1980 and 1985, and about 41,000 households were resettled. However, the programme ran out of steam after 1985, and subsequently the TNDP targets were missed by a long way. By the 1990 only an additional 15,000 families had been resettled (Doré 2009, 9).

The slow pace of resettlement in the 1980s, particularly after 1985, may be explained by a combination of increasing budgetary constraints, and the rising prices of commercial farmland due to the buoyancy of that sector. In addition, a growing number of members of the country's political and economic elite themselves became large-scale commercial farmers thereby weakening their interest in land reform that would benefit others, with an increase in the number of black commercial farmers joining the Commercial Farmers Union. It is noteworthy that Government interest in the programme also seemed to have flagged, undermining ZANU-PF's repeated claims that it has always seen this as the most important development challenge facing the country, with one analyst pointing out that the allocation for resettlement as a percentage of the national budget fell from 1.3 percent in 1981/82 to 0.2 percent in 1990/91 (Masiiwe 2004, 6).

In addition, the diminishing sense of urgency in land acquisitions for resettlement purposes may be attributed to a rise in output in smallholder agriculture in the early post-independence period, with significant increases in the output of maize and cotton. However, this boom in smallholder output did not prove sustainable.

Smallholder maize production had grown very rapidly in the first half of the 1980s, reflecting attractive prices as well as marketing and production subsidies. In 1984, for example, communal farmers delivered about 925,000 tonnes of maize to the markets, almost meeting national requirements. The latter had partly been driven by the switching of the priority focus of agricultural research and extension services from the commercial to the smallholder sector, a massive expansion in the availability of credit, as well as highly favourable prices set by the state-owned Grain Marketing Board (GMB).

However, output in this sector declined in the latter half of the decade, partly because banks reduced their lending to smallholders as a result of poor loan repayment rates (Rohrback et al. 1990). At the same time it also became clear that the boom in smallholder output was largely restricted in geographical terms to the Mashonaland Highveld, and depended on "a small minority of better-off peasants, who were able to respond to improved price incentives and to the provision of credit, extension and research facilities once offered to white farmers alone" (Palmer 1990, 172). In addition, the GMB incurred a growing deficit as it sought to encourage smallholder maize production through its pricing policy which paid smallholders above the market prices for their produce, with government policy then also requiring the GMB to sell this maize at subsidised prices in urban areas.[4] Clearly smallholder agricultural intensification had its limits, and did not represent a comprehensive and sustainable solution to the problem of overcrowding in communal areas in the absence of a robust process of economic structural transformation.

In 1990 the government tried to reboot the land programme following the expiry of the 'willing buyer, willing seller' provision entrenched in the 1980 Lancaster House constitution. It is worth recalling that the provision had guaranteed that commercial farmers who wished to keep their land could do so and would not be expropriated, the exception being "underutilised land" for which "adequate compensation" would be paid.[5] In 1990 the government announced plans to purchase another 5 million hectares of land on which 110,000 families would be resettled. Although a much-amended Land Acquisition Act (1992) provided for the compulsory acquisition of land, the pace of resettlement nevertheless remained slow such that by 1997 a total of only 71,000 farmers had been resettled on 3.5 million hectares – and only 17,000 of them since 1990 against the targeted 110,000 – and this in a context in which population growth between 1980 and 1997 would have added an additional 350,000 households in the communal areas (Doré 2009, 9).

A number of aspects of the programme up to 1997 are worth highlighting to account for the slow pace of land reform and resettlement, some of which as noted above had already manifested themselves by the mid-1980s. Firstly, the gradual move towards a top-down approach to the issues of land acquisition, resettlement, and the reorganisation of communal areas to improve the livelihoods of households through smallholder agricultural intensification, translated into ever greater centralisation of the decision-making process, a burgeoning bureaucracy, growing pressure on the limited capacity of state agencies to deliver, and declining rates of execution and in the transparency of allocation decisions.

This dirigisme was most apparent in attempts at the establishment of 'consolidated villages' in communal areas, as laid out in the government's 1986 Communal Land Development Plan (GOZ 1986). These units required the reorganisation of land in communal areas through its demarcation into grazing, planting and residential areas, and the movement of dispersed settlements into new planned villages intended to facilitate the provision of the necessary infrastructure and support services. Significantly, the state was then to issue leases to individuals in an attempt to supplant existing customary tenure arrangements. These leases were, however, not tradable, and upon their expiry land was to revert to the state. A similar arrangement in resettlement areas, i.e. former commercial farm land, involved the granting of temporary permits to reside and work the land, also leading to uncertainty of tenure, and impacted negatively on the willingness to invest in improvements.[6]

In the event, a combination of capacity and budgetary constraints on the part of key implementing agencies, coupled with the establishment of unwieldy bodies such as the Coordinating Committees involving 20 ministries and departments, meant the rate of progress in terms of implementation of the 1986 Plan aimed at the modernisation of the communal areas was glacial.[7] The Government's own Land Tenure Commission, reviewing the slow progress, concluded in 1994 that:

> The main reason is the over-centralization of government with the relevant technical ministries using top-down methods of planning and implementation. The second problem is the poor coordination of the technical

ministries who continue to exhibit territorial behaviour with no evidence of a well thought-out coordinated strategy. (GOZ 1994, 35)

Secondly, as already noted, there was also growing disinterest in land reform on the part of the ruling party elite, notwithstanding regular ruling party pronouncements to the contrary. Not only may this be attributed to the initial positive performance of communal area smallholders after Independence, which seemed to indicate that this sector was not only able to attain food self-sufficiency but even produce a marketable surplus given the right conditions, but also to the growing numbers of those within the new political and economic elite who had managed to acquire large farms on the open market after Independence, thereby diluting their interest in land reform. As observed by one foreign analyst "For some members of government…land redistribution might now signify taking land for themselves, rather than giving it to peasants" (Palmer 1990, 175).

This trend was eventually to erupt into the so-called 'land grab scandal' of 1994, with the independent media carrying stories of public funds being used to purchase or lease white commercial farms for the benefit of individual members of the ruling elite. Land acquired by Government and earmarked for resettlement was increasingly being used not for its stated purpose to benefit the poor from communal areas, but was rented out at purely nominal rates under lease agreements to politicians, civil servants and senior members of the defence forces (International Crisis Group 2004, 49–50). In an effort to counter popular criticism, and a foretaste of what in the 2000s would become the standard party line, the Government began to blame the slow pace of implementation on the non-fulfilment of promises made by London to provide the necessary funding for land acquisition.

It is noteworthy that the aforementioned 1994 Land Tenure Commission had put forward a number of suggestions which might have relieved the burden on the national budget of land acquisition costs (as well as reduced the country's dependence on donor contributions to the exercise). However, their adoption would have required a smaller role for the state in the process of identification, acquisition and allocation of land, a greater reliance on the market, and a more gradual approach to land reform.

So, for example, the Commission recommended the introduction of a progressive land tax which would serve as an incentive for commercial farmers to subdivide their land holdings and dispose of excess land to new farmers. The latter would also enjoy freehold title to their holdings which they could use as collateral for improvements. The Commission also tackled the issue of security of tenure in resettlement areas, recommending that beneficiaries be granted long-term leases, with an option to eventually purchase their holdings outright. Despite the technical soundness of many of the recommendations contained in the Commission's report, they never gained the necessary political traction to be implemented, arguably because their adoption would have removed the state from centre-stage as the sole allocative mechanism in agriculture and reduced the scope for patronage.

But rising popular discontent with the state of the economy in the wake of ESAP, a growing organised political opposition in the form of the MDC, and rumblings of discontent from within its own support base exemplified by the increasingly vocal demands of the war veterans for compensation for their sacrifices during the liberation struggle which had also included demands for land, all contributed to a significant step change in 1996 with the establishment of the National Land Acquisition Committee. This body, and its provincial offshoots, was tasked specifically with identifying land for resettlement. By the end of 1997, 1,500 commercial farms covering around 4 million hectares were listed for compulsory purchase by the state.

Before the end of 1997, tensions between London and Harare were raised further when the Secretary of State for International Development of the new Labour government elected that year, Clare Short, stated in a letter to the Zimbabwean Minister of Agriculture that the UK did not have "a special responsibility to meet the costs of land purchase in Zimbabwe. We are a new government from diverse backgrounds without links to former colonial interests" (Clare Short 1997). As far as Harare was concerned this was proof positive of British perfidy, and it would disseminate the letter widely to justify its subsequent actions on the land question.[8]

Nevertheless, in 1998 the Government convened a donor conference for land resettlement. It sought funding of US$1.9 billion over five years to resettle 90,000 families, and presented a plan that made clear that while the 1992 amended Land Acquisition Act allowed for compulsory purchases, the process of compulsory acquisitions would be based on a number of strict criteria. These included that targeted land would be underutilised land, or belong to absentee landlords or farmers who had multiple land holdings, or that were oversized, i.e. exceeded 1,500 hectares in Agro-Ecological regions 1 and 2.

The conference agreed a formula for compensation and approved the establishment of a UNDP Technical Support Unit that would assist in undertaking the purchase of 118 farms on a willing buyer, willing seller basis. But this was soon overtaken by events in the form of a clause in the new draft constitution proposed by ZANU-PF that provided for expropriation without compensation. Although as noted earlier, the entire draft constitution was rejected in a popular referendum in 2000, the responsibility for compensation was, nevertheless incongruously formally shifted to the former colonial power, Britain, through a legally invalid Constitutional Amendment No.16 of 2000, with one analyst pointing out the amendment was "*ultra vires* because it is beyond the powers of one state to unilaterally impose an obligation on another in its constitution. It therefore had no basis in international law" (Doré 2012, 3).

The Collapse of the Commercial Sector

Following the rejection of ZANU-PF's draft constitution at the February 2000 referendum, and which the MDC had campaigned against, the government adopted a radicalised two-pronged approach to regime preservation. On the one hand the list of farms for acquisition was rapidly expanded to 3,000 by mid-2000, while on the other thousands of ZANU-PF-sponsored war veterans moved on to commercial farms and evicted the owners, thus presenting the commercial sector with a *fait accompli*. By mid-2000 some 1,600 commercial farms had been taken over. Given that many commercial farmers were known to be sympathetic to the MDC, and had provided the party with financial support, the takeovers had the additional political advantage of seriously weakening the MDC's financial resource base.

This takeover campaign also coincided with the June 2000 parliamentary elections. ZANU-PF lost most of its seats in urban areas, while retaining overall control in the countryside, amidst well-documented systematic violence and intimidation against its opponents headed by the War Veterans and ZANU-PF youth (Amnesty International 2000). The MDC captured 57 seats against ZANU-PF's 62, though as a result of the constitutional provision allowing the President to appoint an additional 30 parliamentarians, ZANU-PF enjoyed a substantial working majority.

Nevertheless, it was clear that the 2000 election results were a shock to the ruling party, and confirmed its worst fears. ZANU-PF now faced, with Presidential elections scheduled for 2002, its most formidable political opposition since Independence, and one that had clearly also made inroads into ZANU-PF previously impregnable support base in its rural heartlands.

The government then went on to publish its FTLRP under the title *People First* (GOZ 2001), in a clear attempt to retrospectively impose a policy framework on the land invasions which by then were already well underway. The document set out two resettlement models for the future of agriculture. Under the A1 Model, each household was to be allocated 3 hectares of arable land with shared grazing rights, while A2 farmers would be allocated medium and large-scale commercial farms on a 99-year lease basis.

By 2005, over 80 percent of commercial farmland had been redistributed. Some 5.7 million hectares had been allocated to 130,440 households under the smallholder A1 scheme, and a further 1.9 million hectares to 12,560 A2 farmers under the scheme for new commercial producers. By 2009, the figures were to rise to around 148,000 benefiting from the A1 scheme, and around 16,000 from the A2 scheme (FAO/WFP 2009).

Large-scale commercial farming effectively collapsed, as evidenced by the output of the sector in terms of both exports and cash crops. By 2007 it has been estimated that overall commercial sector output had fallen to 42 percent of its 1998 levels. Cotton, for example, disappeared completely, while tobacco and coffee dropped to 31 percent and 10 percent respectively of their 1998 output levels. As a key contributor to the country's deteriorating food security and its growing reliance on food aid, both maize and wheat production from commercial farms had contracted to 31 percent and 23 percent respectively of their 1998 levels (UNDP 2008, 155).

When in 2000 the CFU had made its first estimates of the likely impact of land redistribution, it projected declines of around 25 percent in both output and exports along with the loss of 150,000 jobs on commercial farms – about 45 percent of the total formal agricultural sector workforce. This estimate was, however, based on the assumption that 5 million hectares would be acquired for resettlement. In the event the actual figure was much higher, as a result of which by 2007 commercial sector production of all crops and livestock had fallen by 58.5 percent to 957,000 tonnes from over 2.3 million tonnes in 1998. Over the period 2000–2007, the share of commercial production in total farm output had shrunk from two-thirds to just under half. Between 2000 and 2008, value added in total agriculture declined 49 percent in US dollar terms, while the sector's contribution to GDP fell by five percentage points to 13.9 percent compared with an average of 16 percent between 1985 and 1999 (ZIMSTATS National Accounts (various)).

By 2009 the large-scale commercial farming area had been reduced from 15.5 million hectares, or 39 percent of the total, to around 2.6 million hectares or 6 percent. The stake of small-scale agriculture of all kinds had increased from 45 percent to almost 65 percent, while another 7.4 percent was held by A2 'new farmers' operating large-scale commercial plots from which the former owners had been evicted (Rukuni 2011). It had taken almost three decades to achieve the transformation that ZANU-PF had promised, but at tremendous cost.

Inevitably there have been efforts by some academics such as Scoones (Scoones et al. 2010), much trumpeted by the Government-controlled press, to demonstrate that although the FTLRP brought serious economic and social dislocation in its wake, the long-term empowerment of millions of black Zimbabweans justifies this. One such example is the claim that evidence of investment in their holdings by beneficiaries of the FTLRP, and recent growth of smallholder tobacco production, is a measure of the programme's success, though the findings in the Scoones study have been challenged on grounds of both the robustness of the research methodology adopted, and the conclusions derived from the evidence generated.[9]

It was undeniable that the situation inherited at Independence was both socially and politically unsustainable. There was unquestionably land hunger amongst the rural poor, and as Scoones shows (at least as concerns Masvingo province) there was also an element of spontaneity in the land invasions which were not all, at least initially, entirely orchestrated by the state. Large numbers of black Zimbabweans did gain access to land for the first time in their lives as a result of the FTLRP, and as the Scoones study indicates in some cases smallholders did manage to turn it to productive use against the odds (most notably the collapse of agricultural extension services and markets, and lack of tenure security and inputs).

However, it is the failure to thoroughly compute the long-lasting damage caused by the FTLRP in terms of Zimbabwe's economy and its governance system detailed below, its disastrous humanitarian consequences, and the negative impact on human development indicators, human rights, the rule of law and levels of corruption, that is the major shortcoming of the Scoones study. On the cost side, not only was there the damage done to the economy as a result of the severing of previously close symbiotic linkages between agriculture and industry, a rupturing that was a significant contributor to the negative growth rates of the crisis decade (see below), but also the severe weakening of the country's institutional fabric following the FTLRP which will take decades to repair. At the household level there was the breaking up of family units through the loss of members, compelled as a survivalist strategy to join the diaspora or to engage in the urban informal economy, and a rise in the number of vulnerable and poor households (see Chap. 7) which must all be factored into any cost-benefit analysis.

There was long-lasting damage done to the prospects for future generations of exiting poverty, and increasing the scope for the inter-generational transmission of poverty. Declining nutritional standards amongst children, as evidenced by data on the incidence of growth stunting, and the collapse of educational outcomes, particularly in rural areas, were directly attributable to the violence and insecurity prevalent during the FTLRP, as well as deteriorating economic conditions (most notably rising unemployment and the descent into hyperinflation) which severely eroded household incomes and the ability to meet essential expenditure. Successive vulnerability assessments showed a rapid rise in the recourse by households to extreme coping mechanisms, such as the skipping of meals and the distressed selling of assets. Other reports indicated a rise in the withdrawal of children from schools and increased use of child labour (*IRIN NEWS* 2012), and in rates of child prostitution and human trafficking (*Daily News* 2012).

This was coupled with the diminishing ability of the state, due to growing financial and human resource constraints directly attributable to the havoc wrought by the FTLRP, to provide the most basic of services, most emblematically in terms of public health and the control of epidemics (see Chap. 7). That over 17 years after the launch of the FTLRP Zimbabwe remains a major recipient of emergency food assistance – and that the UN's World Food Programme has been forced to launch successive international appeals to feed Zimbabwe's population – is the ultimate indictment of the radicalisation of Zimbabwe's land reform for narrow political ends by its ruling party.

Collateral Damage: The Rule of Law

The destruction of commercial agriculture as a result of the FTLRP was only the tip of the iceberg – the collateral damage in terms of the wider economy was much more extensive. Given commercial agriculture's role as the dynamo of the economy given its extensive linkages with other sectors, it was inevitable that the disruptions associated with the land programme would have seriously adverse repercussions. Not only did production and employment fall across the entire economy, but the chaotic and often violent land reform programme changed investor and donor perceptions permanently, setting the country on the road to ostracism and targeted sanctions imposed by the West against members of the regime.

The rule of law was an early casualty of the FTLRP, though there had been plenty of previous warning signs of ZANU-PF's willingness to ride rough shod over the principle. Already in 1990, with the expiry of the Lancaster House provisions, the Government had moved quickly to introduce Constitutional Amendment No.11 concerning property rights. This substituted the previous provision for "prompt payment of adequate compensation" (the standard formulation in international economic law) in the case of expropriation, for "prompt payment of fair compensation payable within a reasonable time". This was followed up by Constitutional Amendment No.13, which denied the right of property owners to contest through the courts the amounts of compensation which were to be established by the state, as well as the period over which the payments would be made.

In order to give effect to the constitutional amendment, in 1992 the Government amended the Land Acquisition Act of 1985 – according to which the state had been granted the first option on any commercial land placed on the open market at market prices. To all intents and purposes, the 1992 amendment buried the 'willing buyer, willing seller principle', compulsory acquisition was given legal sanction on all land, and the 'fair' land price was to be established by administrative fiat through the application of a complex body of principles by a Compensation Committee.

Additional legislation then followed, further eroding the right of commercial farmers to compensation. The Land Acquisition Act was amended again in 2000 to restrict compensation for 'improvements' made by farmers to their holdings, but not for the land itself despite the fact that many had acquired their properties after Independence, while another amendment of the Act in 2004 granted the government the right to seize any remaining farms, as well as plantations, wildlife parks and agro-industrial property. That same year the Acquisition of Farm Equipment and Materials Act legalised the seizure of the equipment and stock of farmers, with Constitutional Amendment No.17 removing from the courts the right to adjudicate in land disputes, nationalising all farmland that had been gazetted for resettlement (i.e. listed in the official state gazette), and restricting compensation to 'improvements' undertaken by former owners and not the land itself.

While this battery of legislation was gradually put in place, legal judgements were ignored by the Government and the land invaders. The police were often bystanders to the takeovers, telling farmers as they were being evicted that because this was a political matter they were powerless to intervene. Furthermore, there was evidence of extensive involvement of security forces themselves in the land invasions, with one report based on extensive field work carried out in the course of 2001 concluding that the

Central Intelligence Organisation (CIO), the army and police helped to plan and provided logistical support to the war veterans who constituted the 'shock troops' of the ruling party, undermining Government claims that the land invasions had been entirely spontaneous (Human Rights Watch 2002).

There was a sustained assault on the independence of the judiciary. The Chief Justice of the Supreme Court was eventually forced to resign in 2001 under intense pressure, which included the invasion of the Supreme Court by War Veterans and threats to the lives of judges in November 2000 (Gubbay 2009, 17), after having presided over a Court order which declared the land invasions unlawful both in terms of the constitution and the provisions of the Land Acquisition Act. This left the way clear for the new Chief Justice, a ruling party loyalist, together with three newly appointed judges, to set aside the Supreme Court's earlier judgement and to rule favourably on the legality of the government's land acquisition policy in late 2001.

As the former Chief Justice of the Supreme Court of Zimbabwe was to subsequently observe in a lecture he gave in 2009, recalling the Supreme Court's ruling of 2000 which had highlighted both the chaos of the FTLRP and damage down to the rule of law in Zimbabwe:

> The settling of people on farms has been entirely haphazard and unlawful…War veterans, villagers and unemployed townspeople, have simply moved on to farms. They have been supported, encouraged, transported and financed, by party officials, public servants, the CIO and the army. The rule of law has been overthrown in the commercial farming areas and farmers and farm workers on occupied farms have been denied the protection of the law. (Gubbay 2009, 15–16)

He also noted the logic underpinning the process of compromising of the Judiciary wherein "the avowed policy of the executive was to appoint as judges to both the Supreme and High Courts persons known to be sympathetic to its political ideology" (Ibid., 2).

Further undermining the independence of the judiciary was the fact that some judges had allowed themselves to become beholden to the Executive by accepting largesse offered by the government, with one source claiming that by 2010 sixteen Supreme and High Court judges had received farms under the land reform programme (*Zim Online* 2010). As one international law association noted:

> Some Supreme Court and High Court Judges have been allocated land under the Government's commercial farms allocation scheme and hold that land at nominal rents and at the Government's pleasure. The deleterious effect that this has for judicial independence is too obvious to require stating. (International Council of Advocates and Barristers 2004, 2)

In a further indication of the undermining of the rule of law, after being denied access to the Zimbabwean courts a group of former commercial farmers filed an application before the Southern African Development Community (SADC) Tribunal (SADC(T)) challenging the land acquisition programme. In its judgement of 2008, the Tribunal ruled that Zimbabwe was in breach of the SADC Treaty establishing the regional organisation on the grounds that the applicants had been discriminated on the basis of race, and that Zimbabwe was in breach of the relevant article of the Treaty concerning non-discrimination on the grounds of gender, religion, political views, ethnic origin, culture, etc. (Article 6.2). The Tribunal also directed Harare to take measures to protect the applicants' ownership of their land and ensure that they were not evicted. In addition, those applicants whose property had already been expropriated were to be paid compensation by Government, with a deadline for the latter being set for June 2009. Significantly, the Tribunal also ruled that Constitutional Amendment 17, in which Harare put great store in terms of providing legal cover for its radicalised land reform, was in breach of the SADC Treaty, and that 'fair compensation' had to be paid to expropriated farmers that was not restricted to 'improvements' but which included the land itself (SADC (T) Case No.2/2007). Harare's reaction was simply to withdraw from membership of the Tribunal in August 2009.

The growing partisanship of the Office of the Attorney-General and the country's public prosecutors also became evident. Harassment of members of the MDC and its allied organisations such as independent trade unions and NGOs took the form of abuse of the law through the regular opposition of the Attorney-General and public prosecutors to the granting of bail to such individuals subsequent to their arrest, regardless of the merits of individual cases (Human Rights Watch 2008).

One summation of the state of the rule of law during the crisis decade provided a sober reminder of the damage that had been done:

> Over the past decade, Zimbabwe's ruling party has progressively and systematically compromised the independence and impartiality of Zimbabwe's judiciary and public prosecutors, and instilled one-sided partisanship into the police. Since 2000 it has purged the judiciary, packed the courts with ZANU-PF supporters and handed out "gifts" of lands and goods to ensure the judges' loyalty. It has provided instructions to prosecutors to keep opposition members in jail for as long as possible. It has transformed Zimbabwe's police force into an openly partisan and unaccountable arm of ZANU-PF. (Bar Council UK 2010, 1)[10]

Collateral Damage: The Creation of Dead Capital

The chaos triggered by the land invasions was compounded by the opaqueness of the subsequent allocation processes and disregard for qualification requirements. There were numerous reports of ruling party notables and their affiliates in the state apparatus seizing more than one commercial farm against the ruling party's stated policy of 'one man, one farm'.[11] The problem of multiple farm ownership was even brought up by the Government's own committee established to look into the status of the FTLRP, headed by the former Secretary to the Cabinet Dr Charles Utete which released its findings in 2003.

Notwithstanding the constraints it operated under in terms of detailed information that members of the committee were willing to place in the public domain, the Utete report noted, for example, that in Mashonaland Central Province "members of the District Land Identification Committee were accused of allocating land to themselves…Double allocation and multiple ownership had occurred in many districts" (GOZ 2003, 47–48). In Mashonaland West it referred to "double allocations, multiple allocations and favouritism in land allocations" (Ibid., 55) while in Matabeleland North it reported that a "few cases of double ownership were noted. Although the verification that was done on this matter was not exhaustive, what emerged could be a tip of the iceberg" (Ibid., 63).

Another report highlighted the extent to which the objectively verifiable need for land on the part of A1 beneficiaries was trumped by party political affiliation. Support for ZANU-PF, demonstrated by the production of a ZANU-PF membership card, became the key criterion for qualification (Human Rights Watch 2002). And the tenuousness of such security was particularly useful at election time, with one astute observer noting that, "since the new land occupiers have no title to the land and can be easily removed, loyalty to the party is the mortgage they must pay to keep the land" (Magaisa 2017).

This trend was also noted in another study which highlighted the looting and chaos that accompanied the process. Earlier criteria applied to the selection of beneficiaries, and which had at least focused to some extent on skilled and well-resourced entrepreneurial farmers, was increasingly trumped by political connections:

> A new breed of farmers, some experienced in communal farming, others without any idea of what farming entailed, took charge of productive land. The euphoria of owning a piece of land, of grabbing a farmhouse, of seizing a farmer's produce and household property, engulfed the farming areas. A new breed of people termed the "pirates of the land" emerged who were on a perpetual search for new farms as their own booty…Their targets were not just white-owned farms but also A-1 farms that they thought were "nicer" than the ones they already had…The result was that the fast-tracked commercial areas became places for competition for access to resources rather than competition for production and use of the land. (Kanyenze and Kondo 2011, 104–105)

The rule of the strongest and politically connected in rural areas was to remain a feature throughout the FTLRP. Based on findings from Masvingo province, Scoones noted that as late as the run-up to the establishment of a new inclusive government in 2008–09 (and with it the prospect that land seizures might be brought to an end) there was a wave of new land invasions, "resulting in the eviction of several white farmers who had, supposedly, been secure. In each of these cases, the evictions were precipitated by the claims of top officials who had previously not been rewarded with land" (Scoones et al. 2010, 199).

And in a clear sign of the failure of the new inclusive government which took office in 2009 to restore the rule of law in rural areas and rein in the predatory tendencies of the ZANU-PF elite, land seizures continued even after the opposition was brought into government. The search for new sources of patronage to ensure the preservation of the regime underpinned the FTLRP – and in the opinion of the present authors was the dominant motive behind ZANU-PF's radicalised approach to the land question – and is recognised even by those such as Scoones who seek to uncover positive outcomes from the FTLRP:

> In the post-Independence period, calls for land reform coincided on a regular basis with elections. Populist and nationalist rhetoric, however, covered up elite manoeuvres that allowed the capture of land and resources for personal gain…As the state's resources declined, land became one of the main sources of patronage…Disgruntled security officers were paid off, wayward politicians were pulled into line and solid supporters were rewarded with the only resource that the state had access to – land. Violence and intimidation, and an abuse of the rule of law, were often used to effect this. (Ibid., 252)

While senior political leaders grabbed entire commercial farms, those subsequently subdivided into smaller A2 commercial holdings were distributed amongst members of the other key pillars of the regime. Scoones, in his study of Masvingo province, reported that 16.5 percent of the A2 farms went to civil servants, 3.7 percent to members of the security forces, and 4.8 percent to business people (Ibid., 53).

Many farms lay idle in the course of the land invasions, as groups of grassroots ZANU-PF supporters competed amongst themselves to occupy former commercial farms, often then to be shunted aside in turn by notables from ZANU-PF and the security apparatus.[12] That this should have led to increased tensions in the rural areas given ongoing uncertainties over ownership, further impacting negatively on output levels, was hardly surprising. The shock troops of the land invasions, namely the self-designated 'war veterans' (many too young to have even been born before Independence) "argued that it was they who should be getting the largest areas of prime land, and not the "chefes" (top officials from town), or those who could fill in the forms" (Ibid., 194). While there were initial attempts by the Ministry of Lands, Agriculture and Rural Resettlement to ensure that the allocation of the larger A2 farms was based on a means test for qualification purposes (proof of agricultural training and experience in farming, as well as a technically sound production plan and financial resources), this was eventually set aside by central government, provincial governors and even district level officials as they handed out farms to political associates and friends in an orgy of patronage.

Reports at the time indicated that farming equipment was extensively looted, simply destroyed, or eventually seized up through lack of maintenance due to the financial constraints facing both small and large-scale beneficiaries of the FTLRP. Both groups also soon faced problems with purchasing seeds, fertilizer and other agricultural inputs. Banks were reluctant to extend credit to new A2 farmers given concerns over the security of their title as they were initially only granted 'offer letters' and had to wait for the issuing of 99-year leases, as well as their lack of a credit worthiness track record, while A1 farmers were in an even worse position and only granted 'temporary occupation licences'. The Utete Committee established by the government in 2003 reported that the absence of some form of title for land allocated under the A2 model meant that "beneficiaries could not secure support from financial institutions which invariably require collateral security of one form or another" (GOZ 2003, 88).

The tenuousness and insecurity of title should be seen as intentional. Because the new occupiers did not own the land, and so could be evicted without notice or due process, it necessarily strengthened their dependence on the goodwill of ZANU-PF and government officials through manifestations of loyalty to the ruling party. One consequence was the creation of vast amounts of 'dead capital', i.e. assets that could not be bought, sold, valued or used as collateral given uncertainty regarding ownership.[13] What to all intents and purposes had taken place was the further informalisation of the economy given the tenuous nature of the new forms of title issued, and their short 'notice to quit' provisions, which few observers doubted the government would ignore should further dispossessions help to further regime survival.

The speed with which the FTLRP was implemented was telling, and indicative of the extent to which it was a response to the short-term imperatives of regime survival, with the Utete Committee finding that:

> impediments to Programme implementation included limited financial and other resources and administrative difficulties encountered by an over-stretched bureaucratic apparatus suddenly called upon to implement a complex programme in great haste. (GOZ 2003, 6)

In addition, it commented that "Budgetary allocations for the Programme remained woefully inadequate. So also for infrastructure, tillage and inputs" (Ibid., 31). It was clear that the evisceration of the commercial agricultural sector, and the releasing of land for distribution to regime supporters, were ends in themselves, but also that little thought had been given to the long-term prospects of the country's agriculture and consequences for the wider economy.

The Failure to Decongest Communal Areas

While the FTLRP had as one of its stated objectives the decongestion of the communal areas which had been a permanent feature of stated post-independence national policy, the results on this count ended up far short of the mark. One study calculated that while around 55 percent of A1 settlers originated from the communal areas, through natural population increase their numbers would have been replaced in the communal areas within a period of 4–5 years. Particularly in those communal areas contiguous to former white-owned commercial farms, many of those resettled engaged in rational hedging, maintaining their communal homes and therefore a foot in both resettlement and communal areas (Doré 2009, 17).

This would explain seemingly puzzling references in the Utete report to the fact that in the province of Mashonaland East there was "consensus among officials, traditional leaders and settlers that there was no significant decongestion in the Province as a whole" (GOZ 2003, 52). And this was not an exception, since for Manicaland province the Utete findings also included the observation that "Provincial Governor, the Chiefs and those interviewed agreed that the impact of the resettlement programme on decongestion in the communal areas was quite negligible" (Ibid., 42), while for Mashonaland West it stated that "Statistics from the data collection teams and comments from interviewees suggest that decongestion has not significantly taken place in the communal lands" (Ibid., 56).

Economic Contagion

Former commercial farmers held on to their old title deeds, forlornly clinging to the hope that at some point in the future a different government would agree to pay compensation. Those on the side-lines of the chaos included potential domestic and foreign investors and donors, who took note of developments and drew their own conclusions regarding prospects for economic stability, the predictability and soundness of national decision-making processes, and prospects for the rule of law.

The collateral damage caused by the Zimbabwean state's cavalier attitude to property rights as evidenced in both the period prior to and during the FTLRP, as well as the violence which had accompanied the land seizures, had effects far beyond the agricultural sector. Coupled with indications of future government policy on the 'indigenization' of other sectors of the economy, this led to a dramatic decline in rates of investment. The share of private sector investment in GDP dropped from 22.5 percent in 2000 to a low of 2 percent in 2008, and which in US dollar terms represented a reduction of $1.5 billion. Over the whole period between 2001 and 2008, private sector investment averaged just 7 percent of GDP (ZIMSTATS, Various National Accounts).

As noted by a group of legal experts, the negative impact was hardly unexpected:

> No rational investor would consider investing substantial capital in a country where, for example, lawful performance of a contract depends not on what the parties agreed but on political interest in the transaction or where court orders are routinely disregarded by those who consider themselves politically immune from obedience to them. (Bar Council UK 2010, 7)

The spill-over effects on the wider economy were disastrous. As already noted, commercial agriculture had been the driver of the economy, along with manufacturing industry with which it was closely integrated. In the mid-1990s, over half the inputs into agriculture were supplied by the manufacturing sector, while in the reverse direction 44 percent of agricultural output was sold to the manufacturing sector. Of this, over 94 percent was supplied by the commercial farming sector and the balance by small-scale communal producers.

The disarticulation of the linkages between the two sectors, and their ripple effects throughout the rest of the economy, were felt rapidly and in dramatic fashion. Between 2000 and 2008, value added in manufacturing declined by 62 percent. The onset of the FTLRP also triggered negative GDP growth rates which were to become the pattern for the whole period until 2009 with the establishment of a multi-party Inclusive Government and return of macroeconomic stability. Because agriculture, spearheaded by tobacco which was dominated by commercial agriculture, accounted for 45 percent of merchandise exports, the collapse of commercial farming resulted in a precipitous decline in foreign earnings. Agricultural exports in 2000 were worth just over US$1 billion. By 2008 they had collapsed to US$367 million (IMF 2005).

The direct and indirect effects of the FTLRP on employment levels were also profound. Historically the number of commercial agriculture farm workers fluctuated between 300,000–350,000, and represented the largest component of the country's formally employed population (Sachikonye 2003, 17) Already by early 2002 an estimated 50 percent of jobs had been lost, rising to 65 percent by February 2003 (Ibid., 19) By 2009 survey results confirmed that around 66 percent of commercial farm workers had left their farms, and of these 71 percent had been evicted (GAPWUZ 2009, 40–41), with less than 1 percent of them benefiting from any land that was redistributed (Ibid., 43). It is reasonable to assume that many former commercial farm workers simply drifted to the cities in search of new livelihoods, and there were forced to take part in an expanding informal sector given the decline in urban formal sector jobs.

State Control and Fiscal Dominance

As output levels in the agricultural sector fell and had knock-on effects throughout the rest of the economy, the availability of both essential agricultural inputs which the new farmers needed, as well as basic commodities for the general population, rapidly worsened. The ruling party's response was to greatly extend the level of state intervention and controls in the economy as it came to adopt a fire-fighting approach to economic management.

The January 2001 monetary policy statement by then Governor of the RBZ, Leonard Tsumba, in effect abandoned previous attempts to finance excessive government spending in as non-inflationary a manner as possible. With inflation approaching 50 percent a year at the time, there was a powerful economic case for higher interest rates and tough monetary and fiscal restraint.

In the event the new Finance Minister, Simba Makoni, and the RBZ Governor, opted for interest-rate controls that put a 30 percent cap on the cost of official borrowing from the market. This forced all financial institutions to offer negative real interest rates on deposits and make loans also at negative rates, thus establishing a pattern for the rest of the decade. This 'easy money' policy fuelled inflation which rose above 350 percent annually in 2003/4. It was to reach an estimated 231 million percent by the time that ZIMSTATS abandoned its attempts to compile meaningful inflation figures in July 2008.

In July 2001, maize and wheat were declared 'controlled products', forcing producers to sell them to the parastatal GMB which became the sole official buyer of these products. In December 2001 new regulations were introduced, compelling farmers to deliver their stocks no later than 14 days after harvest, with those who did not comply having their stocks seized (UNDP 2008, 154).

Government setting of prices both for agricultural inputs and outputs (eventually to be extended to other sectors of the economy) became standard practice, and led to significant price distortions. So, for example, while in 2006 the GMB fixed the producer price of maize at Z$33,000 per ton, it sold maize on to millers at Z$600 per ton. Needless to say the

GMB's losses resulting from these subsidies had to be paid for by the fiscus, which they were through the increasingly frenetic printing of money by the RBZ.

Even more direct controls were used as the economic situation deteriorated, culminating in Operation *Dzikisa Mutengo* (Reduce Prices in Shona) of June 2007, an attempt to bring down inflation (then running at 4,500 percent annually) by slashing government controlled prices on a range of goods including agricultural inputs such as fertilizer and seed. Given that the cost of producing fertilizer was running at between six to ten times the government controlled selling price, it was not surprising that fertilizer firms produced just 16,000 tons against a national requirement of 600,000 tons for the 2007/08 agricultural season (Doré 2009, 14).

The appointment of Gideon Gono as the Governor of the Reserve Bank in 2003 heralded a new phase of government intervention in the economy and the centralisation of economic decision-making and power at the Reserve Bank. By 2005 Gono had firmly established himself as the country's Economic Czar, and was able to over-rule cabinet ministers, including the Finance Minister to whom he was nominally responsible. With his direct line to the President, Gono side-lined the then Finance Minister to the point that when in mid-2006 Gono revalued the Zimbabwe dollar by cutting zeroes from the currency, he publicly informed the Minister, who was in the audience for his monetary policy presentation, that for reasons of secrecy it had not been possible to inform him in advance of the move to redenominate the currency.

The RBZ also gradually assumed many of the functions of other ministries. In 2005 total government budget spending totalled US$1.4 billion, but additional quasi-fiscal spending by the central bank amounted to a further US$1.1 billion. Between 2005 and 2008, off-budget quasi-fiscal expenditure amounted to US$4.3 billion (30 percent of GDP), swamping budgeted spending of US$2.8 billion or 19.5 percent of GDP. Initiatives under the control of the central bank included facilities such as the Agricultural Sector Productivity Enhancement Facility, the Agricultural Mechanisation Programme and the Grain Procurement and Commodity Producers Support Prices Programmes. In one form or another, all the latter involved the creation of money by the RBZ with which it procured goods and services for, or provided subsidies to, an ailing agricultural sector, with widespread reports of the diversion of resources and from which regime elites benefitted disproportionately, with RBZ initiatives to repair the leaking dykes eventually extending to all other sectors of the economy.

Off-budget spending in the form of the central bank's quasi-fiscal activities, financed by central bank credit creation, eventually came to replace tax revenues as the main source of government income. Tax revenue fell 86 percent between 2005 and 2008, slumping to just 4 percent of GDP in 2008 from 25 percent in 2005. By the end of 2007 inflation had reached 108,850 percent, money supply was increasing at 180,000 percent annually, and the downward trajectory of GDP and employment growth and living standards speeded up.

The RBZ's use of monetary and fiscal policy to seek to arrest the process of economic collapse also provided unique opportunities for the ruling party to engage in extensive patronage. Subsidised (or free) farming equipment, seed and fertilizer, as well as increasingly scarce fuel and loans at negative rates of interest, were targeted at those able to prove their loyalty to the ruling party through the presentation of party cards, and meant that monetary and fiscal policy became important political tools for ensuring regime survival.

For example, through the RBZ's control of exchange rates, arbitrage opportunities abounded. It ensured that the political and military elite enjoyed preferential access to foreign currency at the official exchange rate. Given that the parallel market exchange rate diverged significantly from the official, the rent-seeking elite that were able to buy US dollars at the RBZ's official exchange-rate window, and sell them on the black market, became immensely powerful economically and acquired businesses and properties at bargain basement prices. Reckless credit creation in the form of Zimbabwe dollars printed by the RBZ greased the wheels of this glorified Ponzi scheme, and like the seizure of commercial farms represented a variant of the sharp end of the spoils-based political economy created by ZANU-PF, characterised by a zero-sum extractive form of accumulation.

It was crony capitalism at its worst, with the military, the politicians and business people who had thrown in their lot with ZANU-PF accumulating obscene wealth while impoverishing the vast majority of the population, driving the middle-class and unemployed youth into economic exile, and forcing those who remained behind into the informal economy. The rationale for vital economic decisions that affected the livelihood of millions of people was the preservation of ZANU-PF rule, regardless of human cost.

Notes

1. In official historiography, the First *Chimurenga* refers to the late 19th century revolt by the Shona and Ndebele people against the rule of the British South Africa Company in what was to become Zimbabwe. This was followed by the guerrilla war launched in 1966 against the white minority Rhodesian regime, known as the Second *Chimurenga* leading to Independence in 1980. While the launching of the FTLRP in 2000 was couched by ZANU-PF in terms of a Third *Chimurenga*, over the course of the crisis years it became clear that the correcting of historical wrongs was not limited to the question of land, and gradually expanded to include all sectors of the economy.
2. British Foreign Secretary Lord Carrington, chairing the talks, informed a plenary session of the parties in October 1979 that the UK government agreed to contribute to the costs of a land resettlement programme, but qualified this by stating that this would be "within the limits imposed by our financial resources. The costs would be very substantial indeed, well beyond the capacity, in our judgement, of any individual donor country, and the British Government cannot commit itself at this stage to a specific share in them. We should however be ready to assist the government of independent Zimbabwe to obtain international assistance for this purpose" (UK Parliament 2003). Notwithstanding the lack of binding commitments, the expectation on the part of both ZANU and ZAPU was that the sums involved would be substantial. Significantly, a figure of US$1.5 billion appeared in the document setting out Zimbabwe's needs in the context the country's first donor conference, ZIMCORD, held in 1981. This in turn appeared to be derived from a proposal developed in the context of an earlier peace initiative led by the then US Secretary of State Henry Kissinger as the amount necessary to cover resettlement and land acquisition compensation costs (GOZ 1981, 1).

3. In an attempt to clarify issues around land reform, in 2009 the UK Parliament's Africa All Party Parliamentary Group (AAPPG) carried out an inquiry, which *inter alia* sought to establish "what proposals were made and what commitments were given by UK and Zimbabwe representatives at the Lancaster House talks in 1979" (AAPPG 2009, 13), and produced a report based on its analysis of both written and oral evidence including those of key players at the time, Zimbabwean, American and British (one of which a written submission from the Government of Zimbabwe of February 2009). Amongst its conclusions regarding Lancaster House commitments were that "of all the evidence received… by far the most interesting is that from the Government of Zimbabwe. Despite what President Mugabe and other ZANU-PF figures have alleged and implied, at no point in their account did they state that an explicit sum of money was agreed upon and set aside at Lancaster House for land reform. Nor did their evidence touch upon the oft-repeated claim that Britain later reneged upon a specific promise made at Lancaster House on land" (Ibid., 25).
4. As noted by one agricultural economist, this then led to the incongruous situation of smallholders selling their maize to the GMB at favourable prices, and then purchasing maize meal in urban areas at subsidised prices for their own consumption (Doré 2009, 8).
5. Any commercial farmer wishing to sell land was legally bound to first offer it to the Government. If the latter decided that it did not wish to purchase the land (for financial reasons, or because it was judged unsuitable for resettlement purposes), it then issued a certificate of 'no present interest' with a one year validity which then allowed the owner to dispose of the land on the open market.
6. Though the Zimbabwean villagisation programme never made enough headway to evolve into the 'ujamma villages' that characterised the rural transformation policy of the Tanzanian government under President Nyerere in the 1960s and 1970s, or efforts to enforce socialist rural transformation in Machel's Mozambique in the 1980s under that country's 'communal villages' programme, it was nevertheless evident that the intention was to gradually socialise relations of production in the communal areas in line with the wider transformation of the economy and society along socialist lines. That the Zimbabwean programme gradually lost some of its attractiveness may well have resulted from Harare's reading of the growing RENAMO rebellion in Mozambique which had been stoked by popular discontent with the Marxist policies of the FRELIMO govern-

ment. One key contributor to the rapid spread of the armed conflict in Mozambique's countryside was growing peasant resistance to FRELIMO's communal villagisation programme. The latter had been characterised by the replacement of traditional authorities by state functionaries in rural areas, the forced movement of peasants to new locations, in some cases the state's appropriation of their assets, and the increasing use of heavy-handed tactics in order to ensure compliance. Harare's growing understanding of the drivers of the civil war in Mozambique would have been greatly facilitated by first-hand experience of the nature of that dissidence, as Harare reciprocated Mozambique's previous assistance during the liberation struggle by sending Zimbabwean troops to guard the vital Beira transport corridor linking the two countries. For the seminal study on peasant alienation from the Marxist state in Mozambique see Geffray (1990).

7. One study pointed out that in a specific district between 1986 and 1990, plans had been prepared for only four out of ninety proposed villages, while "government funding had not yet been made available for the implementation of any projects" (Doré 2009, 9).
8. It should be noted, however, that the Clare Short letter did in fact confirm the UK government's willingness to continue funding Zimbabwe's land reform, but also made clear that financial support depended upon land reform being "part of a poverty eradication strategy, but not on any other basis", with the additional requirement that the process had to be "completely open and transparent", all preconditions entirely in line with the then Western donor consensus on international development priorities (see Chap. 8), while also possibly reflecting concerns about the possible misuse of additional donor funding given reports of elite capture of landholdings. Needless to say, these aspects of the letter were studiously ignored by ZANU-PF's propaganda machinery.
9. So, for example, the lack of benchmarks derived from reliable data sets against which to measure progress to support claims of improved levels of investment by small-scale beneficiaries of the FTLRP, or the failure to compare productivity in new and old resettlement areas, or between new resettlement areas and former commercial farms. For a comprehensive elucidation of some of the methodological shortcomings in the Scoones study see Doré (2012).
10. This report on the state of the rule of law in Zimbabwe was produced in the wake of a mission conducted in 2009. Team members included representatives from the Commonwealth Lawyers Association, the Bar Human Rights Committee of England and Wales, the General Council of the Bar of England and Wales, and the NGO Avocats Sans Frontières.

11. One report from 2010 observed that 2,200 politically connected members of the elite ended up controlling up to half of the land seized from white farmers, with the President, ZANU-PF ministers, senior officers from the military, CIO and Police, provincial governors, ZANU-PF members of Parliament, judges and heads of parastatals owning 5 million hectares, with some senior figures having multiple farms. Though difficult to verify, ZANU-PF's continued reluctance to carry out a land audit lends credence to the findings of this report (see *swradioafrica* 2010).
12. The latter became known amongst Zimbabweans as 'weekend' or 'mobile phone' farmers, occasionally visiting their new farms or issuing instructions to farm managers from their homes in urban areas.
13. The concept of dead capital is most closely associated with the work of the Peruvian economist Hernando de Soto (de Soto 2000).

References

AAPPG. 2009. *Land in Zimbabwe: Past Mistakes, Future Prospects*, December. London: House of Commons.

Amnesty International. 2000. *Zimbabwe: Terror Tactics in the Run Up to Parliamentary Elections*, June. London.

Bar Council UK. 2010. *A Place in the Sun Zimbabwe – A Report on the State of the Rule of Law in Zimbabwe After the Global Political Agreement of September 2008*. London.

Clare Short. 1997. *Letter*. http://Zimbabwe-image.blogspot.co.uk/42007/12/Claire-shorts-letter.html.

Daily News. 2012. Zim New Hub of Human Trafficking: IOM, November 11. https://www.dailynews.co.zw/articles/2012/11/01/zim-new-hub-of-human-trafficking-iom.

de Soto, H. 2000. *The Mystery of Capital: Why Capitalism Triumphs in the West and Fails Everywhere Else*. New York: Basic Books.

Doré, Dale. 2009. *Recovery and Transformation of Zimbabwe's Communal Areas*, Comprehensive Economic Recovery in Zimbabwe Working Paper Series, No. 4. Harare: United Nations Development Programme.

———. 2012. *Myths, Reality and the Inconvenient Truth About Zimbabwe's Land Resettlement Programme*. http://www.sokwanele.com/myths_reality_and_the_inconvenient_truth_about_Zimbabwes_land_resettlement_programme_131112.

FAO/WFP. 2009. *Crop and Food Supply Assessment Mission to Zimbabwe*, June. Rome: Food and Agricultural Organization and World Food Programme.

GAPWUZ. 2009. *If Something Is Wrong… The Invisible Suffering of Commercial Farm Workers and Their Families Due to 'Land Reform'*. Harare: General Agricultural and Plantation Workers Union of Zimbabwe.

Geffray, Christian. 1990. *La Cause des armes au Mozambique: Anthropologie d'une Guerre Civile*. Paris: Karthala.

GOZ. 1981. *Zimbabwe Conference on Reconstruction and Development (ZIMCORD)*. Harare.

———. 1986. *Communal Land Development Plan: A 15 Year Development Strategy*. Harare.

———. 1994. *Report of the Commission of Inquiry into Appropriate Land Tenure Systems*. Harare.

———. 2001. *People First*. Harare.

———. 2003. *Presidential Land Review Committee Report on the Implementation of the Fast Track Land Reform Programme 2002–2003 ("The Utete Report")*. Harare.

Gubbay, A. 2009. *The Progressive Erosion of the Rule of Law in Zimbabwe*. Lecture at the Bar Council of England and Wales, December 9.

Human Rights Watch. 2002. *Zimbabwe – Fast Track Land Reform in Zimbabwe*, March. New York.

———. 2008. *Our Hands Are Tied, Erosion of the Rule of Law in Zimbabwe*, November. New York.

IMF. 2005. *Zimbabwe Selected Issues and Statistical Appendix*, Country Report 05/359. Washington, DC.

International Council of Advocates and Barristers. 2004. *The State of Justice in Zimbabwe: A Report to the International Council of Advocates and Barristers by Five Common Law Bars into the State of Justice in Zimbabwe*. Brisbane.

International Crisis Group. 2004. *Blood and Soil: Land, Politics and Conflict Prevention in Zimbabwe and South Africa*, Report No. 85/AFRICA, September 17. Brussels.

IRIN NEWS. 2012. *Child Labour on the Rise*, February 24. http://www.irinnews.org/report/94939/zimbabwe-child-labour-rise.

Kanyenze, Godfrey, and Timothy Kondo, eds. 2011. *Beyond the Enclave – Towards a Pro-poor and Inclusive Development Strategy for Zimbabwe*. Harare: Weaver Press.

Magaisa, Alex. 2017. *Big Saturday Read: Battle for Hearts and Minds of Rural Zimbabwe*, June 10. https://www.bigsr.co.uk/single-post/2017/06/10/Big-Saturday-Read-Battle-for-hearts-and-minds-in rural-Zimbabwe.

Masiiwe, Medicine. 2004. *Land Reform Programme in Zimbabwe: Disparity Between Policy Design and Implementation*, May. Harare: Institute of Development Studies, University of Zimbabwe.

Palmer, Robin. 1990. Land Reform in Zimbabwe, 1980–1990. *African Affairs* 89 (335, April 1): 163–181.

Rohrback, David D., et al. 1990. *Agricultural Growth and National Food Security.* Proceedings of the First National Consultative Workshop on Integrating Food, Nutrition and Agricultural Policy in Zimbabwe, University of Zimbabwe, Harare.

Rukuni, Mandivamba. 2011. Unpublished Paper for *Zimbabwe Poverty Reduction Workshop*, August. Harare.

Sachikonye, Lloyd. 2003. *The Situation of Commercial Farm Workers After Land Reform in Zimbabwe*, Report Prepared for the Farm Community Trust of Zimbabwe, May. Harare.

SADC (T), *Mike Campbell (Pvt) Ltd and Others v Republic of Zimbabwe* (2/2007) [2008] SADCT 2 (28 November 2008), Windhoek.

Scoones, I., et al. 2010. *Zimbabwe's Land Reform: Myths and Realities.* Oxford: James Currey.

Swradioafrica. 2010. *Zimbabwe's Land Barons.* Harare. http://www.swradio-africa.com/pages.landbarons 301110.html.

UK Parliament. 2003. *Annex A – Zimbabwe: UK Approach to Land Reform' Select Committee on Foreign Affairs Minutes of Evidence*, May 27. London. https://publications.parliament.uk/pa/cm200203/cmselect/cmfaff/339/3032509/htm.

UNDP. 2008. *Comprehensive Economic Recovery in Zimbabwe: A Discussion Document.* Harare: United Nations Development Programme.

Zim Online. 2010. 16 Judges Benefit from Mugabe Land Grab, February 16. http://www.zimbabwesituation.com/old/feb16a_2010.html.

ZIMSTATS. *National Accounts* (Various).

6

Regime Survival and the Attack on the Urban Poor

The rapid rise in open unemployment and informal employment referenced in previous sections, coupled with the state's response to the phenomenon, were some of the most prominent features of the country's economic regression during the crisis years. They were also a powerful reminder of the destructive effects of poorly designed economic policies anchored on the narrow and short-term objectives of regime preservation.

More so than arguably any other aspect of Zimbabwe's regression and increasing fragility, it was the growing informalisation of the economy that best captured the anti-developmental consequences of the ruling party's policies. ZANU-PF's policies towards the informal sector in the aftermath of the FTLRP, while dealing with short-term threats to the ruling party, only served to compound state fragility in the longer-term. As with other features of ZANU-PF rule, it destroyed markets and livelihoods, deepened poverty, increased outward migration and internal displacement, compounded popular estrangement from national authorities, and weakened state legitimacy.

M. Simpson, T. Hawkins, *The Primacy of Regime Survival*,
https://doi.org/10.1007/978-3-319-72520-8_6

Zimbabwe's Informal Sector in the Pre-crisis Period

Like other aspects of Zimbabwe's economic regression such as rising inflation and negative GDP growth rates, the growing informalisation of the economy during the crisis decade was unprecedented in global terms for a country not suffering from open conflict. Both workers and enterprises operating in the formal sector were, in increasing numbers, forced into the informal sector as formal enterprises and employment collapsed. Capacity utilisation declined as a result of shrinking domestic markets (itself a reflection of falling incomes), while enterprises faced growing difficulties in accessing foreign exchange to purchase inputs and spare parts.

As government revenues shrank, so did public expenditure on infrastructure maintenance, and enterprises suffered from worsening electricity power cuts, problems with water supply, and deteriorating road and rail transport. Firms laid off workers in increasing numbers, forcing households to supplement income through engagement in informal activities. As a result of rising levels of inflation which impacted on real incomes, even those who kept their formal sector jobs were often also forced to work part-time in the informal sector. In a very real sense, as the economy deteriorated, this 'subterranean economy' became to all intents and purposes the real economy for growing numbers of Zimbabweans.

At the same time it is important to note that such informalisation preceded the onset of the crisis years. Reference has been made in other chapters to the relatively poor growth rates, low levels of employment creation, and the mixed results of successive efforts at structural adjustment during the 1980s and 1990s. In addition, the economy that ZANU-PF inherited at Independence was already characterised by high levels of informal economic activity both in rural and urban areas. In the case of the latter, such activities had developed notwithstanding some attempts by the former colonial state, and subsequent white minority governments, to restrict informality in urban areas in line with efforts at spatial and racial segregation. This was accompanied by efforts to suppress indigenous economic activities (save that of subsistence agriculture) that might compete with white economic interests, and thereby ensure a regular supply of black wage labour for the country's agricultural, mining and manufacturing sectors. As regards the pre-independence regulatory framework applied to urban areas, this included a battery of by-laws, zoning regulations and licensing requirements, all of which sought to restrict the informal economy.

During the period 1986–1990, and in line with the pattern followed by many other developing countries, as already noted formal sector employment was increasing at a slower rate than that of the rate of new additions to the labour market (Kanyenze 2009, 4).[1] Even more sobering was the fact that the Government itself reported that while formal sector employment had grown by just over 52,000 between 1979 and 1984, over 250,000 school leavers had entered the labour market just between the years 1983–1985 (GOZ 1986, 5). By 1991 the gap between the growth in formal sector employment and that of the labour force had widened even further, with "about 200,000 school leavers each year, but only 20,000 to 30,000 new jobs being created in the formal sector" (GOZ 1991, 2). The International Labour Organization (ILO) reported that by the end of the 1980s less than 25 percent of the labour force was employed in the formal sector (ILO 1991).

As detailed in Chap. 4, when Zimbabwe adopted an Economic Structural Adjustment Programme (ESAP) in 1991 it had been hoped that the policy package would trigger more robust growth rates and in turn impact positively on employment levels. In the event, employment growth was disappointing, with formal employment growth rates dropping further from the 2.5 percent registered in the period 1986 to 1990, to 1.2 percent between 1991 and 1996.

Evidence that many of those who found themselves in the informal sector had previously been employed in the formal sector – i.e. those in the informal sector were not only recent school leavers but also victims of retrenchments under ESAP – is provided by a 1993 survey of informal enterprises conducted in some of the country's main cities. 21 percent of respondents indicated that they had previously been employed in the formal sector prior to ESAP. An average of 58 percent of respondents in Harare and Bulawayo indicated that their main reason for engaging in informal activities was the lack of alternative employment, i.e. informal activities constituted a fall back, survivalist strategy rather than a freely chosen employment option. In addition, the typical enterprise was found to be a one-person enterprise, indicating the small size of such undertakings, and low levels of capitalisation and profit margins (Mhone n.d., 25–27).

These features of informality were confirmed by a set of surveys of Zimbabwe's Small and Medium Enterprises (SMEs), commissioned by the United States Agency for International Development (USAID) in 1991, 1994 and 1998.[2] They showed that between 1991 and 1994 there was an increase in the proportion of one-person undertakings, a reliable indicator of a trend towards what should be seen as desperate self-employment, with the 1994 report also noting that close to two-thirds of SMEs made "less profit than the equivalent minimum wage for domestic workers …[and] 88 percent …[making] profits below the average employee earnings within the formal sector" (USAID 1994, 24–25). The increasing importance of such undertakings as coping mechanisms for poor households in the context of rising unemployment is reinforced by data generated by the 1998 survey, which noted that "profits [were used] primarily for household needs and school fees …[and that] only between 10 percent and 15 percent of proprietors reinvest profits into their businesses" (USAID 1998, 57). Therefore, while there may have been elements of dynamism and growth prospects for some SMEs, it was clear that for the majority their growing numbers reflected poor economic growth and employment in the wider economy.

In addition, state support for the development of SMEs had been sorely deficient throughout the post-independence period. It was not until 2002 that the Government developed a comprehensive policy framework for SMEs, with a new Ministry being established for the purpose of leading implementation. This new policy framework noted the limitations of past support programmes. These were judged to have been piecemeal, and the report pointedly observed that notwithstanding previous commitments to improve the regulatory environment, it remained the case that the "process of registering a business, getting the necessary licenses and the cost of compliance can be a major deterrent for small-scale entrepreneurs …[and that] the deregulation agenda is still unfinished" (GOZ 2002, 7).

That the Zimbabwean legal and regulatory environment was burdensome – though in this respect it did not substantially differ from that prevailing in most developing economies as shown in the work of the Peruvian economist Hernando de Soto referenced above[3] – is borne out by an ILO report on the situation in Zimbabwe in the 1990s. The latter highlighted the specific and byzantine regulatory burdens that acted as disincentives for formalisation in Zimbabwe, "blocking the expansion of small-scale business development and … suffocating the dynamic section of the informal sector" (ILO 1993, 13). The result was to increase the vulnerability of many small-scale informal operators to punitive state actions after 2000, as their numbers swelled and their presence increasingly came to be regarded by the ruling party as a threat to the political status quo, such antagonism being compounded by its more general hostility to private enterprise of any size.

During the first two decades of independence, despite the constraints such enterprises operated under– ranging from lack of access to credit from the formal banking sector, low profitability, onerous licensing and other regulations which acted as disincentives to formalisation, to occasional harassment from police and municipal officers – the relationship between informal sector operators and the state might be characterised as one of benign neglect on the part of the latter rather than outright antagonism. While many by-laws inherited from the colonial and UDI years restricting the operations of the informal sector remained on the statute books, their enforcement was usually *ad hoc*, with the payment of bribes ensuring that the eyes of officialdom were averted at relatively low cost.

By the end of the 1990s, a comprehensive survey of 110 countries estimated the size of the informal sector in Zimbabwe as a percentage of official GNP at 59.4 percent, significantly higher than the average 42 percent of the 23 African countries in the sample (Schneider 2002). On the basis of such figures, as the country entered the new millennium it was clear that its informal sector was acting as a significant absorber of both new entrants into the labour market, as well as those displaced from an increasingly stressed formal sector.

Informality in the Crisis Decade: A Collapsing Formal Sector

While the problem of growing informality therefore preceded the crisis years, the pace and breadth of informalisation of the economy in the post-2000 period was both quantitatively and qualitatively different. The process was also one in which the role of the state in terms of the negative impact of its acts of omission and commission was much starker than previously.

A number of forces were at work during the crisis years which resulted in the rapid increase in the growth of Zimbabwe's informal sector. The marked deterioration in the quality of macro-economic management translated into declines in all macroeconomic indicators, with worsening levels of growth, savings, investment, output, and exports. Coupled with the country's inflation rates which reached 'off the chart' levels by 2008, this led to a severe contraction in both real wages and the country's domestic markets.

The shrinkage of the economy is most evident when one looks at employment figures. As Zimbabwe entered the new millennium, GDP growth collapsed to −7.4 percent, setting the trend for the rest of the decade such that between 1997 and 2004 employment growth averaged −1.6 percent (UNDP 2008, 103) with one labour economist estimating that by 2009 only 13 percent of the country's labour force was employed in the formal sector (Kanyenze 2009, 26). In contrast to the 1980s and 1990s when the economy had failed to keep pace with the numbers of new entrants to the labour market, but was nevertheless still creating new jobs, the next decade saw formal employment shrinking rapidly in absolute terms.

In addition, as noted earlier, one consequence of the FTLRP was the large number of farm workers who lost their jobs. Though reliable data is scarce given the difficulties faced by researchers in accessing rural areas during these turbulent times, it is safe to assume that with the exception of that segment of the commercial sector agricultural workforce composed of migrant labour from neighbouring countries such as Malawi and Mozambique who may have returned to their home countries, workers were forced to migrate to urban areas in search of new livelihoods. Finding restricted opportunities for formal sector employment, they were then forced into the informal economy, contributing further to the growing numbers of those engaged in such activities.

Mirroring the downturn in the commercial agricultural sector, a survey of the manufacturing sector conducted by the Confederation of Zimbabwe Industries (CZI) showed that by 2007 the country's industrial output had dropped to less than 30 percent of its 2003 levels, and that 75 percent of industrial concerns were operating at less than 50 percent capacity utilisation (CZI 2008). In addition, the same report noted that most workers were not earning a living wage, with salaries unable to keep pace with rising inflation, forcing even those in formal employment to supplement household income through engagement in informal activities.[4]

Informality in the Crisis Decade: Operation Murambatsvina, State Control and Livelihoods Destruction

Variously translated from Shona as Operation 'Clear the Trash' or 'Clear the Filth', designated officially by the Zimbabwean government as 'Operation Restore Order', and known colloquially as Zimbabwe's 'Tsunami', Operation *Murambatsvina* was launched by the Government in May 2005. This was a clean-up operation of the country's urban and peri-urban areas, purportedly aimed at enforcing by-laws inherited from the pre-independence period and still on the statute books concerning 'illegal activities'. This attribution of illegality to the activities of informal sector operators was to become increasingly shrill as *Murambatsvina* progressed, and the government faced increasing domestic and foreign pressure and felt compelled to justify its actions in legal terms.[5]

As a result of natural population growth coupled with limited housing, and the displacement of farm workers from commercial farms in the context of the FTLRP, many high density, peri-urban settlements had expanded to accommodate new arrivals through the construction of both extensions to existing homes, as well as makeshift habitations. Due to the increasing reliance of households on informal income-generating activities, many dwellings had also become the site of backyard workshops, covering activities as varied as vehicle and domestic appliance repairs, brick-making and furniture construction, small retail outlets, hairdressing, beer brewing, hair salons, bars and restaurants. In addition, numerous informal markets had mushroomed to cater for the needs of inhabitants. However, according to existing legislation, not only were many of these constructions in violation of building regulations, but the economic activities that they accommodated were in breach of zoning by-laws which banned commercial activities from these areas. The rationale for *Murambatsvina* was therefore couched in official pronouncements in terms of an offensive against criminality, justifying the extensive involvement of the country's police.

Gradually spreading outwards from Harare to cover other cities and rural towns, and lasting until mid-June 2005, *Murambatsvina* resulted in the bulldozing and burning of thousands of homes, workshops housing small-scale enterprises, and informal markets, as well as the confiscation and destruction of equipment and goods. This was often done indiscriminately, as many who had built according to planning regulations, or who had secured official vending licenses, were also caught up in the dragnet of the Operation and saw their assets and livelihoods destroyed.

Murambatsvina was also accompanied by the widespread use of a punishing violence against any attempts at resistance, and the arrest of thousands of informal traders. Even in the context of Sub-Saharan Africa where such slums clearances are an unfortunately common occurrence, *Murambatsvina* stands out for its geographical scope, the numbers of those affected, and the brutal efficiency with which it was carried out.

In addition to the destruction of the housing of the poor, the impact on the informal economy was devastating. As the UN's Special Envoy for Human Settlement Issues in Zimbabwe, appointed and dispatched by the UN Secretary-General to report on the situation, was subsequently to note:

> The livelihoods of all directly affected households have been either destroyed or placed in serious jeopardy. In many instances, there is compounded suffering as homeless and displaced people are unable to pursue their occupation or maintain their source of income … Many traders in the informal sector … have had their stock confiscated or destroyed. The loss of capital is therefore substantial … Thousands of those who used to work in the

> informal sector have lost their livelihoods as a result of the crackdown on flea markets, tuck-shops, craft markets, vending stalls and urban agriculture … Markets in rural growth points have been closed and roadside vending has been banned, resulting in net loss of livelihoods. (United Nations 2005, 35–36)

The UN report went on to estimate that 700,000 people were directly affected by the demolitions, i.e. losing their homes, their livelihoods, or both, with a further 2.4 million indirectly affected (as a result of declining markets for goods they produced, or loss of income for extended family members in rural areas dependent on remittances from urban income earners). One Government source quoted in the report proudly published figures according to which over 32,000 'illegal' SMEs had been demolished, as well as 78 'people's markets' in the city of Harare alone (Ibid., 85).

A survey, subsequently conducted in 2006 by the ILO in one area on the outskirts of Harare that had been particularly prominent in terms of its small-scale furniture making concerns, revealed that between 82–88 percent of those working were engaged in informal activities, with 73 percent of those interviewed stating that their work situation had been negatively impacted by *Murambatsvina* due to the destruction of their work premises. In addition, and though more difficult to quantify, it was also clear that the population displacements triggered by the Operation, as the newly homeless moved on in search of new shelter and sources of income, resulted in further depressed demand for goods and services provided by informal operators (ILO 2008, 36–37).

The destructive impact on the economy as a whole by *Murambatsvina*, and more specifically on the livelihoods of the most vulnerable in society, was poignantly conveyed by the leader of the MDC opposition, Morgan Tsvangirai, who stated that:

> Government's claim that such action is in the public interest is disingenuous. Street vendors are not sabotaging the economy; it is the government which is sabotaging the economy through mismanagement and corruption. Teachers, doctors, nurses, factory workers and people from all walks of life have been forced into becoming street vendors as it has become the only means of survival … A government that destroys the properties of

> people who are trying to make an honest living is evil. It is people-insensitive. Millions of Zimbabweans have been made poor and jobless by this regime … the people's belongings have been stolen by the government … it ploughed through their properties and looted their goods. That is unforgiveable. (*Daily Mirror* 2005)

That *Murambatsvina* would have a hugely negative impact on the country's already high poverty levels was entirely predictable. A study subsequently commissioned by UNDP-Zimbabwe commented on the increasingly 'survivalist' aspect of the country's informal sector:

> Extremely high levels of informality in Zimbabwe, in particular a large number of micro or single worker concerns at the "survivalist" end of the spectrum, is a sign not of huge reservoirs of entrepreneurial skills, let alone a conducive environment for small enterprises, but rather of high levels of "desperate employment" and of the frenzied search for coping mechanisms amidst vertiginous rates of economic regression. (Simpson and Ndlela 2010, 21)

Nor was such destruction limited to physical capital, the disruption of trade networks and loss of income-generating opportunities. One survey, focused on a specific settlement on the outskirts of Harare and carried out by the Zimbabwe Lawyers for Human Rights (ZLHR) and researchers at the University of Zimbabwe, noted there were extensive negative impacts in terms of people's access to health and education services as a result of their forced displacement and loss of assets (ZLHR 2006). This had a crippling effect on an already poor and vulnerable population as borne out by another comprehensive survey conducted by an international NGO. Covering over 23,500 households, it reported that 22 percent of households had children who were not attending school as a result of *Murambatsvina*, while 54 percent of households had become food insecure. In addition, large numbers suffered from loss of access to HIV/AIDS Anti-Retroviral Therapy. This was profoundly damaging given that at the time Zimbabwe had the fourth highest HIV/AIDS prevalence rate in the world, while systems of home-based care were also severely disrupted as many of those affected became Internally-Displaced Persons

(IDPs) (ActionAid International 2005). In sum, adding to the loss of livelihoods and the destruction of economic assets and trading networks, *Murambatsvina* also had a profoundly damaging effect on the country's human capital base. That the Operation took place in the depths of Zimbabwe's harsh winter only compounded the misery of those affected.

Murambatsvina, Market Destruction and Regime Survival

The ruling party's motives for launching *Murambatsvina* – besides official justifications concerning the need to combat criminality and remove the eyesore of informal activities from the country's cities – as well as its timing, have both been the subject of intense speculation and analysis. One common view is that *Murambatsvina* is best understood as a form of punishment, meted out by ZANU-PF party to the urban poor for their support to the opposition MDC in the general elections held earlier in March 2005 – elections that had seen the MDC win almost all the parliamentary seats in the country's two largest cities of Harare and Bulawayo – thus showing them in no uncertain terms the costs of voting for the Opposition.

Murambatsvina has also been interpreted as a pre-emptive strike against the possibility of an urban-based popular uprising against ZANU-PF's rule. The use of an iron fist against the urban poor, and the destruction of their sources of livelihood, forced large numbers of them into the countryside where a network of ZANU-PF appointed chiefs could more easily control and monitor popular discontent.[6]

> Rural areas are ZANU PF strongholds. The traditional leadership control access to all communal resources – and the right to Grain Marketing Board maize sales, the only source of grain in rural areas, most of which are currently facing starvation. People are being forcibly removed from MDC dominant urban centres to ZANU PF dominant rural areas; it is simple, those translocated will have to show allegiance to ZANU PF or face a real risk of starvation this winter. (Solidarity Peace Trust 2005, 27)

In addition, *Murambatsvina* also added to the numbers of those fleeing the country in search of new sources of livelihood outside Zimbabwe, further weakening the ranks of anti-ZANU-PF elements within urban areas.

The two objectives are, of course, not mutually exclusive. What they share in common is the goal of weakening political opposition to the continued rule of ZANU-PF, the element of physical intimidation after the 2005 elections dovetailing with the intentional building up of pressures on the poor to leave urban areas through the destruction of their homes and livelihoods.

That the Government was subsequently to fail dismally to provide alternative accommodation for those whose homes were destroyed by *Murambatsvina* – and also proved to be extremely obstructive to the efforts of international agencies to erect temporary shelters *in situ* and provide other forms of humanitarian assistance to those affected by the demolitions – lends credence to the view that the intention was to move those affected away from their destroyed homes and neighbourhoods to rural areas, and to discourage their return. At the time there were numerous reports of the forced transportation of affected communities to rural areas, and these were extensively documented by both Zimbabwean and international organisations.

> In different areas across the country Zimbabwe Republic Police threatened, harassed, or beat the IDPs, forcing them to relocate to the rural areas where many have no homes or family and where social service provision and economic opportunities are minimal ... In addition, the government tried to compel the relocation by ensuring that international assistance is not provided to those who choose to stay in urban areas, meanwhile using the food packages as an incentive for families to move to the villages. (Human Rights Watch 2005, 3)

The numbers of those subjected to such involuntary resettlement during *Murambatsvina* should be added those forced to move during the FTLRP. As one faith-based regional NGO was to observe "Zimbabwe has become a nation of internally displaced people, where its own citizens are refugees within the borders of what should be their home" (Solidarity Peace Trust 2006, 8).

To these largely political considerations behind the Operation might be added others with more distinct economic features, though these also reflected the regime's political interests and survival imperatives. The driving rationale in this case was that the growing informal sector, operating according to its own logic and outside the control of the state, had come to constitute an obstacle to the ruling party's increasing hold on all aspects of the economy, and weakened its capacity to engage in patronage.

Informal sector operators, by and large, did not owe their livelihoods to party or state functionaries. But their dispossession in the context of a shrinking economy created opportunities for ZANU-PF to distribute stakes in the informal economy to lower level state functionaries and party members. This was, in fact, subsequently done through the distribution of the spoils of *Murambatsvina* via the allocation of new stalls in markets and tuck shops, the granting of licenses to operate enterprises such as workshops and hairdressing salons, and preferential treatment in terms of whatever new plots of land, low-cost housing, vending stands and credit facilities the government was subsequently able to provide to those able to present a ZANU-PF party card.[7] Reports of looting of the stock of informal traders by police during the Operation should also be seen as part and parcel of the logic pursued by the regime to ensure the continued loyalty of security forces upon which it had increasingly come to rely. The manner in which it was carried out also reflected a pattern of growing involvement of security forces in all areas of policy, including the economy, as well as significantly its designation as an 'Operation'.

Patronage considerations, and the opportunities for the distribution of largesse opened up by *Murambatsvina*, therefore reflected the same logic as that which had driven the distribution of former white-owned commercial farms to party notables in the course of the FTLRP, and other forms of 'economic empowerment' or 'restitution by take-over'. Even in the context of a rapidly collapsing economy, there were still opportunities (and an added urgency) to replenish the trough of patronage, notwithstanding the longer-term consequences for the majority.

An additional economic motive attributed to *Murambatsvina* was that it reflected a desire on the part of Government to destroy the foreign-exchange black market which had become an integral part of the informal economy, in particular that component made up of remittances from the Zimbabwean diaspora. With a widening gap between the official and parallel foreign-exchange rates, and growing popular recourse to the black market, the temptation to eliminate informal currency dealers would have been a strong one. This would have enabled the RBZ to capture these increasingly scarce sources of hard currency by compelling buyers and sellers to convert at the highly controlled official rate. The foreign-exchange thus accumulated could then also used as additional largesse in the context of the ruling party's patronage requirements.[8]

Given the extensive linkages between the informal and formal economies in Zimbabwe, it is safe to attribute to *Murambatsvina* a significant role in the ongoing process of a declining GDP and government revenues, shrinking formal sector employment, growing out-migration of Zimbabweans and increasing reliance of households on diaspora remittances, collapsing domestic markets, falling real wages and purchasing power, and a rapid rise in national poverty levels and decline in the country's human development indicators. As with the FTLRP, short-term political considerations translated into an anti-developmental extractive form of accumulation, and trumped any concerns about the longer-term consequences of the Operation on the welfare of the most vulnerable of the country's citizens.

Notes

1. Another analyst, who examined data for the period 1980–1987, puts the figure for average formal sector employment growth at only 0.7 percent (Mhone, 12).
2. It is important to note that while these USAID surveys did not distinguish between informal and formal enterprises, they were comprehensive, covering the same sites over the course of all three surveys. Nearly 5,600 enterprises were surveyed in 1991, rising to nearly 7,400 in the 1998 survey, and the data therefore provide unique insights into the historical development of the sector.
3. The work of Hernando de Soto served to draw attention on the extent to which, in addition to the problems the poor face in securing legal title to their assets which can be used as collateral for credit, other regulatory

burdens act as an obstacle to formalisation. The essence of the argument is that government regulation and registration requirements, burdensome both in terms of cost and time expended, lead informal sector operators to opt to continue operating informally (de Soto 2000).

4. One indicator of the extent of collapse in the purchasing power of formal sector wages (and the growing shortages of basic foodstuffs and consumer goods) is provided by a study of informal cross-border trading. This form of economic activity was dominated by women, who brought back goods purchased in neighbouring countries, in particular South Africa, for resale in informal markets, while also acting as carriers for Zimbabwean produced goods which could not be sold on the depressed local market, in particular arts and crafts which suffered from a shrinking foreign tourist market. The study revealed that the incomes earned by those in formal employment were no longer sufficient to cover household needs such as rent, food, school fees and uniforms. In the case of the country's large number of security guards, their average monthly wage was Z$1 million, whereas through one trip across the border to South Africa a trader could net between Z$3–4 million (Ndlela 2006, 22).
5. Another important feature of the global experience with informality concerns its association with criminality, which should be highlighted given it played such a prominent role in Zimbabwe both before and after Independence, and particularly so in the events of 2005. In the eyes of the governments of many developing countries, informality comprises economic activities that fall outside the reach of state structures and their regulatory frameworks, and therefore informality and illegality have often been conflated even though the goods and services produced are not themselves illegal. It is then but a small step – and one which was easily taken by the authorities in Zimbabwe – to ascribe attributes of criminality to all such unrecorded forms of employment, production and exchange. Such an association added to the already onerous burdens faced by informal sector operators. On this point see Potts 2007.
6. One often overlooked aspect of this growing support amongst the urban poor for the MDC is that of the role of ZCTU which was historically closely allied to the opposition party. The ZCTU, against the background of a shrinking membership that in turn reflected falling formal sector employment, had been reaching out to informal sector operators, helping them to organise and thus increasing the regime's concerns about a possible urban uprising based on the poor and informal sector operators.

7. In an attempt to counter mounting international criticism of *Murambatsvina*, in the course of the visit of the UN Special Envoy the Government announced the launching of Operation *Garikai/Hlalane Khule* (OGHK) which can be translated as Operation Reconstruction/New Life in Shona and Ndebele respectively. The stated intention was to build new homes for those who had lost their shelter as a result of *Murambatsvina*, and figures of up to 300,000 new homes were regularly mentioned in the official press. In the event OGHK rapidly fizzled out as the sums required had not been included in that year's budget, itself a good indication of the haste with which the initiative was devised. Even assuming a genuine intention to provide housing to those affected (unlikely given the political objective of moving the urban poor out of the cities), subsequent delivery was dismal. As the NGO Solidarity Peace Trust noted in its report, as regards the situation in Bulawayo city one year after the launch of OGHK not a single house had been built, whilst elsewhere the allocation process of those few units built was characterised "gross irregularities, with houses being allocated to government officials, children of cabinet ministers, police, army, multiple house-owners and others who were not on any official housing list" (Solidarity Peace Trust, 32).
8. Some credence is lent to this linkage by the fact that the Governor of the RBZ, in a monetary policy statement released the same day as the official launch of *Murambatsvina* on May 19, 2005, lambasted the "iniquitous parallel market rates for foreign currency and goods in short supply currently prevailing in this market…most of which are being set and determined in some dark alleys and street corners of our cities…The activities of this grey market pose the single largest threat to our battle against inflation and the turnaround program. This will not be tolerated" (RBZ 2005, 17).

References

ActionAid International. 2005. *The Impact of 'Operation Murambatsvina/Restore Order' in Zimbabwe*. Harare.

CZI. 2008. *Manufacturing Sector Survey*. Harare.

Daily Mirror. 2005. Is Clean-Up Punishment?, May 27. Harare. http://www.zimbabwesituation.com/old.may27.2005.html#link8.

de Soto, Hernando. 2000. *The Mystery of Capital: Why Capitalism Triumphs in the West and Fails Everywhere Else*. New York: Basic Books.
GOZ. 1986. *Zimbabwe: Socio-Economic Review 1980–1985*. Harare.
———. 1991. *Zimbabwe: A Framework for Economic Reform 1991–1995*. Harare.
———. 2002. *Small, Micro and Medium Enterprises (SMMEs)—The Engine for Growth: Policy and Strategy Framework*. Harare.
Human Rights Watch. 2005. Zimbabwe: Evicted and Forsaken – Internally Displaced Persons in the Aftermath of Operation Murambatsvina. *Human Rights Watch* 17(16 A). New York.
ILO. 1991. *Employment/Unemployment in Southern Africa in the Late 1980s*. Report Submitted to the 12th Meeting of the Southern Africa Labour Commission, Tanzania.
———. 1993. *The Urban Informal Sector in Zimbabwe: From Insignificance to the Employer of Last Resort*, ILO Working Paper (WEP 2-19/W61), February. Geneva: World Employment Programme Research.
———. 2008. *Decent Work and Informal Employment: A Survey of Workers in Glen View, Harare*, Issues Paper, No. 33. Harare: ILO Sub-Regional Office for Southern Africa.
Kanyenze, Godfrey. 2009. *Labour Markets and the Rebuilding of Human Capital*, Comprehensive Economic Recovery in Zimbabwe Working Paper Series, No. 3. Harare: United Nations Development Programme.
Mhone, Guy C.Z. n.d. *The Impact of Structural Adjustment on the Urban Informal Sector in Zimbabwe*, Issues in Development. Discussion Paper, No. 2. Geneva: ILO.
Ndlela, Daniel B. 2006. *Informal Cross-Border Trade: The Case of Zimbabwe*, Occasional Paper, No. 52. Johannesburg: Institute for Global Dialogue.
Potts, Deborah. 2007. *The State and the Informal in Sub-Saharan African Urban Economies: Revisiting Debates on Dualism*, Crisis States Working Paper Series, No. 2. London: Crisis States Research Centre, London School of Economics.
RBZ. 2005. *The 2005 Post-election and Drought Mitigation Monetary Policy Framework*. Harare.
Schneider, Friedrich. 2002. *Size and Measurement of the Informal Economy in 110 Countries Around the World*, July. Paper Presented at a Workshop of the Australian National Tax Centre, Australian National University, Canberra.
Simpson, Mark, and Daniel Ndlela. 2010. *The Informal Economy, SMEs and the 'Missing Middle' in Zimbabwe: Some Observations*, Comprehensive Economic

Recovery in Zimbabwe Working Paper Series, No. 9. Harare: United Nations Development Programme.

Solidarity Peace Trust. 2005. *Discard the Filth – Operation Murambatsvina*, June 27. Harare.

———. 2006. *'Meltdown'—Murambatsvina One Year On,* August 30. Harare.

UNDP. 2008. *Comprehensive Economic Recovery in Zimbabwe: A Discussion Document*. Harare: United Nations Development Programme.

United Nations. 2005. *Report of the Fact-Finding Mission to Zimbabwe to Assess the Scope and Impact of Operation Murambatsvina*. New York: United Nations.

USAID. 1991. *Micro and Small-Scale Enterprises in Zimbabwe: Results of a Country-Wide Survey*, December. Washington, DC: USAID.

———. 1994. *Changes in the Small-Scale Enterprise Sector from 1991 to 1993: Results of a Second Nationwide Survey in Zimbabwe,* March. Washington, DC: USAID.

———. 1998. *Zimbabwe: A Third Nationwide Survey of Micro and Small Enterprises,* September. Washington, DC: USAID.

ZLHR. 2006. *Report on the Impact of Operation Murambatsvina – The Case of Hatcliffe Extension*. Harare.

7

Regime Survival: Poverty Creation, Mass Migration and Elite Enrichment

Throughout the period 2000–2008, both domestic and foreign observers – in particular those concerned with the humanitarian consequences of Zimbabwe's economic meltdown – witnessed a dizzying rise in the country's poverty levels, a rapidly deteriorating humanitarian situation, and growing dependence on emergency international assistance. The seemingly irreversible downward spiral in the living conditions of the vast majority of the population was accompanied by a growing exodus of Zimbabweans to both neighbouring countries and further afield. These outflows both contributed to, and were a consequence of, the collapsing economy and deteriorating political environment, and severely weakened the country's human capital base. Those who could afford to and possessed the necessary qualifications and skills migrated legally, while those desperate enough to be willing to live as illegal migrants in host countries also voted with their feet and left in search of greener pastures.

Observers also regularly noted that the worsening conditions facing ordinary Zimbabweans took place against the backdrop of apparent government indifference to the plight of large numbers of its citizens. Every official government 'turnaround' programme designed to reverse the decline – and such programmes were to be launched with increasing

M. Simpson, T. Hawkins, *The Primacy of Regime Survival*,
https://doi.org/10.1007/978-3-319-72520-8_7

regularity as a fire-fighting mentality took hold and planning horizons shortened – was either not implemented, or where it was had the opposite effect of that intended.[1] Even when such programmes might have gone some way towards reviving production and arrested the decline in output levels and employment, they were often obsolete by the time they were launched such was the quickening pace of regression which made both the baseline data and intended targets irrelevant almost as soon as they were announced.

In addition, amidst this growing poverty and deepening humanitarian crisis, there was increasing evidence of significant levels of personal enrichment on the part of an elite that seemed to be thriving notwithstanding (or arguably because of) the economic meltdown and its social consequences. More so than negative news on GDP growth, inflation rates, industrial capacity utilisation or agricultural export earnings, it is the human consequences of the destruction of markets and livelihoods, and the disastrous management of the economy, that constitute the most egregious aspects of increasing state fragility in Zimbabwe resulting from the primacy given by the ruling party to the maintenance of its continued monopoly on power.

Unemployment, Poverty and the Humanitarian Crisis

Previous chapters have noted that the country's growth rates, as well as the rate of formal sector employment creation, were already anaemic prior to the onset of the crisis in 1997/8. A critical ingredient of employment creation and poverty reduction, namely robust growth, was therefore already missing prior to the onset of the crisis decade.

But it was in the new millennium that both GDP growth rates and employment growth rates were to move strongly into negative territory after the violence that accompanied the elections of 2000 and the launch of the FTLRP in 2000–2001. GDP contracted by an average of 4 percent per annum over the whole period between 2000 and 2008, with per capita income in international dollar terms shrinking by 5.25 percent per annum (IMF 2010).

The impact of this collapse in GDP on employment levels resulted in a catastrophic decline in real average earnings and rising poverty. One study usefully conveyed the extent of the squeeze on wages and salaries by calculating the percentage share of the former in total Gross Domestic Income (GDI) for the period 1985–2007; from an average of 49.4 percent of GDI between 1985 and 1990, wages and salaries had fallen to 35.3 percent over the period 2000–2007 (Kanyenze 2009, 8). To this must be added the effects of rising rates of inflation which eroded the purchasing power of wages. The same source calculated that based on a real average earnings index (adjusted for inflation), this had peaked at 120 in 1982, and collapsed to 10 by 2004 (Ibid., 6). Thereafter, as inflation accelerated dramatically, real wages fell even further.

A vicious cycle set in, with declining purchasing power brought about by rising unemployment and the corrosive effects of inflation on real incomes leading to falling demand for goods and services. This in resulted in a decline in capacity utilisation amongst enterprises and further lay-offs. By 2008 the CZI was estimating that capacity utilisation had collapsed to less than 10 percent (CZI 2008).

Government's 'corrective' measures throughout the crisis years only compounded the meltdown, with successive price control offensives aimed at bringing down inflation forcing many enterprises to operate at a loss, resulting in further closures. Amidst declining tax receipts given rising levels of unemployment and the collapse of companies, the Government was unable to maintain the country's basic infrastructure (in particular utility services such as water and electricity). This, in turn, came to constitute an additional burden on enterprises as the provision of services became increasingly erratic, and contributed to further downsizing and more job losses.

One problem facing labour economists – in addition to the dearth of regularly updated employment data and concerns about their reliability – was the narrow definition of employment used by the national statistics office, whereby those engaged in as little as one hour of work during the reference week were classified as employed. One incongruous result was that the Labour Force Survey of 2004 showed an unemployment rate of only 4.4 percent (GOZ 2006a). Using such strict criteria, a person spending a single hour at the traffic lights of an intersection selling a bag of tomatoes would have been classified as employed. There was recognition, even by the official statistics office, of the nonsensical nature of the figures arrived at through this methodology when it noted that:

> In the labour force framework, unemployment is considered to be an extreme situation of total lack of work. In many developing countries there is either none or a very limited number of workers covered by unemployment insurance or other public relief schemes. Under these conditions, very few people can afford to be unemployed for any period of time. As such most people would be engaged in some economic activity, i.e. they get employed although it may be inadequate. Therefore the employment status cannot be fully described by unemployment data alone. (Ibid., 70)

A better indication of the problems of both unemployment and extensive underemployment in the economy was provided by Zimbabwe's Poverty Assessment Study Survey-PASS II (GOZ 2006b). This used a broader definition of unemployment, and included amongst others those workers who were involuntarily in the informal sector. Using this definition, the unemployment rate shot up to 63 percent in 2003. By 2009, unemployment figures over 90 percent were being put forward by some economists. Whereas at Independence 14 percent of the population was employed in the formal sector, this had declined to 10 percent by 2004, and was estimated to have declined further to 6 percent by 2007 (UNDP 2008, 103).

After 2007 data on wages became increasingly meaningless as the country descended into hyperinflation, and the Zimbabwe dollar ceased to function both as a useful medium of exchange and unit of account. The living standards of those on fixed incomes such as pensioners plummeted as a result of inflation, with many simply no longer bothering to collect their monthly pension payouts as a single bus journey cost more than the money to which they were entitled. At the height of hyperinflation in 2008, many civil servants, nurses and teachers often received less than the equivalent of US$10 as their monthly wage, insufficient to even cover their transport costs. To the extent that they turned up for work at all it was increasingly to use their workplaces as venues to barter goods and services, while those operating at the frontline of service delivery applied 'under the counter' tariffs for services rendered to the public as a form of income supplementation.

Zimbabweans in both the public and private sectors, as well as those engaged in informal activities and subsistence agriculture, sometimes commented that they had been reduced to 'hunter gatherers'.[2] Hours were spent queuing up for increasingly scarce basic goods such as bread, cooking oil and maize meal. Vehicle fuel was also rationed, and only available to those able to purchase coupons with foreign exchange. With rising inflation, and the growing worthlessness of the Zimbabwe dollar, these fuel coupons became a widely accepted substitute medium of exchange.

As the decade progressed and the printing presses failed to keep up with the demand for local currency, the RBZ imposed daily withdrawal limits on the banked segment of the population, this policy of restricting people's access to their money being justified by the RBZ as an anti-inflationary measure. This in turn led to the increasingly common phenomenon of people at the end of the month camping overnight outside banking outlets in order to be first in line to withdraw as much as they could of their salaries, followed by a frenzied rush to the nearest shop in order to purchase anything which might hold its value and be traded.

If many Zimbabweans were now hunter gatherers, they also sought to adapt to what had to all intents and purposes had become a pre-monetary barter economy. It is a supreme irony that notwithstanding the stated objective of Operation *Murambatsvina* in 2005, namely the elimination of informal activities in urban areas, by 2008 the vast majority of Zimbabweans had by force of circumstance become operators in the informal economy.

It was the informal sector that picked up the slack in terms of employment, though as already noted in the previous chapter it was a sector characterised by poor growth prospects, low levels of profitability and wages, and 'desperate employment'. This necessarily translated into even higher levels of poverty, confirmed by the findings of the PASS II, with 61 percent of those in the urban informal sector below the Total Consumption Poverty Line (TCPL)[3] as opposed to 46 percent of those engaged in what remained of the formal sector.

Any observer familiar with Zimbabwe's trajectory in the first two decades of independence would have been shocked by what they witnessed by the mid-2000s. An early morning visit to the industrial sites around Harare, Bulawayo, Masvingo and Mutare would have been rewarded with the sight of people queuing up outside factory gates in the hope of daily piece work, while a detour to any metropolitan rubbish dump would have been yielded scenes of large numbers of families scavenging amongst piles of trash.

Attempts by analysts to understand what was happening on the economic front became increasingly challenging. Access to information was restricted, with many economists forced to rely on extrapolations from past trends, estimates and insider information. The national statistics agency could not but have been negatively affected by the nationwide deterioration in institutional capacity, as well as a growing lack of government interest in funding the collection, processing, analysis and dissemination of national statistics. Its budgets were slashed, surveys became increasingly infrequent, and the comprehensiveness and quality of data analysis deteriorated as qualified staff left the service. As noted by the IMF in 2004, "Zimbabwe's economic data suffer increasingly from poor coverage, time lags, and worsening reliability of reporting units, all of which hamper Fund surveillance" (IMF 2004, 1). The official attitude of neglect was understandable given what the available data showed.

Notwithstanding such data constraints, there was plenty of reliable evidence that both the incidence and depth of poverty was rapidly increasing during the crisis years. One useful document, which surprisingly did see the light of day notwithstanding its extremely sobering content, was the aforementioned nation-wide poverty assessment conducted in 2003.[4]

While the country's 1995 poverty survey had found that 55 percent of the population were living below the TCPL, i.e. were unable to meet their basic food and non-food requirements, by 2003 the poverty headcount had increased to 72 percent of the population. The data also showed a particularly worrying increase in the depth of poverty, evidenced by the growing percentage of the population unable to meet even their basic nutritional needs, i.e. the extreme poor. The figure for those falling below the Food Poverty Line (FPL) based on minimum calorific requirements increased even more dramatically from 29 percent in 1995 to 58 percent in 2003. In other words, more than half of the country's population was not consuming the recommended minimum daily number of calories.

According to one assessment of urban household vulnerability, data showed a rapidly deteriorating food security situation in peri-urban and high-density locations where the urban poor were concentrated, with 33 percent of surveyed households being 'food insecure' (falling below the ideal daily caloric intake) in 2009 as compared to 24 percent in 2006. Over the same period the proportion of those consuming three meals a day declined from 54 percent to 23 percent, while the adequate dietary diversity score showed that households were consuming less diversified diets, the figure having declined from 87 percent in 2006 to 59 percent in 2009. The skipping of meals, the shrinking of portion sizes and the consumption of less nutritious foods, became increasingly common coping strategies for poor households in the face of the multiple pressures they confronted, as did the distressed sale of assets and the switching of expenditure from education and health to food items (ZimVAC 2009).

The nutritional status of the country's children showed a particularly marked deterioration. The 2005/06 Demographic and Health Survey found that 17 percent of children in Zimbabwe were malnourished, an increase of 13 percent over the last survey conducted in 1999, while three provinces (Midlands, Harare and Bulawayo) registered a shocking 70 percent increase in child malnutrition rates (GOZ 2006c, 8).

No national poverty surveys were conducted after 2003, though by 2008 economists were 'guesstimating' that the TCPL headcount was over 85 percent due to a combination of the corrosive effects of inflation and rising unemployment on household real incomes. In a useful exercise which provided unique insights into the impact of inflation on income levels and household food security – as well as of the extent of the decline since the PASS II report based on 2003 survey data – the UN's Food and Agriculture Organization (FAO) and World Food Programme (WFP) calculated that by April 2007 the statutory minimum wage rate represented only 10 percent of the TCPL, and just over 20 percent of the income needed to reach the FPL (FAO/WFP 2007, 27).

By the mid-2000s, and notwithstanding Government reluctance to publicly accept that Zimbabwe was facing a humanitarian crisis, international agencies were providing emergency food assistance to growing numbers of Zimbabweans. In 2007 the FAO and WFP estimated that 4.1 million would be needing food aid until the next harvest in 2008 (Ibid., 4). By mid-2008 these agencies were projecting that the figure would increase to 5.1 million by January–March 2009 (FAO/WFP 2008, 5).

There was a growing realisation amongst international agencies of the complex factors driving the dire humanitarian situation. The regularity with which the country began to suffer from food deficits was recognised as being caused by a range of factors other than simply poor rainfall patterns requiring the occasional provision of emergency food aid. From their Harare offices, these agencies came to terms with the extent to which official policies had caused – and continued to compound – the food crisis, though to access target populations the language they used in their funding appeals had to necessarily be circumspect, if not obtuse, with frequent references to unspecified national 'challenges' facing the country.

Over and above the highly visible destruction of the previously vibrant commercial farming sector, agencies also took note of acts of apparent self-immolation, such as the officially sanctioned and gradual takeovers of the few remaining white-owned commercial farms left over from the FTLRP after the high watermark of the land invasions had passed. In addition, there was the deterioration of rural infrastructure such as roads, water, electricity and the provision of agricultural extension services necessary for agricultural production, processing and marketing, profligate monetary policies and the effects of inflation which placed inputs beyond the reach of most small-scale agricultural producers, poorly targeted fiscal policies and the lack of incentives to produce a marketable surplus in the context of extensive price controls. To many aid agencies their work increasingly resembled plugging holes, on a recurrent basis, in a dam that was being actively undermined by those responsible for its upkeep.

Broader indicators of development shone further light on the human costs of multiple deprivations due to the country's regression. One insight into the pace of degeneration was provided by the widely accepted UNDP composite HDI. In 1990 Zimbabwe had occupied 78th position out of the total 130 countries in the HDI global rankings (UNDP 1990, 124), and throughout much of the 1990s it had been placed in the Medium Human Development category of countries. By

2003, however, it had fallen to 145th position out of 175 countries, this also being the year in which it dropped into the Low Human Development category. By 2010 Zimbabwe had fallen even further to last place out of a total of 169 countries in the index for which the relevant data were available. This decline reflected the fact that the country had experienced an average negative HDI growth rate of −1.81 percent over the whole period since Independence in 1980 to 2010, the only country out of the 169 countries whose data was recorded in the 2010 report to have registered a negative average performance over those three decades. This was largely attributable to the crisis years, with the HDI growth rate having deteriorated at an average rate of −5.05 percent between 2000 and 2010 (UNDP 2010, 148).

Scrambling for the Door and Hollowing Out National Institutions

As already noted, the crisis years led to a rapid rise in the number of Zimbabweans seeking to emigrate. What began as a trickle in 2000 following widespread employment of violence by the state against the political opposition in that year's legislative elections, soon turned into a flood as declining economic conditions went hand in hand with a state which used heavy-handed tactics in the implementation of its FTLRP, resorted again to violence in the course of the 2002 Presidential elections and 2005 legislative elections to intimidate opposition parties, strong-armed the urban poor in its offensive against the informal economy during Operation *Murambatsvina* in 2005, followed by even higher levels of state-sponsored violence during and after the 2008 Presidential and legislative elections.

Between 2000 and 2008 daily life became increasingly oppressive and unpredictable as the state ignored its primary duty to protect its citizens. The judiciary was restructured in order to be more amenable to ensuring the interests of the ruling party were safeguarded, media laws were modified to circumscribe the independence of the press, and a battery of new legislation was introduced strengthening the powers of the Presidency and the security forces, such as the infamous Public Order and Security Act (POSA) of 2002 which granted virtually unlimited powers of detention to the Zimbabwe Police. If the growing numbers of those seeking to eke out a living in the informal sector was an indication of 'desperate employment', the increasing numbers of those leaving the country showed that the forces of 'desperate migration' were also at work.

These push factors were felt particularly strongly by the unemployed youth, with many risking life and limb to undertake hazardous journeys to cross illegally into South Africa and other neighbouring countries in search of refuge and jobs. The sense of despair was such that the numbers willing to take the risk increased significantly during the crisis years. As one anonymous respondent to a comprehensive study on the importance of migrant worker remittances on household wellbeing poignantly stated:

> How can you expect me to survive in these difficult moments? Government should support the elderly and those struggling to support their families, but today we have a government that believes in destruction and human suffering. Government leaders are the biggest liars. Our people are dying of hunger. For the past 25 years the government has been farming poverty. (Bracking and Sachikonye 2006, 8)

The link between increasing outward migration and deteriorating conditions inside Zimbabwe can be gauged from figures on the Zimbabwean migrant population in the major host country, South Africa. Based on official South African census figures, in 2001 there were 131,886 Zimbabweans in South Africa. One source estimated that by the end of 2009, the total figure for Zimbabwean migrants in South Africa, based on data from various surveys, stood at around 2 million. The same source estimated that by 2010 the total number of Zimbabweans which had emigrated both legally and illegally to South Africa and other countries in the region such as Botswana, and further afield to countries such as the UK, the US, Australia and Canada, to be between 3 and 4 million. The higher figure represented 25 percent of the country's estimated total population (Makina and Kanyenze 2010, 9).

Based on data collected in 2005, another study highlighted the effects of out-migration on the country's human capital base, noting that the:

> Majority of migrants (72%) are under the age of 40 with most of those (56%) in the 25 to 39 age group. In other words, migrants are generally individuals in their prime working years. They are also well-educated compared to migrants from other SADC countries. Less than 1% have no schooling and over 50% have a post-secondary diploma, undergraduate degree or post-graduate degree'. (Tevera and Chikanda 2009, 16)

From the point of view of ZANU-PF, such an exodus was not necessarily unwelcome and may even have been actively pursued. The country's dwindling urban middle class, unionised groups such as teachers and health workers, as well as the country's youth, were all segments of society that were not only aligned or at least sympathetic to the MDC, but also those most likely to contest ZANU-PF's continued rule. In the case of unemployed youth, they were also the ones most likely to take to the streets. As one analyst insightfully pointed out:

> With up to a quarter of the country's population out of the country – a majority of them Zimbabwe's best and brightest – the implications for political protest and activism are potentially enormous. The country has been stripped of a critical mass of risk-takers who could take part in collective action with the potential to undermine the authoritarian regime. (Masunungure 2011, 53)

Public statements by the authorities lent credence to such an interpretation. In 2002 Didymus Mutasa, a leading figure within ZANU-PF, was to chillingly answer when asked about the Government's response to growing food insecurity in the country, the impact of the HIV/AIDS pandemic, and reports of growing numbers of Zimbabweans leaving the country, that 'We would be better off with only six million people, with our people who support the liberation struggle. We don't want all these extra people' (Institute for War and Peace Reporting 2004).

The impact on the national skills base of such haemorrhaging of human capital, in particular of professionals, skilled and semi-skilled workers, is brought home by sector-specific data. One report conducted by a national research institute in 2003 found that 24.6 percent of emigrants were either doctors, nurses or pharmacists, a further 24.6 percent were engineers or scientists, with an additional 20 percent being teachers (Chetsanga and Muchenje 2003, 44).

Another study noted that by 2000 the country was losing an average of 20 percent of its health care professionals every year to emigration (Chikanda 2005, 1). This was significantly above the rate at which national health training institutions were able to replace losses as they themselves were crippled by the brain drain. By 2007 the country's main medical training institution, the University of Zimbabwe's College of Health Sciences, was reporting an overall vacancy rate of 60 percent, with some departments such as haematology not having a single specialist in post (Kanyenze 2009, 13). The effects in terms of deteriorating health service delivery were predictable; PASS II data showed that only 48 percent of health units had filled at least 80 percent of established posts for doctors, while the figure for nurses stood at 45 percent.

To put a human face on the consequences of such an exodus, the Maternal Mortality Rate (MMR) which had stood at 283 per 100,000 live births in 1994 had risen to 725 per 100,000 live births by 2007, a deterioration that is at least partly attributable to a growing lack of skilled birth attendants in the country (GOZ and UN 2010, 28). The same source also noted that as of 2010, 80 percent of midwifery posts in the public sector were vacant (Ibid., 29).

The increasing lack of public funds available for infrastructure maintenance, and the loss of skilled and semi-skilled technicians, also had an impact on the health status of the population, with a survey in 2009 showing the proportion of people in rural areas with access to safe drinking water falling from 70 percent in 1999 to 61 percent in 2009 (Ibid., 42). The population's access to adequate sanitation facilities such as improved latrines also decreased, from 60 percent in 1999 to 30.5 percent in 2006 (Ibid., 38).

The situation of the country's health system was not more catastrophic only because of increased donor assistance in the context of a deepening humanitarian crisis. That the public health system was able to retain any of its staff at all was due to the fact that in 2008 donors began to supplement the salaries of all categories of workers, from cleaning staff, nurses and laboratory technicians to doctors, in an effort to arrest the sector's decline (see Chap. 10).

The effects of the skills exodus were also felt in the country's education system. This sector's achievements had been a source of great national pride during the first two decades of independence given the very high levels of school attendance and literacy achieved. The reversal was therefore all the more marked. The shortage of learning materials was particularly stark, with some surveys showing that by 2009 an increasing number of urban and rural primary schools respectively had no textbooks at all (Ibid., 12). Together with the gradual deterioration of school facilities given the lack of maintenance funds, the migration of thousands of teachers due to collapsing real wages and worsening working conditions, and the contribution of HIV/AIDS to the attrition rate of teachers, there was a slow but steady reversal of previous gains.

Examination achievements in the last year of primary education provided insights into the rapid drop in the quality of primary education. If in 2003 46 percent of children managed a pass in all four subjects tested, by 2009 this had fallen to 20 percent. An additional indication of the drop in educational attainment levels, as well as the stress placed on households by the economic meltdown, is provided by primary school completion rates, i.e. the percentage of children who started and completed primary school. Between 1996 and 2006, completion rates fell from 82.6 percent to 68.2 percent (Ibid., 10). One of the likely causes – in addition to lack of teachers, high rates of teacher absenteeism, poor facilities and the dearth of learning materials – was increased pressures on households to use their children to contribute to household income, either as unpaid labour in small-scale subsistence agriculture or in the urban informal economy.

The civil service also suffered as a result of the economic meltdown, and any characteristics of 'Weberianness' it had once possessed were gradually undermined. It lost growing numbers of staff due to financial difficulties as they struggled to subsist on Zimbabwe dollar salaries, as well as the increasingly oppressive requirement to demonstrate loyalty to the ruling party. Promotion based on purely meritocratic criteria soon became a distant memory, as did the notion of a clearly defined and predictable career path, critical elements for building competent civil services as highlighted in Chap. 2. The exodus was most marked amongst technically competent and experienced civil servants who were able, without great difficulty, to find alternative employment either in the private sector, with international organisations, or outside the country. Even short-term planning became an exercise in futility, since due to inflation budgets were irrelevant as soon as finalised. Morale collapsed, except for those few at the very apex of the system who chose to remain, and these were looked after by the ruling party which ensured their continued loyalty through a share in the national spoils, be this a former commercial farm, an imported car, fuel coupons or preferential access to foreign exchange.

It was not only public services that suffered from the effects of out-migration. The private sector also reeled under the effects of the decline in real wages leading to an exodus of workers, compounding sector-specific difficulties such as falling output, shrinking domestic markets, increasing difficulties in accessing foreign exchange with which to import inputs, and rising inflation. One CZI survey noted that the majority of "workers are not earning a living wage, with low-level employees earning an equivalent of $8 to $10 a month" (CZI 2008, 28). It is hardly surprising, given such conditions, that another report cited an interviewee who stated his company was losing about half of its qualified artisans every year (UNDP 2008, 127).

The difficulties facing the country's mining sector painted a stark picture of the consequences for Zimbabwe of this 'rush for the door' by skilled personnel. By 2007, more than half of the mining industry's skilled workers had left for greener pastures. Given the close links between private enterprise and public tertiary educational establishments, the knock-on effects of stress on the latter could not but have been felt by human resources in the former. While the industry's annual need for graduates in mining-related disciplines was in the order of 480–550 per year, the University of Zimbabwe's maximum capacity was 124 students per year, in a context in which the geology department had only three persons in post against an establishment of sixteen (Hawkins 2009, 9). By 2009, both academic and support staff throughout the University of Zimbabwe were being given monthly food packs which included bags of maize meal and cooking oil to compensate for salaries whose value in terms of real purchasing power had all but disappeared.

Keeping Households Afloat: The Role of Diaspora Remittances

As the economy collapsed and the financial stress on households increased, so the role of migrant remittances (both monetary and in-kind) grew in importance as a means of mitigating the effects of declining household incomes and increasing shortages of basic food and non-food items within Zimbabwe, while at the same time injecting scarce foreign exchange into an economy which had suffered from a marked decline in export receipts. Though notoriously difficult to measure, particularly in an economy in which monetary remittances were overwhelmingly informal given the artificially low official exchange rates imposed by the Reserve Bank, one attempt to do so arrived at a figure of nearly US$1.4 billion by 2009, and this in the context of a rapidly shrinking GDP which according to one estimate then stood at only US$4.39 billion (Makina and Kanyenze 2010, 19).

In terms of their impact on household security, one study served to highlight the extent to which such remittances had become an essential coping mechanism, representing anywhere between 80 and 93 percent of total expenditure, and covering everything from food to clothing, medical expenses and school fees (Pendleton et al. 2006). Significantly, analysis of data from another survey conducted in 2005 found that 50.8 percent of households sampled had used remittances to buy food which they would not otherwise have eaten (Bracking and Sachikonye 2006, 35). As the crisis deepened, it became increasingly difficult to find an extended household in Zimbabwe which did not have at least one member in the Diaspora.

In line with the increasingly desperate and predatory tendencies of the ruling party to secure additional assets in the face of economic meltdown, there were repeated efforts to capture migrant remittances. International best practice recommends that such flows be treated as private flows, and successful labour exporting countries have adopted enlightened policies to encourage the flow of remittances through official channels, such as preferential interest rates, the establishment of migrant service bureaux in host countries, and legislation permitting the holding of foreign currency accounts. In stark contrast, in the case of Zimbabwe the state's *dirigiste* attitudes once again made themselves felt.

In a clear attempt by the ruling party to secure whatever valuable resources were available in a rapidly shrinking economy, the authorities sought to compel funds to be remitted through official channels by attempting to destroy the foreign-exchange black market (or at least that part of it which it did not itself control) through interventions such as *Murambatsvina*, and made the holding of foreign currency a criminal offence. In addition, a number of state schemes were set up to secure these flows of foreign exchange. Most famously there was the RBZ's Homelink initiative in 2004, which sought to encourage the Diaspora to remit their funds through official channels in order to build or acquire homes in Zimbabwe. Given the increasing gap between the official and black market exchange rates – as well as understandable Diaspora mistrust of official state institutions such as the RBZ – the initiative was largely stillborn. One survey conducted in South Africa in 2007 found that only 2 percent of Zimbabwean migrants there used formal channels to remit funds to Zimbabwe, with the remaining 98 percent using a variety of informal channels ranging from cross-border taxi drivers to giving cash and goods to relatives on home visits (Makina 2007).

Replenishing the Trough: Success for Some Amidst Generalised Collapse

The hardships imposed on the overwhelming majority of Zimbabweans were not shared by a small minority whose lot seems, in fact, to have improved as a result of the economic meltdown. The process of national pauperisation detailed above went hand in hand with growing income inequality, with the country's Gini coefficient increasing from 0.53 in 1995 to 0.61 in 2003 (GOZ 2006b), an indication not only of the shrinking share of the poor in national income, but also of the growing share captured by a small elite.

To return to the distinction made by Stewart and Brown referenced in Chap. 2 between the concept of state 'unwillingness' and objectively verifiable capacity deficits as contrasting explanations for the lack of development in fragile states, Zimbabwe's experience during the crisis years seems to have represented an extreme case of disinterest. Not only was the state unwilling to deliver on certain basic domestic responsibilities along the lines detailed by Ghani and Lockhart, but its acts of commission and omission placed the country firmly on the path of regression and growing state fragility.

Arguably, what one is faced with when analysing Zimbabwe's crisis years and more recent developments is the progressive and intentional destruction of markets and the production of poverty, as well as the unrelenting weakening of human security defined as safety from threats such as hunger, disease, politically-inspired repression and sudden disruptions to the pattern of the daily lives of the general population. Despite the brain drain, technical capacity to design appropriate policies to reverse the decline never disappeared completely, in addition to which advice was regularly proffered by Zimbabwean economists and sector specialists working both inside and outside the country, and by international agencies such as the IMF, World Bank and the UN system.

One plausible, if disconcerting, explanation for the relentless and seemingly intentional destruction of the economy therefore remains. The undermining of markets, the seemingly illogical budgetary processes and fiscal and monetary policies, the weakening of legislatures, the compromising of judicial systems and security forces beholden to the ruling party, and the gradual entrenchment of opaque decision-making processes regarding production and distribution, all served one objective, namely the conscious pursuit of elite economic power and profit.

In other words, the undermining of independent operators within the private sector not beholden to the ruling party, the decline in private sector output, growing hunger and the collapse in provisioning of public goods such electricity, water, health and education, as well as the gradual but seemingly inexorable entrenchment of the notion that holders of political office have a personal claim on the assets that they are supposed to be administering on behalf of the citizenry, may not in fact have been seen as governance failures by the ruling elite. Rather, they constituted essential means for achieving the primary objective of regime preservation and enrichment.

It follows that this elite set out in a planned fashion to establish systems which enabled it to exert predatory control over resources deemed essential to its own survival. A monopoly over the levers of political power, the enforcement capacity that went along with this, the use of material inducements to buy support, were all essential in facilitating the seizure of former commercial farmland, sources of foreign exchange, scarce commodities such as food, fuel, agricultural fertilizer and seed, diamonds following the diamond rush to the Marange fields in the east of the country beginning in 2006 (see Chap. 12), the destruction of independent, small-scale informal sector operations during *Murambatsvina*, as well as later efforts to takeover 'non-indigenous' companies under the guise of 'economic empowerment'. Despite their differences, all such interventions shared in common the fact that they were meant to yield spoils which could then be distributed to its support base.

The distortions introduced into the economy by government policy also greatly increased the scope for arbitrage profits for those with the right contacts. Throughout the crisis decade, loans with strongly negative real interest rates, and heavily subsidised foreign exchange, were available from the RBZ as it increasingly engaged directly in lending to selected private sector operators. According to one economic assessment conducted by a bilateral donor which drew on IMF data, between 2000 and 2005 the real interest rate on bank loans was negative, averaging −27.7 percent (USAID 2007, 27). As one commentator put it, "Credit was provided at derisory nominal interest rates to favoured sectors whose prospects of repaying were so low that these credits should more properly be viewed as subsidies" (Makina 2009, 13–14). The latter source also noted that by end 2007, the share of RBZ lending to the private sector had increased from 0.6 percent in 2004 to 43 percent (Ibid., 13).

The criteria for the RBZ's allocation decisions were, unsurprisingly, not open to scrutiny by the general public, nor was Parliament able to exercise any oversight role, while what increasingly amounted to the central bank's own fiscal activities were often couched in the language of 'emergency needs'. By 2007 the RBZ had become the epicentre of economic policy-making through its monetary powers and its 'quasi-fiscal operations'. The relentless printing of money enabled it to engage in the purchase of agricultural equipment and other inputs and their distribution to 'new farmers', the gifting of imported vehicles to senior members of government, the civil service, judiciary and security forces, transfers to bankrupt parastatals headed up by members of the regime, and the provision of heavily subsidised loans and foreign exchange to selected clients.[5]

In the case of those granted access to the RBZ's foreign exchange, the scope for making huge arbitrage profits was immense. While in June 2007 the official exchange rate stood at Z$250 to US$1.00, on the parallel market it was valued at anywhere between Z$250,000 and Z$400,000. Stories were rife at the time that the RBZ was itself a major player in this market, printing Zimbabwean dollars and then passing these on to its own 'runners' who bought foreign exchange from dealers operating in the black market who had been able to access currency from sources such as diaspora remittances. Under such circumstances, 'round-tripping' of foreign exchange became a highly lucrative activity for those with the right contacts.

In addition, those 'party-capitalists' with privileged access to scarce commodities such as maize meal through the Grain Marketing Board which enjoyed a monopoly on grain purchases from farmers, were also able not only to survive but to thrive, acquiring goods at highly discounted rates and selling them on at market rates. Another example of the highly profitable nature of such arbitrage operations – made possible by growing government control of all factor markets – is provided by those farmers who had benefited from the FTLRP. A UN report into the country's crop situation noted that these farmers could make significant profits by selling their monthly diesel fuel allowance on the open market, which at the time they were able to access at the highly subsidised rate of Z$600 per litre, whereas other consumers had to pay a rate of Z$3,000 per litre (FAO/WFP 2007, 11). Needless to say, such speculative activities resulted in this scarce commodity not being used for its intended purpose, further contributing to the country's food deficits and hunger. As noted by the IMF in 2004:

> Price distortions, numerous sector-specific incentive programs, and preferential access of a few to cheap foreign exchange, distracts from productive activities and provides significant opportunities for rent-seeking behaviour. (IMF 2004, 21)

There were other methods by which elite accumulation took place, and which had a more direct negative impact on poverty levels. For example, soon after the FTLRP, and in a move widely interpreted as an attempt to facilitate accumulation by the new beneficiaries of large farms, the state deliberately began a policy of suppressing wage levels in the agricultural sector which previously had been freely negotiated through collective bargaining. The Government introduced a derisory minimum wage on the grounds that 'new farmers' who had benefited from the FTLRP were unable to pay previous wage rates.

Unsurprisingly, the minimum wage became the norm. Surveys showed that in some provinces such as Midlands, these 'new farmers' were paying their workers monthly wages just about sufficient to purchase a 50kg bag of the staple maize meal. In other provinces such as Masvingo, the survey found that workers were paid a bar of soap or a cup of salt for a day's labour (FAO/WFP 2008, Appendix 1).

Seen in this light, generalised economic failure was highly profitable for certain well-connected groups, and seems to have been intentionally pursued as a group objective. Amidst increasing and planned scarcity, the value of whatever largesse was available increased exponentially in terms of its power to purchase support for the ruling party amongst the political and military elite, and from rank and file supporters of ZANU-PF, as well as lower-grade personnel within the civil service and security forces.

The latter two groups, who found it more difficult to insulate themselves completely from the economic meltdown, were regularly provided with unique opportunities to engage in more primitive forms of accumulation, such as the looting of goods in the context of militarised operations such as *Murambatsvina* and *Dzikisa Mutengo* (Reduce Prices in Shona), the latter the price control drive launched in 2007 which only led to further scarcities. During both these operations the police and military were empowered, with ZANU-PF youth present to add the required element of intimidation, to 'impound' goods judged to be 'illegal' in the case of *Murambatsvina*, or whose prices had not been appropriately adjusted downwards in the case of *Dzikisa Mutengo*. During the latter operation, if shopkeepers failed to empty their shelves and hide their stock in time, or failed to pay the necessary bribe, they were accused of being speculators and 'economic saboteurs' and had their stock seized, all of it to disappear into the vortex of the spoils redistribution system presided over by the ruling party.

In the context of generalised scarcity and widespread need, the occasional distribution of basic goods such as maize meal and fuel helped to ensure passive compliance on the part of the wider population, particularly in rural areas where the ruling party was easily able to co-opt village headmen with carrots such as vehicles or the extension of electricity to their homes. In exchange, many of them took on the role of ensuring that their wards did not become a source of political unrest and contestation of the status quo.

Once grains were declared 'controlled products' in 2001, thus making their sale to the GMB mandatory, even the surpluses produced by small-scale farmers ran the risk of being confiscated by police as they were being transported to urban relatives. By monopolising the marketing of this basic commodity, and amidst growing hunger and artificially created poverty and scarcity, the state was able to exercise significant leverage on both the urban and rural poor. Stories were rife throughout the crisis years of the use by the ruling party of food aid to secure popular support.[6] And should this prove insufficient and resistance was detected, this could always be backed up by threats of dispossession of assets, or the undisguised application of a punishing violence.

When refracted through such a prism, the seemingly illogical policies pursued by the ruling party were in fact not technically unsound reactions to unfolding and unpredicted developments, but were known *a priori* by some members of the elite to have likely perverse consequences and to be objectively anti-developmental. Imperatives other than the triggering and sustaining of economic growth, the reduction of poverty levels and strengthening of state legitimacy and capacity to provide public goods, had become deeply rooted amongst the ruling party elite that controlled the state apparatus, and these were the preservation of their monopoly on power and continued extraction of wealth from their own citizens.

Notes

1. Amongst the numerous policy frameworks launched during the crisis years were the Millennium Economic Recovery Programme of 2001, the Ten Point Plan of 2002, the National Economic Revival Programme of 2003, the Macro-Economic Policy Framework of 2004, the National Economic Development Priority Programme of 2006, and the Zimbabwe Economic Development Strategy of 2008.
2. In some cases, quite literally so. As conditions deteriorated so the number of reports of poaching on nature conservancies multiplied, as did the reliance of rural populations on other forms of wild food.
3. The TCPL was a composite metric derived from the monthly cost of a basket of essential food and non-food items. Households unable to secure the basket were judged to be below the national poverty line.
4. The report itself was only released three years later in 2006 by the Ministry of Public Service, Labour and Social Welfare, and possibly only because the Government had received significant UN funding to carry out the survey which made any attempt to withhold the results problematic, while Harare also had international obligations to report on progress in the area of poverty reduction in the context of the UN's Millennium Development Goals framework.
5. The extent to which the RBZ felt it had carte blanche to move away from its core business and engage in 'quasi-fiscal' activities, running the economy on behalf of the ruling party elite and ensuring their needs were met, is attested to by the directive it issued in 2007 compelling all commercial banks to lodge their foreign currency holdings with the RBZ. One notable casualty of this move was the donor-funded Global Fund to Fight Aids, Tuberculosis and Malaria (GFATM), which had US$7.3 million of its US$12.3 million Zimbabwe programme funds, which it had deposited with Zimbabwean commercial banks, seized, compromising its ability to operate. At the time not only did this cause serious tensions between Western donors and the RBZ (though the funds were eventually returned), but it also threw light on the amounts of foreign exchange required to fuel the patronage system, the extent to which the slush funds had been depleted, the short-termism that dominated the regime's actions given that it risked jeopardising the country's next funding application to the GFATM, and RBZ's willingness to sacrifice the welfare of the country's

population in the pursuit of the means to maintain the patronage machinery functioning (*Zim Online* 2008).

6. One report, produced by a coalition of Zimbabwean human rights NGOs in the aftermath of the 2005 parliamentary election, highlights this politicisation of food aid. It noted, for example, that villagers were regularly vetted by headmen, with those known to support the Opposition or unable to produce a ZANU-PF party membership card being denied access to food aid by having their names struck off the food register. (On this see Zimbabwe Human Rights Forum 2005, 12–13).

References

Bracking, Sarah, and Lloyd Sachikonye. 2006. *Remittances, Poverty Reduction and the Informalisation of Household Wellbeing in Zimbabwe 2005–6: A Political Economy of Dispossession,* June. Global Poverty Research Group, Economic and Social Research Council UK.

Chetsanga, C.J., and T. Muchenje. 2003. *An Analysis of the Cause and Effect of the Brain Drain in Zimbabwe.* Harare: Scientific and Industrial Research and Development Centre.

Chikanda, Abel. 2005. *Medical Leave: The Exodus of Health Professionals from Zimbabwe.* Migration Policy Series, No. 34. Southern African Migration Project. Kingston: Queen's University.

CZI. 2008. *Manufacturing Sector Survey 2008.* Harare.

FAO/WFP. 2007. *Special Report – Crop and Food Supply Assessment Mission to Zimbabwe,* June 5. Rome.

———. 2008. *Special Report – Crop and Food Supply Assessment Mission to Zimbabwe,* June 18. Rome.

GOZ. 2006a. *Labour Force Survey 2004.* Harare.

———. 2006b. *Zimbabwe 2003 Poverty Assessment Study Survey.* Harare.

———. 2006c. *Zimbabwe Demographic and Health Survey 2005/06.* Harare.

GOZ and United Nations. 2010. *2010 Millennium Development Goals Status Report – Zimbabwe.* Harare.

Hawkins, Tony. 2009. *The Mining Sector in Zimbabwe and Its Potential Contribution to Recovery,* Comprehensive Economic Recovery in Zimbabwe Working Paper Series, No. 1. Harare: United Nations Development Programme.

IMF. 2004. *Zimbabwe-Staff Report for the 2004 Article IV Consultation*, June 19. Washington, DC.

———. 2010. *World Economic Outlook Database*. Washington, DC: IMF.

Institute for War and Peace Reporting. 2004. *Whatever Happened to Didymus Mutasa*, October 6. https:/iwpr.net/global-voices/whatever-happened-didymus-mutasa.

Kanyenze, Godfrey. 2009. *Labour Markets and the Rebuilding of Human Capital*, Comprehensive Economic Recovery in Zimbabwe Working Paper Series, No. 3. Harare: United Nations Development Programme.

Makina, Daniel. 2007. *Survey of Profile of Migrant Zimbabweans in South Africa: A Pilot Study*. http://archive.kubatana.net/docs/migr/mpoi_zdrf_makina_profile_zweans_in_sa_0708.pdf.

———. 2009. *Recovery of the Financial Sector and Building Financial Inclusiveness*, Comprehensive Economic Recovery in Zimbabwe Working Paper Series, No. 5. Harare: United Nations Development Programme.

Makina, Daniel, and Godfrey Kanyenze. 2010. *The Potential Contribution of the Zimbabwe Diaspora to Economic Recovery*, Comprehensive Economic Recovery in Zimbabwe, Working Paper Series, No. 11. Harare: United Nations Development Programme.

Masunungure, Eldred V. 2011. Zimbabwe's Militarized, Electoral Authoritarianism. *Journal of International Affairs* 65(1, Fall/Winter): 31–45.

Pendleton, Wade, et al. 2006. *Migration, Remittances and Development in Southern Africa*. Southern Africa Migration Project (SAMP) Series, No. 44. Kingston: Queen's University.

Tevera, Daniel, and Abel Chikanda. 2009. *Migrant Remittances and Household Survival in Zimbabwe*. Southern African Migration Project (SAMP) Series, No. 51. Kingston: Queen's University.

UNDP. 1990. *Human Development Report 1990*. New York: United Nations Development Programme.

———. 2008. *Comprehensive Economic Recovery in Zimbabwe: A Discussion Document*. Harare: United Nations Development Programme.

———. 2010. *Human Development Report 2010 – The Real Wealth of Nations: Pathways to Human Development*. New York: UNDP.

USAID. 2007. *Zimbabwe Economic Performance Assessment: A Benchmark Study*. Washington, DC: USAID.

Zim Online. 2008. *Reserve Bank of Zimbabwe Fails to Account for US$ 7 Million in Global Fund Aid*, November 5. http:www.zimbabwe.co.za/Article.aspx?Articleld+3862.
Zimbabwe Human Rights Forum. 2005. *It's the Count That Counts: Food for Thought – Reviewing the Pre-election Period in Zimbabwe*, March. Harare.
ZimVAC. 2009. *Urban Food Security Assessment*. Harare.

8

International Isolation and the Search for New Friends

No account of Zimbabwe's collapse during the crisis years is complete without reference to the country's external relations. A key feature of Zimbabwe's economic regression and growing fragility of the Zimbabwean state was the robust correlation between socio-economic decline and deteriorating political governance on the one hand, and on the other increasing recourse by the ruling party to the language of 'economic sovereignty'. This was accompanied by a deepening estrangement from the West and the country's exit from the 'development mainstream.'[1] As the economy shrank, and living conditions deteriorated for the majority of Zimbabweans unable to insulate themselves from hyperinflation, job losses, collapsing infrastructure, and worsening service delivery, and as the gap between *de jure* and *de facto* sovereignty as defined by Ghani and Lockhart widened, so the mobilising language of the ruling party increasingly characterised its domestic and external policies and actions in terms of a 'Third *Chimurenga*' or Third War of Liberation. In fact, the more the domestic situation deteriorated, the shriller the revolutionary language used by the ruling party.

The state media gradually came to depict Zimbabwe as a country under siege from imperialist forces. The latter were often depicted as

M. Simpson, T. Hawkins, *The Primacy of Regime Survival*,
https://doi.org/10.1007/978-3-319-72520-8_8

being in alliance with subversive domestic elements which included white commercial farmers, segments of the private sector, the independent press, NGOs and the Movement for Democratic Change (MDC), and eventually anyone who came to be classified as an 'economic saboteur'. These forces were intent on overthrowing the Mugabe government in order to recolonise the country, exploit its natural resources, enslave its people, and in particular reverse the land reform programme.

The Third *Chimurenga* was also seen as necessary to complete the 'unfinished business' of the national liberation struggle, by which was meant final and irreversible 'indigenous' control of the country's resources. Though couched in the language of 'restitution', what in fact state policy translated into was indigenisation through seizures of privately-owned assets, empowerment through takeovers, increasing state control of the economy, and the development of a complex and opaque system of spoils distribution with a restricted number of people being the major beneficiaries.

As the economy declined, and there was growing recourse to violence by the ruling party to intimidate the domestic political opposition, so the country was increasingly put on a war footing. There was a gradual though unmistakable militarisation of the daily business of government and policy formulation, with an increasing role for the police, the armed forces, the CIO, ZANU-PF youth militia and the war veterans in the planning and execution of the various 'Operations' launched throughout the crisis years. This militarisation was justified in terms of the need to counter the threat of both the ruling party's domestic enemies, and an expanding assemblage of external counter-revolutionary foes. By the mid-2000s the President, Ministers, Generals and the official state media regularly referred to Zimbabwe having to face up to the West engaged in an "unprovoked declaration of war against Zimbabwe" (*The Herald* 2011a).

The enemies ran the whole gamut from the UK and the US, the Commonwealth, the World Bank and IMF and the EU, and expanded over time to eventually include all foreign actors who failed to vigorously endorse the Third *Chimurenga* and its objectives. This, on occasion, came to encompass some UN agencies which criticised specific aspects of government policy such as Operation *Murambatsvina*, Harare's human rights record, its obstructionist attitudes towards international humanitarian efforts, or its agricultural policies which led to recurrent food deficits.

Nor were other African countries spared Harare's lashings when they also voiced concerns about the deteriorating situation in Zimbabwe.[2]

As the ruling elite's process of accumulation of spoils extracted from its own citizens progressed, facilitated by the gradual undermining of the rule of law, so the number of Western countries and international organisations critical of the deterioration in the country's political and economic situation grew. Particular concern was expressed about the rising levels of poverty and worsening human development indicators such as in health and education, as well as the growing numbers of Zimbabweans fleeing the country. In addition, attention was drawn by some Western countries to Harare's failure to abide by the provisions of certain international legal commitments it had entered into with many countries, such as the numerous Bilateral Investment Promotion and Protection Agreements (BIPPAs) which had been violated through seizure of foreign-owned assets without compensation, starting with former commercial farms.

Exiting the Development Mainstream

One consequence of deteriorating relations between the West and Zimbabwe during the crisis years was that of Zimbabwe's side-lining at a time of profound changes in international aid architecture, the priorities of the Western donor community and those of the BWIs they controlled. Foremost amongst these shifts, which began in the late 1990s, was the new emphasis placed on poverty reduction in the Western approach to development assistance. Western donors and partner (recipient) countries jointly committed to prioritise poverty reduction, and partner countries were to incorporate this objective into their own national development strategies in exchange for ODA.

The new shared priority saw the rise of Poverty Reduction Strategy Papers (PRSPs) as the dominant programmatic frameworks through which Western bilateral agencies and the BWIs interacted with developing countries, and these were closely tied to Western debt relief initiatives.[3] By 1999, both the World Bank and IMF had agreed that all future concessional lending, as well as debt relief, would be made conditional on the development of national PRSPs. In the case of debt relief, the resources freed up from a reduction in debt servicing and debt cancellation were to be directed specifically to poverty reduction activities, most notably through increased investments in health and education.

The PRSP approach, and the global compact underpinning it, was also couched in terms of a new, more open partnership between donors and partner countries based on notions of mutual accountability for results, namely global public goods of reduced poverty and the attainment of other Millennium Development Goals (MDGs).[4] These aspirations would subsequently be incorporated in the Paris Declaration of 2005, signed up to by over 100 developed and developing countries as well as a range of multilateral organisations, and which sought to codify a set of principles aimed at putting donor-partner country relations on a new, more equitable footing.

As Zimbabwe entered the new millennium, its policies were already strongly at variance with the above international consensus on development. Rather than reducing poverty, the country seemed firmly set on the course of poverty production. It was seen to be remiss in terms of its fiscal and monetary policies, while its military intervention in the DRC was taken as an indication of a lowering of the importance granted by government to investments in health and education relative to defence and internal security. The quality of its public financial management system was assessed as having deteriorated significantly, while its credibility in terms of meeting a range of economic targets agreed with the BWIs and other donors in exchange for their support was increasingly questioned given recurrent 'slippages'. This all took place against the backdrop of the country's growing foreign debt, and a diminishing ability (and apparent willingness) to service these obligations.

The Late 1990s and Souring Relations with the Bretton Woods Institutions

By the late 1990s, Zimbabwe's relations with the World Bank and IMF had already been deeply coloured by continuing controversies over the impact of the Economic Structural Adjustment Programme (ESAP) which the country had implemented in the early to mid-1990s under the supervision of the Washington-based institutions, but which had not yielded the intended results. As noted earlier, with the 1997 awarding of unbudgeted gratuity and monthly pension payments to the war veterans, any hopes of budget reduction efforts that were essential for the achievement of the overall objectives of the successor ZIMPREST reform package were dashed.

Further damage was done to the budget deficit reduction efforts recommended by the BWIs when, as noted in Chap. 4, Zimbabwe sent troops to the DRC in support of President Laurent Kabila, who was at the time fighting Ugandan- and Rwandan-backed rebels in the east of the country. By 2000 it was estimated that up to one-third of the country's defence forces were operating in the DRC. This was accompanied by a growing number of reports that high ranking Zimbabwean Defence Force personnel, ministers and other members of the political and business elite, had been granted extensive and highly profitable mining concessions by Kabila in his mineral rich country, as well as agricultural land and transport contracts.[5] That the intervention in the DRC had been motivated by concerns other than the need to help preserve the territorial integrity of a fellow member of SADC was confirmed by Mugabe himself on Armed Forces Day in 2001, when he stated that:

> The business community should not look at the peace that was created by your Defence Forces in the Democratic Republic of Congo as an end in itself. The business community must now make aggressive follow-ups and open up business ventures in that country in areas like mining, road construction, agricultural development, food supplies and several others.' (Mugabe 2001, 48)

The military intervention in the DRC contributed significantly to the further deterioration in already strained relations with the IMF. In the course of negotiations for another IMF loan in 1999, the then Minister of Finance stated in a memo to the IMF that the outlays associated with Zimbabwe's involvement in the DRC had been limited to US$1.3 million in 1998, and had risen to only US$3 million in 1999 (IMF 1999). Reports that the figure was in fact ten times higher then led to delays in the approval of a standby arrangement with the IMF worth close to US$200 million.

Stand-Off with the International Financial Institutions (IFIs) During the Crisis Years

By the end of 2000, and following an IMF mission to Harare in the context of Article IV consultations[6] with the Zimbabwean authorities, the IMF's Executive Board through a Public Information Notice (PIN), stated that its Directors:

> expressed deep concern about the decline in per capita income and the deterioration in social conditions of the past several years as a result of Zimbabwe's weak macroeconomic policies, the rapid spread of the HIV/AIDS pandemic, poor governance, and escalating tension and uncertainty related to the government's land reform programme. (IMF 2000)

Furthermore, the PIN placed the responsibility for these problems squarely on the shoulders of national economic policy decision-makers, referring obliquely to the costs of the country's involvement in the DRC conflict, and highlighted a problem which would continue to plague Zimbabwe's relations with the IFIs, namely its growing external debt burden:

> the slump in economic performance in 1999–2000 was due mainly to the pursuit of unsustainable fiscal policy driven by large wage and defence overruns, and by governance problems that have undermined investor confidence. Economic activity has contracted, inflation has accelerated, and the balance of payments position has weakened significantly, as evidenced by the depletion of foreign reserves and the emergence of external payments arrears. (Ibid.)[7]

Relations with the IMF continued to deteriorate further in the new millennium. In March 2000, the Executive Board of the IMF had adopted a set of new global measures in response to instances of misreporting and allegations of misuse of IMF resources by central banks of a number of member countries. Central banks, as the primary recipients and custodians of IMF disbursements, would now be obliged to introduce external audit mechanisms according to international accounting standards. These were to be accompanied by a set of staged procedures for dealing with arrears to the Fund, and which might result in remedial measures (sanctions) in situations where the Executive Board of the IMF decided that 'active cooperation' on the part of members to deal with their outstanding obligations was lacking.

By February 2001, Zimbabwe's outstanding obligations to the IMF totalled US$53 million. In September 2001, the IMF's Executive Board declared Zimbabwe ineligible to use the funds in its General Resource Account (GRA), as well as resources under the highly concessional Poverty Reduction and Growth Facility (PRGF), due to accumulated arrears. By June 2002, arrears had increased to about US$132 million. That same month the Executive Board adopted a 'declaration of non-cooperation' with Zimbabwe, which resulted in the suspension of technical assistance to Zimbabwe (IMF 2002). Zimbabwe's voting and related rights were suspended in June 2003 given its continued non-settlement of arrears.[8]

By November 2003, Zimbabwe's total arrears had reached US$273 million, and in December 2003 the Executive Board decided to trigger compulsory withdrawal procedures against Zimbabwe (IMF 2003) However, in the event this ultimate sanction was not implemented, and the IMF continued to send annual missions to Harare to hold Article IV consultations with the Zimbabwean authorities. In October 2004, however, the IMF did take the step of closing down its offices in Harare on the grounds that the size of its lending programme with Zimbabwe did not justify a permanent in-country presence. The IMF's unwillingness to apply the ultimate sanction of compulsory withdrawal was helped by Zimbabwe's decision in August 2005 to pay US$120 million towards its arrears to the GRA, though this still left it with total arrears to both the GRA and the PRGF of around US$175 million (IMF 2005).

In February 2006 Zimbabwe finally settled its outstanding arrears to the GRA. While this led to the rescinding of the compulsory withdrawal threat, Zimbabwe's voting and related rights were not restored, nor was the IMF's declaration of non-cooperation with Zimbabwe reversed. The country's access to both the GRA and PRGF funds were also not restored on the grounds of its continued arrears to the PRGF.

Throughout this process of estrangement, the IMF noted that in addition to Zimbabwe's growing arrears problem the Zimbabwe government had consistently failed to adopt corrective policy measures to reverse the country's economic decline. As the organisation had diplomatically noted in December 2003 "the IMF regrets that the authorities have not adopted comprehensive and consistent policies needed to address Zimbabwe's serious economic problems" (IMF 2003).

The Government's reluctance to undertake the necessary changes in its economic policy, and take on board external advice, was to be a constant feature of its relations with the IFIs and Western donor community throughout the rest of the crisis years. In December 2006, for example, in the wake of another Article IV consultation mission during which an IMF team had discussed the country's economic policies with national authorities and proposed a set of corrective measures, the IMF observed that:

> Inflation has accelerated while shortages of food, fuel, basic consumer goods, and essential agricultural inputs remain acute. Progress on structural reforms has been limited and uncertainty over property rights continues to depress investor confidence...Zimbabwe's economic crisis calls for the urgent implementation of a comprehensive policy package...Without a fundamental change in policies, prospects are for a continued deterioration in the economic situation. (IMF 2006)

With only minor adjustments in the above language to take account of ever-worsening economic indicators, such IMF advice has been repeated ever since.

One consequence of this estrangement from the IMF was that in addition to being cut off from IMF funding sources, the signalling effects of the increasingly dismal economic situation in the country depicted in IMF reports meant Zimbabwe was also cut off from access to loans and debt rescheduling arrangements on offer from other multilateral lenders such as the World Bank, the African Development Bank and the Paris Club of 19 official bilateral creditors. This had additional knock-on effects in terms of the country's diminishing credit-worthiness in the eyes of private international creditors, as well as foreign direct investors.

The World Bank also downgraded its relations with Zimbabwe as a result of growing arrears to its two main lending facilities, namely loans provided by the International Bank for Reconstruction and Development

(IBRD) and the highly-concessional loans provided by the International Development Association (IDA). Zimbabwe was placed on 'non-accrual' status in October 2000, which meant that no new lending was forthcoming. By May 2007, Zimbabwe had accumulated arrears totalling US$ US$496 million to the World Bank (World Bank 2007). Like the IMF, the World Bank also downgraded the status of its office in Harare, and its subsequent activities were limited to analytical work and the provision of policy advice and 'dialogue', the latter largely one-sided given that the Government was clearly intent on ignoring any economic advice on offer.

The same situation obtained with regard to the African Development Bank (AfDB). Like the World Bank and the IMF, the AfDB had also undertaken significant lending operations in the context of support to the earlier ESAP. By March 2007, Zimbabwe had accumulated arrears totalling US$348.8 million to the AfDB (AfDB 2007, v). This IFI had also placed Zimbabwe on non-accrual status in 2000, frozen its lending operations, and subsequently restricted its activities to humanitarian assistance, analytical work and dialogue with Government.[9]

Given the extent of Zimbabwe's continuous failings, the IFIs were eventually compelled to engage in some deep soul-searching. In an uncharacteristically candid piece of introspection and critical assessment of its own past failings to read the political economy of Zimbabwe correctly, in 2004 the World Bank's Operations Evaluation Department (OED) released an evaluation of the organisation's past country assistance strategy. This highlighted a number of shortcomings in terms of its operations during the 1990s. Particular criticism was reserved for its numerous adjustment loans granted during the period of ESAP and its successor ZIMPREST, meant to assist Zimbabwe implement the necessary structural reforms:

> the Bank…should have been more forceful in ensuring that credible steps to achieve fiscal sustainability were incorporated in adjustment lending, and should have formed a judgement not only about macroeconomic/fiscal targets, but also about the likelihood of their implementation…In the absence of ownership from the political leadership, the Bank should have insisted that conditions be fulfilled and not proceed to lend on the basis of promises. The Bank's willingness to lend sent the wrong message to the client and to the partners. (World Bank 2004, vi)[10]

In addition, the same report highlighted the fundamental failure to understand the extent of resistance to market-based reforms amongst the country's leaders:

> From the start of the adjustment program in 1991, the Bank did not factor in its strategy the divisions on major reform issues. On the one side were a small circle of technocrats (e.g. officials of the economic ministries) committed to market based reforms, and in the other were the anti-reformers, the President and other members of the party. The important characteristic of the anti-reformers was that they did not believe in the market's efficacy in redistributing wealth…Ultimately, reforms were not sustained because power lay not with individual ministries and technocrats with whom the Bank engaged, but with the anti-reformers whose trust the Bank was unable to gain. (Ibid., 28)

A less sanguine assessment might have concluded that the root of the problem was not that the BWIs had failed to grasp the extent of mistrust regarding the role of markets in redistributing (and creating) wealth on the part of Zimbabwe's anti-reformers. Rather it was their failure to see that the role of markets was perfectly well understood by the ruling party's inner circles, but that another logic entirely informed internal decision-making, priorities and therefore economic outcomes.

The reforms the BWIs pushed for would have undermined the key objective of the anti-reformers, namely to strengthen their grip on the levers of economic power through dirigiste policies, and prevent the formation of markets over which they had limited control and the rise of an indigenous class of entrepreneurs that was not beholden to the ruling party for their enterprises. To the anti-reformers, any accumulation outside party networks was anathema. As the country's subsequent trajectory was to show, such centralised control of the economy enabled the distribution of largesse in a manner that both facilitated further elite accumulation and ensured regime survival through the selective purchasing of broader acquiescence and support. Therein lay the internal logic of resistance to the reforms advanced by the IFIs and Western donors, both during the ESAP period as well as subsequently.

The World Bank's blind spots as regards Zimbabwe are in no way unique, either to that institution or the ZANU-PF party-state. They reflect a widespread failure, in attempts by international development agencies to promote economic reforms in developing countries, to simultaneously recognise the need for more inclusive political institutions, and specifically in the case of Zimbabwe a lack of understanding of the historical links between extractive political and economic institutions that were established, nurtured and managed by the ruling party:

> Attempts by international institutions to engineer economic growth by hectoring poor countries into adopting better policies are not successful because they do not take place in the context of why bad policies and institutions are there in the first place…The consequence is that the policies are not adopted and not implemented, or are implemented in name only. (Acemoglu and Robinson 2013, 442)

At the height of the process of economic meltdown in 2008, Zimbabwe was to find itself in the worst of all worlds. Its access to concessional development financing from the IFIs had been shut down, and amidst declining export revenues Zimbabwe found it increasingly difficult to service its external debt (which in contrast to its domestic debt could not simply be inflated away by an expansionary monetary policy). And to all intents and purposes it had given up making any effort to do so, though it proved useful to the ruling party's propaganda machine to use the restrictions placed on Zimbabwe ability to borrow from the IFIs as proof of a wider Western conspiracy.

Zimbabwe came to suffer from an increasingly severe case of debt overhang, as its external debt significantly exceeded future capacity to repay its obligations. By end-2008, the IMF estimated that the country's public and publicly guaranteed external debt stood at US$5.1billion, which represented 166 percent of the country's GDP, (IMF 2009, 27) while the latter had in turn shrunk to US$3.18 billion in nominal terms (Ibid., 26). Arrears for the country's total external debt stood at US$ 3.8 billion representing 120 percent of GDP, while gross foreign reserves at end-2008 stood at US$6 million dollars which provided import cover for less than 1 week (Ibid., 6).

Missing Out on Debt Relief

Because of its estrangement from the IFIs and the Western donor community, Zimbabwe was unable to benefit, unlike many other developing countries, from two important and comprehensive international debt relief initiatives, namely the Highly Indebted Poor Country (HIPC) initiative[11] and the Multilateral Debt Relief Initiative (MDRI).[12] As a result, not only did Zimbabwe's foreign debt become an increasing constraint on economic growth, but it also contributed to the country's deepening poverty.

The comprehensiveness of the various programmes which Zimbabwe was excluded from, and the costs that resulted from exclusion, can be gauged from certain global end-2007 figures which serve as a useful counter-factual. The total debt relief provided under the HIPC and MDRI initiatives by the BWIs, regional development banks such as the AfDB, Paris and non-Paris Club bilateral and commercial creditors, amounted to US$117 billion (IDA and IMF 2008, 6). Those countries that benefited from the full delivery of debt relief under these programmes found their external debt burden reduced by about 90 percent. Significantly for a country such as Zimbabwe with a serious problem of debt overhang, post-completion countries, i.e. those countries which had benefited from full, irrevocable debt relief under HIPC, were in a significantly better position in terms of their debt to export ratios than those which had not benefited from the programme.[13]

Even more damaging for Zimbabwe's growing numbers of poor, these debt relief efforts also represented a missed opportunity by the country's rulers to relieve the burden of poverty on its people, since such programmes also made progress in terms of another of its key objectives, namely to help highly indebted countries free up resources and to channel these into priority poverty reducing areas such as health and education. As a result of the importance attached by the international donor community to developing countries designing technically sound PRSPs, and the commitment of beneficiary countries to the implementation of such strategies and achievement of the MDGs, between 1999 and 2006 poverty reducing expenditures increased by around 2 percent of GDP in those HIPCs which benefited from debt relief (Ibid., 14).

While Zimbabwe objectively met the debt sustainability threshold criteria, because of its failure to meet the necessary policy-related criteria such as demonstrating a track record of sound economic management and a commitment to an arrears clearance strategy required to access these international debt relief programmes, Harare found itself unable to benefit from these global initiatives. Its debt burden, and the situation of 'debt distress' it found itself in as well as its worsening poverty profile, were to continue to deteriorate over the course of the crisis years as it accumulated further arrears.

Western Bilateral Donors and Zimbabwe During the Crisis Decade

As political relations between the West and Harare continued to sour throughout the crisis years, so bilateral development assistance also dried up. Western donor agencies based their decisions on growing concerns regarding Zimbabwe's economic policies and its effects, its worsening human rights record, the undermining of the rule of law, violence associated with elections and the FTLRP, and Zimbabwe's violations of the BIPPAs signed with a number of countries from the Western donor community (Germany, the Netherlands, Switzerland and Denmark).[14]

Western bilateral donor agencies and their Zimbabwean Government counterparts increasingly spoke at cross-purposes. They found themselves at loggerheads over the country's development priorities and the policies to be pursued to achieve these. Such disagreements ran the whole gamut from the country's health, education, land and agricultural policies to its monetary, fiscal, and trade policies, with diametrically opposed positions being taken on issues such as price and exchange-rate controls, the Government's policy on parastatals, and its hostility towards both foreign investment (at least that originating from the West) as well as the country's private sector (at least those enterprises controlled by individuals not directly associated with the ruling party).

Particularly sharp exchanges between the two sides were reserved for disagreements about both the need, and the delivery mechanisms, of humanitarian assistance. Western donors regularly raised concerns that humanitarian assistance was being 'politicised' and diverted to those communities that supported the ruling party, and withheld from those known to support the MDC. The Government often countered that the country's humanitarian needs were grossly exaggerated by foreign governments intent on depicting the country in a negative light, and that the resources of these relief programmes were being channelled to local and international NGOs that operated according to a well-known anti-government agenda as portrayed in its 2013 election propaganda, since "virtually all …have been founded and funded by the same countries that have imposed illegal sanctions against Zimbabwe for purposes of effecting illegal regime change"(ZANU-PF 2013, 43).

Nowhere, however, was this entrenchment of antagonistic positions more evident than in the area of political governance, with Western diplomatic missions voicing their objections to the growing battery of laws which sought to restrict the operations of NGOs, the independent press, and trade unions. Harare responded that such concerns constituted interference in Zimbabwe's internal affairs, and constituted clear evidence of the West's 'regime change' agenda. While the West attributed the Zimbabwe's regression to poor economic and political governance, Harare hit back by blaming Western efforts to instigate 'regime change' in the wake of the FTLRP for everything from hyperinflation, shortages of basic commodities, recurrent poor harvests, to electricity cuts, the out-migration of its citizens and collapsing transport infrastructure. So, for example, collapsing agricultural output and deteriorating national food security were attributed to "the destructive hands of our enemies seeking to undermine our grain importation programme…[since] food is the latest of their weapons in their regime change agenda', while the country's record-breaking hyperinflation of 2008 was a result of 'an insidious foreign hand in the destabilisation of our currency" (Mugabe 2008).

Harare's cosmology was perfectly encapsulated in an economic recovery plan launched by the President in the course of 2000. Entitled the 'Millennium Economic Recovery Programme' (MERP), and meant to replace ZIMPREST and provide a framework for the country's economic recovery, the document emphasised:

> the deleterious effects of neo-imperialist machinations aimed at limiting national sovereignty over the redistribution of national assets such as land in favour of indigenous Zimbabweans. These machinations are aimed at frustrating national efforts to transform the Zimbabwean economy so that it cannot reach higher levels of development as well as withstand acts of economic destabilisation. (GOZ 2000, 13)

The role of domestic economic saboteurs was also highlighted in this document. The country's economic problems were being:

> exploited by crime syndicates and corrupt businesses who illegally externalise funds, destabilise foreign exchange markets through speculative behaviour which in some cases is foreign inspired in order to frustrate economic stabilisation efforts by government. (Ibid., 14)

By 2005, and following Operation *Murambatsvina*, relations had reached a nadir from which they were not to recover for the rest of the crisis years. Western donor agencies ceased to interact with government ministries and officials in support of national plans, with the notable exception of initiatives judged by Western donors to have a clear humanitarian component such as the national HIV and AIDS programme and emergency food assistance, both of which continued to receive donor funding. The government was in turn increasingly forced to rely on rapidly shrinking internally-generated resources to implement broader national and sectoral development plans. Given high levels of perceived fiduciary risk, Western donors also moved away from channelling resources through state institutions in favour of directly funding local and international NGOs as well as UN agencies, thus bypassing the Treasury, the Central Bank and government ministries.

As a result of the prioritisation of emergency humanitarian aid as opposed to development assistance by Western bilateral donors, there were negative consequences for a whole range of local institutions. Universities, agricultural research institutes and the national statistics office that had come to rely on Western donor assistance for their operations were severely affected. Some bilateral donor agencies, such as the Danish International Development Agency (DANIDA), simply shut up shop in Harare while others, mirroring the positions taken by the BWIs, downgraded their presence in terms of staffing numbers and the range of activities they undertook.

One landmark event in the deterioration of relations between Zimbabwe and the West was the passing of a US Act of Congress in 2001. In the wake of violence associated with both the 2000 parliamentary elections and the early stages of the FTLRP, the US Congress passed the Zimbabwe Democracy and Economic Recovery Act (ZIDERA) in December 2001. Given the weight of the US's voting rights in organisations such as the World Bank and the IMF, ZIDERA effectively imposed economic sanctions on Zimbabwe. The legislation prohibited all key international financial institutions (both the Bretton Woods Institutions and the regional development banks) from extending loans or credit guarantees to Zimbabwe, and also proscribed any extension of debt relief by both the US government and the IFIs to Zimbabwe. The rationale presented in the Act, based on the findings of Congress, was that:

> Through economic mismanagement, undemocratic practices, and the costly deployment of troops to the Democratic Republic of the Congo, the Government of Zimbabwe has rendered itself ineligible to participate in International Bank for Reconstruction and Development [World Bank] and International Monetary Fund programs, which would otherwise be providing substantial resources to assist in the recovery and modernization of Zimbabwe's economy. (United States Congress 2001, Section 4(a)(1))

These measures were intended to remain in place until such time as Zimbabwe met a number of criteria. These included the restoration of the rule of law, which was to be measured by:

> respect for ownership and title to property, freedom of speech and association, and an end to lawlessness, violence, and intimidation, sponsored, condoned, or tolerated by the Government of Zimbabwe, the ruling party, and their supporters. (Ibid.: Section 4(d)(1))

In addition, ZIDERA referred to the need for improvements in the conditions under which elections were held, as well as a commitment on the part of Harare to an "equitable, legal and transparent land reform program" (Ibid.: Section 4(d)(3)), an independent and free press, and the subordination of the country's security forces to civilian government.[15] It is noteworthy that the responsibility for Zimbabwe's decline was placed by the US Congress squarely on the shoulders of individual members of the ruling elite, and the ZIDERA required the US President to work with other governments to identify those Zimbabweans responsible, and to implement targeted sanctions and travel bans against them.

This US action was soon followed up in 2002 with a tightening of the noose by the EU, which further isolated Zimbabwe from the mainstream of international development, and strengthened its status as a pariah state in Western eyes. In reaction to the violence of the Presidential elections held that year –attributed by Brussels to the Zimbabwean Government – and following the expulsion of the head of the EU observer delegation to the 2002 elections, the EU severely restricted its assistance programme, ending direct budgetary and project support to the Zimbabwean Government.

The justification presented by Brussels was that Zimbabwe was in violation of the EU-ACP Cotonou Agreement[16] of which it was a signatory, and which in its Preamble noted that the states-parties recognised that:

> peace, security and stability, respect for human rights, democratic principles and the rule of law, and good governance is part and parcel of long term development. (EC-ACP: *Preamble*)

In 2002 the EU ratcheted up the pressure further on those it specifically held responsible for violations of the above Cotonou principles, when its Council of Ministers adopted a 'Common Position' which became binding on its member states. This introduced 'targeted measures', renewable on an annual basis, against Zimbabwe's ruling elite. Harare was subsequently to characterise these as 'illegal sanctions', the attribution of illegality arising from the fact that these sanctions has not been authorised by the UN Security Council.

These measures included visa bans and asset freezes applied to specific individuals and companies connected to the ruling party, as well as an arms embargo. Amongst those caught up in the dragnet were the President and Deputy Presidents, senior ZANU-PF officials, a number of parliamentarians and managers of parastatals and private companies with close ties to the ruling party, Government ministers, the Governor of the

Reserve Bank, and senior members of the defence and security forces. A range of non-EU countries soon followed suit, with Canada, Switzerland, Japan, Norway, Australia and New Zealand adopting similar sets of measures against the Harare government.

Zimbabwe's growing isolation was compounded by its suspension from the Commonwealth in 2002. This followed a negative report from a Commonwealth elections observer group that had monitored the 2002 Presidential elections.[17] The organisation subsequently judged that Zimbabwe had violated the organisation's core principles and values as embodied in the Commonwealth's Harare Declaration of 1991,[18] and a decision was taken to suspend the country for one year from the organisation. Rather than risk eventual expulsion, Harare chose to voluntarily withdraw from the organisation in 2003, and characterised the Commonwealth's decision as reflecting the racism of its white member states which it argued dominated the organisation. Thereafter, Harare was no longer able to access a range of Commonwealth development assistance programmes, many of them with a longstanding presence in the country.

With the exception of the years of coalition government between 2009 and 2013 (see Chap. 10), this stand-off between Western donors and the Zimbabwe government was to remain in place. Zimbabweans that found themselves on various sanctions list were prevented from visiting Western countries, while Western ministers refrained from visits to Zimbabwe in a clear sign of non-engagement with the Harare government and disapproval of its policies. Despite a growing Western contribution to humanitarian relief efforts in Zimbabwe, this tended to be studiously ignored by the state media, with the role of UN agencies being highlighted whenever there was any reference to outside assistance (even though much of the funding for these UN operations came from disbursements by Western donors in response to successive annual UN humanitarian appeals).[19]

Pivoting East for Counterweights

Harare's anti-Western diatribes were accompanied by an effort – arguably the product of both pressing economic necessity and pre-existing ideological inclinations[20] – to realign the country's international economic relations away from dependence on Western private capital flows and corporations, and Western-dominated international financial institutions and bilateral donor agencies, towards the emerging Asian economies, most particularly the People's Republic of China (PRC). Cut off from Western sources of debt relief and development finance, coupled with growing domestic political contestation to its continued rule, ZANU-PF sought new non-Western partnerships and the revival of old ones in the hope of both economic assistance and diplomatic alliances that would help it to stand up to an increasingly hostile West, as well as deal with internal dissent.

Based on the common denominator of shared hostility to the West, two countries it sought to cultivate relations with were Venezuela and Iran. In the case of Venezuela, the 'resource nationalism' President Hugo Chavez applied to his country's oil resources, his anti-American foreign policy and populist economic policies, all chimed with Mugabe's own land reform programme, Zimbabwe's evolving policy on indigenisation, and ZANU-PF's party's anti-British and broader anti-Western and anti-imperialist discourse. The leaders of both countries often waxed lyrical about each other's revolutionary and anti-Western credentials, with particularly laudatory coverage by Zimbabwe's state media when Chavez died in 2016 (*The Herald* 2016). Similar interests were at work in terms of efforts to deepen relations with Iran, another country smarting under Western-imposed sanctions. Both Venezuela and Iran also enjoyed substantial foreign-exchange reserves derived from their oil exports. For a Zimbabwe reeling under the effects of increasing foreign exchange and fuel shortages, the hope was that over and above expressions of collective Third World anti-Western solidarity there might also flow concrete economic benefits from strengthening ties with these countries.

Though there is little evidence these overtures translated into enduring and substantive aid programmes for Zimbabwe, judging by the extensive state media coverage of state visits such as Mugabe's to the Islamic Republic of Iran in 2006, Ahmadinejad's to Zimbabwe in 2010 and meetings between Chavez and Mugabe, there were nevertheless clearly advantages to be derived from investing in such bilateral relations. One of these was to demonstrate to a domestic audience that Zimbabwe was not as isolated internationally as the West portrayed, that its leader enjoyed prestige within particular foreign circles, and that with countries such as Iran there was "support for each other against the common enemy of imperialism" (*The Herald* 2011b).

But it was in terms of cultivating relations with Asian countries that most diplomatic effort was expended. In 2003, Harare announced its 'Look East' policy. This was to focus on China, Indonesia, India and Malaysia, all seen as promising partnerships which could make up for the shortfall in Western development assistance, investment and defence cooperation. These links would also provide the country with new diplomatic alliances to compensate for its growing isolation from the West.

Over time, the Look East policy increasingly came to focus on the PRC. Harare hoped to reap benefits from China's extraordinary economic growth, its seemingly insatiable demand for raw materials, and Beijing's willingness to take on an increasingly active role in international affairs as champion of the developing world. In the face of the Western arms embargo, there was the expectation that Beijing would be willing to revive its military assistance programme to ZANU-PF which dated back to the days of the liberation struggle. In addition, given a rapid decline in the number of Western tourists as a result of the increasingly negative international publicity surrounding the country, and the importance of the tourism sector to the economy, there were high hopes that Chinese tourism would be able to pick up the slack following Beijing's granting in 2004 of 'approved destination' status to Zimbabwe.

Mugabe, in the course of an interview in 2006 with the official Xinhua Chinese news agency, encapsulated Harare's expectations, stating that Zimbabwe appreciated past ties forged during the liberation struggle:

> In most recent times, as the West started being hostile to us, we deliberately declared a Look East policy…we said these were the friends we relied upon during the liberation struggle and they will not let us down. (zimbabwe-journalists.com 2006)

Beijing's approach to Zimbabwe reflected its wider economic diplomacy towards Africa, underpinned by China's hunger for the raw materials required to feed its economic growth, in particular minerals and agricultural commodities. It is therefore hardly surprising that Beijing should have evinced a strong interest in gaining access to Zimbabwe's rich mineral resources such as iron, chrome, and in particular platinum, with Zimbabwe home to the world's second largest reserves after South Africa of the latter mineral. In contrast to other African countries with large and vibrant economies which could be exploited by Chinese exporters and entrepreneurs, in the case of Zimbabwe with its shrinking domestic markets and the reduced purchasing power of the majority of the population it was clearly Zimbabwe's natural resources that was the primary driver of Chinese policy towards Zimbabwe.

In addition to diplomatic support, Harare's Look East Policy with its primary focus on the PRC aimed to secure external assistance at a time when its foreign-exchange reserves, and its ability to import capital goods for industry, agriculture and deal with the country's collapsing infrastructure, were at all-time lows. And amidst widening and increasingly vociferous domestic popular contestation of the status quo, there was also an urgent need to modernise the capacity of the Zimbabwe's intelligence and security forces to deal with this dissent. Beijing was to provide support on all these fronts.

Like other 'new donors' who are not members of the Organization for Economic Co-operation and Development-Development Assistance Committee (OECD-DAC) which remains the major international source of data on this issue, China does not report on the type, volumes and beneficiaries of its development assistance to that organisation. One problem facing analysts of Chinese aid relates to the fact that the official Chinese definition of what constitutes 'aid' or 'development assistance' differs from that used by the OECD-DAC,[21] with analysts often forced to rely on official information from beneficiary countries, itself of varying reliability. In addition, a standard Chinese practice seems to be for many deals to be protected by non-disclosure clauses. The gathering of information on Chinese aid flows is therefore fraught with difficulties, all the more so in the case of its assistance to Zimbabwe as ZANU-PF has never felt a strong obligation to strengthen parliamentary oversight of international agreements, or to systematically publish data on Zimbabwe's external relations. Nevertheless, a number of conclusions can be drawn from information sifted from a range of sources.

In terms of development assistance, over the course of Zimbabwe's crisis years a number of deals were struck with the PRC covering support to Zimbabwe's agricultural, mining, transport sectors, and most notably a U$S1 billion China Import-Export Bank loan for the rehabilitation of the country's largest electricity power station (*Reuters* 2015). The modalities have included outright grants (usually in the form of in-kind contributions rather than cash), technical assistance and training programmes, and concessional and commercial loans. Given Zimbabwe's foreign exchange problems, some arrangements have included an element of barter trade which has proved beneficial to Zimbabwe, with Harare being given loans in exchange for selling forward commodities such as minerals (in particular chrome, platinum and increasingly diamonds) and cash crops such as tobacco to the Chinese. Other initiatives have involved the sending of Chinese medical teams to Zimbabwe, and the training of Zimbabweans at Chinese institutions through an extensive scholarship programme, and the provision of humanitarian assistance. As intended by the 'Look East' policy, significant changes in Zimbabwe's trade patterns have also taken place. Total trade between Zimbabwe and the PRC rose from U$191 million to U$1.1 billion in between 2003 and 2013 (National Bureau of Statistics of China *'National Data'*).

An additional and increasingly significant benefit to Harare flowing from its deepening relationship with Beijing lay in the field of military cooperation. As the arms embargo imposed by the West made itself felt, and the country's defence and security forces found it difficult to replace and repair increasingly obsolete equipment, so Beijing stepped into the breach and became Zimbabwe's major source of external military assistance. China was able to capitalise on pre-independence relations with senior figures within the Zimbabwe defence forces, many of whom had been trained at Chinese military academies.[22] Such information as does percolate into the public domain indicates that Chinese assistance includes the supply of fighter jets (*The Guardian* 2005), military vehicles and arms and ammunition to the Zimbabwe Defence Forces, training programmes and the extension of a loan to build a new National Defence College (*Zimbabwe Independent* 2005).

Harare also hoped that Beijing would provide verbal support to the policies pursued by ZANU-PF. Coming from an economic superpower and permanent member of the UN Security Council, and which had historically taken a strong position on the principle of non-interference in the internal affairs of other states, such endorsements would help validate both the ruling party's domestic and foreign policy decisions, and demonstrate that notwithstanding its ostracism by the West Zimbabwe had trusted and powerful friends.

In the event, the policy of strengthening links with Beijing in the hope the PRC would help to shield Zimbabwe from Western-backed international pressure yielded important positive results on a number of occasions. Beijing quickly came to play the role of a critical alternative international political patron at a time when Zimbabwe was increasingly bereft of friends, most notably in 2008 when the PRC blocked the efforts of Western countries to table a resolution calling for the imposition of mandatory sanctions against Zimbabwe in the UN Security Council in the wake of the election violence that year. In a statement that would have been welcomed by Harare given it reaffirmed the importance attached by both parties to the principle of sovereignty and non-interference in the internal affairs of other states, China's representative at the UN argued that the situation in Zimbabwe "had not exceeded the context of domestic affairs and did not constitute a threat to international peace and security" (United Nations 2008).

Zimbabwe was also not disappointed in the returns from its investments in the relationship with China by what the state media chose to depict as the PRC's recognition of historic ties, and most importantly Beijing's support for ZANU-PF's internal policies which the latter found useful for rallying its internal support base. For example, in the run-up to a state visit by President Xi Jinping in 2015, ZANU-PF's invocation of its historic ties with China were not overlooked by the Chinese President, who noted that during "the national liberation struggle in Zimbabwe, the Chinese people stood steadfastly behind the Zimbabwean people as comrades in arms." And providing further comfort to Harare, he also added that "China firmly supports Zimbabwe's efforts to safeguard national sovereignty, security and development interests and its choice of development path that suits its national interests" (*The Herald* 2015).

Notes

1. The concept of a *development mainstream* is used here to denote the approaches shared by the members of the Organization for Economic Co-operation and Development (OECD)'s Development Assistance Committee (DAC). It is exemplified by the DAC's support for the principles of the Paris Declaration which govern donor-recipient country

relations, the Poverty Reduction Strategy Paper (PRSP) approach to poverty reduction and debt relief, and above all the importance attached to 'good governance' principles in the development equation. In addition to the purchase within the Western aid community that these principles enjoy, there is the fact that the vast majority of developing countries also subscribe to them, as evidenced by the large numbers of signatories to the Paris Declaration and its subsequent iterations, as well as those who chose to apply for various Western-led international debt relief initiatives.

2. Particular venom was reserved for neighbouring Botswana, whose leadership consistently expressed concerns about the deteriorating situation in Zimbabwe, and the effects it was having on Botswana in terms of the movement of Zimbabwean refugees into the country. In the particularly tense aftermath of the 2008 elections in Zimbabwe, Botswana called for SADC to isolate Mugabe. Harare responded by accusing Botswana of providing military training to elements of the MDC-T on its territory with the intention of destabilising Zimbabwe.
3. PRSPs were to contain country-specific poverty eradication targets, a sound macroeconomic framework meant to trigger both growth and poverty reduction, and commitments to a range of public sector reforms such as in Public Financial Management systems and regulatory frameworks.
4. Agreed at the UN Millennium Summit 2000, the MDGs were a comprehensive set of 8 development goals agreed to by all member states and subscribed to by the major international development institutions. The first goal was that of reducing by half the global levels of extreme poverty by 2015.
5. For a detailed examination of the economic aspects of Zimbabwe's intervention in the DRC conflict, and comprehensive analysis of the Zimbabwean actors involved and their institutional and corporate links see Nest (2001).
6. Article IV of the IMF's Articles of Agreement allows for Fund missions to member countries to collect data and discuss policies with national authorities. On the basis of these findings the missions prepare a report for the consideration of the Executive Board which is then shared with the country authorities.
7. It is noteworthy that the table of economic indicators in the PIN projected a negative real GDP growth rate of −5.5 percent for 2000, a

collapse in gross reserves from US$882 million in 1995 to US$198 million in 2000, while Zimbabwe's debt service as a percentage of exports was to increase from 19 percent in 1995 to an estimated 29 percent for 2000.

8. This meant that Zimbabwe would no longer be able to appoint a representative to the IMF Board of Governors, participate in the election of an Executive Director to the IMF's Board of Directors, or cast a vote in IMF policy decisions.
9. The AfDB document notes that the institution sent five missions to Zimbabwe between 2001 and 2007 to discuss the country's arrears, all to no avail despite specific and repeated Government undertakings to deal with its outstanding obligations.
10. The World Bank's 'partners' include, amongst others, bilateral donors and other IFIs, all of whom would have closely monitored the Bank's lending programme in Zimbabwe, and on the assumption that due diligence had been exercised by the Bank responded positively to the signalling effect of the approval of new World Bank credits to Zimbabwe in terms of their own programmes.
11. The HIPC, launched in 1996 and subsequently modified in 1999, aimed to provide low-income countries with substantial debt relief subject to them meeting a number of eligibility criteria. These were that a country's external debt levels were judged to be above sustainability levels. The latter were set in 1996 as a ratio of external debt to exports above a threshold of 250 percent, while the ratio of debt to government revenue was set at 280 percent. These ratios were subsequently lowered in 1999 to 150 percent and 250 percent respectively in order to facilitate the access of more countries to the programme. In addition to these debt sustainability criteria, countries had to meet a number of other conditions. These included the adoption of an adjustment and reform programme supported by the World Bank and IMF, demonstration of a track record of macroeconomic stability (again determined by the BWIs), the designing of a PRSP which met World Bank and IMF quality standards, a commitment to use resources freed up by debt relief for poverty reduction purposes, as well as reaching an arrears clearance agreement with the BWIs and other multilateral creditors.
12. International debt relief under HIPC was taken one step further in 2005, when in the form of the MDRI the G-8 countries proposed that the IMF, World Bank and the AfDB cancel 100 percent of their debt claims on those low-income countries that had met HIPC criteria. The

initiative was specifically cast in terms of assisting those countries to free up resources that might have been expended to support debt servicing on national efforts to meet the Millennium Development Goals.

13. So, for example, post-completion point countries had an average debt to exports ratio of 63 percent in contrast to those HIPCs which had not yet received any debt relief and had average debt to export ratios of 200 percent (IDA and IMF 2008, 37–38).
14. In general terms these BIPPAs followed the standard pattern of Bilateral Investment Treaties, laying out a series of undertakings between two countries to reciprocally promote and protect investments of their nationals and companies in their respective jurisdictions. All contain provisions on expropriation and nationalisation which is lawful, but certain conditions must be met such as the payment of compensation which is usually required in its standard formulation to be 'prompt, adequate and effective'. It was particularly in regard to this last requirement that Zimbabwe was seen to be most remiss, and therefore in violation of its international treaty obligations by the West.
15. This provision was a clear sign that Western capitals were concerned by the fact that as the crisis deepened in Zimbabwe, the role of the 'securocrats' in government decision-making processes became increasingly evident.
16. The Cotonou Agreement is a treaty signed between the EU (European Union) and the ACP (African, Caribbean and Pacific) group of countries which came into force in 2003. In contrast to its predecessors, the Yaoundé and Lomé Conventions which had previously governed EU-ACP trade and development cooperation, the Cotonou Agreement emphasised the importance of 'good governance' as fundamental to relations between both groups of countries. Article 96 stated that violations of these good governance principles would lead to the suspension of development cooperation between the EU and the ACP country in question (EU-ACP 2000).
17. The observers report noted that "the Presidential election in Zimbabwe was marred by a high level of politically motivated violence and intimidation, which preceded the poll…it is our view that most of these were perpetrated by members/supporters of the ruling party against members/supporters of the opposition…conditions in Zimbabwe did not allow for a free expression of will by the electors" (Commonwealth Secretariat 2003, 43).

18. Amongst the key principles adopted by the Commonwealth Heads of State at the Commonwealth summit, held ironically in Harare in 1991, was that of an "individual's inalienable right to participate by means of free and democratic political processes in framing the society in which he or she lives" (Commonwealth Secretariat 1991, 1).
19. Even the UN was, however, on occasion, added to the list of external agents plotting regime change. So, for example, in the wake of the visit of the UN's Under-Secretary-General for Humanitarian Affairs in 2005, and the negative report that he produced on the overall humanitarian situation in Zimbabwe and in particular the lack of progress in terms of government assistance to those affected by Operation *Murambatsvina*, Mugabe stated in the course of ZANU-PF party conference: "You can see how they raise this, so that the rest of the international community can say human rights are being violated, people are suffering in the hope that the United Nations can support the British in their evil campaign to try and have control here…I'm going to tell the Secretary General not to send us men, or women, who are not his own but agents of the British" (*Zim Online* 2005).
20. It is worthwhile noting that in the context of the Sino-Soviet split of the 1960s and 1970s, when both Moscow and Beijing competed for ideological leadership of Third World liberation movements, ZANU had followed Beijing's line, most particularly its Maoist prescriptions on guerrilla warfare, and received both training and armaments from the PRC.
21. So, for example, in contrast to OECD-DAC members the Chinese include the construction of sports facilities and military assistance in their external assistance figures, and also exclude debt relief and administrative costs of these programmes from their figures, again in contrast to standard OECD-DAC practice. For an excellent overview of the definitional differences see Bräutigam (2011).
22. For example, Emmerson Mnangagwa, current President of Zimbabwe, was trained in China in the 1960s.

References

Acemoglu, Daron, and James A. Robinson. 2013. *Why Nations Fail – The Origins of Power, Prosperity and Poverty*. London: Profile Books.

AfDB. 2007. *Zimbabwe Country Dialogue Paper 2007*, April.

Bräutigam, Deborah. 2011. Aid 'With Chinese Characteristics': Chinese Foreign Aid and Development Finance Meet the OECD-DAC Aid Regime. *Journal of International Development* 23 (5): 752–754.

Commonwealth Secretariat. 1991. *The Harare Commonwealth Declaration*, October 20. London.

———. 2003. *Zimbabwe Presidential Election, 9–11 March 2002, The Report of the Commonwealth Observer Group*. London.

EU-ACP. 2000. *Partnership Agreement Between Members of the African, Caribbean and Pacific Group of States of the One Part, and the European Community and Its Member States, of the Other Part, Signed in Cotonou on 23 June 2000*, (2000/483/EC). Brussels: European Commission.

GOZ. 2000. *Millennium Economic Recovery Programme*. Harare.

IDA and IMF. 2008. *Highly Indebted Poor Countries (HIPC) Initiative and Multilateral Debt Relief Initiative (MDRI) – Status of Implementation*, September 12. Washington, DC.

IMF. 1999. *Memorandum on the Economic Policies of the Government of Zimbabwe for 1999*, July 16. http://www.imf.org/external/np/loi/071699.htm.

———. 2000. *IMF Concludes Article IV Consultation with Zimbabwe*, Public Information Notice No. 00/17, December 13. http://www.imf.org/en/News/Articles/2015/09/04/53/pn00107.

———. 2002. *IMF Adopts Declaration of Noncooperation for Zimbabwe and Suspends Technical Assistance*, Press Release No. 02/28, June 14. http://www.imf.org/en/News/Articles/2015/09/14/01/49/pr0228.

———. 2003. *IMF Initiates Compulsory Withdrawal Procedures for Zimbabwe*, Press Release No. 03/210, December 3. http://www.imf.org/en/News/Articles/2015/09/14/01/49/pro03210.

———. 2005. *IMF Executive Board Concludes 2005 Article IV Consultation with Zimbabwe*, Public Information Notice No. 05/139, October 4. http://www.imf.org/en/News/Articles/2015/09/28/04/53/pn05139.

———. 2006. *Statement by IMF Staff at the Conclusion of the 2006 Article IV Consultation Discussions in Zimbabwe*, Press Release No. 06/282, December 18. http://www.imf.org/en/News/Articles/2015/09/14/01/49/pr06282.

———. 2009. *Zimbabwe: 2009 Article IV Consultations – Staff Report*, Country Report No. 09/139, May.

Mugabe, R.G. 2001. *Inside the Third Chimurenga*. Harare: Department of Information and Publicity, Office of the President and Cabinet.

———. 2008. *Full Text of Speech by President Robert Mugabe at the Opening of the First Session of Zimbabwe's Seventh Parliament on Tuesday, August 26, 2008.*

http://robertmugabespeeches.blogspot.co.uk/2009/08/president-mugabes-speech-to-zimbabwes.html. 10 June 2017.

National Bureau of Statistics of China. *National Data*. http://data.stats.gov.cn/english/easyquery.htm?.cn=1017.

Nest, Michael. 2001. Ambition, Profits and Loss: Zimbabwean Economic Involvement in the Democratic Republic of the Congo. *African Affairs* 100 (400, July 1): 469–490.

Reuters. 2015. China's Xi in Zimbabwe to Sign Power, Infrastructure Deals, December 1. http://reuters.com/article/us-china-africa-zimbabwe-idUSKBNDTK3Q320151201.

The Guardian. 2005. Zimbabwe Buys Six Fighter Jets, April 14. https://www.theguardian.com/world/2005/apr/14/zimbabwe.

The Herald. 2011a. Sanctions a Declaration of War: Mutasa, July 7. http://www.herald.co.zw/sanctions_a_declaration_of_war.

———. 2011b. Buddies Take Imperialists Head-On, September 8. http://www.herald.co.zw/buddies_take_imperialists_head_on.

———. 2015. Statement by Chinese President Xi Jinping: Let the Sino-Zim Flower Bloom with New Splendour, November 30. http://www.zimbabwesituation.com/news/zimsit_w_statement-by-chinese-president-xi-jinping-let-the-sino-zim-flower-bloom-with-new-splendour-the-herald/.

———. 2016. Ode to Zimbabwe's Loyal Friend, March 4. http://www.herald.co.zw/ode-to-zimbabwes-loyal-friend.

United Nations. 2008. *Security Council Fails to Adopt Sanctions Against Zimbabwe Leadership and Two Permanent Members Cast Negative Votes*, July 11. www.un.org/press/en/2008/sc9396.doc.htm.

United States Congress. 2001. *Zimbabwe Democracy and Economic Recovery Act*, Public Law 107–99, December 21. Washington, DC.

World Bank. 2004. *Zimbabwe Country Assistance Evaluation*, Report No. 29058, May 21. Washington, DC.

———. 2007. *Further Elaboration of a Systematic Approach to Arrears Clearance*, June 2007. Washington, DC.

ZANU-PF. 2013. *Team ZANU-PF 2013*. Harare.

Zim Online. 2005. Mugabe Brands UN Envoy Hypocrite and Liar, December 10. http://www.zimbabwesituation.com/old/dec10b_2005.html.

Zimbabwe Independent. 2005. Zimbabwe 'Looks East' for Military Training/Hardware, June 17. http://www.theindependent.co.zw/2005/06/17.

Zimbabwejournalists.com. 2006. *President Mugabe Hails Zimbabwe-China Ties*, October 26. http://www.zimbabwesituation.com/old/oct28_2006_html#Z14.

9

Economic Meltdown and Elections

In the run-up to Zimbabwe's Presidential, legislative and local council elections in March 2008, few external and domestic observers would have predicted either that the country was about to enter one of the most violent phases of its post-independence history, or that 2008 would also be remembered by the quickening pace of economic collapse, and that new depths would be plumbed and records set for negative economic performance. Even fewer would have been able to foresee the extent to which ZANU-PF, together with the defence, police and intelligence apparatus upon which it had increasingly come to depend, was willing, irrespective of the consequences for the welfare of the Zimbabwean population, to use even greater and more extensive violence to crush the Opposition to maintain its hold on the key levers of power.

The fraught and violent 2008 elections, in which ZANU-PF lost its majority in Parliament while Mugabe eventually succeeded, after a second round in which he ran uncontested, in retaining the post of President, were followed by protracted inter-party negotiations mediated by regional neighbours. These eventually led to the signing of a Global Political Agreement (GPA) in September 2008 whereby ZANU-PF was forced to concede elements of genuine power to other political parties, and the

M. Simpson, T. Hawkins, *The Primacy of Regime Survival*,
https://doi.org/10.1007/978-3-319-72520-8_9

formation of an Inclusive Government (IG) in February 2009 in the form of a power-sharing arrangement between ZANU-PF, MDC-T and MDC-M.[1] While the IG was a necessary evil as far as both the Opposition and ZANU-PF were concerned, it did seem to nevertheless seem to offer an opportunity for the country to begin the process of reversing its seemingly relentless socio-economic and political downward trajectory, rebuild the credibility and capacity of state institutions, and restore popular trust in these bodies.

Hitting the Bottom: Economic Freefall and Its Human Costs

As a result of the RBZ's policy of printing money to finance a growing government deficit, by July 2008 the official inflation rate had reached 281 million percent, the last time official figures were published. By mid-November 2008, independent analysts were estimating that the inflation rate had hit a mind-numbing 79 billion percent, which translated into a daily inflation rate of over 90 percent, while the IMF estimated it had peaked at an even higher 500 billion percent by September 2008 (IMF 2009, 5).

The full extent to which the RBZ had over time stepped completely outside its mandate, usurped the role of the Ministry of Finance, and through its damaging quasi-fiscal activities reconstituted itself as the centre of economic policy formulation and patronage, were subsequently laid bare by the IMF in May 2009. The RBZ's quasi-fiscal activities were:

> Estimated at US$1.1 billion (36 percent of GDP) in 2008…they included election-related expenses, transfers to parastatals, subsidised directed lending, below-cost provision of equipment and fertilisers to farmers, and allocation of foreign exchange at subsidised exchange rates. These expenses were mainly financed by surrender requirements on export proceeds, the retention of foreign exchange earnings of the gold and agricultural sectors in excess of the mandatory surrender requirements, the confiscation of most foreign currency deposits, external borrowing, purchases of foreign exchange at the parallel market exchange rates, and monetization. (IMF 2009, 7)

In a forlorn attempt to bring down the inflation created by his own policies, between 2006 and early 2009 the Governor of the RBZ, Gideon Gono, had ordered three redenominations of the currency resulting in the elimination of a total of 25 zeros.[2] The printing presses often failed to keep up with orders, and the banking public was faced with daily cash withdrawal limits imposed by the RBZ. By the end of 2008 Zimbabweans had effectively abandoned the local currency, and were conducting their transactions in foreign exchange, fuel coupons or through the barter of goods and services.

The country's workforce and its factories stood idle as protracted electricity and water supply cuts (often lasting days) became the norm, and imports of raw materials and equipment ceased due to the lack of foreign exchange, except for those with privileged access to the RBZ Governor. According to IMF figures, over the course of 2008 Zimbabwe's GDP contracted a further 14.0 percent, a figure to be added to the cumulative decline of 40 percent over the period 2000–2007 (IMF 2009, 4). IMF data also showed that while in 2000 Zimbabwe had contributed 3.2 percent to SADC's total GDP, and was ranked as the fourth largest economy in the regional grouping, by 2010 its share had fallen to below 1 percent, making it the grouping's third smallest economy after Swaziland and Lesotho (IMF 2010).

The country's balance-of-payments situation continued to deteriorate, with exports declining from US$2.192 billion in 2000 to an estimated US$1.652 billion in 2008 (Hawkins and Ndlela 2009, 24). In addition to the collapse of the agricultural sector, another indication of the wrenching changes that had taken place in the economy was that of the country's increasing reliance on a narrow range of mineral exports. This shift away from what – at least by the standards of the continent – had been a relatively diversified economy with major contributions to export earnings from agricultural and manufactured exports, as well as tourism and services – to one in which extractive industries dominated the economy, increased the country's vulnerability to external shocks because of growing export concentration.[3]

In the post-2008 elections period, poor management of the country's mineral wealth would also significantly reduce the scope for comprehensive recovery (in particular the need to address accumulated deficits in terms of investments in health, education and the country's infrastructure). ZANU-PF's continued control of these resources enabled it to prioritise and channel resources to support its own regime maintenance objectives. As a result, Zimbabwe rapidly came to manifest, and in extreme form, all the symptoms associated with the resource curse (see Chap. 2), as mineral wealth provided ZANU-PF with a pipeline of resources which allowed it to run what, in effect, became its own parallel revenue collection and fiscal policy for party political ends.

Budget revenues fell from almost US$1 billion in 2005, which represented 25 percent of GDP, to US$133 million and 4 percent of GDP in 2008, while total public expenditure shrank from US$1.4 billion in 2005 to US$258 million in 2008 (IMF 2009, 9). Given that budgetary allocations were made at the beginning of the year in Zimbabwean dollars, under conditions of hyperinflation their value in real terms was rapidly eroded.

Reflecting the increasing pace of economic decline and a shrinking revenue base – and a microcosm of the impact of hyperinflation on the performance of the overall public sector as the real value of the government budget shrank – was the rapid deterioration in the quality of services provided by the public health system. According to one source drawing on official data, between 2005 and 2008 per capita public expenditure on health fell from an already low US$2.33 to a derisory US$0.05 (USAID 2010, 33).[4] By the beginning of 2009 the public health system – with the exception of donor-funded programmes such as those in the areas of HIV/AIDS, malaria and tuberculosis and vaccination programmes – had to all intents and purposes ceased to operate, and the majority of the population was forced to fend for itself. As subsequently noted by a group of public health experts:

> hospitals in the country were hardly operating with massive shortages of essential medicines and supplies…The physical infrastructure of most government health facilities is decrepit, and ambulances sparse…Although some [health care professionals] heroically continued to work for minimal wages, by the end of 2008 many had stopped working. By this time, a government doctor's salary had fallen to less than $1 per month. (Todd et al. 2010, 606)

By 2009 the Ministry of Health and Child Welfare was reporting vacancy rates of 69 percent for doctors, 80 percent for midwives and 50 percent for pharmacy, radiology and laboratory personnel (GOZ 2009, 8). Even these figures may well be significant underestimates of the actual vacancy levels, as many health workers simply failed to report to work – due to transport difficulties or because they decided it was an exercise in futility given the regular stock-outs of medicines and medical supplies – without ever officially resigning. Even those few Zimbabweans fortunate enough to have employer-based or private health insurance schemes soon found themselves in difficulties as the capital base of those schemes was eroded by inflation, and private health facilities increasingly demanded payment in foreign currency.

This funding crisis, rooted in the wider economic malaise, translated directly into worsening health indicators during this period of 'deep crisis'. Ambulances became increasingly scarce due to lack of maintenance and fuel shortages. Medical equipment was not repaired, and supplies disappeared from dispensaries. Household incomes available for health spending shrank, while demands for 'unofficial' payments for services increased as health staff struggled to survive. Pregnant mothers and their relatives were forced to bring along with them everything from bed sheets to cotton wool for their deliveries in health units, and basic maternal and neo-natal care became increasingly difficult to access for the vast majority of Zimbabwean women.

The extent of the collapse in the public health system, as well as the deterioration of the country's water and sanitation infrastructure, was made clear in the starkest possible terms with the outbreak of a cholera epidemic in August 2008. This was to eventually infect close to 90,000 people and claim over 4,300 lives. According to one specialist source reporting in March 2009, the epidemic registered "the largest number of infections ever recorded in a single outbreak on the continent" (Chambers 2009, 993).

Not only did Zimbabwe's public health system – once a source of great national pride – prove unable to respond in a timely manner to the outbreak without significant external assistance, but the speed with which the cholera spread (not helped by initial official denials of the existence of the problem) brought to light the extent to which the country's public health system was now incapable of responding to a national health emergency, as well the poor condition of water treatment and distribution and sanitation systems. Years of underinvestment in both expansion and maintenance of such infrastructure came home to roost as broken water pipes, open sewers, the collapse of rubbish collection services and the lack of funds to purchase water treatment equipment and chemicals, all converged to produce ideal breeding grounds for the virus. By the time the epidemic was brought under control in early 2009, the country was peppered with tented treatment centres more reminiscent of refugee camps in countries affected by armed conflict or major natural disasters.

Zimbabwe's other 'crown jewel', its public education system built up during the first decade of independence, was likewise crippled. Mirroring to a large extent the collapse of the public health system, the high rates of absenteeism amongst staff, deteriorating infrastructure, and lack of teaching materials, led to a severe deterioration in quality. By late 2008 there were reports that most rural schools, and large numbers of schools in urban areas, had simply ceased to operate.

There was a growing gap between ZANU-PF's vitriolic defence of its *de jure* sovereignty on the one hand, and the reality of its failure to meet its most basic obligations to its own people in line with the concept of inward looking *de facto* sovereignty expounded by Ghani and Lockhart (see Chap. 2). The more the ZANU-PF controlled state reneged on its domestic responsibilities, the wider the chasm between the state and the general population, as well as the more frayed the relations between the liberation party and those it had freed from white minority rule. And as the national implosion gathered pace, the more paranoid, shrill and violent ZANU-PF became.

The Elections of 2008 and Its Aftermath

It was against the backdrop of this quickening pace of economic, social and institutional disintegration that Mugabe called for joint Presidential, legislative and municipal elections to be held on March 29, 2008. The ruling party hoped that it would be able to count on goodwill and gratitude generated by the redistribution of land under the FTLRP, and that this would be sufficient to ensure victory at the polls. Insulated as its senior leadership was from hardships, it seemed unable to grasp the full extent and depth of the suffering faced by the general population as a result of the policies it had adopted. Yet this did not mean that the full toolkit of coercive instruments, used to help ensure victory in previous elections, would not also be deployed for these elections as in the past.

Opposition parties were forced to contend with the regime's regular recourse to the battery of repressive legislation at its disposal to obstruct their campaigns, such as the Public Order and Security Act (POSA) which outlawed meetings of 5 or more people without prior police authorisation, and which was rarely granted to opposition parties. War veterans and ZANU-PF youth militia were deployed to intimidate both voters and opposition campaigners in an effort to create no-go zones for the Opposition, particularly in rural areas.

Members of the Opposition also faced threats – both veiled and explicit – from leaders of the security forces, some of whom made it clear that they would be unwilling to respect the results of the elections if these translated into an overturning of the status quo. In early March 2008, for example, Constantino Chiwenga, Commander of the Zimbabwe Defence Forces, revealed the full extent of the partisanship of the country's defence and security apparatus, and the manner in which senior securocrats saw their forces as simply an extension of the ruling party as had been the case during the liberation struggle. Chiwenga put the Opposition on notice that even in the event they won the ballot, there was no guarantee that they would be allowed to take power:

> Elections are coming and the army will not support sell-outs and agents of the West before, during and after the presidential elections. We will not support anyone other than President Mugabe who has sacrificed a lot for the country. (*The Standard* 2008)

By depicting the MDC-T and its leader Morgan Tsvangirai as creations of the West, as a fifth column intent on advancing the recolonisation project of London and its allies, it was but a small step for ZANU-PF to convince the defence establishment that the use of force as applied during the years of the liberation struggle would again be necessary if the ruling party's monopoly of power should come to be threatened. The careful nurturing of senior members of the army, air-force, police, intelligence and prison services by ZANU-PF during the crisis years – ensuring that they were given scope to accumulate riches and were sufficiently insulated from the economic meltdown taking place around them – would then yield the hoped for results as they shored up the ruling party and regime and helped to neutralise an electoral threat (see Chap. 11). The 2008 elections were therefore to be treated as a war against the West and its perceived local proxies.

In addition to the dangers arising from the strict subordination to, and identification of the interests of the country's military with those of ZANU-PF, opposition parties also expressed growing concerns about possible gerrymandering of the electoral process by officials appointed by Mugabe to the Zimbabwe Electoral Commission (ZEC). In the case of the Chairperson of ZEC, this post was held by a retired Brigadier-General and former fighter in ZANU-PF's armed wing during the liberation struggle. This constituted not only a further indication of the militarisation of the country's key state institutions that had become of increasing concern to both Zimbabwean democracy activists and Western observers, but also raised strong suspicions regarding the partisanship of the electoral body. Opposition leaders also expressed reservations concerning the validity of the country's electoral roll given that the Registrar-General responsible for its maintenance and updating was also an open supporter of the ruling party, and had consistently obstructed their access to the electoral roll.[5] Their concerns were compounded by the fact that while invitations to send electoral observers were issued to international bodies judged by ZANU-PF to be acceptable, such as the SADC and AU (African Union), other bodies such as the EU, the highly regarded Atlanta-based Carter Center, and even the UN were excluded.

Following election day on March 29 2008, there were protracted delays in the announcement of results by ZEC. Every day the public was drip fed results on television and radio, in a clear effort to attempt to show that the two main parties, MDC-T and ZANU-PF, were neck and neck. However, and based on projections from a partial Parallel Voting Tabulation (PVT) exercise, preliminary results, which soon became common knowledge, pointed to a serious defeat for ZANU-PF in both the legislative and Presidential polls.

Many observers believed the drawn-out process of releasing the results reflected the fact that ZANU-PF had been caught completely by surprise by the popular verdict, and was using its influence within the ZEC to delay announcement of the final results while it decided how it was going to react to the unthinkable, while simultaneously engaging in rear-guard actions such as massaging the figures in an effort to improve ZANU-PF's performance. To the immense frustration of the opposition parties, the final official tally of the March 29 elections was only announced over four weeks later on 2 May 2008.

The results showed ZANU-PF had lost control of its parliamentary majority in the House of Assembly. As a result of three by-elections in June 2008 due to the death of candidates, the final tally for the two MDCs was a total of 110 seats (100 seats for MDC-T and 10 for the smaller MDC-M faction) against ZANU-PF's 99 seats, with the remaining seat going to an Independent candidate. In addition, the ZEC announced that Tsvangirai had won the first round of the Presidential elections with 47.9 percent, with Mugabe gaining 43.2 percent, and a third candidate, Simba Makoni, gaining 8.3 percent.[6] However, and at least according to the official figures announced by the ZEC, Tsvangirai failed to achieve the necessary threshold of 50 percent plus one vote necessary to avoid a run-off with Mugabe.

Most shocking for ZANU-PF was the fact that the results showed that both MDCs had made significant inroads into its rural strongholds, with many rural voters clearly having chosen Opposition parties, notwithstanding that a key objective of the FTLRP had been to rebuild ZANU-PF's peasant support base. But after the initial shock and a period of stock-taking, it was soon to regroup to ensure regime survival.

It was during the interregnum between the first and second rounds of the Presidential elections that ZANU-PF launched a comprehensive and coordinated campaign of violence and intimidation, coordinated by the Joint Operations Command (JOC),[7] against the MDC-T and its supporters. Known as Operation *Mavhoterapipi* (How Did You Vote?), its objectives were redolent of the logic which had informed Operation *Murambatsvina* three years earlier. They included a mixture of meting out punishment to those who had voted for the MDC-T, intimidation of former ZANU-PF voters who had switched sides such that they returned to the fold come the second round of the Presidential elections, and cleansing the rural areas of the Opposition through the forced displacement of MDC-T supporters (who would lose their right to vote in the districts where they had registered), thereby crippling MDC-T party structures and changing the political landscape in favour of ZANU-PF.

ZANU-PF quickly revealed the extent to which it was willing to use all means at its disposal to perpetuate its grip on power. Mugabe himself made clear to the electorate in no uncertain terms what lay in store for them should they not cast their votes for him in the second round: "We fought for this country, and a lot of blood was shed. We are not going to give up our country because of a mere X. How can a ballpoint fight with a gun?" (*The Times* 2008).

Areas in which such state-sponsored violence was unleashed were sealed off to outsiders, while journalists, trade unionists and members of human rights and local election observation groups were detained on a regular basis so as to prevent information reaching the public sphere. However the latter proved difficult, since as the reign of terror took hold many victims sought both refuge and medical assistance in urban areas, thus revealing the full extent of the violence that was sweeping the countryside.

The period between the two rounds also highlighted the degree to which the country had to all intents and purposes been subjected to a creeping military coup, with the security chiefs in the JOC usurping the role of Cabinet and becoming the *de facto* national policy-making body, the culmination of a process of militarisation of national life which had been underway for a number of years. By September 2009 one Zimbabwean defence analyst was to characterise the situation as one in which "the securocrats had appropriated most of the levers of state power and coercion" (Chitoyi 2009, 8).

Being amongst those with most to lose if ZANU-PF should be ousted from power, and haunted by the prospect of an MDC-T government initiating a process of transitional justice in which they would be held accountable for past human rights abuses, and in the course of which the source of their wealth might also become the subject of investigations, the securocrats gained the upper hand in the highest decision-making circles as the centre of gravity in terms of policy formulation shifted from Cabinet to the JOC.[8] The latter convinced the civilian leaders within

ZANU-PF that the best option was to adopt a scorched earth policy aimed at crippling the MDC-T, and then presenting Zimbabweans and the world with an electoral *fait accompli.* In contrast to the first round where the Opposition parties had been granted access to state TV for their campaign messages, in the run-up to the second round media restrictions were re-imposed. The MDC-T found itself obstructed at every turn from holding rallies, and its leaders were regularly harassed and arrested on spurious charges.[9]

The country's largest civil society election observer group, the Zimbabwe Elections Support Network (ZESN), which had deployed over 8,600 national observers in the first round of the elections and played a key role in the PVT exercise, was also subject to harassment and attacks on its observers. It was subsequently informed by the Minister of Justice, Patrick Chinamasa, that only 500 of its election monitors would be invited by his ministry and accredited by ZEC for the run-off. ZESN was eventually to withdraw from the second round election monitoring process when there were delays in accrediting even this severely reduced number of its observers (*Zimbabwe Independent* 2008).

Given the success of ZANU-PF's scorched earth policy that had shattered his grassroots party structures, and the rising death toll amongst his supporters, Tsvangirai eventually withdrew from the run-off on the grounds that he could no longer risk the lives of his supporters. It may also have become obvious to him that even if he were to contest the second round, the process and results would be manipulated in such a way as to ensure that Mugabe emerged victorious. Prior to the second round, Tsvangirai felt compelled to seek refuge in the Netherlands Embassy in Harare after a number of his lieutenants had been arrested on various trumped up charges, while there were rumours that he was the target of an assassination plot. As many were to later conclude, in a Zimbabwe under ZANU-PF rule, victory at the ballot box for the Opposition did not translate into securing power.

Ignoring a call from SADC for the election to be postponed, Mugabe ran unchallenged in the second Presidential round held on 27 June 2008. However, in an attempt to provide a modicum of legitimacy for the outcome, the ZEC ruled that Tsvangirai's filing of his notice to withdraw on 24 June was too late, as a result of which his name was to remain on the ballot paper. Mugabe, unsurprisingly, won by a landslide, polling 2,150,266 votes against Tsvangirai's paltry 233,000. In stark contrast to the delays experienced in the first round, the results were announced 48 hours later on the 29 June 2008. One hour after the announcement of the results, Mugabe was rapidly sworn in for another term as President by the Chief Justice, and the *fait accompli* of regime continuity was presented to Zimbabweans and the international community.

The full extent of the violence used to secure victory for Mugabe in the second round was gradually revealed. The Washington Post reported that:

> In the three months between the March 29 vote and the June 27 runoff election, ruling-party militias under the guidance of 200 senior army officers battered the Movement for Democratic Change, bringing the opposition party's network of activists to the verge of oblivion. By election day, more than 80 opposition supporters were dead, hundreds were missing, thousands were injured and hundreds of thousands were homeless. (*The Washington Post* 2008)

One group of African observers, which had been invited back to observe the second round, was to issue a hard-hitting report on the period between the first and second rounds which proved profoundly embarrassing to the government. The report was also indicative of the extent to which ZANU-PF could no longer, irrespective of the policies it pursued, automatically count on the sympathy of the African continent. The Pan-African Parliamentary Group, composed of members of the AU's legislative body, stated that its members had "observed traces of intimidation and violence in all the provinces it visited. Houses burnt down, people assaulted" and that "the victims of the violence were largely aligned to MDC" (Pan-African Parliament 2008, 11–12). The report also stated that on the basis of what it had observed "the mission found it difficult not to believe in the widespread allegations that the security forces were not only permissive but actually perpetrated violent acts against suspected opposition supporters" (Ibid., 15). The group was to conclude "that the atmosphere prevailing in the country, at the time, did not give rise to the conduct of free, fair and credible elections" (Ibid., 20).

It was clear to observers – possibly even to Mugabe himself though maybe not the less politically astute and economically literate securocrats with which he had increasingly surrounded himself and come to depend upon to keep him and his party in power – that his victory was an extremely problematic if not hollow one. Firstly, the results of the first round of the elections had shown conclusively to both domestic and international audiences the full extent of popular disenchantment with his party, and that his claims to enjoy overwhelming popular support for both himself and his party's policies were threadbare. As poignantly put by a church-based NGO in its analysis of the violence that followed the first round of the elections:

> it is the violence that has been unleashed by the Mugabe regime on Zimbabwean citizens that has demonstrated the hollowness of Mugabe's anti-colonial message, with the real targets of his party's onslaught being the impoverished and battered citizens of the country. (Solidarity Peace Trust 2008, 6)

In addition, the need for economic stabilisation was an increasingly incontrovertible and urgent one. Amidst the high drama of the country's election processes it was evident, even to those who in the recent past had themselves supported, designed and implemented the ruling party's market destroying and poverty producing policies, that the economic collapse would have to be arrested irrespective of which party was in power.

The complete meltdown of the economy in the course of 2008 also severely constrained the scope for further accumulation on the part of ZANU-PF elites and their associates. At its most basic, the patronage trough was now largely empty as most commercial farms had already been seized and redistributed, control of parastatals had already been allocated to party notables and retired securocrats, while the *de facto* abandonment by the general public of the Zimbabwe dollar and the catastrophic decline in export receipts meant that the RBZ had severely limited scope to engage in foreign exchange arbitrage and money printing to support patronage efforts.

The imperative of restocking the larder meant that in the course of 2007–2008, and while it still commanded a majority in Parliament, ZANU-PF had introduced legislation aimed at ensuring control of new sources of largesse, and in the run-up to the 2008 elections it made attempts to shore up its declining support base by holding out the promise of securing and distributing more wealth to supporters in years to come. The 'Indigenization and Economic Empowerment Act', signed into law by Mugabe in April 2008, required all foreign owned and local 'non-indigenous' owned companies (which meant white-owned) operating in Zimbabwe to cede 51 percent of their shares or interests to 'indigenous' Zimbabweans.[10] Yet this would take time to implement, and the patronage requirements were pressing (see Chap. 12).

The urgency of replenishment was compounded by the fact that the economic meltdown of 2008 had eroded the value of those assets appropriated in the course of the crisis years by party notables and their affiliates. Put simply, a shrinking domestic market, the by now negligible purchasing power of the vast majority of the Zimbabwean population, coupled with growing disinterest from traditional sources of FDI in bringing capital into Zimbabwe given the country's shredded reputation in terms of political and economic stability and notoriously poor history of respecting property rights, all converged to ensure that significant long-term returns could not be realised on those assets which had been seized. Elite control over a vast panoply of fixed assets, ranging from farms and factories to banks, transport companies and private housing stock, was largely meaningless and represented 'dead capital' if they could not be made productive, profitable and transacted. Transforming them into productive assets required inputs and markets (both of which had largely disappeared by 2008), or alternatively that they could at least be sold (which presumed there were interested buyers, either foreign or domestic, both groups increasingly conspicuous by their absence).

The tension between these conflicting imperatives was stark. If on the one hand there was an overwhelming need for a measure of stability and predictability in terms of national economic policy, this had to be balanced against the need to ensure that new sources of wealth were identified to feed ongoing patronage requirements amongst groups whose loyalty had to be secured and maintained. During the crisis years the message had been widely disseminated that the ruling party, through its control of the state, was the only route to personal enrichment as it monopolised a shrinking pool of national resources. This in turn led to a revolution of rising expectations, even if the economic policies pursued to ensure the loyalty of those benefiting from an ever expanding patronage network ran counter to the need felt by other beneficiaries of past largesse for some form of economic stabilisation.[11]

Changes in African perceptions may also have played a role in ZANU-PF's eventual decision to share power. The reaction of the many sections of African public opinion and African governments to the events of 2008 made it clear that Mugabe's former high standing and legitimacy amongst his African peers, flowing from his role as leader of a liberation movement and founding father of Zimbabwe, was at an all-time low. Whereas throughout much of the post-independence period he could count on the unreserved support of almost all his fellow African leaders, there were now voices amongst them that left little room for doubt they were increasingly embarrassed by developments in Zimbabwe, and by Mugabe himself.[12] The 'Zimbabwe question', a regular item on the agenda of continental and sub-regional meetings, coupled with continuous efforts by Western powers to have the Zimbabwe situation referred to the UN Security Council, had become a source of growing concern to Africa in general, and a burden to SADC in particular. It was clear that the issue would not be allowed to rest, particularly as Western countries gave notice that 'targeted measures' against ZANU-PF notables and their affiliates were to be tightened even further in the aftermath of the violence which had plagued the second round of the 2008 elections.

There had been much sympathy expressed in African circles for Mugabe's land reform programme when first launched, especially when couched in terms of anti-imperialism and demands for restitution for past colonial wrongs. Even with regards to those governments who might have taken a more critical stance concerning the manner in which it was carried out, Harare was able to benefit from widespread and longstanding adherence to the principle of non-interference in the internal affairs of other African states contained in the founding charter of continental bodies such as the Organization for African Unity (OAU), the precursor to the African Union (AU).

By 2008, however, what had become increasingly clear was that the ultimate objective of the President was solely that of maintaining himself in power, preferably on a monopolistic basis, and irrespective of the costs either to Zimbabwe, or the reputation of the sub-region and the continent. Mugabe's efforts to depict his country's travails as being the result of foreign machinations orchestrated by forces intent on regime change, and his attempts to clothe ZANU-PF policies in anti-imperialist rhetoric and as a struggle against the former colonial master and its local proxies, principally the MDC-T, lost some of its purchase at a time when the African continent as a whole was seeking to convince the world through a number of continent-wide initiatives that the precepts of 'good governance', and the pursuit of sound economic policies, had gained a more solid footing on the continent.[13]

The Formation of the Inclusive Government (IG)

Developments in another part of Africa were to have an important influence on post-elections Zimbabwe. Following extremely violent elections in Kenya in December 2007, the UN/AU launched a joint mediation effort in early 2008. This eventually led to the establishment of a coalition government in which Kenya's head of state, Mwai Kibaki, retained his post as President, while his main opponent Raila Odinga took on the newly-created post of prime minister, with both dividing the rest of the spoils in terms of government posts between their respective parties. In addition, the parties agreed to jointly address problems seen to have contributed to the political crisis, such as the need for judicial reforms and revisions to Kenya's constitution and electoral system.

Given this recent precedent, it was perhaps not surprising that African leaders should have sought a similar solution as a way out of the impasse created by the 2008 elections in Zimbabwe. In July 2008 at a summit in Egypt, the AU adopted a resolution calling for the formation of a government of national unity in Zimbabwe. Under pressure from the AU appointed mediator, South African President Thabo Mbeki, and following protracted negotiations, the leaders of ZANU-PF, MDC-T and the smaller breakaway MDC-M faction eventually signed the Global Political Agreement (GPA) in September 2008 (GOZ 2008b).

As far as the opposition parties were concerned, the most important provision of the GPA was arguably the undertaking to establish a

Parliamentary Select Committee to oversee the development of a new constitution through public hearings and consultations, and which would subsequently be subjected to a referendum (Ibid., Article 6.1), seeing this as a mechanism through which they might begin to overhaul the ZANU-PF state's extractive political and economic institutions. Given their recent experiences at the hands of state organs such as the ZEC and the security forces, they were also clearly the prime movers behind the inclusion of a commitment in the GPA to "ensuring that all state organs and institutions strictly observe the principles of the Rule of Law and remain non-partisan and impartial" (Ibid., Article 13.2(b)). The battering their supporters had received at the hands of ZANU-PF youth militia known as the 'Green Bombers'[14] also explains the inclusion of the restructuring of the National Youth Service established by the Government in 2001 which "shall not… be used or deployed for partisan political work" (Ibid., Article 15.1(c)). Their interest in opening up political space for themselves, heavily restricted during the 2008 election campaign, were catered for by provisions such as that "all political parties are able to propagate their views and canvass for support, free of harassment and intimidation" (Ibid., Article 10), and in addition "that steps be taken to ensure that the public media provides balanced and fair coverage to all political parties for their legitimate political activities" (Ibid., Article 19.1(d)).

Finally, and given the commitment of both MDCs to the recovery of the country's economy and an improvement in the conditions facing the majority of Zimbabweans, the signatories committed their parties to work together "on a full and comprehensive economic programme to resuscitate Zimbabwe's economy, which will urgently address the issues of production, food security, poverty and unemployment" (Ibid., Article 3.1(a)). Significantly, the GPA also committed the new Inclusive Government (IG) to "conduct a comprehensive, transparent and non-partisan land audit during the tenure of the Seventh Parliament of Zimbabwe for the purpose of establishing accountability and eliminating multiple farm ownerships" (Ibid., Article 5.9(a)).

In return, ZANU-PF was able to secure the acceptance from both MDC formations of some of its strongly held historical positions. So, for example, the GPA noted that the parties "Accepted the irreversibility of the said land acquisitions and redistribution" (Ibid., Article 5.5) and that "the primary obligation of compensating former land owners for land acquired rests on the former colonial power" (Ibid., Article 5.6). Given the interest of the ZANU-PF elite in bringing an end to the isolation imposed on them by the West, the GPA also included as an objective "that all forms of measures and sanctions against Zimbabwe be lifted in order to facilitate a sustainable solution to the challenges that are currently facing Zimbabwe" (Ibid., Article 4.6(a)), with the parties agreeing to work together to achieve that objective.

The new governance arrangements established by the GPA were indicative, however, (though this was only to become clearer in the course of the cohabitation arrangement), of only minor shifts in the balance of power, or at least the balance of 'hard power'. The new post of Prime Minister was granted to Tsvangirai, while two Deputy Prime Minister posts were taken up by Mutambara as leader of the breakaway MDC-M faction, and another senior MDC-T politician, Thokozani Khupe. Mugabe, however, was to continue as President, Head of State and Commander in Chief of the Armed Forces, and to chair Cabinet and significantly the National Security Council (NSC), with the new Prime Minister as deputy chair of the former and only a member of the latter. In addition, the President retained the right to make all key appointments to state positions, subject only to the requirement that he do so "in consultation with the Prime Minister" (Ibid., Article 20.1.3(p)). As likely intended, the extent and nature of such consultation was left open to interpretation by the Head of State, and as events were to prove, Mugabe's disdain for Tsvangirai meant the PM was often to find out about such appointments only once officially announced by the President's spokesman.

While a new body, the Council of Ministers, was to be created and chaired by the PM, this was to only exercise limited powers, most notably in terms of overseeing implementation of Cabinet decisions, coordination of Cabinet business, and reporting to Cabinet on progress (Ibid., Article 20.1.5). Numerous delays – partly a result of horse-trading between the parties for control of specific ministries (in each ministry headed up by a representative of one of the signatories, the opposing party received the post of deputy minister), but largely due to ZANU-PF's delaying tactics aimed at ensuring that it retained as much control as possible over those ministries in which it had primary interest and that the MDC-T was kept as its junior partner in government – meant that the new government was to eventually only take office in February 2009.[15]

An analysis of the division of ministerial portfolios shows a clear pattern that again speaks to the analytical framework developed by Ghani and Lockhart, and in particular the relevance of their expanded definition of sovereignty and its various components. ZANU-PF sought to maintain its hold over the means of domestic coercion through oversight of the security forces and the justice delivery system, as well as administrative control of the national territory (through the Presidential process of appointing of provincial governors over which Mugabe continued to exercise complete authority despite GPA provisions regarding the need to consult with his PM), in addition to defence, justice and foreign policy. It was clearly less interested in responsibility for the other attributes of *de facto* sovereignty highlighted by Ghani and Lockhart, such as the establishment of the rule of law,[16] sound management of public assets and finances, the formation and deepening of markets, public investment in human capital through health and education programmes, and the design and implementation of economic development and poverty reduction strategies.

The final distribution of government posts was therefore profoundly instructive, reflecting the divergent logic driving ZANU-PF and the MDCs. As a result of the bargaining that preceded the installation of the IG, ZANU-PF was able to retain control of what in its eyes were the most important ministries, (Defence, Justice, Foreign Affairs, Agriculture, Lands and Rural Resettlement, Mining, Information and Publicity, and Local Government amongst others, while also ensuring that it co-chaired Home Affairs). It also secured the Ministry of Youth Development, Indigenisation and Empowerment which had been responsible both for nurturing shock troops such as the Green Bombers thrown into the frontline of anti-MDC violence during the 2008 elections, as well as the formulation of indigenisation policy which would assist ZANU-PF to secure new resources for patronage purposes.

In addition, the post of Minister of State for National Security in the President's Office responsible for oversight of the CIO went to a former Defence Minister and ZANU-PF stalwart, further weakening the prospects of any meaningful security sector reform being initiated during the lifetime of the IG. Also noteworthy was the fact that, notwithstanding repeated demands from MDC-T, Mugabe pointedly refused to replace the Governor of the Reserve Bank,[17] or the existing Attorney-General, the latter a critical position if there were to be any serious prospects of prosecutions being initiated relating to the electoral violence of 2008, and human rights violations during *Murambatsvina*, *Gukurahundi* or any other dark chapter in the country's history.[18]

The two MDCs were put in charge of what might broadly be termed service delivery ministries, namely Labour and Social Welfare, Housing, Education, Health, Energy, Public Works, Public Service, Water Resources, Industry and Commerce, and State Enterprises. These were all sectors profoundly damaged by the country's extended decline, and also the most challenging to turn around as they required the most resources (both financial and human), and comprehensive and technically policies that took into account the complex challenges facing the country. In addition, MDC-T also secured the two Ministries of Economic Planning and Finance which provided them with platforms to develop the overarching economic recovery framework for Zimbabwe referenced in the GPA.

However, one key requirement for the implementation of the required reforms was a modicum of cross-party consensus on both the root causes of the country's decline, as well as the remedial measures required. As events were to prove, however, such common ground proved elusive, as diagnoses of the causes, consequences and solutions to the country's fragility were often diametrically opposed.

The fault lines were deep, severely compromising the prospects of success of the IG from its inception. As noted at the time:

> power sharing was no leader's first choice. Each signed the GPA under duress and with considerable reluctance. Tsvangirai, having learned that he could win elections but still not achieve power, accepted the need for change in political strategy that allowed the MDC to get a foot in the door of national government. Mugabe, humiliated in the 2008 elections and having lost support among fellow African leaders, needed to buy time in order to work out a fresh survival strategy…one side saw the GPA as a step towards completing a democratic transition and restoring a developmental agenda, whereas the other saw it as an opportunity to shore up [its] fading power and protect the privileges of its leaders. (Bratton and Masunungure 2011, 32)

The power-sharing deal was a bitter pill for ZANU-PF to swallow. To all intents and purposes it had been forced through a combination of international pressure and domestic realities into an arrangement with a centre of opposition to its rule which it had always characterised as an unpatriotic and alien body set up by hostile foreign interests. Acceptance by ZANU-PF of the IG was a purely tactical move born out of overwhelming necessity, to be tolerated only as long as strictly necessary.

A Glimmer of Hope

Notwithstanding widespread scepticism both domestically and internationally regarding the IG's prospects, there was immediate popular relief in the aftermath of the signing of the GPA agreement as the incidence of political violence fell dramatically. This was particularly so in MDC-T strongholds that had been battered by state-sponsored violence before, during and in the immediate aftermath of the 2008 elections, as attacks by ZANU-PF aligned groups of youth militia, 'war veterans' and security forces ceased.

The abating of violence was accompanied by the introduction of new monetary policies, (most notably the belated official introduction of a multi-currency regime and abandonment of the Zimbabwe dollar), which had an immediate positive impact in terms of macroeconomic stabilisation by putting an end to hyperinflation. It also provided some immediate reassurance to Zimbabweans who, for the first time in many years, enjoyed a positive supply-side response from producers and retailers, with factories reopening and goods once more available in stores.

However, only the most starry-eyed of observers would have suggested that the country's efforts to reverse fragility – even if cross-party consensus could be reached and working relations established between all the disparate groups now in government – were going to be easily rewarded by rapid and irreversible gains in terms of economic growth and employment, improved provision of health, education and other public services, and the enhanced security of citizens and impartial delivery of justice. The legacy of years of extremely poor economic management had resulted in an economy that bore little resemblance to that of the 1980s and

1990s, having regressed in terms of all significant indicators. In addition, the political turbulence of the years from 1997 to 2008 had led to high and seemingly irreversible levels of political polarisation and deep mistrust. This had been accompanied by the extensive undermining of the legitimacy of state institutions and their hollowing out in terms of capacity, the growing and overt partisanship of the security forces, the centralisation of power in the Presidency, and widespread corruption nurtured by strongly entrenched patronage networks.

The list of challenges facing Zimbabwe was a daunting one. They included the need to open up the national decision-making process to public scrutiny – which over time had come to be concentrated in the hands of senior members of ZANU-PF in alliance with the JOC – by restoring the oversight role of Parliament in regard to the Executive. Other urgent tasks included ensuring transparency and accountability in the management of public finances as a basic precondition for kick-starting economic growth, reinstituting the rule of law and respect for human rights, rebuilding relations with Western donors and the BWIs, and the rolling back of a corpus of draconian legislation restricting press freedom and civil rights built up during the crisis decade.

Taken individually, each of the items required its own comprehensive reform programme involving significant investments of time, effort and human and financial resources. Taken together, for the reform-minded elements within the IG they meant a Herculean effort would be necessary to reverse the onerous legacy that they had inherited. Put succinctly, it implied nothing less than the prising apart of the ruling party, government, security establishment, state apparatus and the economy, which under ZANU-PF had been collapsed into a single entity.

The task ahead would be a formidable one given the dominant mindset within ZANU-PF and the sources of its legitimacy. As astutely noted by a South African based NGO, ZANU-PF had drawn:

> its legitimacy less from a representative and democratic state than from its legacy in the liberation struggle. The party's conception of sovereignty is thus based on its self-perception as a revolutionary vanguard party that embodies the general will of the people of Zimbabwe, not through elections but because of blood spilled under its auspices during the war of liberation…it

> views itself as a privileged minority that persistently distinguishes itself from the rest of the citizenry through a state it regards as a party state…while it controls this state it also regards itself as above any structures of accountability within it. (Solidarity Peace Trust 2011, 7)

A necessary component of such a reform programme was the dismantling of the deeply entrenched vested interests, systems and structures which had underpinned the way the former ruling party had governed since Independence. During the crisis years these had largely catered to the needs of a small elite whose objective at times seemed to be the maintenance of high levels of state fragility as a facilitator of elite consolidation of power and profit, and it was clear that the way the state did business would have to be reformed if the necessary gains in terms of recovery were to be made. That these entrenched economic interests, buttressed by ZANU-PF's monopoly of political and coercive power, would not surrender their privileges easily was a foregone conclusion.

Such reform efforts would also have to take place against the backdrop of growing calls, both prior to and following the signing of the GPA, for some form of transitional justice to be launched to hold accountable those responsible for past human rights violations. Such demands emanated from groups within Zimbabwean civil society, as well as international organisations such as Amnesty International. Encouraged by developments such as the establishment of the International Criminal Court and the Special Courts for Rwanda, Sierra Leone and the Former Yugoslavia, and closer to home South Africa's Truth and Reconciliation Commission, they demanded that those responsible for past 'Operations' such as *Gukurahundi*, *Murambatsvina*, and the violence that had accompanied the land invasions and the country's elections since 2000, be brought to book, and that the culture of impunity that had characterised the country's recent past be ended.[19]

However, the lack of a clear break with the past in 2008–2009, and the compromises reached in order to establish the IG and its cohabitation arrangements, led to what might be characterised as an 'arrested transition'. On a practical level, for the opposition parties this meant working in ministries they now shared with ZANU-PF politicians who had been appointed as their seniors or deputies, and with a senior civil service (permanent secretaries and departmental directors) that had been appointed by the former ruling party on the basis less of their technical competence than their loyalty to ZANU-PF. Any reform initiatives were thus forced to take place within the context of high levels of mistrust between the uneasy partners. Mistrust also characterised relations between citizens (and in particular the country's private sector) and the state given the country's long history of policy unpredictability, which meant that the credibility of reform initiatives was handicapped at the outset by significant scepticism.

A number of additional constraints faced the opposition parties as they entered the IG. Firstly there was the inexperience of their new ministers and deputy ministers, and in particular their lack of economic expertise, forcing them to rely on civil servants whose professionalism and loyalty could not be taken for granted. Secondly, the reality of an arrested transition and lack of a clear break with the past made the essential work of rebuilding relations with international capital markets, foreign investors and the donor community all the more problematic as many investors adopted a wait and see attitude, and international donors took a guarded approach to the new dispensation.

Concerns regarding the irreversibility of any future reforms in general, and particularly the protection of foreign investment and proper use of any international development assistance that might be forthcoming given Zimbabwe's high levels of fiduciary risk, were to loom large in the calculations of many external actors, and condition the amount of resources that the IG could raise for recovery initiatives. As regards international development assistance, it was also unfortunate timing for Zimbabwe that the global financial crisis of 2008 would see a downsizing of the aid budgets of the major Western bilateral donors, accompanied by increased demands from their respective domestic constituencies that such resources as might be provided should be subjected to ever stricter criteria in terms of 'value for money'.

Finally, there was the ever present risk of the 'Zanufication' of those MDC members who had made it into government and other positions of power, i.e. their gradual adoption of the patterns of behaviour of their former ZANU-PF foes, and now 'colleagues'. For the new MDC holders of office, there was the danger that once in power this might result in an inflated sense of entitlement, the misuse of public office and appropriation of state resources for personal gain, and the development of their own systems of patronage.

In the event, the capacity of Zimbabwe's extractive political and economic institutions established by Mugabe and ZANU-PF to endure in the face of pressures for reform was to prove formidable. Their resilience was an indication of the extent to which they had become entrenched in national life, and able to adapt to changed circumstances while preserving their essential nature and role as props of the regime. What happened during the lifetime of the IG lends support to the observations made by Acemoglu and Robinson in their comparative study of state success and failure, namely that the "synergy between extractive economic and political institutions create a vicious circle, where extractive institutions, once in place, tend to persist" (Acemoglu and Robinson 2013, 430).

Notes

1. Founded in 2006, the MDC-M party was a breakaway faction of the MDC led by Arthur Mutambara, (hence the M in the party's acronym), following internal disagreements on a range of issues, with the old rump MDC led by Morgan Tsvangirai thereafter adopting the MDC-T label. The leadership of the breakaway faction would subsequently be taken over by Welshman Ncube, and the party become known as MDC-N.
2. In one particularly cynical effort at 'spin', in the course of one of the redenomination exercises the RBZ printed and circulated posters showing the new currency under the slogan 'From Zeros to Heroes'. This took place at the same time as notices were going up in whatever public conveniences still existed requesting the public to refrain from using Zimbabwean banknotes as toilet paper as these were blocking the flush toilets.
3. As a result of the boom in global commodity prices in the 2000s, and notwithstanding falling production figures, the value of mineral exports increased from 27 percent in 2000 to 53 percent by 2008 of export revenues. This was accompanied by a decline in the value of both commercial agricultural and manufacturing exports, which fell from 72 percent to 43 percent over the same period (Hawkins 2009, 1).

4. In contrast, and an indication of the enormous funding gap that had opened up during the second half of the 2000s, in 2011 the Ministry of Health calculated that in order for Zimbabwe to provide an essential package of health services and achieve its health-related Millennium Development Goals (MDGs), the country would have to spend (and should have been spending) US$34 per capita per annum on health (GOZ 2011, 16).
5. The Registrar-General's party political affiliation was subsequently to become even clearer when he was accredited as a ZANU-PF delegate to a Constitutional Conference in 2012. It was only after the 2008 elections that the full extent of manipulation of the electoral register was revealed. As a result of the work of an investigative journalist working for the South African Institute of Race Relations, the roll used in 2008 was shown to have a total of 5,727,902 registered voters. This figure is highly suspect given the large numbers of Zimbabweans who had left the country, estimated at between 3 and 4 million. Given the historical average of some 60 percent of Zimbabweans under the voting age of 18, and even accepting a higher range figure of 10 million Zimbabweans remaining in the country, this would leave a maximum possible electorate of 4 million. The researcher concluded that the difference would mean that "Such fictitious votes could be added to totals wherever Zanu-PF was vulnerable" (Johnson 2011, 9). These figures were shown to be even more implausible when the updated electoral roll for 2010 was examined. This showed an increase in the size of the electorate of close to 140,000, and in addition contained 132,540 persons over the age of 90 and 41,000 voters over the age of 100 in a country where life expectancy had dropped to an average of between 42–45 years by the second half of the 2000s. As the journalist opined this was "an impossible figure. The United Kingdom, with a total population of over 60 million and an average life expectancy more than 30 years longer than Zimbabwe's, has only 10,000 centenarians" (Ibid., 7).
6. Simba Makoni was a well-respected technocrat, a former Finance Minister from 2000 to 2002 and member of ZANU-PF's Politburo. He announced in February 2008 that he would run as an independent candidate in the Presidential race, and was soon thereafter expelled from the ruling party.
7. The JOC brought together the heads of Zimbabwe's police, prison services, defence forces and intelligence bodies.

8. In the years immediately prior to the 2008 elections there had been regular debates, led by civil society and church groups, on the appropriate forms of transitional justice that might be applied in a post-Mugabe era. These were often extensively reported in the local independent press, as well as Zimbabwean radio stations operating outside Zimbabwe, and the securocrats would have been aware of such discussions (see Chap. 11).
9. In one incident on 25 April 2008, the police raided the National Headquarters of the MDC-T in Harare, with large numbers of people being arrested, many of them having sought refuge there from the ongoing political violence in rural areas.
10. According to the Act, an indigenous person was defined as "any person who, before 18th April 1980 [the date of Zimbabwe's Independence] was disadvantaged by unfair discrimination on the grounds of his or her race, and any descendant of such person, and includes any company, association, syndicate or partnership of which indigenous Zimbabweans form the majority of members or hold the controlling interest" (GOZ 2008a, Section 2(1)).
11. One possible contributing factor in Mugabe's reluctant decision to eventually share power, over and above that of external pressure, was that ZANU-PF realised that it had lost any international credibility in terms of management of the economy, while the MDC-T could assist with the necessary stabilisation by helping to turn on the taps of international development assistance and also help to secure the removal of Western sanctions against the ZANU-PF leadership.
12. Mugabe could usually count on the friendship of those Southern African leaders who headed up political parties born out of a former liberation movement past. These included ruling parties in South Africa, Angola, Mozambique and Namibia with longstanding links with ZANU-PF, and with whom Mugabe's anti-imperialist discourse and inter-African solidarity still resonated, as well as others such as Joseph Kabila of the DRC, who like his father had benefited from Zimbabwean military assistance during that country's civil wars. In contrast other regional leaders, who did not share that history of armed struggle, such as Ian Khama of Botswana, were more openly critical of Mugabe and his policies. For a time during the period between the first and second rounds of the 2008 Presidential elections, Tsvangirai was to base himself in Gaborone, and the Botswana government pointedly refused to recognise the results of the June 2008 run-off as legitimate.

13. Most notable amongst these efforts was the launching of the New Partnership for Africa's Development (NEPAD) in 2001. The latter reflected the African Union's vision of a continental framework for accelerating socio-economic development and cooperation amongst African countries. Central to the framework was the recognition that commitments to good governance, democracy and human rights were essential for the establishment of an environment conducive for economic growth and social progress. One of its offshoots was the African Peer Review Mechanism (APRM), an AU instrument set up in 2003 for those member states that voluntarily acceded to it (and as of this writing Zimbabwe still has not) which would ensure adherence to the principles contained in the AU's 2002 Declaration on Democracy, Political, Economic and Corporate Governance, and allow scrutiny by fellow Africans of progress in terms of meeting the standards set out in the Declaration. The latter, *inter alia*, referred to the importance of the rule of law and protection of the independence of judiciaries, transparent and accountable governments, and the right to participation in free and credible democratic political processes.
14. Known in popular parlance as the 'Green Bombers' due to the colour of their fatigues, these youths gained national and international notoriety in the aftermath of the first round of the 2008 elections when they played a key role, together with the war veterans, in the anti-MDC violence.
15. Mugabe also delayed swearing in the new Parliament in which ZANU-PF had lost its majority. Equally significant was his refusal to swear in Tsvangirai's appointee as new Deputy Minister of Agriculture, Roy Bennett, the white MDC-T's Treasurer who comfortably won his seat in the 2008 elections and who was known as an implacable foe of ZANU-PF. Days after his nomination for the post Bennett found himself in jail on the grounds of having committed 'treason', and though subsequently acquitted he went into exile in South Africa. His access to confidential files in the Ministry of Agriculture might have proved profoundly embarrassing to ZANU-PF in terms of details as to who had benefited from the land reform programme, who had breached the law in terms of owning multiple farms, and who had enjoyed RBZ largesse to support agricultural production. Most notorious, however, was ZANU-PF's reluctance to relinquish control over the Ministry of Home Affairs which had oversight over the police. The deadlock over this posi-

tion threatened to scupper the whole agreement, though an incongruous and profoundly dysfunctional compromise was eventually found which involved the ministry being co-chaired by two ministers, one from ZANU-PF and the other from MDC-T.

16. The distance between the two sides was most evident in ZANU-PF's reluctance to relinquish control of the justice delivery system, with Mugabe insisting on appointing the Attorney-General and the Supreme Court judges (understandable in light of the aforementioned concerns within ZANU-PF and the security force regarding the possibility that they might be held accountable for past misdemeanours), while the stated objective of both MDCs was to restore the rule of law. The latter entailed, *inter alia*, ensuring the independence of the judiciary, fairness in the application of the law, equality before the law, an end to arbitrary arrests, and reducing the scope for discretion in the behaviour of the government and its agents.
17. In the context of the *de facto* and eventual *de jure* dollarization of the economy, monetary policy could no longer be set by the Reserve Bank, while at the same time the scope for the Central Bank to engage in fiscal policy through continued quasi-fiscal activities via expansion of the money supply was also eliminated. Analysts at the time interpreted Mugabe's decision to retain the RBZ Governor within the fold of ZANU-PF as based on Gono's in-depth and highly sensitive knowledge of the internal financial dealings of the Party, and of those who had benefited from his largesse.
18. On this point, the GPA stated that "the prosecuting authorities will expedite the determination as to whether or not there is sufficient evidence to warrant the prosecution or keeping on remand of all persons accused of politically related offences arising out of or connected with the March and June 2008 elections" (GOZ 2008b, Article 18.5(j)).
19. The general public (and more so the ranks of ZANU-PF and the security forces) were well aware of these international legal developments which were extensively reported by the independent media in Zimbabwe. Notable amongst cases were those of the former President of Liberia, Charles Taylor, indicted in 2006 by the Special Court for Sierra Leone for war crimes and crimes against humanity and eventually extradited to the International Criminal Court (ICC) in the Hague where he stood trial, as well as that of the President of Sudan, Omar Al-Bashir, the first sitting Head of State to be indicted by the ICC for war crimes and crimes against humanity perpetrated during the conflict in Darfur.

References

Acemoglu, Daron, and James A. Robinson. 2013. *Why Nations Fail – The Origins of Power, Prosperity and Poverty*. London: Profile Books.

Bratton, Michael, and Eldred Masunungure. 2011. *The Anatomy of Political Predation: Leaders, Elites and Coalitions in Zimbabwe, 1980–2010*, Developmental Leadership Program Research Paper, No. 9, January. University of Birmingham, UK.

Chambers, K. 2009. Zimbabwe's Battle Against Cholera. *The Lancet*, Special Report 373 (9668, March 21): 993–994.

Chitoyi, Knox. 2009. *The Case for Security Sector Reform in Zimbabwe*, Occasional Paper, September. London: Royal United Services Institute.

GOZ. 2008a. *Indigenisation and Economic Empowerment Act [Chapter 14:33]*. Harare.

———. 2008b. *Agreement Between the Zimbabwe African National Union-Patriotic Front (ZANU-PF) and the Two Movement for Democratic Change (MDC) Formations, on Resolving the Challenges Facing Zimbabwe*, September 15. Harare.

———. 2009. *National Health Strategy 2009–2013*. Harare.

———. 2011. *Health Transition Fund*. Harare.

Hawkins, Tony. 2009. *The Mining Sector in Zimbabwe and Its Potential Contribution to Recovery*, Comprehensive Economic Recovery in Zimbabwe Working Paper Series, No. 1. Harare: United Nations Development Programme.

Hawkins, Tony, and Daniel Ndlela. 2009. *Foreign Trade, Competitiveness and the Balance of Payments*, Comprehensive Economic Recovery in Zimbabwe Working Paper Series, No. 6. Harare: United Nations Development Programme.

IMF. 2009. *Zimbabwe: 2009 Article IV Consultation – Staff Report*, Country Report No. 09/139, May. Washington, DC.

———. 2010. *World Economic Outlook Database 2010*. Washington, DC: IMF.

Johnson, R.W. 2011. *Preventing Electoral Fraud in Zimbabwe – A Report on the Voters' Roll in Zimbabwe*, May. Johannesburg: South African Institute of Race Relations.

Pan-African Parliament. 2008. *Report on the Presidential Run-Off Elections and House of Assembly By-Elections, Republic of Zimbabwe*, June 27. Pan-African Parliament Election Observer Mission. Midrand, South Africa.

Solidarity Peace Trust. 2008. *Punishing Dissent, Silencing Citizens: The Zimbabwe Elections 2008*. Johannesburg.

———. 2011. *The Hard Road to Reform*. Johannesburg.
The Standard. 2008. I'll Only Salute Mugabe, Not Sell-Outs: Chiwenga, March 9. Harare. http://www.zimbabwesituation.com/old/mar9a_2008.html#Z12.
The Times. 2008. Robert Mugabe Warns Zimbabwe Voters: How Can a Pen Fight a Gun?, June 17. London.
Todd, Charles, et al. 2010. What Is the Way Forward for Health in Zimbabwe? *The Lancet* 375 (375): 606–609.
USAID. 2010. *Health System Assessment Zimbabwe*, June. Washington, DC.
Washington Post. 2008. Inside Mugabe's Violent Crackdown, July 5.
Zimbabwe Independent. 2008. Zesn Withdraws from Observing Polls, June 27. https://www.theindependent.co.zw/2008/06/27/zesn-withdraws-from-observing-polls/.

10

The Challenges of Cohabitation

Amidst much fanfare, and not a little popular scepticism given that many saw it as simply the latest in a long list of discredited turnaround strategies, in March 2009 the new IG launched its Short-Term Emergency Recovery Programme (STERP). The overarching strategic objective of this multi-sectoral programme was that of restoring economic growth. This was to be done by freeing up markets and prices, increasing levels of savings and investment, and which together with the exercise of strong fiscal discipline and improved revenue collection would strengthen government's revenue base. This, in turn, would allow government to rebuild the country's dilapidated infrastructure and restart basic service delivery. The enormity of the STERP's resource requirements was made clear in the document, which set out a budget for the necessary priority actions costed at over US$5 billion, higher than Zimbabwe's 2008 GDP of US$3.18 billion in nominal terms according to the IMF, and many times a multiple of severely constrained government revenues.

Starting from such a low government revenue base, and given a profoundly debilitated private sector, it was not only obvious that the right macroeconomic conditions would have to be put in place to restart

M. Simpson, T. Hawkins, *The Primacy of Regime Survival*,
https://doi.org/10.1007/978-3-319-72520-8_10

growth, but that the country's investment climate would have to be significantly improved for the necessary recapitalisation to take place:

> The Inclusive Government is, therefore, instituting measures to guarantee the consistency and predictability of the country's business environment targeted at both domestic and foreign investors. (GOZ 2009, 56)

Given the dire state of public finances, it was also evident that for STERP to succeed required substantial injections of ODA, which in turn meant rebuilding of bridges with the BWIs and Western bilateral development partners.

Early Gains

A number of early gains were made in terms of a return to a semblance of economic normality. Most importantly, there was the almost immediate quashing of inflation following dollarization (officially a multi-currency regime including the South African Rand, the Euro, the British Pound and the Botswana Pula in addition to the US Dollar, though the latter became the principal currency). Though this was officially announced in the STERP in March 2009, it was in fact simply a belated acceptance of reality.[1] In April 2009, the Zimbabwe dollar was declared to no longer be legal tender, and the IG's first national budget of 2009 was denominated in US dollars, with the Reserve Bank of Zimbabwe (RBZ) and the overall banking system maintaining accounts in US dollars, and the Stock Exchange trading in that currency.

As a result of a combination of measures such as prices and import liberalisation and elimination of surrender requirements of exports earnings to the RBZ, there was a rapid resumption of growth, with official figures showing GDP growth of 8.7 percent in 2009, 15.4 percent in 2010, 16.3 percent in 2011 and 13.6 percent in 2012, as a result of which GDP (in constant US$) grew from US$4.41 billion to US$14.05 billion over the same period (World Bank Database). Capacity utilisation in the manufacturing sector, which had been estimated to have fallen to below 10 percent in 2008, increased to 32 percent in 2009 (CZI 2009, 2).

Three additional aspects of economic policy outlined in STERP represented radical departures from that of the previous government, and would also yield some early positive results. Firstly, there was a firm commitment to the elimination of the central bank's quasi-fiscal activities via the adoption of a cash-budgeting approach to public expenditure, i.e. the enforced matching of expenditures to revenue. Secondly, and making a virtue out of necessity given dollarization, the new government committed to a policy of "no printing of money" which effectively restricted the RBZ to its mandated regulatory and supervisory role, it no longer even being able to play the role of lender of the last resort given its lack of reserves (GOZ 2009, 83).[2] Thirdly, the STERP committed government to new levels of transparency and accountability in the management of public funds, most notably resources earmarked for the STERP. These would be channelled to the Consolidated Revenue Fund (CRF) of the Treasury, and therefore placed under the control of the Ministry of Finance, while a programme implementation unit would be established in order to ensure "transparency and full accountability in the use and management of resources mobilised for funding STERP" (Ibid., 120). The latter decision was clearly an attempt by the new MDC-T Minister of Finance to exercise firm control over revenue, as well as to convince Zimbabwe's estranged international development partners of the seriousness of his intent to restore stability and transparency to the country's wrecked public finances, and thereby address their fiduciary risk concerns regarding financial support to the IG.[3]

In addition to macroeconomic stabilisation and a resumption of growth, early gains accrued to the health and education sectors, the revitalisation of which figured prominently as key national objectives in the STERP. Both MDCs had strongly stated their commitment to the immediate improvement of the welfare of the Zimbabwean people during their election campaigns, and affirmed the responsibility of the state for social provisioning. The fact that the Ministries of Health and Education were headed up by members of MDC-T and MDC-M respectively helped convince a number of Western donors that they could resume the channelling of funds to support those sectors, and thereby move away from what had previously been strictly emergency humanitarian assistance flows to Zimbabwe.

The supply-side response from the donors was quick. Following the establishment of the IG, the Ministry of Education set up an Education Trust Fund (ETF). In order to allay donor concerns regarding the channelling of money through government systems, under the ETF all funds were managed by UNICEF which accounted for expenditures through regular reports to donors, and also conducted its procurement according to UN regulations and not government tender procedures. As a result, Western donors eventually felt sufficiently comfortable with procedures to fund the programme to the tune of US$54 million. The main activity of the ETF was to ensure that schools had the wherewithal in terms of didactic materials such as textbooks and other teaching equipment to reopen. A total of 23 million textbooks for both primary and secondary had been procured by October 2011, such that the ratio of pupils to textbooks improved dramatically to 1:1 from the previous low of 10:1 in 2009 (UNICEF 2011).

A similarly creative scheme was established for the health sector. The Ministry of Health under a new MDC-T minister was quick to reach out to donors, and sought their technical advice. A National Health Strategy (NHS) 2009–2013 was rapidly developed. This was candid in terms of its assessment of the severely debilitated state of the sector and poor health status of the Zimbabwean population, as well as comprehensive, realistic and technically sound in terms of proposed remedial measures.

Reflecting a Primary Health Care approach, and focused on ensuring equity, the NHS reflected a commitment to rapidly improve the health status of all Zimbabweans through the provision of a basic package of health services. The strategy became a widely accepted template for external support, and the rapid and positive response of donors was a clear demonstration to Zimbabweans of the benefits of re-engagement with the Western donor community. A donor funded Health Workers Retention Scheme (HWRS), initially launched during the 2008 cholera epidemic, recognised the impact of low wages on levels of absenteeism and out-migration amongst health workers. The Scheme was expanded, and through salary supplementations the gains were soon visible as staff returned to their places of work and health centres reopened throughout the country. A Health Transition Fund (HTF) was subsequently established, again managed by UNICEF, allowing Western bilateral donors both to overcome their self-imposed restrictions on direct development assistance to the Zimbabwean government – as opposed to life-saving humanitarian aid – as well allaying their concerns around the proper use of the resources provided. In addition to improved salaries for health sector workers, funds under the HTF were used to improve the availability of medicines, medical supplies, equipment, and the quality of training and health sector planning.

The positive impact of such cooperation between the new IG and Western health sector donors was soon evident. For example, between February–March 2009 and April–June 2011, the percentage of health facilities suffering from a complete stock-out of essential medicines and health commodities dropped from 3 percent to 0 percent, while the percentage of those with over 80 percent of essential medicines and health commodities rose from 8.3 percent to 82.5 percent over the same period (Takavarasha 2011, 20). In terms of human resources, the average vacancy rate for nurses, which stood at 31 percent in 2008, dropped to 14 percent by 2010 (DFID 2012, 18). The percentage of health facilities with functional maternal units increased from 85 percent in April–June 2009 to 99.5 percent by July–December 2010, and the percentage of Institutional Live Births (i.e. the percentage of live birth deliveries in health facilities) rose from an average of 51.4 percent in 2009 to 76.2 percent in 2011 (Ibid., 67).

Early successes were also registered in terms of improved freedom of information through the loosening of previous constraints operating on the independent media. There had been a provision in the GPA of September 2008 for a new Zimbabwe Media Commission to be established, and the MDC-T had committed itself to the repeal of the Orwellian Access to Information and Protection of Privacy Act (AIPPA) of 2002 which had been used to muzzle the independent press. While the MDC-T met with strong resistance from ZANU-PF in terms of its efforts to repeal AIPPA, and was ultimately unsuccessful, some progress in terms of greater media freedom was nevertheless made.

A number of previously banned newspapers were able to relaunch, licenses were granted to new ones, and restrictions lifted on Western broadcasting agencies such as the BBC and CNN. While the situation remained far from satisfactory, with the state media continuing to be highly partisan and broadcasting ZANU-PF propaganda, and with the Ministry of Media, Information and Publicity remaining in ZANU-PF's hands, the independent media was nevertheless able to report on national developments with relative ease compared to the situation prior to the establishment of the IG.

The Opposition also faced ZANU-PF obstructionism concerning the repeal of the equally Orwellian Public Order and Security Act (POSA), which had been invoked on numerous occasions by previous ZANU-PF governments to restrict the operations of other political parties, trade unions, and civil and human rights campaigners. Nevertheless, while the POSA was to remain on the statute books during the period of the IG, the overall political decompression of the period, added to the need for ZANU-PF to be seen by the guarantors of the GPA (in particular South Africa) to be respecting the spirit of that agreement, meant that the police were to adopt a more relaxed attitude in terms of applying POSA's provisions.

Reducing Fragility: Long-Term and Binding Constraints

While there were indications of a rebound in the economy following macroeconomic stabilisation, accompanied by improvements in the country's performance in terms of social provisioning, subsequent developments were to show that these in fact constituted the easy and quick wins. It gradually became clear that such progress was not an indication of a long-term and sustainable reversal of the country's fragility, let alone that ZANU-PF had relinquished its hold on power in any meaningful way, nor that its capacity to obstruct any progress that it saw as threatening its ability to turn back the clock at any moment of its choosing had been seriously weakened. A team of Zimbabwean economists were to presciently caution in 2008, just prior to the formation of the IG, that:

> profound damage has occurred over time, some aspects of which are easily reversible, others less so. For example, while the correction of price distortions and the restoration of reliable supplies of water and electricity may

> lead to a quick rebound in the mining sector, tourism and in some areas of manufacturing, the damage done to public sector capacity and the loss of the country's human capital base may well take decades to reverse…This cautionary note is necessary in order to guard against misplaced enthusiasm and a misreading of positive signals in the early years of a recovery scenario. While there will be a bounce back effect, possibly a strong one as current idle capacity is brought on stream…this may well peter out unless the necessary measures are taken to sustain this rebound…an early rebound in a post-crisis scenario might be misinterpreted…as translating into a sound and sustainable longer-term growth model. (UNDP 2008, 5–6)

The full extent of the damage inflicted during the crisis years on the country's infrastructure, its markets and productive sectors, its human capital base and institutional capacity, its domestic and external finances, its economic competitiveness ratings, governance and legal systems, as well as the full extent of the 'looting' that had taken place, only became clearer as access to information improved following the inauguration of the IG. MDC ministers demanded to see data that truly reflected the reality of the sectors over which they had been assigned responsibility, as did the IFIs and bilateral donors as they sought to re-engage with the Ministry of Finance under its new MDC-T leadership.

The uneasy cohabitation between MDC ministers and senior civil servants who owed their sinecures to ZANU-PF, inevitably contributed to tensions as bureaucratic obstructionism quickly made itself felt.[4] The difficulties facing reform-minded elements within the IG as they sought to assess the full extent of regression, and design and implement remedial measures, were compounded by a dysfunctional government as political tensions between members of the enforced cohabitation arrangement ebbed and flowed. It quickly became clear that the systems and procedures inherited from the past were deeply entrenched, and that strong vested interests were going to prove extremely difficult to dislodge.

In mid-October 2009, and therefore less than 8 months after the swearing in of the IG, MDC-T announced that it was suspending its cooperation with ZANU-PF, and would boycott meetings of the Cabinet and Council of Ministers. The reasons given were ZANU-PF's obstructionism and its failure to adhere to key elements of the GPA, including the need for consultations between the principals prior to the appointment of senior state officials such as the Attorney-General, a GPA provision which Mugabe had studiously ignored from the very beginning of the IG, as well as the fact that the NSC had been convened by Mugabe only once since its establishment nine months earlier (*SW Africa Radio* 2009).

After the October 2009 walkout, and though the MDC-T ministers and deputy ministers were eventually to return to their positions under SADC pressure, tensions surrounding the fundamental issues of constitutional, electoral and security sector reform – vital to the MDC-T but on which no discernible progress was being made – were to continue to plague relations with ZANU-PF. A renewed SADC sanctioned mediation effort by the new South African President, Jacob Zuma, eventually led to detailed 'roadmap' of reforms in 2011. The roadmap was intended to lead to both a new constitution and new elections, and raised SADC's hope that the 'Zimbabwe question' could then be finally put to rest. Even with SADC pressure, however, reforms continued to be painfully slow as ZANU-PF fought rear-guard actions on every front.

Foreign Debt

The MDC-T incumbent of the post of Minister of Finance, Tendai Biti, found that the problem of the country's foreign debt burden he had inherited was to prove intractable. Furthermore, he also soon realised that his efforts to make progress on this issue were subject to intense ZANU-PF interference.

It is worth recalling, as detailed in Chap. 8, that by the end of 2008 the IMF had estimated that Zimbabwe's total public and publicly guaranteed external debt stood at US$5.1 billion dollars representing 166 percent of the country's estimated GDP, while arrears on its total external debt represented 120 percent of GDP. Zimbabwe was therefore in a situation of severe debt distress when the IG took office in February 2009, and it was clear that a comprehensive solution would be required to deal with the problem. The new Finance Minister hoped that a debt relief programme agreed with creditors might also potentially unlock new flows of development assistance to deal with some of the country's critical recovery backlogs, and that as Harare demonstrated its commitment to settle its arrears this would have positive signalling effects and strengthen the overall investment climate and Zimbabwe's credit ratings.

When he took office, Biti initially indicated he was willing to follow the tried and tested HIPC route to debt relief outlined in Chap. 8, and recommended that Zimbabwe enter the process. However, this soon ran into problems as ZANU-PF Ministers in Cabinet raised strong objections to the proposal, with their positions widely reported in the state media. Relying on nationalist rhetoric, they expressed an unwillingness to accept that the country should be classified as a HIPC, even though it objectively (and easily) met the necessary qualifying criteria in terms of GDP per capita and its debt burden as a percentage of both GDP and export receipts.

The more vociferous amongst the ZANU-PF leadership chose to characterise the new Finance Minister's efforts as another example of the MDC-T acting as lackeys of Western imperialism, with debt relief associated with a 'regime change' agenda. Their objections were couched in the language of 'economic sovereignty', and they argued (all evidence to the contrary) that Zimbabwe was in fact a rich country that should not be grouped with other low-income countries. Copious references were also made to the negative consequences the last time Zimbabwe had extensively engaged with the BWIs, namely the ESAP of the 1990s, while the impact of international 'sanctions' was put forward as the key explanation for the country's economic difficulties rather than the ruling party's own mismanagement of the economy.

A more likely, if mundane, explanation for the objections raised, lay in the understandable reluctance of those with a long history in government to have to address questions as to how Zimbabwe had become so poor under the rule of ZANU-PF, how it had become so indebted, who had contracted loans and on what terms, and what use these funds had been put to. In regard to the latter, and following the installation of the IG, there were soon voices within civil society demanding that an audit be conducted on Zimbabwe's external debt. Such public voices were encouraged by the fact that the new Minister of Finance set up a Debt Management Office in his ministry in order to reconcile data on the country's debt, precisely because of serious problems with lack of information regarding the full extent of the country's indebtedness, and the conditions under which loans had been contracted.[5]

There was clearly also growing disquiet within ZANU-PF ranks that one of the requirements for debt relief under HIPC would be a joint IMF/World Bank Staff Monitored Programme (SMP). This would have implied a level of oversight and intrusion by the BWIs into Zimbabwe's economic affairs which ZANU-PF saw, notwithstanding the power-sharing arrangement, as its continued preserve.[6] As the debates on how to deal with the foreign debt problems continued both within Cabinet and outside, so the total arrears stock mounted as additional principal and interest payments became due. In 2012, IMF figures showed that between 2010 and 2011 the country's total external debt had risen from US$9.018 billion to US$10.727 billion, with arrears alone accounting for US$6.344 billion of the latter figure (IMF 2012, 3).

Biti was eventually forced to compromise, with the IG developing the Zimbabwe Accelerated Arrears clearance, Debt and Development Strategy (ZAADDS), officially launched in March 2012. The document outlined a dual-track hybrid debt relief strategy, premised on the simultaneous pursuit of "traditional debt relief" and the "leveraging of the country's natural resources to achieve sustainable economic development" (GOZ 2012, xvii). Details as to how precisely the country's natural resources (mainly its mineral wealth) were to be used for debt relief purposes were conspicuous by their absence, while the option of engaging with the International Financial Institutions (IFIs) under a SMP was significantly not referenced in the strategy.

The extent of the splits within the IG, and indications of how dysfunctional it was, were evident in the mixed messages individual members of government sent out to domestic and external audiences, While ZANU-PF sought to ensure that the IFIs were kept at arm's length and made clear its position through the state media, the Minister of Finance was more sanguine about the benefits of re-engagement with these institutions in his search for a solution to the country's debt distress, and also publicly shared his views. Therefore, while the IMF Article IV consultation report of 2011 noted that "The Authorities have expressed interest in a staff-monitored programme" (IMF 2011, 24), it was unclear to observers where exactly decision-making power rested.

However, notwithstanding ZANU-PF intransigence, cold water was regularly poured on the idea that Zimbabwe could keep the IFIs at a distance, and still resolve the problem of its debt overhang through the use of its mineral wealth, by following a 'homegrown' heterodox path. The IFIs repeatedly reiterated that renewed access to funding would not be possible until Zimbabwe settled its debt arrears, while the IMF also pointed out the fundamental flaw in one key assumption of the ZAADDS by noting that "the net present value of Zimbabwe's mineral wealth was less than that of the country's total external debt" (Ibid., 24).

While some restrictions were lifted by the IFIs following the formation of the IG – such as restoration of Zimbabwe's IMF voting rights in 2010 after the elimination of exchange controls and multiple exchange rates which had previously constituted breaches of the IMF's Articles of Agreement, as well as reactivation of IMF technical assistance in 2012 – Zimbabwe's external debt situation continued to deteriorate as there was no comprehensive resolution of its arrears problem upon which parties within the IG, and the IG and Zimbabwe's creditors, could agree.[7] It therefore remained unable to access Western donor and IFI concessional development finance, and the country had to resort increasingly to external non-concessional financing.[8]

Ghost Workers and the Securocrats

Further evidence of the degree to which ZANU-PF had managed, over the course of its long monopoly over of power, to deeply entrench its support structures, was provided by post-2009 developments in the areas of civil service and security sector reform. Both these areas proved to be highly contentious ones, in which reform-minded elements within the IG found it extremely difficult (and eventually impossible in the case of security sector reforms) to make any headway in terms of dismantling these ZANU-PF props.

Mirroring the phenomenon of 'ghost voters' on the electoral roll in the 2008 elections referenced in Chap. 9, there had been persistent rumours prior to the formation of the IG that previous ZANU-PF governments had boosted the ruling party's support base (and the number of shock troops that it was able to throw into the fray in the 2008 elections and the second presidential round) by placing large numbers of its youth militia on the public sector payroll as civil servants. A 2010 audit, conducted by an international accounting firm and financed by the World Bank, confirmed that large numbers of ZANU-PF Youth League members had been recruited into the civil service in the run-up to the 2008r elections, many of whom did not possess the necessary educational qualifications to make even the lowest grade of the civil service. Though the report was then embargoed by Cabinet despite repeated calls by the opposition-dominated Parliament for its release, figures as high as 70,000 'ghost workers' made into the independent press, which if true represented around 30 percent of the total civil service's authorised establishment.

The state-controlled Herald newspaper predictably argued that the "statistical misrepresentation of facts on the ground is a clear sign of Western machination on (sic) Zimbabwe" (*The Herald* 2011). The Ministry of Public Service subsequently conducted its own audit. This served to confirm that large numbers of youth (between 6,000 and 7,000) had been incorporated into the civil service 'irregularly' by the ZANU-PF controlled Ministry of Youth Development, Indigenisation and Empowerment prior to the 2008 elections, though it was not until March 2012 that they were removed from the government payroll.

The difficulties thrown up by this inherited problem impacted negatively on recovery efforts in a number of ways. On the one hand the IMF had, soon after the establishment of the IG, flagged the issue of ghost workers as one which needed to be resolved urgently as a precondition for a stock-taking exercise that might lead to an SMP. Positive results in this area were seen, both by the IFIs and the Western donor community, as a significant progress indicator in terms of overhauling the country's Public Financial Management systems. Delays caused by ZANU-PF obstructionism in resolving the issue represented yet another obstacle in the path of the country's re-engagement with the international donor community, and only served to compound their fiduciary risk concerns.

In addition, there was the drain on the public purse of these ghost workers. There were those who had been irregularly employed such as the youth militia, those who were found to not even exist, and those who were deceased but whose salaries were still being drawn to the benefit of unknown persons. This scandal erupted at a time when the Treasury was struggling under the cash-budgeting approach to cover on a monthly basis the public sector wage bill, and when the Finance Minister's reluctance to grant wage increases was quickly seized upon by the state media and trumpeted as a sign of MDC-T's indifference to the plight of workers. The drain on the fiscus of ghost workers, and the weight of the overall public sector wage bill in the budget, meant less was available for essential capital expenditures, in particular investments in both productive and social infrastructure, as well as essential maintenance. Employment costs were estimated by the IMF in 2010 to consume 68 percent of total revenue. By 2011, Zimbabwe's civil service wage bill as a percentage of total government expenditure was the highest in Sub-Saharan Africa (IMF 2012, 23).

The difficulties faced by the MDC-T Finance Minister to overcome such ZANU-PF obstructionism were unsurprisingly interpreted by external observers as an indication of the real balance of power within government notwithstanding the supposedly equitable power-sharing arrangement, and one that was not favouring the MDCs.[9] They were also left to draw their own conclusions regarding the prospects of success and irreversibility of the reform measures that the MDCs were attempting to introduce. Such conclusions further contributed to the wait and see attitude on the part of Western donors on the provision of significant amounts of development assistance, and of FDI in the case of investors.

The Poisoned Chalice and 'Zanufication' of the MDC

After years spent in the political wilderness, the establishment of the IG provided an opportunity for members of the MDC groupings to both exercise power (even if constrained by ZANU-PF's red lines) as well as enjoy the trappings of office. It was unsurprising, even if disappointing to many, that some MDC members should have taken to the latter with alacrity, and quickly came to display patterns of behaviour that were all too similar to those of ZANU-PF. This was to become true of members of the Opposition at all levels, from its leaders, its ministers and deputy ministers, members of parliament and those in local government.

The phenomenon clearly demonstrated the extent to which ZANU-PF attitudes towards the public purse, the erosion of the ethics that were supposed to underpin the exercise of public office, the self-seeking and intolerant political culture and rise in corruption which had taken root during the years of ZANU-PF dominance, had pervaded wider society and came to be considered the norm. It is also worth remembering that in the past many in the ranks of the Opposition had themselves been part of ZANU-PF structures before their individual acts of dissidence, and as such could not but have absorbed traces of the governance ethos of the ruling party.

What did catch many observers by surprise was the speed with which the Opposition's commitments to frugality, sound and transparent management of public resources, and proclaimed concern for the downtrodden, were discredited by growing evidence of members jostling for a space at the trough. Though less obvious when seen in isolation, each incident of malfeasance and greed seemed to indicate a process of 'Zanufication' was underway, particularly within the MDC-T.

This meant an additional obstacle to the recovery effort was erected, as it damaged in the eyes of the public the credibility of MDC-T's stated commitment to transparency, good governance and improving the welfare of the Zimbabwean people. It also meant that the critical rebuilding of trust between governors and the governed was compromised. While it is impossible to know if this reflected a well-thought out strategy by ZANU-PF to co-opt and discredit its opponents through the enticement of largesse and granting of a place for the leadership of the MDC-T in the country's extractive political economy, it was nevertheless the case that this is what occurred, and in the longer-term would prove extremely costly politically to the MDC-T.

MDC-T and MDC-M ministers and deputy ministers in the IG were quickly offered the material benefits of public office in what was already an extremely bloated and costly government by international standards, and certainly one that was excessive for a country with Zimbabwe's poverty levels.[10] An early sign of the absorption by the MDCs of the deeply embedded attitudes towards the public purse of their ZANU-PF partners in government was their decision in 2009 – one widely criticised by rank and file MDC supporters – to accept imported luxury vehicles attached to their positions as new cabinet members. The total fleet was valued at US$20 million, at a time when the country was facing both a dire humanitarian situation with large emergency food assistance needs, and still reeling from the effects of the cholera epidemic.

Reports that Tsvangirai had agreed to the expenditure of significant public funds for the acquisition and upgrading of his new Prime Ministerial official residence, and that much MDC-T time and effort was spent ensuring that Tsvangirai was granted the appropriate number of vehicles and outriders for his motorcade, were also greeted with disdain by many rank and file supporters. Foreign travel became another source of concern to observers sympathetic to the MDCs, as MDC officials, mimicking the longstanding practices of their ZANU-PF colleagues, took every opportunity to travel on official business. The Finance Minister eventually felt compelled to publicly announce in his budget statement of mid-2011 that the total costs of foreign travel for the previous 6 months from January to June 2011 had amounted to a staggering US$29.6 million. This represented 3 percent of total government expenditure, higher than public expenditure on priority capital projects in the areas of energy and water and sanitation (GOZ 2011, 58–61).

That there was more than a grain of truth in the increasing number of accusations that members of both MDCs had joined the ZANU-PF gravy train was confirmed in the course of 2012 when scandals erupted concerning the personal enrichment of a large number of MDC-T local councillors. When 12 MDC-T councillors were eventually expelled from the party, it was revealed that their corrupt practices had ranged from questionable procurement deals and tenders, as well as the awarding of business stands and residential building plots to themselves, friends and relatives (*Zimbabwe Independent* 2012). The revelations were profoundly damaging to the MDC-T, and the ZANU-PF controlled media was not slow to capitalise on the scandal. It severely damaged the credibility of key MDC-T's election commitments, namely that it would restore sanity to public finances, ensure sound management of public assets, and thereby rebuild the frayed social (and more specifically fiscal) contract between the citizenry and the state.

ZANU-PF's long game plan to retain the key levers of power was also greatly facilitated by MDC-T ineptitude, especially at the top, where Prime Minister Morgan Tsvangirai cut an increasingly forlorn and powerless figure, and was depicted as such in the state media which never missed an opportunity to remind the public that Mugabe remained Head of State, Head of Government and Commander in Chief. Tsvangirai was repeatedly outwitted by the President as key aspects of the GPA agenda were either delayed, or manipulated to suit ZANU-PF interests. With the notable MDC-T exceptions of Tendai Biti in his role as Finance Minister, Elton Mangoma as firstly Minister of Economic Planning and Investment Promotion and subsequently as Minister of Energy,[11] and David Coltart[12] from the breakaway MDC-M in his role as Minister of Education, MDC ministers and deputy ministers were manifestly unable to make any significant headway in terms of pushing back against ZANU-PF and ensuring progress in terms of reforms.

Tsvangirai's failure to take an early and principled stand on the issue of the President's refusal to accept the nomination of the MDC-T's Roy Bennett as Deputy Minister of Agriculture (see Chap. 9), was not surprisingly interpreted by ZANU-PF as indicative of his willingness to make major sacrifices in order to keep the IG afloat. As Tsvangirai himself, in a much belated recognition of reality, conceded in an interview in March 2012:

> Mugabe has appointed governors, when in the power-sharing agreement all appointments should be in consultation with me. He has appointed ambassadorial deployments without consulting me. He extended the appointment of some of the key security positions like Commissioner of Police beyond their term without consulting me. The litany of unilateral decisions is endless. (*This is Africa* 2012)

Over the course of the IG, Tsvangirai was compelled to make increasingly frequent – and vain – appeals to SADC, directly to the new South African President Jacob Zuma who had taken over the role of SADC-appointed mediator from his predecessor Mbeki, and to Western and other African governments, in the hope that they might compel Mugabe to fully implement the terms of the GPA. And as the IG ran its course, it became increasingly clear that the diplomatic skills of the MDC-T leadership were also seriously deficient. They consistently misread SADC and AU dynamics and the position of both organisations in regard to the 'Zimbabwe question', failing thereby to understand that the priority of most countries in the region was 'stability', the objective to be rid of an embarrassing problem as soon as possible. This involved cajoling Zimbabwean actors towards a new constitution that was minimally in line with accepted international standards, and on that basis to support elections which could also be declared 'generally free and fair', even if this required accepting that expected ZANU-PF obstructionism would mean implementation of the detailed provisions of the constitution would likely be sorely deficient, and electoral institutions and systems remain largely unreformed.

ZANU-PF increasingly made clear its views on the IG as a necessary but only temporary truce in its efforts to recover its monopoly on power through the positions it took on four key elements of change required by the GPA. These were constitutional and electoral reform and 'national healing' for victims of the country's political violence, the latter seen by many within Zimbabwe's organised civil society as well as both MDCs as an opportunity to launch some form of transitional justice process, and one referred to only obliquely in the GPA, but arguably the *sine qua non* for progress in all other areas, namely security sector reform.

Notes

1. The previous ZANU-PF Minister of Finance had been forced to bow to the inevitable as early as September 2008, when 1,000 retail outlets were granted licenses to transact in foreign currency. His ZANU-PF successor as acting Minister of Finance announced in January 2009 that it would no longer be illegal for all Zimbabweans to conduct their business in any convertible currency of their choosing.
2. Money supply was now a function of the performance of the overall economy in terms of export earnings, in addition to inflows of foreign exchange from remittances, FDI and any loans and grants from international development agencies.

3. Further efforts to improve Zimbabwe's financial management systems included the Public Financial Management Act and the Audit Office Act, both of 2009, which contained provisions which would enhance transparency, accountability and oversight, as well as increasing financial reporting requirements for line ministries.
4. It was also widely believed that some ministry staff were either members of the CIO, or reported to the CIO on the activities and views of MDC ministers and other members of staff who might have been sympathetic to the efforts of their new political masters.
5. The problem was particularly acute with regards to terms under which non-concessional loans had been secured from non-Paris Club bilateral lenders such as Russia and China, as well as the magnitude of the loans contracted by the country's parastatals which had been guaranteed by central government.
6. In the event, such concerns regarding the level of intrusiveness of a SMP were not misplaced, as over the course of 2011–2012 both the IMF and the World Bank developed detailed recommendations on how to increase transparency and revenue collection in the precious minerals sector for the consideration of the Minister of Finance.
7. A good indication of the lack of progress was the singularly uninformative and passing reference to the ZAADDS in the Minister of Finance's November 2012 presentation to Parliament, a clear sign that there had been no major breakthrough on the external debt problem.
8. The IMF's restrictive measures on Zimbabwe did not preclude the country from benefiting from the organisation's injection of the equivalent of US$283 billion into the international financial system in 2009 in order to deal with the global liquidity crisis. This took the form of Special Drawing Rights (SDRs) whose value is based on 4 key international currencies and which could be exchanged for convertible currencies. Zimbabwe benefited to the tune of SDR324 million (equivalent to US$512 million). The new Minister of Finance found himself under pressure from his Cabinet colleagues to quickly draw down and spend these resources, against the advice of the IMF which was that given Zimbabwe's poor reserves and export cover position, these SDRs should be used to build up the country's foreign-exchange reserves. In addition, the IMF also reminded the Zimbabwean authorities, to no avail, that the SDR allocation was a loan on non-concessional terms and not a grant, and would therefore only add to the country's external liabilities.

9. Additional civil servants continued to be recruited in the aftermath of the formation of the IG without the knowledge of the Minister of Finance who had not catered for them in the budget, and he was eventually forced to announce a recruitment freeze in mid-2012.
10. As a result of the horse-trading during negotiations leading to the IG, Zimbabwe ended up with a total of 32 ministers (a number of completely new ministries being created to accommodate them), 32 Deputy Ministers, additional Ministers of State in both the President and the PM's office, as well as 2 Vice-Presidents and 2 Deputy PMs.
11. Elton Mangoma's combative style in Cabinet meetings, added to his efforts to clean up the operations of parastatals responsible for fuel imports and distribution as well as electricity, meant that he quickly became a thorn in the side of ZANU-PF. He was arrested and later acquitted on trumped up charges of flouting tender procedures in fuel procurement in 2011, and then again in 2012 for allegedly having insulted Mugabe at an MDC-T event.
12. David Coltart was responsible for the turnaround in the education sector, and quickly built up a reputation as a competent minister amongst the Western donor community. This was eventually to lead to the establishment of the donor-funded education trust fund referenced above.

References

CZI. 2009. *2009 Manufacturing Sector Survey*. Harare.

DFID. 2012. *Impact Assessment of the Zimbabwe Health Worker Retention Scheme*, February 1. Harare.

GOZ. 2009. *Short-Term Emergency Recovery Programme (STERP): Getting Zimbabwe Moving Again*, March. Harare.

———. 2011. *Mid-Year Fiscal Policy Review 2011*, July 26. Harare.

———. 2012. *Accelerated Arrears Clearance, Debt and Development Strategy*, March 16. Harare.

IMF. 2011. *Zimbabwe – Staff Report for the 2011 Article IV Consultation*, Country Report No. 11/135, May 11. Washington, DC.

———. 2012. *Zimbabwe – Staff Report for the 2012 Article IV Consultation-Debt Sustainability Analysis*, Country Report No. 12/279, September 11. Washington, DC.

SW Africa Radio. 2009. Zimbabwe in Crisis as MDC Cuts Off Contact with ZANU PF, October 16. http://www.zimbabwesituation.com/old/oct172009.html.

Takavarasha, Felicia. 2011. *Vital Medicines and Health Services Survey, Round 8, (April–June 2011)*. Harare: Collaborating Centre for Operational Research and Evaluation.

The Herald. 2011. PSC Disputes Payroll and Skills Audit, February 15. http://www.herald.co.za/psc-disputes-payroll-and-skills-audit/.

This is Africa. 2012. Morgan Tsvangirai, Prime Minister of Zimbabwe, March 5. http://www.thisisafricaonline.com/Policy/Morgan-Tsvangirai-Prime-Minister-of-Zimbabwe.

UNDP. 2008. *Comprehensive Economic Recovery in Zimbabwe: A Discussion Document*. Harare: United Nations Development Programme.

UNICEF. 2011. *Education Transition Fund, Fourth Progress Report*, October. Harare.

World Bank. *World Bank Database*. http://data.worldbank.org/topic/economy-and-growth?location=ZW.

Zimbabwe Independent. 2012. MDC-T Jumps on Zanu PF Gravy Train, August 31. Harare. https://www.theindependent.co.zw/2012/08/31/mdc-t-jumps-on-zanu-pf-gravy-train/.

11

Protecting the ZANU-PF State: Safeguarding Extractive Political Structures

In contexts such as post-independence Zimbabwe, where a ruling elite had monopolised political power for an extended period, and structured and entrenched both political and economic institutions of its creation in such a way as to ensure the continuation of its rule, the challenges facing reform-minded groups are daunting. The establishment of exclusive political institutions enables such elites to adopt the economic institutions that are best suited to the extraction of wealth for their own enrichment. This is done through the control, and if necessary the destruction, of markets even should this result, as was the case in Zimbabwe, in the impoverishment of large numbers of people. In turn, the development of exclusive and extractive economic institutions controlled by elites provides them with the resources to further consolidate their monopoly over political institutions, trapping countries in a vicious downward spiral. The resilience of such non-inclusive political and extractive economic institutions is therefore directly related to the fact that they are mutually reinforcing.

Securing and monopolising the instruments of coercion further strengthens the symbiotic nexus between non-inclusive political and extractive economic institutions. Zimbabwe's experience, and in particular ZANU-PF's melding of its interests with those of the country's security

M. Simpson, T. Hawkins, *The Primacy of Regime Survival*,
https://doi.org/10.1007/978-3-319-72520-8_11

forces, fits neatly into a historical pattern whereby control over valuable resources and the wealth they provide enables regimes such as ZANU-PF's "to build armies and security forces to defend their absolutist monopoly of political power" (Acemoglu and Robinson 2013, 81–82).

In post-independence Zimbabwe, an increasingly voracious regime had erected and nurtured an exemplar of a profoundly predatory state in which "significant amounts of otherwise investible wealth tend to be extracted [and] little is returned to the populace by way of investment in public goods" (Bavister-Gould 2011, 2), and which over time became the very antithesis of the Weberian, plan-rational, developmental state capable of delivering sustained economic growth and improved welfare indicators outlined in Chap. 2. Because of the longevity of both the regime and the state it controlled, this led to the development of a predatory society characterised by pervasive corruption and increasing use of coercion for short-term personal gains. Predatory behaviour permeated all walks of life and become the norm, with those at the top of the power structure using their alliances and means of coercion to use the state to steal from those too weak to resist, and steal from the state itself.

Where extreme forms of predatory rule take hold such as in Zimbabwe – where the state was transformed into a starkly anti-developmental agent of its elites, and the welfare of large segments of the population was sacrificed in order to preserve the regime's monopoly on power and elite wealth – reform of a country's political and economic institutions to trigger broad-based economic growth, market formation, poverty reduction, and political stability and social progress, is unlikely to happen either quickly or easily. Sustained and substantive reform requires a clear break with the past in the form of a new set of political masters with an agenda markedly distinct from its predecessors in terms of the systems of political and economic governance to be adopted, the most pressing national priorities to be pursued, and what is judged to be required to rebuild a revived, viable and effective state apparatus.

The GPA, and IG it gave birth to, were not conducive to, and in fact prevented, such a transition, enforcing the cohabitation of ZANU-PF and Opposition political parties that were deeply divided, leading to a profoundly dysfunctional government in which different ministries were controlled by different parties with widely differing views on national priorities. In the aftermath of the setbacks it had faced in 2008, ZANU-PF also soon made clear its view on the IG as a necessary but only temporary truce in its efforts to recover its complete monopoly on power, and revert to the status quo ante.

ZANU-PF's dismissive views on the IG quickly became evident through the positions it took on two of the key reforms required by the GPA, and which both domestic and external actors hoped would help finally put the Zimbabwe question to rest, namely constitutional and electoral reform. The position of the MDCs was that successful reform on these two linked issues would enable Zimbabwe to conduct elections under an improved constitution and electoral law, and the results of future elections would be recognised internationally, regionally and domestically as free and fair as a result of which a new administration would enjoy unquestioned domestic legitimacy and international support, essential preconditions for the country to embark on a comprehensive recovery programme.

In addition, the fundamental questions of both justice for the victims of past political violence as well as security sector reform also loomed large during the IG, though both had been referenced only obliquely in the GPA, a clear indication of their sensitivity for ZANU-PF. At the time of the GPA negotiations, concerns had been expressed in certain quarters, particularly amongst Zimbabwe's CSOs, that the GPA in effect rewarded ZANU-PF for deploying violence to overturn the results of the first round of the 2008 Presidential ballot and maintain itself in power. The events of 2008 had brought to the surface, in the starkest possible terms, the extent to which the country's security forces had become an instrument of repression in the hands of the ruling party, their willingness to commit human rights abuses in order to prevent regime change, and the existence of widely held assumptions of impunity for perpetrators and lack of redress for victims.

Failure to address transitional justice and security sector reform would only serve to give credence to ZANU-PF's deeply held view that violence was both a legitimate and the ultimate arbiter in determining national political outcomes, a means of avoiding accountability for past atrocities, as well as ensuring the indefinite postponement of any reforms in the country's political economy that might weaken its hold on power. As argued by one analyst:

> it is a tried and tested tactic of ZANU PF to threaten and deploy intense violence as a strategic bargaining tool. Since independence the party has singularly distinguished itself among Zimbabwean political parties by demonstrating a capacity for – and indeed claims the right to wage – mass violence in defence of its "national" interests…such an arrangement [a Government of National Unity] would deny the popular voice and reward anti-democratic, flagrantly illegal and often murderous behaviour – while only deferring, and certainly not solving, the problem of organising the transition to a new political order. (Kwinjeh 2008, 1–2)

Since the security and defence establishment provided ZANU-PF with the means to frustrate any reforms that threatened their common interests, and constituted the last line of defence against the introduction of accountability for past human rights violations, cnsuring progrcss on these issues would come to represent the most important challenge facing anti-ZANU-PF forces and the prospects of success of their overall reform agenda. It was clear that comprehensively overhauling the existing extractive political and economic system set up by ZANU-PF necessarily required significant progress in these areas. Unsurprisingly, reform initiatives were subject to a continual test of strength between the regime and anti-ZANU-PF forces.

In terms of the constitution-making process, analysts took note of the fact that in addition to efforts to protect and reinforce its support base in the security forces, ZANU-PF also sought to rebuild its credibility amongst two other key constituencies, with its eyes firmly set on new elections and therefore the roles these groups would play in helping securing victory at the polls. These were the war veterans, who provided the party with significant historical and ideological legitimacy as well as the capacity to act as shock troops whenever necessary, and the country's traditional leaders who played the critical role of ZANU-PF's eyes and ears at local level in rural areas.

The Opposition and GPA Structures

Despite the formidable challenges they faced, and notwithstanding the fact the GPA itself was couched in unclear language thus leaving the scope and meaning of many of its provisions open to interpretation, there was nevertheless some initial optimism within the ranks of both MDCs that the oversight and compliance mechanisms catered for in the Agreement might serve to constrain ZANU-PF's ability to manipulate implementation of GPA provisions for its own ends. In particular, high hopes were deposited in the body established to ensure the "speedy and full implementation" of the GPA, namely the Joint Monitoring and Implementation Committee (JOMIC). This was composed of representatives of each of the three signatory parties, and provided the MDCs with a platform from which they could try and ensure ZANU-PF compliance.

JOMIC, however, lacked any enforcement authority. It could only conduct assessments and recommend remedial actions to the IG, and was always likely to suffer from a lack of unity of purpose given the wider political divisions within the IG. Its monitoring of progress on implementation of the GPA was additionally handicapped by the fact that, with the exception of the provisions governing the constitution-making process, none of the other GPA articles had specific timelines attached to them, thus making any attribution of responsibility for implementation delays problematic. JOMIC was also handicapped by the player-referee contradiction, as those who had drafted the GPA had also, through JOMIC, made themselves responsible for ensuring its implementation.

Over the lifetime of the IG – and particularly in the face of persistent anti-MDC hate speech in the state-controlled press, restrictions on the operations of human rights activists, continued invasions of commercial farms and police violence against MDC supporters – JOMIC increasingly came across as a neutered body, eventually reduced to issuing anodyne public statements reminding the signatories to the GPA of the commitments they had entered into while studiously avoiding attributing responsibility for violations of the agreement to one side or the other. Given its design flaws, it was not surprising that

JOMIC rapidly became first immobilised, and then irrelevant, as any recommendations it was able to produce were ignored with impunity. To the extent that deadlocks in terms of implementation of the GPA (of which there were many) were resolved at all, this was only after direct negotiations between the principals, coupled with intense pressure from external bodies such as SADC.

Electoral Reform

The inclusion of electoral reform issues in the GPA was unsurprising given that contested elections – consistently marred by violence, controversy over the role of electoral bodies and the massaging of results – had been a perennial feature of Zimbabwe's political landscape, a major contributor to instability, and therefore a regular item on the list of reforms demanded by the Opposition. The key accusations levelled against the country's electoral bodies, and in particular the ZEC and Office of the Registrar-General, were that they had proven to be easily manipulated by ZANU-PF, and staffed by officials appointed on the basis of loyalty to the ruling party.

The way the elections of 2008 had been conducted had served to confirm the partisanship of the electoral bodies. Extended delays in the release of results for the first round were widely interpreted in terms of the ZEC having to wait for instructions from ZANU-PF as the latter decided how to deal with the novel situation of ZANU-PF losing its majority in the National Assembly and Mugabe having been bested by Tsvangirai in the Presidential race. Further evidence of ZEC's partisanship lay in its subsequent report on the 2008 elections. This studiously downplayed the violence which had plagued both the first and second rounds and been copiously documented by both domestic and external observers. In its report, ZEC even stated that it had fulfilled its mandate in terms of ensuring that the elections had been conducted "efficiently, freely, fairly, transparently and in accordance with the law", notwithstanding all evidence to the contrary (ZESN 2009, 2).

Throughout the elections of the 2000s the Registrar-General, who was appointed by the President, was regularly accused of obstructing the access of Opposition party representatives to the country's electoral rolls, of refusing to allow audits of the rolls, of presiding over rolls of increasingly questionable reliability as a result of revelations of numerous irregularities such as the inclusion of long deceased persons. He was also often accused of discriminating against urban and Opposition leaning areas to the benefit of ZANU-PF during voter registration exercises.

Similar concerns regarding partisanship had been expressed by Opposition parties in regard to the role of the Delimitation Commission (DC). The DC had often been accused of manipulating constituency delimitation exercises, of not consulting opposition political parties, and not making the maps and data used to inform the delimitation of constituencies available. The Opposition alleged that such practices had resulted in ZANU-PF strongholds being split into multiple constituencies, thus securing the ruling party a larger number of elected representatives (Kabemba 5, 9–27).

Transitional Justice

The widespread violations of human rights in Zimbabwe's post-independence history, resulting from the state's regular employment of violence and torture against its opponents, had been extensively documented by a range of domestic and international organisations. If this onerous legacy was to be overcome and meaningful 'national healing' take place, any transition to a new Zimbabwe required some form of redress for past crimes.

While reference was made to the need for the latter in the GPA, the precise mechanism to be established and the process to be followed were, like many GPA provisions, left unspecified. It is likely that this ambiguity was intentional given that ZANU-PF would have been unwilling to sign up to an agreement that set out detailed steps on a process of transitional justice for human rights violations. As a result, the commitment contained in the GPA was a nebulous one, kicking the can down the road through the establishment of a "mechanism to be set up to advise on what measures might be necessary and practicable to achieve national healing, cohesion and unity in respect of victims of pre- and post-independence political conflicts" (GOZ 2008, Article 7.1(c)).

Soon after the establishment of the IG, an Organ on National Healing, Reconciliation and Integration (ONHRI) was set up, led by three ministers representing the three GPA signatories. The primary task of this body was to formulate recommendations for a mechanism to implement the objectives laid down in Article 7.1 above. Not surprisingly, the work of the ONHRI, as with other bodies and processes set up by the GPA, was plagued by profound disagreements between the parties as to the nature and brief of any future mechanism and process.

The existence of an immense gulf between the two sides became obvious at the launch of the ONHRI's first stakeholders conference. There was scant reference in ZANU-PF interventions during the event to the need for justice and reparations, let alone the establishment of personal and institutional responsibility on the part of senior leaders for past violations of human rights. It became clear that ZANU-PF would not permit members of the security apparatus, ZANU-PF aligned paramilitaries such as the war veterans, or its own rank and file supporters, to be subjected to a non-partisan and civilian led justice process. MDC-T, on the other hand, emphasised the need for the assigning of responsibility, for justice to be done, for reparations for victims, and for an end to impunity given Mugabe's extensive use in the past of his Presidential pardon prerogatives (see Chap. 3).

Initially, Zimbabwe's human rights activists and the victims of human rights violations had high expectations that a process of transitional justice would be launched by the IG. The fundamental question that arose was whether this would emphasise the judicial investigation of past crimes and the prosecution of those judged responsible, i.e. retributive justice, or whether the process and mechanism would more closely resemble a non-judicial Truth and Reconciliation Commission of the kind adopted by neighbouring South Africa in the aftermath of apartheid, with its emphasis on the revelation of abuses (nature of violation, perpetrators and victims) so as to develop as complete as possible a historical account of past atrocities without this necessarily being accompanied by criminal prosecutions.[1]

In the event, during the four years of its existence under the IG, and not withstanding extended consultative processes with a range of interested parties, the ONHRI was unable to establish what precise form transitional justice should take in Zimbabwe. It even struggled to define its own role against the backdrop of ongoing reports of politically inspired human rights violations during its tenure.

The ONHRI's experience showed the issue of transitional justice in Zimbabwe to be one plagued by significant, if not irreconcilable, differences between ZANU-PF and its partners in the IG. In a clear indication of the extent to which progress was hostage to ZANU-PF interests, there was not a single prosecution for human rights violations during the IG. The original lack of clarity in the GPA regarding the ONHRI meant no substantive process of transitional justice was ever launched, a problem which was to be carried over to its successor body established under the new 2013 constitution, namely the National Peace and Reconciliation Commission (NPRC) which was to suffer from the same ZANU-PF obstructionism (see below).

Security Sector Reform

The country's recent history, and in particular the violence that characterised the 2008 elections, showed the extent to which that the security forces had come to constitute ZANU-PF's most important prop. Events at the time also made it clear that senior securocrats would do whatever was necessary to remain above the law with minimal Parliamentary oversight and accountability, answerable only to the President as their Commander in Chief whom they saw as possessing the necessary liberation struggle credentials to lead the country, thus enabling them to maintain their power of veto, through control of the means of coercion, over the direction of travel of the IG's programme. National security as a concept came to be defined increasingly as the preservation of ZANU-PF's monopoly on power, and of the maintenance of Robert Mugabe as

Head of State, Head of Government and Commander in Chief of the Defence Forces.

The relationship between ZANU-PF and security forces was both strong and mutually beneficial. Evidence of its symbiotic nature lay in the willingness of leaders of the Zimbabwe National Army (ZNA) to allow their forces to be deployed in what were essentially domestic enforcement operations against unarmed opponents, and the use of the police against supporters of the MDC formations in the elections of 2008. Through intimidation, and when this proved to be insufficient extreme violence before, during and after the first round of the 2008 elections, the security forces had secured for ZANU-PF's leadership a new lease on life, as well as a renewed flow of valuable resources by deploying the necessary muscle to first wrest control over, and then secure, the Chiadzwa/Marange diamond fields (see Chap. 12).

Over the course of the IG the senior securocrats relied, in turn, on the civilian leadership of ZANU-PF to deal with opposition parties in the legislature and their representatives in Cabinet, as well as with a hostile West, on a variety of issues of vital importance to them. So, for example, the securocrats were concerned with ensuring that any attempts to trigger transitional justice initiatives – as a result of which they might be held accountable for past human rights violations – were fended off by ZANU-PF in both domestic and international fora, that their farming interests acquired as a result of the FTLRP were not subjected to a comprehensive land audit, that security sector budgets were protected to the extent possible and if Treasury cuts were imposed that alternative sources of funding would be found, that those who had come to occupy sinecures in state and parastatal enterprises were not removed as a result of public sector economy drives and specifically state enterprise reform initiatives,[2] and that their income flows from diamond interests were not subjected to scrutiny by either Parliament or opposition Cabinet members.

The existence of such a symbiosis between ZANU-PF and the security forces, and of the power of the latter to determine the country's political future, was well understood by members of both MDCs, as well as the country's CSOs. As stated by one MDC-T official in an interview with an international think tank:

> We can implement the GPA to the last line, but if we don't deal with the contentious issue of the security leadership in this country, we will be haunted by it at the next elections…if the military is left with free rein to dictate and influence key decisions with regards to political developments in the country, including national leadership. (International Crisis Group 2010, 11)

If there were any doubts as to the depth of hostility towards the MDC-T felt by senior securocrats, these had been laid to rest at the very genesis of the IG. During Tsvangirai's inauguration ceremony in February 2009, senior military, intelligence and police representatives were either conspicuous by their absence, or pointedly refused to salute him as the country's new Prime Minister.

Early on in the IG, ZANU-PF made a point of reciprocating the loyalty expressed by senior commanders. It did so by repeatedly reassuring the security forces that it would act as a bulwark against attempts at security sector reform. So, for example, at ZANU-PF's December 2009 Party Congress, Resolution No.6 was passed which proclaimed that:

> ZANU PF as the Party of Revolution and the people's vanguard, shall not allow the Security Forces of Zimbabwe to be the subject of any negotiation for a so called "security sector reform" that is based on patent misrepresentations of Zimbabwe's heroic history and to the mere purpose of weakening the state so that it can be overthrown. (ZANU-PF 2009)

ZANU-PF warnings that security sector reform was not an issue up for discussion meant it had not been adequately addressed in the course of the 2008 negotiations leading to the signing of the GPA. Other than a single reference in Article 13 to the need for the country's uniformed forces to undergo training in the areas of human rights, international humanitarian law and statute law, they were simply lumped together with other "state organs and institutions" which "do not belong to any political party" and which were called upon to remain "non-partisan and impartial" (GOZ 2008, Article 13).

Unsurprisingly, post-GPA progress in this area was negligible. While the GPA had made provision for a reconstituted NSC which would strengthen cross-party oversight of the security sector, and which was to be chaired by the President with the PM as a member, it would be six months into the IG's existence before the President convened an introductory meeting of the NSC, and it would only meet intermittently thereafter. It was also widely believed that the JOC continued to meet behind closed doors with senior ZANU-PF figures, and in the absence of representatives of either MDC formations.

In the course of the IG there was to be no meeting of the minds on the concrete and practical steps needed in order to ensure that the country's security services, as required by the GPA, did in fact become politically neutral and professional. As with its control of diamond resources, so ZANU-PF's maintenance of its exclusive control over the security forces strengthened the impression that not only were there parallel economic activities and revenue streams which fell outside the purview of the Opposition members of the IG, but that the same applied to activities of entire state institutions such as Zimbabwe's defence forces, and its police, prison and intelligence services.

To add insult to injury, service chiefs regularly and publicly castigated Tsvangirai for his attempts to initiate reforms in their sector, and in particular MDC-T's efforts to enhance civilian and Parliamentary oversight and strengthen accountability and transparency. One senior commander went so far in 2011 as to comment that the military viewed the Prime Minister as a "major security threat…he takes instructions from foreigners who seek to effect illegal regime change in Zimbabwe."[3] The President himself menacingly put the MDC-T on notice that their interference in such matters was likely to have negative consequences for them:

> As Commander-in-Chief of the security forces, I want to make it clear that no one should meddle with the command…The so-called security sector reforms, all of them emanate from Western interests, and are a proposition from an enemy who wishes to weaken us. We are not in the habit of taking advice from our enemies. (*Mail and Guardian* 2011)

As late as May 2013, and despite numerous frustrated efforts by the MDC-T leadership to reach out to senior securocrats, it was clear that the latter felt sufficiently invulnerable in their positions, and enjoyed the full backing of the leadership of ZANU-PF, not to hide their blatant partisanship. That month General Chiwenga, in an interview with a state-owned weekly (and therefore reflecting officially sanctioned views) stated:

> We have no time to meet sell outs. It is just not possible for me to entertain the MDC-T leader...As the defence forces we will not respect or entertain people who do not value the ideals of the liberation struggle...Who the hell does Tsvangirai think he is? No one can make us turn our back on the ideals of the liberation struggle. (*Sunday Mail* 2013)[4]

The extent to which these views were shared by the civilians within ZANU-PF was made clear that same month by the ZANU-PF spokesman, Rugare Gumbo:

> The leaders of Zimbabwe's security forces that we have today did not emerge out of the blue, they have a history, one of the liberation struggle... You cannot expect them to be non-partisan and neutral. The perception is that the MDC is sponsored by the British...to effect regime change in Zimbabwe so our security forces cannot be neutral in light of that. They simply cannot. (Human Rights Watch 2013)

The timing of both the Chiwenga and Gumbo statements in May 2013 was significant given that at the time the country had already begun preparations for the holding of new Presidential and legislative elections. The effect of such threats on the electorate should not be underestimated. They served to remind the electorate of ZANU-PF's power to trigger punishing violence if the results of upcoming elections were not to its liking, and thereby intimidated voters with still vivid memories and scars of the violence unleashed against those who had supported the Opposition parties in 2008.

Such statements were also timed and carefully calibrated to help reassure ZANU-PF's own rank and file support base that, notwithstanding the years of IG cohabitation, the party's coercive capacity both to protect its own, and as a tool to achieve specific regime objectives, remained intact. In addition, lack of progress in the area of security sector reform clearly showed up the inability of the MDC-T leadership to make significant inroads in terms of reforming the extractive political and economic institutions controlled by ZANU-PF. This again redounded to the latter's benefit, as it was able to depict Tsvangirai and his lieutenants as weak, and therefore both unworthy and incapable of leading the country.

The timing of both May 2013 statements was also significant as they were made shortly after approval of a new constitution in a popular referendum in March 2013. In effect, senior securocrats and ZANU-PF personnel in the IG, and the President himself, were willing to publicly position the security services beyond the purview of the country's new national charter, and suggest that liberation struggle credentials were sufficient to trump the will of the people as expressed through elections. It was a clear indication of how little progress had been made since the establishment of the IG in terms of shifts in the balance of power between the two sides, as well as in the mind-set of the inner circles of ZANU-PF and the security establishment, both of which were preconditions for triggering and then sustaining comprehensive security sector reform.[5]

Constitutional Reform

Article 6 of the GPA stated that within two months of the establishment of the new IG, a Constitutional Parliamentary Select Committee (COPAC) would be put in place to oversee the drafting of a new constitution. The composition of the twenty-five member COPAC would reflect the balance of power within Parliament, with eleven members from the MDC-T, ten from ZANU-PF, three from MDC-M and one representative of the country's traditional leaders. It was headed by a troika of senior representatives from the three parties.

The GPA specified that the constitutional revision process required extensive popular consultations. It also stipulated that after the consultative phase, a further period of twelve months would be set aside for a COPAC body to prepare and then submit to Parliament a draft constitution for debate in the legislature, after which a referendum on the new draft constitution would be held within a period of three months. Therefore, according to this calendarisation, new Presidential and legislative elections could be held by March 2010 under a new constitution.

It was later to prove significant that the GPA both referenced and annexed a previous draft constitution known as the Kariba draft, with the parties having 'acknowledged' this draft. This had been negotiated in September 2007 behind closed doors between representatives of ZANU-PF and the two MDC formations, in meetings facilitated by SADC's mediator, South African President Thabo Mbeki, who sought to establish appropriate conditions in Zimbabwe so as to avoid a repeat of the violence which had marred the earlier 2005 elections.

Representatives of civic organisations such as those which came together under the umbrella of the National Constitutional Assembly (NCA) – the latter with close and historic links to the MDC-T and which had helped lead the campaign for the rejection of the 2000 draft constitution (see Chap. 5) – were of the opinion that the Kariba draft, negotiated behind closed doors, simply repeated the shortcomings of the 2000 draft and rejected it outright.[6] They also saw its acceptance by the MDC-T at the Kariba meeting as a major betrayal of the alliance which had worked so successfully in the campaign against the 2000 draft constitution. The dispute would eventually lead to the collapse of the alliance between the NCA and MDC-T, with the former subsequently launching a boycott campaign of the COPAC process which it saw as catering to party political as opposed to popular interests.

Therefore, in addition to lack of clarity in the GPA itself as to how exactly the provisions of Article 6 governing the revision of the constitution were to be implemented, disagreements between the parties over the precise status of the Kariba draft led to serious delays in launching the process. ZANU-PF took the position that the Kariba draft – which was to its liking given its maintenance of a highly centralised and powerful Presidential system, and whose existence it pointed out all parties had in any case been "acknowledged" in the Agreement – should be used as a basis for the outreach consultation process. In ZANU-PF's eyes, the consultative phase would thereby largely become an exercise in validating the Kariba draft.

While not subscribing entirely to the 'people led', bottom-up process advocated by the NCA which might have relegated Parliament and political parties to a secondary role in the drafting process, neither of the MDC formations saw the outreach component of the COPAC-led process as merely an optional extra, let alone a threat. While Parliament in the form of the three parties represented in the COPAC was to lead the process, they stated that their expectation was that the process would be genuinely participatory, with the views of the Zimbabwean people contributing substantively to the shaping of the final product.

The turbulence that was to characterise the country's entire constitutional revision process made itself felt right from its inception. A first all-stakeholders conference was held in Harare in July 2009 to induct representatives in the process, establish the relevant thematic committees, and develop a programme for the subsequent national outreach exercise. In a foretaste of the problems the whole exercise would run into, proceedings on the first day of the conference were brought to an abrupt end as a result of outbreaks of violence between supporters of political parties, with the police forced to intervene to restore order (*Sokwanele* 2009).

As the outreach component was rolled out, reports of ZANU-PF intimidation at public meetings became increasingly common. This phase of the process was characterised by extremely acrimonious consultation sessions, with all political parties being accused of 'coaching' participants to ensure that specific views were both expressed and recorded by rapporteurs, with ZANU-PF elements particularly notorious in this regard. ZANU-PF's strategy seemed to be to seek to manipulate the deliberations in order to ensure that the core elements of the Kariba draft, and in particular the centralisation of power in a strong Executive President, were preserved in the final draft constitution. As observed by an umbrella civil society grouping, the Civil Society Monitoring Mechanism (CISOMM), established specifically to monitor implementation and compliance with the GPA:

> Some political parties, particularly ZANU-PF, have gone ahead to coach citizens on what to say during sessions…[there have been] numerous reports of intimidation and coercion of citizens, particularly in rural areas, by military, para-military and (mainly ZANU-PF) party supporters; with reports of uniformed forces…campaigning for the ZANU-PF-backed Kariba Draft and threatening MDC supporters with assault. There is widespread evidence that in a bid to silence citizens, ZANU-PF launched

> *Operation Chimumumu* (Operation Dumbness) where citizens were instructed to remain silent and allow a selected few to contribute during COPAC meetings. (CISOMM 2010, 39)

Such tensions were to be carried forward into the discussions of the technical committees, with acrimonious disputes over how the conclusions of their deliberations were reported, the process of compiling the views expressed, the uploading of data collected during the more than 4,700 popular consultation meetings held nationwide, over the weight to be attributed to popular submissions and therefore their inclusion or exclusion in the final draft, as well as disputes over the impartiality of the outreach rapporteurs. As a result of extensive delays in completing the exercise, and as the prospect of new Presidential and legislative elections loomed ever larger on the horizon, the tense atmosphere would be carried over into the drafting process.

Despite the best efforts of the COPAC outreach teams to ensure frank, open and peaceful meetings, varying degrees of harassment and intimidation were reported throughout the process, with one civil society consortium, established specifically to monitor the constitution-making process, concluding in its final report that:

> to a great extent, the operational framework for constitutional outreach consultations was inhospitable to open debate. At most meetings…debate was generally subdued…The likelihood of producing a constitutional draft that primarily reflects ZANU-PF proposals, as enunciated in its flyers, remains high if not certain. (ZZZICOMP 2011, 58)

The drafting stage, which began in December 2011, saw ZANU-PF attempting to undermine the credibility of COPAC and the drafting team by regularly accusing them of deliberately ignoring and failing to incorporate those inputs from the popular consultations which were to its liking. In the event, after numerous delays, a draft constitution was finalised by the COPAC in July 2012, and significantly signed off by representatives of all three parties.

Contrary to the logical conclusion that since representatives of all three parties in COPAC had approved the COPAC draft this meant they were in agreement with its contents, in August 2012 ZANU-PF then unexpectedly presented COPAC with a new 29 page document. This contained its demands for significant changes to the agreed July 2012 draft which ZANU-PF had already begun to label a 'regime change' draft constitution.[7] At the time, the reason presented by ZANU-PF for this unexpected development was that its own soundings of participants in the outreach phase had not been sufficiently reflected in the COPAC draft.

An alternative interpretation was that ZANU-PF had decided to throw a spanner in the works of the constitutional revision exercise so as to collapse the entire process by triggering a prolonged deadlock. This would have allowed Mugabe to call for new Presidential, legislative and local elections under the existing constitution, and therefore to be able to count on unreformed electoral and judicial bodies as well as unreconstructed security forces. It is worth recalling that the constitution had been amended nineteen times since Independence to strengthen and preserve ZANU-PF rule and the role of a powerful Executive President, and that its provisions helped to shape the uneven electoral playing field which had always benefited ZANU-PF; any non-ZANU-PF inputs were therefore always going to be resisted.

Finally, and only after intense closed doors negotiations between members of a Cabinet Committee composed of the Chairpersons of the COPAC and the negotiators of the GPA, as well as significant pressure from SADC, the COPAC draft was completed and presented to a second all-stakeholders conference. Following that conference, a final draft acceptable to all three political parties was presented to Parliament in February 2013, and approved by both houses of the legislature. Leaders of all three parties to the GPA committed to campaign for a 'Yes' vote in a popular referendum scheduled for March 2013. Given the firm backing of the country's major political parties, and the relatively peaceful conditions prevailing during the referendum, there was an exceptionally high voter turnout, with around 95 percent of those who voted in the referendum approving the draft. On 23 May 2013 Mugabe signed the new constitution into law.

The extent of the horse-trading between the political parties that took place in order to finalise the draft can be gauged by examining the specific provisions that eventually found their way into the new constitution.

Such analysis also helps to highlight the specific red lines insisted upon by ZANU-PF, and which it clearly saw as essential to its survival as a force in national politics and the revival of its fortunes, as well as the prospects for a return to the status quo ante-IG.

On the one hand, the MDCs had been successful in securing the inclusion of a chapter on fundamental human rights and freedom. This Declaration of Rights was comprehensive, and served to bring Zimbabwe into line with existing international norms. It covered a set of civil and political rights such as freedom of expression and association, a free media, freedom from torture and unfair imprisonment, rights to a fair hearing, and freedom to engage in political activity and make political choices freely. It also contained a set of socio-economic rights, and placed obligations on the state to ensure the provision of education, health, shelter, food and water to its citizens (GOZ 2013, 29–44). The MDCs also succeeded in securing the inclusion of provisions governing the devolution of powers and responsibilities to lower tiers of government at provincial, metropolitan and local authority levels, part and parcel of their efforts to weaken the powers of the Presidency and which ZANU-PF had resisted throughout the COPAC process. Such decentralisation would be carried out "wherever appropriate" and subject to the ability of those bodies to carry out those responsibilities "efficiently and effectively" (Ibid., Section 261(1)), with the specific powers to be conferred upon these tiers of government to be determined by a future Act of Parliament.

Attempts by ZANU-PF to retain what were seen by opposition political parties and civil society as prerogatives of the country's longstanding 'imperial' Executive Presidency were strongly resisted in turn by the MDC formations. The result was that the rights and obligations of the President in the new constitution were a product of compromise. Presidential powers were now to be restricted in a number of important areas. For example – and with Zimbabwean involvement in the DRC conflict clearly in the minds of those who sought its inclusion – the Presidential power to declare war was constrained by a new provision. This stipulated that the President had to advise Parliament within seven days of exercising such power, and that the legislature was granted the power to resolve that the declaration of war should be revoked after which the President was compelled to take the necessary measures to disengage the country (Ibid., Section 111).

Similar provisions constrained Presidential prerogatives in terms of declarations of states of emergency. This again had been a longstanding concern of the political opposition and human rights activists given the past use of emergency powers to prosecute operations such as *Gukurahundi* in Matabeleland (see Chap. 3), and the conflation under ZANU-PF of a public emergency with any serious challenge to its rule. States of public emergency would now only be valid for an initial period of fourteen days, with extensions subject to Parliamentary approval. Upon application by an interested party, the Constitutional Court was granted the power to consider the validity of the declaration or extension of a state of public emergency (Ibid., Section 113), while the constitution also stated that a specific set of fundamental rights such as that to a fair trial and the right not to be tortured could not be curtailed during a public emergency (Ibid., Section 87(4)(b)).

Under Section 167, a new Constitutional Court would, *inter alia*, advise on the constitutionality of any proposed legislation and determine whether Parliament or the President had failed to fulfil an obligation such as the duty to defend and protect the human rights and freedoms contained in the constitution. In addition, in the context of elections, the Constitutional Court was to play the role of an electoral court, allowing it to hear and determine disputes relating to elections for the Office of President (Ibid., Section 167(2)(b)).

The Presidential power to appoint judges was made more dependent on the Judicial Services Commission than in the previous, much amended, Lancaster House constitution. This body would invite nominations from the public and conduct public interviews of candidates, on the basis of which shortlists of nominees would then be presented for Presidential consideration (Ibid., Section 180). It was also at the insistence of the MDC groupings, given the compromising of the judiciary that had taken place throughout the crisis years, and particularly during the FTLRP (see Chap. 5), that the new constitution include a specific proscription on the soliciting or acceptance of "any gift, bequest, loan or favour that may influence their judicial conduct or give the appearance of judicial impropriety" (Ibid., Section 165(5)).

In terms of the defence forces, their functions were defined as being "to protect Zimbabwe, its people, its national security and interests and its territorial integrity and to uphold this constitution" (Ibid., Section 212), while "only the President, as Commander-in Chief of the Defence Forces, has power to (a) authorise the deployment of the Defence Forces" (Ibid., Section 213 (a)). Both these provisions were to take on increased significance following the open intervention of the military in domestic politics that was to take place in the course of November 2017 (see Chap. 14).

Partisan statements from senior commanders of the security forces, even after the approval of the new constitution, were to continue to cast doubts over the extent to which they were willing to abide by its provisions. However, the entrenchment of the principle of political impartiality of the security forces in the new constitution (Ibid., Section 208) was interpreted as a significant victory for the MDC formations and human rights groups.

The new constitution also determined that the protection of Zimbabwe's national security could only be pursued in line with respect for the rights, freedoms, democratic values and the principle of the rule of law the national charter contained (Ibid., Section 206(3)). The security services were now to be "subject to parliamentary oversight" (Section 207(2)). Recourse when abuse by those state bodies took place was to be guaranteed by the establishment of an independent complaints mechanism which would receive, investigate and act upon complaints from the general public concerning misconduct of members of the security services (Ibid., Section 210).

The much feared CIO – whose existence and mandate were not even acknowledged in either the Lancaster House constitution or Act of Parliament – had been notorious for operating outside Parliamentary or Judicial oversight, due largely to the fact that it fell under the responsibility of the Minister of State for National Security, a post that was in turn part of the Office of the President which itself operated autonomously. The new constitution specified that the country's intelligence service was to remain "non-partisan" (Ibid., Section 224(2)), and clarified its chain of command (Ibid., Sections 225–226). Furthermore, as a branch of the country's security services, the intelligence services were subject to the constitution's General Provisions (Ibid., Sections 206–210) governing the proper conduct of its members, the role of Parliamentary oversight, the right of the NSC to request reports on its operations, and would also be accountable to the aforementioned independent complaints mechanism.

The MDC parties and allied CSOs were also gratified by the inclusion of provisions governing the roles and mandates of a set of important 'independent commissions',[8] even if these were subject to Presidential prerogatives in terms of the appointment of their members.[9] These commissions were, *inter alia,* to promote and protect human rights and democratic values, constitutionalism, transparency and accountability in state and government institutions, and "ensure that injustices are remedied" (Ibid., Section 233). Furthermore, their independence was to be ensured by stipulations that they would operate without "fear or favour", while state institutions were obliged to assist them and "protect their independence, impartiality, integrity and effectiveness" (Ibid., Section 235). Parliamentary oversight of these commissions was provided for, as were provisions governing the need for them to report annually to Parliament. A specific section also set out the requirement for members of these commissions to be non-partisan and non-political in the exercise of their functions, and to relinquish their membership of political parties in order to do so (Ibid., Sections 236).

Against these gains for the MDCs and the country's CSOs, ZANU-PF was successful in safeguarding a number of additional core interests. Firstly, ZANU-PF's determination to defend the FTLRP, which it relied upon as a source of both ideological and popular legitimacy as well as patronage to secure essential support, paid off as seen in the inclusion of the relevant sections governing agricultural land, and which reaffirmed provisions contained in the GPA. One indication of the centrality of agricultural land and its 'repossession' by ZANU-PF in its self-ascribed role in Zimbabwean history, as well as the special treatment the land question received in the new constitution, was that the right to agricultural land was treated as distinct from the general property rights detailed in the new constitution.

The new constitutional provisions on land therefore reflected ZANU-PF's specific interpretation of the history of the liberation struggle and the land question in Zimbabwe. The content and language used would have been anomalous in any national constitution, and more suited to a party political brochure, but the elevation of ZANU-PF's rationalisation of the FTLRP to that of a constitutional principle was clearly an essential concession if the MDC groups were to make progress and secure ZANU-PF approval of the overall charter. So, for example, the new constitution stated that the land reform programme should be understood in the context of a number of factors "regarded as of ultimate and overriding importance" namely that under colonial domination the people of Zimbabwe were "unjustifiably dispossessed of their land and other resources without compensation", while the struggle for independence was driven by the decision to "take up arms in order to regain their land and political sovereignty" (Ibid., Section 72(7)(a and b)). As in the GPA, the new constitution reaffirmed ZANU-PF's oft-stated position that the responsibility for the payment of compensation to former owners for the compulsory acquisition of their land for resettlement purposes lay with the former colonial power, while the Government of Zimbabwe was exonerated from any responsibility to pay compensation for that land (Ibid., Section 72(7)(c. i and ii)).

ZANU-PF also sought to ensure the new constitution safeguarded both the irreversibility of the land redistribution that had taken place under the FTLRP, and the future rights of the state to continue to compulsorily acquire agricultural land. The commitment in the GPA entered into by the MDCs as regards land reform, namely that the signatories accepted "the irreversibility of the said land acquisitions and redistribution" (GOZ 2008, Article 5.5), was carried over into the new constitution. Safeguarding the acquisitions that had taken place under the FTLRP, all agricultural land already itemised, identified and acquired under the provisions of the old constitution "continues to be vested in the state" (GOZ 2013, Section 72(4)). The new constitution stipulated that subject to the existence of a "public purpose" for which agricultural land was required by the state, this "may be compulsorily acquired by the state by notice published in the *Gazette*...whereupon the land, right or interest vests in the state with full effect from the date of publication of the notice" (Ibid., Section 72(2)(c)).

Bringing further closure to controversies surrounding the FTLRP, Section 291 entrenched the rights of new occupiers of agricultural land to continue to occupy that land based on an offer letter from the state.

Amendments to the former Lancaster House constitution, introduced during the crisis decade with the aim of ensuring that the FTLRP could not be challenged on the grounds of legality (see Chap. 5), were also carried over to the new constitution. This led to a clear distinction between provisions concerning land on the one hand, and the General Property rights contained in Section 71 of the new constitution which ruled that a person could not, for example, be deprived of their property unless given "reasonable notice of the intention to acquire the property", while also allowing a person "to apply to a competent court for the prompt return of the property if the court does not confirm the acquisition." Constitutional Amendment No.17 of 2005, which had entirely removed from the courts their jurisdiction over cases of compulsory acquisition of land by the state,[10] was carried over to the new constitution which stipulated that where agricultural land had been compulsorily acquired "no person may apply to court relating to compensation, except for improvements effected on the land before its acquisition, and no court may entertain any such application" (Ibid., Section 72(2)(b)).

It was also noteworthy that details of the constitutional provisions governing the establishment of a land commission and the launching of a land audit, another ZANU-PF redline, reflected the latter's interests. Such an audit had been a longstanding demand of both the MDC-T and the international donor community, and it is worth recalling that the GPA had stipulated that a land audit would be conducted during the tenure of Seventh Parliament, with the specific objectives of establishing accountability and eliminating multiple farm ownership. In the event, during the lifetime of the Seventh Parliament and the GPA, the ZANU-PF Minister of Lands and Rural Resettlement unsurprisingly failed to take the necessary measures to launch such an exercise. This task was always likely to remain unfulfilled given that – as with opposition party demands for security sector reform and transitional justice – a land audit ran the risk of profoundly destabilising ZANU-PF's support structures given that the multiple land holdings of senior figures in the regime which might be identified would then become vulnerable to seizure by a new government, while the findings might themselves prove embarrassing given the ruling party's depiction of the FTLRP as having had as its sole beneficiary group the land hungry masses rather than members of the elite.

A land audit did, nevertheless, make an appearance in the new constitution as one of the functions of a new body to be established, namely a Land Commission (Ibid., Section 297(1)(b)). However, close reading of the constitutional provisions governing the mandate and composition of this Land Commission reveal again the extent to which ZANU-PF was unwilling to allow the legality of the FTLRP to be questioned, and run the risk that the land distribution that had taken place might be reversed.

Contrasting sharply with the provisions governing the appointment of members of the 'independent commissions' referenced above, the Chairperson, Deputy Chairperson and other members of the Land Commission were to be appointed directly by the President without the requirements to consult any other institution, to invite nominations from the general public, or conduct interviews open to the public (Ibid., Section 296(1)). Any expectations that it would be able to exercise significant autonomy were soon disappointed as the constitution made it clear that it "must exercise its functions in accordance with any general written policy directives which the Minister responsible for land might give it" (Ibid., Section 297(3)). Under such condition, it was safe to assume that the work of the Land Commission would, as intended by ZANU-PF, be restricted to that of a purely advisory body to Government on land issues, that it would be composed of members sympathetic to both ZANU-PF and the FTLRP, and therefore unlikely to constitute a threat to the land holdings of members of the regime.

Another issue on which it was clear the MDC groupings had been compelled to make concessions in order to secure ZANU-PF agreement to the COPAC draft concerned the issue of the Diaspora vote. Given the significant (and in electoral terms potentially decisive) number of Zimbabweans who had migrated to other countries during the crisis decade in order to escape economic and political instability, the MDCs had made repeated efforts to ensure that revisions to electoral legislation and constitutional amendments enfranchised the Diaspora. Amongst their proposals were postal votes and that Zimbabwean diplomatic missions be charged with conducting voter registration of citizens abroad and setting up polling stations on election day.

ZANU-PF, on the other hand, had consistently sought to prevent this given the threat of what would likely be an overwhelmingly anti-ZANU-PF Diaspora vote. In the event, and despite the fact that the new constitution stated that "every citizen who is eligible to vote in an election or referendum has an opportunity to cast a vote" (Ibid., Section 155(2)(b)), it contained no specific provisions for facilitating the exercise of their right to vote by the Diaspora. As a result, this segment of the population remained disenfranchised unless willing to return to Zimbabwe to vote in their designated wards, and even this only on the assumption that they had been able to make a prior journey in order to register.

As noted above, the MDC groupings would have considered the inclusion of new constitutional provisions governing the role of the security forces, and in particular the requirement for them to perform their duties in a non-partisan manner, as a significant victory, clipping the wings and thereby constraining one of the key support structures of ZANU-PF. However, it was also pointed out at the time by sceptics that such provisions, based on very similar language, already featured in a number of Acts of Parliament and secondary legislation governing the operations of the security forces, and that the country's senior commanders had felt in no way constrained in their partisanship notwithstanding the existence of such laws. Seen in this light, what came across as a major achievement for the MDC groupings would in reality remain hostage to the ability of a non-ZANU-PF party to secure power, manage any subsequent threats of a military coup, and then foster the longer-term behaviour change within the security forces required to ensure the irreversibility of the required security sector reform and attendant dismantling of ZANU-PF's extractive political and economic institutions.

ZANU-PF red lines also meant that the new constitution's provisions regarding transitional justice would disappoint those who hoped that the focus of such a process would be less on the aspect of 'reconciliation' and the granting of amnesties for the perpetrators of past abuses, and more on 'retributive justice', judicial processes and the holding to account of those responsible. The latter were seen as essential components in the process of restoring the rule of law as well as deterring future abuses, and important metrics for gauging progress in terms of a transition to a new post ZANU-PF dispensation.[11]

Like the ONHRI, which during its four years of existence had singularly failed to define what form a process of transitional justice in Zimbabwe should take, the new NPRC was handicapped by the fact that as a new institution, clarity on its specific mandate would have to wait for the necessary enabling legislation in the form of an Act of Parliament. Based on past form, this would in turn be subjected to ZANU-PF efforts to circumscribe the new body's remit in order to reduce the scope for judicial processes. Inter-party negotiations in Parliament related to the drafting of the necessary Act were likely to be protracted and further delay the start of the NPRC's work, to the benefit of ZANU-PF and the human rights violators within its ranks.

While the new constitution stated that the first function of the NPRC was to be to "ensure post-conflict justice, healing and reconciliation" (Ibid., Section 252(a)), it was also noticeable that the term 'justice' was absent from the new body's acronym. Subsections also indicated that the work of the body would be less concerned with ensuring that perpetrators of past human rights abuses were brought to account, and more focused on the promotion of "national healing, unity and cohesion in Zimbabwe, and the peaceful resolution of disputes" (Ibid., Section 252(b)), by "encouraging people to tell the truth about the past" (Section 252(c)).

There was a clear focus on forward-looking and preventive activities, and a de-emphasising of the country's onerous legacy of organised political violence, with the NPRC tasked to "facilitate dialogue …in order to prevent conflicts and disputes arising in the future" (Ibid., Section 252(d)), to "develop mechanisms for early detection of areas of potential conflicts and disputes, and to take appropriate preventive measures" (Ibid., Section 252(g)), and to "conciliate and mediate among communities, organisations, groups and individuals" (Ibid., Section 252(i)). Cast in these terms, the work of the NPRC was unlikely to cause any discomfort to those in ZANU-PF and the security forces concerned with possible prosecutions for human rights violations. They could also rely on the sitting President to ensure that his constitutional prerogatives regarding appointments of commissioners to the NPRC would, as so often in the past with other commissions, result in a compliant if not blatantly pro-ZANU-PF body.

In terms of reform to the country's electoral system and bodies, the constitution contained a number of important provisions welcomed by the MDC formations and CSOs. Apart from the fact that members of the ZEC, like all the independent commissions, were enjoined to act in a non-political manner, the ZEC would take on the responsibility, previously exercised by the Registrar-General, for voter registration and compilation of voters' rolls, and for ensuring the proper custody and maintenance of the latter (Ibid., Section 239(c)(d) and (e)). A number of impediments that had negatively impacted on the electoral performance of the MDCs in the recent past were removed, such as the difficulties they had faced in 2008 in accessing the electoral register, and the severe delays in the announcement of 2008 first round results (see Chap. 9). The new constitution stipulated that it was incumbent on the state to ensure that "all political parties and candidates contesting an election or participating in a referendum have reasonable access to all material and information necessary for them to participate effectively" (Ibid., Section 155(2)(c)), while the ZEC was responsible for ensuring that "the results of the election or referendum are announced as soon as possible after the close of the polls" (Ibid., Section 156(b)). In addition, the ZEC was also given responsibility for ensuring that political parties and candidates were granted "fair and equal access to electronic and print media, both public and private" (Section 155(2)(d)).

Longstanding concerns about the scope for gerrymandering of electoral boundaries to suit ZANU-PF were also addressed through a set of detailed constitutional provisions, foremost amongst which being that "the boundaries of constituencies must be such that, so far as possible, at the time of delimitation equal numbers of voters are registered in each constituency in Zimbabwe" (Ibid., Section 161(3)), while Parliamentary oversight of the delimitation exercise was strengthened through the requirement for ZEC to submit a report to Parliament through the President, with the legislature given the right to refer back to the ZEC any issue "for further consideration" (Ibid., Section 161(8)(b)).

Yet the ZEC's ability to perform its duties, in line with the provisions of the new constitution, also required an enabling electoral law in the form of an Act of Parliament, containing the necessary amendments to the extant electoral law for processes ranging from the nomination of candidates and delimitation of constituencies to the registration of voters and a code of conduct for political parties and candidates. Given that such legislative processes were often subject to extended delays, there was the risk that Zimbabwe would enter a new electoral cycle without the necessary reforms having taken place, and under the extant electoral legislation.[12] It would also not have escaped the attention of analysts that the new constitution contained a provision – the application of which would again redound to ZANU-PF's advantage given Opposition concerns that previous demarcation exercises had been manipulated to the advantage of the former ruling party – namely that "If a delimitation of electoral boundaries is completed less than six months before polling day in a general election, the boundaries so delimited do not apply to that election, and instead the boundaries that existed immediately before the delimitation are applicable" (Ibid., Section 161(2)).

In the run-up to the 2013 Presidential, legislative and local elections, the scepticism of many concerning the prospects of substantive reform of the country's electoral system proved well-founded. Even after years of IG cohabitation which should have given the MDCs the opportunity to access and pressure key state institutions such as electoral bodies towards reform, the bias of the Registrar-General in favour of ZANU-PF, through acts of both commission and omission, was still evident. Rita Makarau, a former ZANU-PF MP and sitting judge of the Supreme Court, was appointed by Mugabe as Chairperson of ZEC in March 2013.[13] Notwithstanding the new provisions concerning ZEC's responsibility for voter registration and the compilation of voters rolls, there was little evidence of ZEC supervising the process, and the May 2013 voter registration process to update the roll in the run-up to the elections remained almost entirely in the hands of the Registrar-General, providing opportunities for further manipulation of the voters roll. As noted by one foreign organisation, the 2013 voter registration:

> showed bias against registration in cities – especially Harare...Civil society organisations assert that as many as two million youths have not been registered; there are more registered voters than adults in almost a third of the 210 constituencies; since 2008 the number of registered urban (traditionally MDC) voters has decreased, while registration in rural resettlement

areas (traditionally ZANU-PF) have increased; and the roll has almost 900,000 duplicate entries. (International Crisis Group 2013, 3–4)

However, it was the issue of Presidential terms, and the abolition of the post of Prime Minister and reaffirmation of a strong Presidency contained in the new constitution, that revealed the extent to which ZANU-PF was confident it would be able to recover ground lost in 2008 and during the IG, reverse extant reforms, and restore its previous monopoly on power. As had happened in 1987 which had seen the introduction of Constitutional Amendment No.7 indicating a clear drift towards a more centralised and authoritarian form of governance (see Chap. 3), the post of Prime Minister created by the GPA was abolished by the new constitution, which also reaffirmed the centralisation of powers in the Presidency, with the occupant of that post remaining as "Head of State and Government and Commander-in-Chief of the Defence Forces" (GOZ 2013, Section 89).

While for the first time the new constitution introduced term limits, with each President restricted to a maximum of two, five-year terms in line with the Kariba draft which ZANU-PF had sought to have adopted during the constitution-making process, it also stipulated that the term limits were not retrospective. This meant that as of 2013 when the constitution was signed into law, Mugabe would have the right to run twice more for President, and if successful remain in office for another decade (Ibid., Section 91(2)).

Strengthening ZANU-PF's Ties with Traditional Leaders and War Veterans

The status of Zimbabwe's traditional leaders, most of which had over time been co-opted by ZANU-PF (and also largely neglected by MDC-T given its strong urban roots), was recognised and guaranteed at the insistence of ZANU-PF during the constitutional negotiations. So, for example, the new constitution recognised their specific functions in customary law as chiefs of their communities, and as custodians of history and customs. In addition, their roles in adjudicating access to resources at local level was reaffirmed in the new constitution, which stipulated that they had "authority, jurisdiction and control over the Communal Land or other areas for which they have been appointed, and over persons within those Communal Lands or areas" (Section 282(2)). Since Independence such power had placed traditional leaders in a strong position given their control over access to this critical resource for rural households, to use such leverage to secure compliance at local level with any political directives emanating from Harare, and in particular ensuring that the Opposition faced difficulties in building support in rural areas. Furthermore, the new constitution reaffirmed the existing strong and direct link between the President and traditional leaders, with the President approving their appointment, removal or suspension (Ibid., Section 283(c)(i)), as well as their remuneration and benefits (Ibid., Section 284(1)).

Clearly focused on the next elections and need to strengthen its support base, ZANU-PF's senior leadership would go on and highlight their concern for traditional leaders in its election manifesto, portraying the party as the natural home of "patriotic" chiefs, and this despite the new constitution containing the standard clauses proscribing partisan political behaviour and even chiefs' membership of political parties. The manifesto highlighted the fact that they had been "at the forefront of Zimbabwe's liberation, especially during the Second Chimurenga and when Zimbabwe indigenised its land during the Third Chimurenga" (ZANU-PF 2013, 106). The manifesto also offered additional sweeteners to secure their loyalty, with the announcement of a Presidential Chiefs Support Programme. This would involve the capacity-building of chiefs in the management of local development initiatives on behalf of their communities, with each chief being allocated the significant sum of US$20,000 per annum to support such activities, thus further strengthening their dependence on central government, and Mugabe specifically, as well as their power over community members (Ibid., 106).

A similar ZANU-PF approach to the country's war veterans was also reflected in the new constitution, though the charter was even more laudatory to this group.[14] So the new constitution stipulated that "the state and all institutions and agencies of government at every level must accord due respect, honour and recognition to veterans of the liberation struggle" (GOZ 2013, Section 23(1)). Furthermore, given their unique contribution to the liberation of Zimbabwe, an Act of Parliament would confer on them "suitable welfare such as pensions and access to basic health care" (Ibid., Section 84). This was clearly aimed at rebuilding a relationship that had undoubtedly been strained by the collapse of the country's health and education systems and the real value of incomes due to hyperinflation from which the war veterans would not have been immune. Furthermore, material enticements to secure their support were also contained in the party's 2013 election manifesto, reassuring them that they would also benefit from the wealth made available through the national indigenisation and economic empowerment programmes.

ZANU-PF: Ensuring Continuity at the Top

For ZANU-PF, the new constitutional provisions governing Presidential terms of office also meant that the thorny issue of the succession to Mugabe could be postponed, if necessary, for yet another decade. Assuming a positive outcome for ZANU-PF in the forthcoming elections, it was expected that Mugabe would be able to continue to act as unifier of the party, mediating between its various often fractious factions and where necessary playing one group off against the other, and exercising the role of its chief ideologue and repository of its revolutionary history. For a party which had never known another leader, and whose history, internal structures, ideology and future prospects were seen as intimately tied up with the person of Mugabe himself, such provisions were a source of reassurance to many supporters. Any risks that the party might have of entering the 2013 elections openly divided along factional lines were thereby mitigated. The prospect of Mugabe at the helm of the Party and Government for another extended period would, *ceteris paribus*, help ensure not only policy and institutional continuity, but also his continued role as protector of the material interests of the regime's elite and those further down the food chain who had also benefited from past economic policies and redistributive exercises.

Most importantly, continuity meant he would remain as the fulcrum of the party's mutually beneficial and supportive relations with the security forces, and lynchpin of the extractive political institutions over which ZANU-PF hoped to regain exclusive control. For his supporters, and in particular those who came to see him as their last line of defence against demands for transitional justice, during a new period in office he would be able to fulfil his unique functions as rallying point for the party faithful, and skilful mobiliser and deployer of ZANU-PF personnel and resources to counter internal and external attempts at regime change and accountability for past actions.

Mugabe could also continue to be the paramount arbiter of largesse allocation to help secure the party's continued rule. However, his ability to continue accessing and distributing resources required, in turn, appropriate conditions that facilitated the perpetuation of ZANU-PF's predatory attitude to the economy and hostility to the independent private sector, as well as the continued functioning of the complex and opaque systems it had established to extract maximum political advantage from control of the economy. As events in late 2017 were to prove, however, expectations that he would be able to continue to exercise his unique skills in containing the factionalism to which the ruling party was always prone, and above all to keep the security establishment onside and protect their interests in what was effectively a two-way protection racket, were to prove misplaced (see Chap. 14).

Notes

1. A landmark event in terms of the evolution of the thinking of non-state actors on the forms that transitional justice might take in a post-2008 Zimbabwe was a meeting in Harare convened by the Zimbabwe Human Rights Forum in September 2008. Amongst the conclusions reached was the need for a set of minimum conditions for a credible transitional justice process. These included no amnesty for crimes against humanity, torture, rape and corruption, that there be no extinguishing of civil claims against perpetrators or the state, no guarantee of job security for those found responsible for gross human rights violations, and that there be comprehensive reparations for victims (Zimbabwe Human Rights Forum 2008).

2. By 2008, the creeping militarization of government and state institutions, which had been proceeding throughout the crisis decade, reached a hiatus, with either serving or retired senior security forces personnel occupying positions in a vast array of strategic institutions. These ranged from Ministers, Deputy Ministers and Permanent Secretaries in the Ministries of Energy and Power Development, Transport and Communications, Trade and Industry, General Managers, CEOs, Chairs of Boards and Heads of bodies ranging from the National Railways of Zimbabwe, the Grain Marketing Board to the Zimbabwe Electoral Commission (Chitoyi 2009).
3. Such pronouncements were in clear violation of the relevant provisions of the GPA which stipulated in Article 13.1 that "State organs and institutions do not belong to any political party and should be impartial in the discharge of their duties."
4. Such expressions of disdain for Tsvangirai by senior security officials, and attempts to delegitimise him, were already evident as far back as the 2002 Presidential elections, when the then head of the Zimbabwe Defence Forces stated the armed forces would not support any leader who had not fought in the liberation war.
5. A review of legislation concerning the composition, operations and oversight of the ZDF and ZRP in existence prior to both the GPA and new constitution (the CIO being the one security institution not regulated by any legislation), shows that relevant Acts and Regulations already affirmed their non-partisan nature and proscribed the active participation of members in politics. That the ruling party had consistently ignored these provisions in the past and used the security services to defend its own narrow political and economic objectives, with the active encouragement and support of senior members of the ZDF and ZRP, meant that popular expectations regarding respect for the implementation of the relevant provisions in the new constitution were not high, and that interference in the political sphere by the security services would likely continue with impunity as in the past.
6. This included the fact that the central role of the President in the appointment of the Judiciary, the Police Commissioner and army commanders, without the need for Parliamentary approval, was left intact. The Kariba draft also left intact the power of the President to dissolve Parliament at will, while a majority vote in Parliament could vest legislative powers in the President, and also ensured immunity from prosecution for acts

committed during a person's tenure as President. Significantly, the Kariba draft also made provision for a limit of two, five year Presidential terms, but which excluded the term of the sitting President, meaning Mugabe could have run for, and served, an additional two terms.

7. Amongst the changes demanded by ZANU-PF for inclusion in the COPAC draft were that the military should be allowed to play an active part in national politics (with, for example, serving members of the security forces being permitted to also occupy positions within party political structures), that there be no devolution of power to provinces as demanded by the MDCs, that executive power should remain vested exclusively in the President as opposed to the first COPAC draft which had vested such power in both the President and the Cabinet, that the President should, in line with the existing Lancaster House constitution, be granted powers to appoint commissions without Parliamentary approval, that there be no limit to the number of ministers and deputy ministers that the President could appoint, and that provisions in the COPAC draft governing Presidential accountability to Parliament for the deployment of ZDF both externally and internally be eliminated.
8. These included the Zimbabwe Media Commission, the Zimbabwe Gender Commission, the Zimbabwe Electoral Commission, the Zimbabwe Human Rights Commission and the National Peace and Reconciliation Commission.
9. The President was to select members after consultations with other competent bodies such as the Judicial Services Commission and Parliament's Committee on Standing Rules and Orders.
10. This had stated in Article 16B(3)(a) that any person having any interest or right in the land "shall not apply to a court to challenge the acquisition of the land by the state, and no court shall entertain any such challenge" (GOZ 2005, *Constitution of Zimbabwe Amendment (no.17) Act 2005*).
11. One opinion survey conducted in 2012 revealed that 75 percent of those interviewed were in favour of holding to account those responsible for political crimes, as opposed to 21 percent in favour of the granting of amnesty, while 52 percent were in favour of the use of Zimbabwe's court system as the most appropriate venue for the process of establishing accountability (Afrobarometer 2012).
12. The same was true of a number of repressive pieces of legislation such as AIPPA and POSA, which would remain on the statute books until such

time as the legislature either abolished or amended them in order to bring them into line with the relevant provisions of the new constitution.

13. In the new constitution, the qualification criteria for chairperson of the ZEC were that they should be "either a judge or former judge or a person qualified for appointment as a judge" (Ibid., Section 238 (2)). This in fact translated into a requirement to select a chairperson from the ranks of those previously appointed by Mugabe.
14. The flattering references to the war veterans, included at the insistence of ZANU-PF during the COPAC negotiations, were a result of not only its reliance on this group to carry out 'spontaneous' demonstrations and its useful intimidatory capacity that could be deployed in support of the party's political agenda as seen during the FTLRP and elections, but also memories of its potential to threaten government when its needs were not met, as in 1997 when groups of war veterans had taken to the streets and forced concessions from the government (see Chap. 4).

References

Acemoglu, Daron, and James A. Robinson. 2013. *Why Nations Fail – The Origins of Power, Prosperity and Poverty*. London: Profile Books.

Afrobarometer. 2012. *Results of the Round 5 Survey in Zimbabwe*, November.

Bavister-Gould, Alex. 2011. *Predatory Leadership, Predatory Rule and Predatory States*. Developmental Partnership Program Concept Paper, No. 1, September. UK: University of York.

Chitoyi, Knox. 2009. *The Case for Security Sector Reform in Zimbabwe*. Occasional Paper. London: Royal United Services Institute.

CISOMM. 2010. *Six Month Shadow Report on the Performance of the Inclusive Government of Zimbabwe*. Harare: Civil Society Monitoring Mechanism.

———. 2008. *Agreement Between the Zimbabwe African National Union-Patriotic Front (ZANU-PF) and the Two Movement for Democratic Change (MDC) Formations on Resolving the Challenges Facing Zimbabwe*, September 15. Harare.

———. 2013. *Constitution of Zimbabwe Amendment (No.20) Act*. Harare.

Human Rights Watch. 2013. *The Elephant in the Room – Reforming Zimbabwe's Security Sector Ahead of the Elections*, June. http://www.hrw.org/report/2013/06/04/elephant-room/reforming-zimbabwes-security-sector-ahead-elections.

International Crisis Group. 2010. *Zimbabwe: Political and Security Challenges to the Transition*, Africa Briefing No. 70, March 3. Brussels.

———. 2013. *Zimbabwe's Elections: Mugabe's Last Stand*, Africa Briefing No. 95, July 29. Brussels.

Kabemba, Claude. 2005. An Assessment of Zimbabwe's Electoral Administration. In *Negotiating the Impasse: Challenges and Prospects for Democratization in Zimbabwe*, ed. Wole Olaleye. Johannesburg: EISA. EISA Research Report No. 9.

Kwinjeh, Grace. 2008. *Staring a Gift Horse in the Mouth – Death Spiral in Zimbabwe: Mediation, Violence and the GNU*, June 18. Harare: Research and Advocacy Unit.

Mail and Guardian. 2011. Tsvangirai Accused of Being a Security Threat, June 23. South Africa.

Sokwanele. 2009. War Vets' and Youths Loyal to ZPF Creating Mayhem at New Constitution Conference, July 13. http://www.sokwanele.com/thisiszimbabwe/archives/4408.

Sunday Mail. 2013. I Have No Time for Sellouts: Chiwenga, May 5. Harare.

ZANU-PF. 2009. *National People's Congress Resolutions, 9–13 December*. Harare.

———. 2013. *Team ZANU-PF 2013*. Harare.

ZESN. 2009. *A Comment on the Zimbabwe Electoral Commission (ZEC) Report on the 2008 General Elections*, May 29. Harare.

Zimbabwe Human Rights Forum. 2008. *Minimum Demands Adopted by Participants at the Transitional Justice Workshop, 9–10 September 2008*. Harare.

ZZZICOMP. 2011. *Final Report: Shadowing the Constitution Outreach Process*. Harare: Zesn/Zpp/Zlhr Independent Constitution Monitoring Project (ZZZICOMP).

12

Protecting the ZANU-PF State: Safeguarding Extractive Economic Institutions

In May 2013, soon after signing the new constitution into law and in clear violation of the Global Political Agreement (GPA) which required that agreement on this issue be reached between the three signatory parties, Mugabe caught many by surprise by announcing a date for new harmonised Presidential, legislative and local elections. While Mugabe had over the course of the IG regularly threatened to call elections under the existing, much modified, Lancaster House constitution and electoral law whenever he felt that his partners in government were constraining his powers and negatively affecting ZANU-PF's interests, these threats were not acted upon, with many observers interpreting them as blackmail and brinkmanship. Most also operated on the assumption that in any election enjoying even a modicum of being 'free and fair', ZANU-PF would suffer a resounding defeat.

Given new constitutional provisions such as those governing reform of the electoral system, freedom of expression, association and of the press and non-partisanship of the security forces, and on the assumption that election monitoring missions from organisations that had previously not been invited by ZANU-PF governments to observe elections in Zimbabwe would be able to do so thereby exerting pressure on electoral bodies to

M. Simpson, T. Hawkins, *The Primacy of Regime Survival*,
https://doi.org/10.1007/978-3-319-72520-8_12

ensure that elections met the necessary standards, many analysts thought that the new, more level, playing field that emerged from the IG would redound to the benefit of the MDCs. Under such conditions, the outcome could not be overturned, either through the manipulation of results by compromised electoral bodies, or through the threat or actual employment of force by the security establishment. Therefore, Mugabe's decision to announce new elections did not appear to make sense.

Set against such optimism were the views of other observers who, over the course of the IG, had concluded that Mugabe had played a masterful long game. They noted that under his leadership, ZANU-PF had single-mindedly focused on the need to ensure that the events of 2008 were not repeated. Reflecting on the broad dynamics operating within the IG, one analyst opined (ominously in terms of the prospects for reversing Zimbabwe's fragility) that "ZANU-PF has, in fact, been more shrewd in its engagement with the transitional process than its political opponents…It has been effectively using the transition arrangement to regroup and reorganise, and is now better organised than it was in 2009" (Muzondidya 2013, 59).

Threats to call elections were not therefore bluffs. Once ZANU-PF's confidence that it could recover lost ground had been restored, and a plan for achieving this developed, its tactics of obstructionism and constant testing of MDC-T patience and willingness to counter its manoeuvres, manifest for throughout the constitutional process, can be seen to reflect calculated brinkmanship. The conclusions it drew may have led ZANU-PF to believe that it could collapse the IG at a moment of its choosing by forcing the MDCs to unilaterally withdraw from the arrangement, and thereby also claim the moral high ground by not being seen by fellow African governments as the guilty party for the termination of the cohabitation arrangement.

As shown in the previous chapter, over the course of the IG ZANU-PF had sought to ensure, through the positions it had taken on a range of MDC and civil society-backed institutional and constitutional reform initiatives, that the political governance systems which it had created and over which it had presided were left largely intact, and most importantly that its alliance with the security forces and paramilitary organisations such as the ZANU-PF youth and war veterans was not weakened. Where it had felt compelled to make concessions to the MDCs, implementation of agreed constitutional provisions could simply be delayed for indefinite periods through stonewalling the necessary enabling legislation, or where there was overwhelming pressure to introduce such legislation to do so and simply wait until it could be reversed once electoral prospects improved and it regained the required majority in the legislature. Oftentimes, one approach adopted was simply to ignore the law. The latter pattern of behaviour did not constitute a radical departure from normal ZANU-PF practise, and reflected a well-established historical pattern:

> At the root of Mugabe's approach to the law is the notion that rules, including the national constitution and its subsidiary laws...are not inviolable. Mugabe and ZANU-PF hold the new constitution to be a mere guideline that the government may adhere to at some unstated time in the future, rather than a sacrosanct document the provisions of which require immediate, absolute and fearful compliance. (Matyszak 2014b, 4)

As with its focus during the IG on the preservation of its extractive political systems, ZANU-PF had also succeeded in ensuring continued control over the extractive economic institutions which were also essential pillars of regime maintenance. The search for new assets to sequester and distribute in order to secure loyalty had always been a tried and tested component of ZANU-PF rule, though during the IG this had taken on an increased sense of urgency as more traditional avenues for wealth accumulation were restricted.

The stock of large-scale commercial farms had already been severely depleted by 2008, and therefore the scope for using these to secure the support of rural inhabitants, senior members of the party, civil servants and members of the security forces, was likewise reduced. The abandonment of the Zimbabwean dollar meant ZANU-PF could no longer simply instruct the Reserve Bank to print money to fund activities that bought it the required support. In addition, MDC-T's control of the Ministry of Finance and the Treasury had resulted in improved transparency and accountability in terms of public financial management, and thus curtailed the scope for diversion of revenues by state institutions to meet ZANU-PF's party political objectives.

ZANU-PF's efforts to ensure that the country's extractive economic institutions remained both intact and under its monopoly control were reflected in its dogged pursuit during the IG of the 'full indigenisation of the economy', irrespective (or more likely because) of its negative impact on MDC-T efforts to recapitalise the economy and attract FDI. The policy, and the promise of significant resources which would become available for distribution, would have been seen as an important if not critical vote winner during the upcoming election campaign, and explains the extraordinary prominence given to indigenisation in its 2013 election manifesto.

Over the period of the IG, ZANU-PF sought to ensure that a large share of the income from the sale of Zimbabwe's diamonds and the royalties of mining companies continued to flow outside state systems, and into its own coffers. Revenue from diamond mining activities became an essential component of ZANU-PF's support structure and its parallel economy, helping to compensate for the loss of Reserve Bank capacity to print money to support 'quasi-fiscal activities'. It was therefore essential that such revenue remained beyond the control of the MDC-T Minister of Finance, and hidden from the scrutiny of MDC members in the IG Cabinet and Parliament.

Indigenisation

During the horse-trading over control of ministries prior to the signing of the GPA, ZANU-PF had insisted it retain control of the Ministry of Youth Development, Indigenisation and Empowerment. This would allow it to determine the pace and scope of one of the central elements of its post-IG economic strategy, and also permitted continued oversight of its highly indoctrinated paramilitary youth and the opportunity to cultivate a bloc of voters which it recognised as being of increasing electoral significance, namely the country's youth.

For an economy such as Zimbabwe's, constrained from receiving large injections of ODA from the West due to debt arrears problem and disagreements over policy, and unable to find fiscal space in the state budget for capital investments, there was a clear economic imperative to attract foreign investment. Yet attempts during the IG to do so were severely and continuously hampered through ongoing efforts by ZANU-PF to implement the next phase of its indigenisation and economic empowerment strategy. This was often painted by party propagandists as the 'Last *Chimurenga*' – following on from the FTLRP characterised as the 'Third *Chimurenga*' – and aimed to strengthen Zimbabwe's "economic sovereignty" and secure final and irreversible "indigenous control" of the economy. This 'Last *Chimurenga*' was therefore cast in terms of "taking back the economy", the "final stage of the liberation struggle", and a requirement for "total independence".

The 'Indigenisation and Economic Empowerment Act', passed by the ZANU-PF dominated Parliament prior to the 2008 elections (GOZ 2008), was then followed during the IG by the necessary Regulations drawn up by the ZANU-PF controlled ministry, and gazetted in 2010. The structures set up by ZANU-PF without consulting its IG partners to oversee the indigenisation effort were illustrative of the extent to which the party had come to depend on the security apparatus for its survival, as well as the mechanisms through which the ruling party was able to ensure that securocrats were ensured a place at the patronage trough. The ZANU-PF controlled Ministry of Youth Development, Indigenisation and Empowerment was led by Savior Kasukuwere, a former member of the CIO. The ministry in turn set up a National Indigenisation and Economic Empowerment Board (NIEEB), tasked with ensuring compliance with ministerial directives, which was headed up by a retired Major-General of the Army.

The 2008 Act provided that when there was a change in the shareholding of a foreign or local non-indigenous owned company, or when a foreign or non-indigenous Zimbabwean investor set up a new company in Zimbabwe, at least 51 percent of the equity of the new or restructured business must be held by indigenous (for which read black) Zimbabweans. However, analysis of the subsequent Regulations of 2010 show that these were *ultra vires* in terms of the Act, as they applied not only to new investments in foreign companies undergoing restructuring, but to all existing companies (Matyszak 2014a, 2–3).

It was also noteworthy that both the Act and the Regulations lacked detail as to how exactly such transfers were to take place, and there was a conspicuous absence of any reference to how designated state bodies were to pay for the shares prior to transfer, raising the possibility – and in the eyes of many operators in the private sector the almost certainty – of compulsory acquisition of majority stakes without compensation. A common theme, constantly repeated in the state media and featuring prominently in ZANU-PF's 2013 election manifesto, was that there was no need for Zimbabweans to have to pay for any assets they secured as the indigenisation process was actually one of restitution on the grounds that such companies had been "unfairly exploiting the country's God-given natural resources over the years, at the expense of its rightful owners" (ZANU-PF 2013, 80) Flowing from this position – and particular note would have been taken of this point by foreign and non-indigenous owners of companies – ZANU-PF's views was that "going forward, there is a need to among other things clarify the fact that indigenous Zimbabweans cannot be expected or required to buy back their God-given natural or economic resources" (Ibid., 35).

Lack of detail and clarity also meant the ZANU-PF Minister of Youth Development, Indigenisation and Empowerment was able to exercise wide discretion in terms of accepting or rejecting any given indigenisation plan submitted by affected enterprises, and more importantly whom the eventual beneficiaries were to be. This was not unintentional, and represented continuity in terms of the way successive ZANU-PF governments had conducted business. Throughout the crisis years economic policies had been increasingly framed to meet short-term political objectives, without much thought given as to how programmes would be funded and what their long-term consequences might be. In addition, the vaguer the rules the greater the scope for discretion and capriciousness, and the more room there was for ZANU-PF and civil servants to shift the goal posts to suit their immediate needs and widen the scope for patronage, graft and corruption – the latter all hallmarks of the fragile state that Zimbabwe had become.

One analyst noted the sheer impracticality of the Act and Regulations, highlighting the basic fact that the legal title to shares in a company lies with the owners and not the company which issued those shares, and therefore a company simply could not force its shareholders to dispose of their shares to meet the 51 percent indigenous ownership requirement.

While one component of the law requiring that all new investments or major share transactions of existing companies, such as mergers or takeovers, should leave 'indigenous' Zimbabweans with a 51 percent holding was legal, the second component requiring all existing foreign and local non-indigenous owned companies to dispose of 51 percent of their existing shares was both invalid and unenforceable (Matyszak 2014a, 2–4).

But in the past such legal niceties had never held ZANU-PF back from implementing policies to strengthen its hold on power. As the same analyst noted, when the unenforceability of the law was pointed out to a government official at a public seminar, the response perfectly encapsulated ZANU-PF's longstanding default position, namely that the government would use "political means" to achieve its goal (Ibid., 4). There were threats emanating from the ministry that work permits would not be granted or extended for employees of foreign-owned firms, and that profit repatriation would be blocked and export permits denied or cancelled unless indigenisation was carried out.

Given the legal and practical difficulties the ministry faced in implementing the Act and the Regulations and securing the compliance of companies – and notwithstanding propaganda carried in the state media prior to the 2013 elections which sought to show that the Minister was successfully compelling foreign companies to indigenise and that ZANU-PF was winning the battle against international capital in defence of rights of Zimbabweans to economic empowerment – the fact was that the only compliance demanded of foreign companies contained in the Regulations was the submission of 'indigenisation plans' for ministry approval. However, this did not mean the absence of the necessary statutory provisions to compel companies to indigenise would be sufficient to deter ZANU-PF from ensuring that its political objectives were achieved through other means. While foreign-owned companies operating in a list of economic sectors simply ignored a notice put out by the ministry informing them of a January 2014 deadline to hand over their businesses to indigenous Zimbabweans, there always remained the concern that ZANU-PF might up the ante at any moment of its choosing, as it had done with its FTLRP, once free of the constraints of the IG.

With memories still fresh of the unleashing of ZANU-PF youth against their enterprises and the accompanying looting that had taken place at the height of the price control operation in 2008, and the violence and wanton destruction that had accompanied the land invasions under the FTLRP, coupled with ZANU-PF's historic unpredictability regarding property rights, it was hardly surprising that the country's private sector opted to keep their heads as far below the parapet as possible rather than confront the issue head-on. With business leaders putting self-preservation ahead of principle, it was easy for government to pursue a divide-and-rule strategy. Throughout the indigenisation debate there was an understandable fear-driven reluctance by the independent private sector to test the legality of the Regulations in the courts.

The Minister was thus able to make up the details of policy on the hoof, and give himself maximum discretion to issue new directives at any moment of his choosing and whenever money was urgently needed. This translated into an ability to extract what might be best characterised as protection money from companies. These took the form of the 'compliance certificates' issued by the NIEEB, and for which companies were charged significant sums of money, as proof of acceptance by that state body of the indigenisation plans that had been submitted, in addition to 'voluntary contributions' to the Youth Empowerment Fund under the control of the same ministry, to be used for funding loans to youth presumably possessing the correct pro-ZANU-PF leanings.

Given plans to call elections in 2013, the unrelenting rhetoric on indigenisation and economic empowerment – even if implementation of policy fell short in terms of its intended objective of actually transferring the remainder of the country's wealth locked up in enterprises into 'indigenous' hands – was essential to advancing the party's objectives. ZANU-PF's discourse on indigenisation and economic empowerment, cast as a logical progression from the FTLRP, provided "a seemingly inexhaustible well of rhetoric about sovereignty and fighting the capitalist-imperialist monster in the form of foreign companies" (Matyszak 2014a, 2). As its election manifesto put it:

> Now Zimbabweans have an historic opportunity to extend the ownership of their land to 14 key sectors of the economy whose control and ownership are in foreign hands as a direct result of colonialism and Rhodesian racist rule. In the same way we have taken back our land as Zimbabweans through the Third Chimurenga, we are now taking back our economy as its rightful owners. (ZANU-PF 2013, 31)

ZANU-PF's role as the guarantor of the aspirations of Zimbabwe's masses, as well as its continued ability to identify, secure and distribute largesse, was continually emphasised, as well as the notion that restitution for past exploitation and dispossessions could only be assured by supporting ZANU-PF:

> To ensure that the goals of the people are won, Zanu PF will work with everyone to take back the economy to benefit the majority of Zimbabweans, building on the same way the Party worked with the people to win Zimbabwe's independence in 1980...When Zanu PF wins at the polls, the people win their goals and benefit in terms of having sustainable livelihoods. (Ibid., 107–108)

Election propaganda also highlighted the enticing prospect of vast sums of money that would be unlocked through indigenisation and directed to the beneficiaries of economic empowerment, with the election manifesto stating that US$7.3 billion would be made available over the period 2013–2018 based on the estimated value of 51 percent of the assets of foreign and non-indigenous companies in the country (ZANU-PF 2013, 79). Through means left largely unspecified, this wealth would be channelled to the coffers of a state that it was assumed would, post-2013 elections, once again be fully under the control of ZANU-PF. According to the election manifesto, this would then allow ZANU-PF to use this wealth to benefit a broad range of Zimbabweans through various schemes such as the rehabilitation of social and economic infrastructure, projects aimed at the economic empowerment of priority groups such as women and youth, and the financing of agriculture.

According to ZANU-PF, on the back of its indigenisation and empowerment programme, economic growth was projected to reach 9 percent per annum by 2018. In addition, a total of 2.26 million new jobs would be created (Ibid., 96), given that "Indigenisation and People's Empowerment is particularly designed to create unprecedented employment opportunities over the next five years" (Ibid., 27).

While the need to create jobs had been a constant feature of MDC-T's economic policy before and then during the IG, this had been less the case with ZANU-PF given the latter's longstanding party line that the fastest and most effective route to 'empowering' Zimbabweans was through the straightforward takeover of existing concerns, be these commercial farms or manufacturing companies. That it changed its position by adopting the MDC-T emphasis on employment creation as the fastest route to economic empowerment in its manifesto, while merging it with the policy on indigenisation, possibly reflected the conclusions it drew from the results of a public opinion survey conducted in 2012. This had shown a clear preference for empowerment through job creation as opposed to the takeover of existing firms (Afrobarometer 2013). This willingness to shift policy emphasis was a clear indication that ZANU-PF was intent on ensuring that its policies and messaging were fine-tuned to voter preferences, even if this should require the partial dilution of previous dogma.

Further evidence of this focus on regaining the support lost in 2008, and a willingness to adopt new approaches to secure this objective, can also be seen in the aforementioned emphasis placed on the country's youth. According to its 2013 manifesto, the country's youth had always been at the centre of the party's attentions, and that "Zanu PF is a natural home for the youth who are the frontline of the people's revolution" (ZANU-PF 2013, 26). The manifesto highlighted the fact that, based on the 2012 population census, the youth defined as those in the 18–35 age group represented not only 37 percent of the total population, but more significantly 61 percent of the total electorate (Ibid., 26). So the promise to establish a Youth Empowerment Fund by the Ministry for Youth Development, Indigenisation and Empowerment, and the manifesto commitment to ensuring that the youth benefited from a future ZANU-PF government through a 25 percent quota for youth participation "across all sectors of the state and economy" (Ibid., 27). A caring ZANU-PF was portrayed as their natural mentor, protector and guide, a role which was required as:

> many young people in this bracket will be voting for the first time and that places a huge responsibility on them which requires historical guidance in the national interest...it is this age group that is most vulnerable to external political, cultural and information manipulation. (Ibid., 26)

Further indications of what were seen as necessary actions to rebuild its support base were its proposed measures for the rural areas, with commitments to address the concerns of those who had benefited from the FTLRP and earlier post-independence resettlement initiatives, and specifically the need for improved tenure security over their redistributed land holdings, with the manifesto committing ZANU-PF to address this long outstanding issue (see Chap. 5). While precise details as to how this would be done were singularly lacking, the manifesto nevertheless committed a future ZANU-PF government to provide "bankable leasehold security of tenure to all agricultural beneficiaries of the Land Reform Programme" (ZANU-PF 2013, 103).

Despite ZANU-PF's efforts to couch indigenisation in terms of rational economic empowerment arguments, many Zimbabweans saw through the populist platform, and viewed the indigenisation policy as simply another attempt by ZANU-PF to perpetuate its extractive economic systems and bolster its popular support by replenishing the patronage trough. One Zimbabwean think tank observed:

> With lucrative white farming enterprises no longer available (the resource having been depleted) the Regulations thus began to create the conditions for a new source of patronage for the ZANU PF elite and a weapon against businesses and individuals perceived to support the MDC ahead of the next election. (Matyszak 2011, 6)[1]

Against the backdrop of these developments, Tsvangirai and his lieutenants had the unenviable task during the IG of seeking to attract badly needed foreign investment, and would often take every opportunity to declare that Zimbabwe was 'open for business'. However, many foreign investors were, not surprisingly, less than comfortable with the idea of exposure to the vagaries of Zimbabwean policy, with many putting their investment decisions on the back burner. While Zimbabwe did receive FDI to the tune of US$166 million in 2010, a figure which increased to US$387 million in 2011, such figures need to be put in perspective, both in terms of the country's enormous and urgent need for capital, as well as in regional terms given that it was competing with neighbours for such inward investment. By way of comparison, its neighbour Zambia received a significantly higher figure of US$1.729 billion and US$1.982 billion in 2010 and 2011 respectively, while another neighbour, Mozambique, received US$989 million and US$2.093 billion in FDI over the same period (UNCTAD 2012, 170).

The issue of indigenisation thus cast a pall over the new Government's overall recovery efforts. At international conferences the MDC-T sought to reassure investors of the safety of their investments, plugging the line that with the establishment of the IG a new page had been turned in terms of Harare's respect for, and protection of, property rights and contract enforcement, while back home ZANU-PF threats directed at foreign-owned companies completely undermined their efforts. The mixed messaging on FDI emanating from the IG was a persistent irritant to the MDCs, a source of considerable confusion to outside observers, and yet another indication of the quarrelsome nature of the relationship between the parties.

After Kasukuwere's Ministry had issued instructions to foreign-owned banks in 2012 to submit their indigenisation plans, and imposed a deadline, the PM's office felt compelled to issue a lengthy statement denying the validity of the instruction:

> The Prime Minister would like to inform the public and concerned stakeholders that there is no such government position because no such issue has been discussed and agreed upon in Cabinet. Government has not sanctioned the Minister's actions that are a threat to investment in the country. The Indigenization and Economic Empowerment Act does not empower the Minister to act and to project an image of a voracious government keen to compulsorily grab almost all institutions and companies in the country. (Office of the Prime Minister 2012)

In April 2012 the MDC-T National Council felt compelled to pass a resolution which served to highlight the profound policy differences between the partners and the increasingly noxious atmosphere in the IG, castigating the indigenisation policy in the strongest possible terms as:

> asset stripping, looting, patronage, clientelism, corruption and self-aggrandisement euphemistically referred to as indigenisation and empowerment…[which] is not demand driven and in any event is based on a

narrow model of transferring shares to a few black elite [sic] that can afford them and does not amount to genuine wealth creation and distribution to poor people of Zimbabwe. (MDC 2012)[2]

Diamonds and Parallel Revenue Flows

Upon taking office in February 2009, the new MDC-T Finance Minister, Tendai Biti, who famously described his new position as the 'worst job in the world' (Kwenda 2009), was faced with empty state coffers, a shrinking GDP, severely depleted revenue collection capacity within the Zimbabwe Revenue Authority (ZIMRA) due to the brain drain, an increasingly onerous foreign debt which constrained the country's ability to borrow externally, deteriorating export performance, a massive infrastructure deficit[3] and sympathetic but cautious international donors and IFIs. It was clear that the success of efforts to rebuild the country was dependent on both large injections of external capital and ensuring that domestic resources were appropriately managed.[4]

One key assumption informing MDC-T economic policy had been that increased revenues from mineral exports, and in particular recently discovered diamonds, would flow into Treasury, providing the country with the necessary fiscal space to meet public expenditure priorities. Coupled with the new cash-budgeting approach adopted by the Ministry of Finance, it was hoped that such revenues could be directed both to growth-enhancing public expenditure and in particular the rehabilitation of the country's physical infrastructure, as well as priority social sector needs, without recourse as in the past to extensive deficit financing or the printing of money.[5] Such optimistic assumptions eventually proved to be profoundly misplaced. The strength and resilience of the country's extractive economic institutions and practices, developed and perfected by ZANU-PF, rapidly became evident once the MDC-T tried to introduce reforms in the areas of revenue collection, accountability and transparency, and ensure that the country's mineral wealth was used to support recovery efforts.

In the wake of the discovery in 2006 of the Chiadzwa/Marange alluvial diamond fields in the east of Zimbabwe close to the border with Mozambique, and at the time hailed as one of the richest diamond deposits in the world and the 'find of the century', there had been a large influx of small-scale prospectors, estimated by one source at up to 20,000 miners (Human Rights Watch 2009). ZANU-PF had initially adopted a *laissez-faire* attitude to the presence of such miners, hoping thereby to gain some political support from this numerically significant component of the informal economy labour force.

However, once the full potential of the fields was revealed, and in order to tackle leakages when it became clear that the miners preferred not to sell their diamonds to the state-owned Minerals Marketing Corporation of Zimbabwe (MMCZ) but rather smuggle them across the country's borders to Mozambique and South Africa, ZANU-PF and the country's security apparatus worked together to rapidly gain control of these resources. An operation was launched (Operation *Chikorokoza Chapera* – meaning 'end to illegal panning') at the end of 2006, with the ZRP being deployed to put an end to the operations of thousands of miners. In the event the police sent to Marange were in many cases themselves eventually to strike deals with groups of artisanal miners, exchanging diamonds for protection.

In October 2008, prior to the formation of the IG, the Government launched yet another operation, Operation *Hakudzokwi* ('You will not return'). This time the Government used the country's defence forces to expel the miners from the fields, and according to one report based on extensive field research extreme violence was used to achieve this objective. One notorious episode which took place between October and November 2008 involved the CIO and units from the army with air force support in the form of helicopter gunships, leading to the death of hundreds of miners (Human Rights Watch 2009). Like the earlier Operation *Murambatsvina*, one of the likely motivations for the decision to have the Zimbabwe National Army (ZNA) spearhead the operation in the diamond fields was to combat growing discontent amongst rank and file soldiers who were also feeling the effects of the economic meltdown during 2008. Operation *Hakudzokw*i thus provided them an opportunity to engage in some direct looting themselves (as the Police had enjoyed during *Murambatsvina* and *Chikorokoza Chapera*), and therefore helped to ensure their continued loyalty to ZANU-PF.

Once ZANU-PF and the security chiefs had secured control of the diamond fields, they set up a complex network of companies in order to manage both the mining operations and revenues from the sale of diamonds, with the ZANU-PF Minister of Mines – a ministry which ZANU-PF had insisted should also fall under its control during the GPA negotiations – responsible for the awarding of concessions and playing a pivotal role in ensuring that this extractive economic sub-system remained beyond the control of its MDC partners in government. As observed by one organisation which has campaigned globally against conflict diamonds, what took place with regards to Zimbabwe diamond wealth was part of a well-established pattern of ZANU-PF behaviour, characterised by "carefully crafted campaigns of economic theft with which to engage in crass patrimonialism to placate key constituencies and buy more time in office" (Partnership Africa Canada 2010, 6).

The exploitation of Zimbabwe's diamond resources rapidly led to the country displaying all the features of the resource curse syndrome outlined in Chap. 2. ZANU-PF grasped the potential for diamond revenues to be used to meet the needs of what was to all intents and purposes a ZANU-PF parallel government. These needs ranged from self-enrichment by the military and the politically well-connected, to the financing of ZANU-PF's party political campaigns and the pro-ZANU-PF state-controlled media, to ensuring that those in its grassroots support base such as war veterans, card carrying members, traditional leaders and youth militia were also looked after. These parallel revenue streams also enjoyed the additional advantage of obviating the need for ZANLU-PF ministries and the Office of the President having to request funds from the Ministry of Finance, and to have to account for their use.

If the dollarization of the economy in 2008 had constrained the Reserve Bank in terms of its role of ZANU-PF's private Treasury, this would now be compensated for by the Ministry of Mines playing party paymaster. This was particularly important to the security forces given budget cuts imposed by the MDC-T Minister of Finance, as during the IG the Ministry of Defence appropriations were heavily downgraded relative to expenditure on health, education and infrastructure, thus making an alternative source of funds for arms purchases essential.

In his 2012 Mid-Term Fiscal Policy statement, Biti was to claim that of the US$600 million his ministry had projected it would receive from diamond sales that year (through royalties and taxes on mining companies), it had received only US$41 million (*New Zimbabwe* 2012a). This was a revealing indication of both the magnitude of the leakages and sophistication of the parallel revenue generating systems set up both prior to and in the aftermath of the establishment of the IG. Diamond smuggling, human rights abuses, corporate skulduggery in the form of outright confiscation of mining concessions and their recycling to companies with close links to the military and ZANU-PF,[6] the refusal of the Ministry of Mines to compel state bodies and companies to make revenue and tax payments to Treasury, were all classic, extreme and visible manifestations of the resource curse at work.[7]

For example, with regards to a Chinese mining company which became the largest concern operating in the Marange fields and was believed to enjoy close relations with Zimbabwe's security establishment,[8] Biti stated in 2012 that:

> We have not received a single cent from Anjin, yet Anjin is seven times bigger than some of the other companies. Clearly, we fear as the ministry of finance that there might be a parallel government somewhere in respect of where these revenues are going...There is opaqueness and unaccountability surrounding our diamonds. (Global Witness 2012b, 18)[9]

The MDC-T Deputy Minister of Justice and Legal Affairs, Senator Obert Gutu, was even more categorical:

> ZANU-PF has misused and abused the inclusive government to resuscitate its waning political fortunes. They have effectively set up a parallel government which is very handsomely funded by the proceeds of Chiadzwa and Marange...Let me tell you that this country is being looted day in, day out. (*Nehanda Internet News* 2012)

The impact of such leakages on the country's finances, and in particular on urgently needed public investment in the country's infrastructure, unsurprisingly had negative consequences on the country's recovery prospects. After high growth rates averaging 8 percent between the start of dollarization at the end of 2008 and 2011, the Minister of Finance was thereafter forced to engage in constant downward revisions of growth projections. After an initial forecast of 9.4 percent GDP growth for 2012, this was subsequently revised downwards to 6 percent. Significantly, the national budget for 2013 was also cut from an initial US$4 billion to US$3.6 billion, with 65 percent having to be earmarked for public sector wages, leaving little for urgently needed capital expenditures.

That ZANU-PF had successfully put in place parallel mechanisms, to sustain its patronage requirements and achieve its political objectives, was evident through its ability to continue to both raise and allocate resources outside the control of central government. So, for example, while the downward revision of growth rates forecasts and public expenditure were taking place, and against the backdrop of growing indications that Presidential, legislative and local elections would be held in 2013, ZANU-PF launched a revamped 'Presidential Well-Wishers Agricultural Inputs Scheme'. This initiative, redolent of the multiple quasi-fiscal support programmes of the RBZ during the crisis years, involved the distribution of seeds and fertilizer to 80,000 rural households in a clear attempt by ZANU-PF to bolster its support base, while the source of the US$20 million funds expended remained unclear (*New Zimbabwe* 2012b).

The above initiative was launched at a time when, due to budget constraints, the Ministry of Finance was only able to allocate a total of US$17.2 million for the rehabilitation of all the country's severely debilitated primary and secondary schools, an even lower US$15.6 million for the revitalisation of all district level hospitals, and only US$18 million for the urgently needed rehabilitation of the country's decrepit electricity generation, transmission and distribution systems (GOZ 2012). Further evidence that ZANU-PF's party coffers were either flush with funds, or that it enjoyed significant goodwill secured through the granting of favours, was provided by the construction of a new and luxurious Chinese-built ZANU-PF conference centre – and costed at US$6.5 million – for the holding of its December 2012 Congress (*NewsDay Zimbabwe* 2012).

MDC-T efforts at damage limitation in terms of ZANU-PF's indigenisation efforts and control over diamond revenues only served to highlight what by 2013 had become clear to both domestic and foreign observers. ZANU-PF treated the MDCs with what could only be described as disdain and as very junior partners in government, and took advantage of every opportunity to do so publicly. Often the content and timing of ZANU-PF initiatives such as the indigenisation policy seemed to be aimed specifically at forcing the MDC-T onto the defensive, both showing up its inability to protect what should have been a critical support base and source of party funding, namely the country's residual independent private sector which had managed to survive and operate outside the bounds of ZANU-PF patronage economics, while also hindering economic recovery by discouraging foreign investment.

Possibly even more significantly, what ZANU-PF obstructionism also did was to remind Zimbabweans that the traditional route to personal enrichment, namely access to ZANU-PF's larder, was still available subject to loyalty to that party's objectives. With elections looming, there were timely reminders that the only really important and still functioning market was that of influence peddling in the corridors of power and patronage networks controlled by ZANU-PF.

What the wealth generated through the exploitation of the Chiadzwa/Marange diamonds also permitted was the cementing of the symbiotic relationship between the leadership of ZANU-PF and the country's defence and security apparatus, and underpinned the mutual reinforcement of extractive political and economic institutions noted by Acemoglu and Robinson:

> Extractive political institutions lead to extractive economic institutions, which enrich a few at the expense of many. Those who benefit from extractive institutions thus have the resources to build their (private) armies and mercenaries, to buy their judges, and to rig elections to remain in power. They also have every interest in defending the system. Therefore, extractive economic institutions create the platform for extractive political institutions to persist. (Acemoglu and Robinson 2013, 343)

Even if such dynamics only compounded state fragility with long-term negative consequences for recovery, ZANU-PF's self-interest lay in the perpetuation of the state systems from which it benefited, and in obstructing the necessary reforms which might threaten the gains that accrued to it through the exploitation of such fragility. If for the opposition party signatories to the GPA of September 2008 the IG had offered the prospect of a transition from the monopoly rule of ZANU-PF to a reformed and pluralistic society, polity and economy, the experience of cohabitation made it clear that this vision was not one ever shared by President Mugabe, ZANU-PF and the securocrats, whose strategy from day one was to undermine the coalition administration and block the MDCs at every opportunity while simultaneously rebuilding the party's power base. The profoundly dysfunctional, and often openly fractious nature of the IG, became increasingly evident over time, as well as the fact that all parties had come to see the coalition as an inconvenience, simply to be tolerated until the next general elections resolved the deadlock.[10]

Notes

1. One modality for such economic empowerment became clear in the course of 2012 when, in a repeat of the FTLRP, there were reports that leading figures in the military and intelligence apparatus had moved into the Save Valley Conservancy, one of the largest privately-owned parks in Africa, and granted themselves 25-year leases under the guise of 'economic empowerment' and 'indigenisation', though central government would eventually intervene in 2014 and rescind those leases (*Zimbabwe Situation* 2014).
2. The accusations levelled by MDC-T at the indigenisation and economic empowerment policy, on the grounds it had been designed to benefit an existing ZANU-PF connected elite and was simply a repeat of the FTLRP which it claimed had also catered to the needs of an undeserving few, clearly hit a raw nerve. ZANU-PF therefore felt compelled, given that the policy had been given prominence based on the expectation that it would be a popular vote winner, to state in its manifesto that as "a revolutionary programme that seeks to meet the goals of the people in line with the objectives and legacy of the liberation struggle as an expression of the people's sovereignty, it is important to understand that the Indigenisation and Empowerment programme is not about benefiting a few well-connected individuals" (ZANU-PF 2013, 82).
3. In 2010 the African Development Bank conducted an in-depth survey focused on the status of Zimbabwe's economic physical infrastructure, i.e. transport (roads, railways and civil aviation), power generation and distri-

bution, Information and Communications Technology and water and sanitation, and estimated the costs of the necessary rehabilitation and expansion of this infrastructure at US$14.2 billion (AfDB 2011, 30).

4. Recourse to the domestic capital markets was not an option. National savings had been decimated by hyperinflation, which while having the advantage of allowing the previous ZANU-PF government to retire large amounts of domestic public debt which were simply inflated away, also caused untold misery to millions as pension funds and other investment vehicles which had invested in government debt found their asset base wiped out.
5. While the latter had become impossible under dollarization, there were soon voices from within the ranks of ZANU-PF demanding the reintroduction of the Zimbabwe dollar as they discovered the constraints the new monetary arrangement placed on the scope for RBZ largesse.
6. A British mining concern, Africa Consolidated Resources, had held the prospecting rights to the area after acquiring them in 2006. These rights were subsequently cancelled by the Government, and its staff were removed from the location by the ZRP, with the mining rights being taken over by the state-owned Zimbabwe Mining Development Corporation (ZMDC) which was then able to select its own mining companies.
7. For details on some of the schemes set up to ensure parallel flows outside central government systems see Partnership Africa Canada 2012.
8. According to one report, amongst the members of the company's Executive Board were the Permanent Secretary of the Ministry of Defence and a Commissioner in the ZRP (Global Witness 2012a, 6).
9. The same report notes that there was information that a key figure within the Chinese syndicate behind the Anjin operation had provided the CIO with US$100 million, and argued that "If true this is a significant sum [and] would free the CIO from having to seek funding from the Ministry of Finance, and would give the CIO considerable freedom to set its own agenda" (Global Witness 2012b, 7).
10. ZANU-PF's views on the GPA and the IG were again made clear in its 2013 election manifesto, in which the IG was seen as an impediment to the realisation of ZANU-PF's revolutionary programme and the product of illegal regime change efforts by the country's enemies, and during which "the last five years of the awkward GPA government have exerted the greatest toll on the people's aspirations" (ZANU-PF 2013, 31).

References

Acemoglu, Daron, and James A. Robinson. 2013. *Why Nations Fail – The Origins of Power, Prosperity and Poverty*. London: Profile Books.

AfDB. 2011. *Infrastructure and Growth in Zimbabwe – An Action Plan for Sustained Strong Economic Growth*. Tunis.

Afrobarometer. 2013. *Zimbabweans' Views on Empowerment: Jobs vs. Business Takeovers*, Briefing Paper No. 115, March.

Global Witness. 2012a. *Diamonds: A Good Deal for Zimbabwe?* February 13. London.

———. 2012b. *Financing a Parallel Government? The Involvement of the Secret Police and Military in Zimbabwe's Diamond, Cotton and Property Sectors*, June. London.

GOZ. 2008. *Indigenisation and Economic Empowerment Act* [*Chapter 14:33*].

———. 2012. *The 2013 National Budget Statement*, November 15. Harare.

Human Rights Watch. 2009. *Diamonds in the Rough – Human Rights Abuses in the Marange Diamond Fields in Zimbabwe*, June 26. New York.

Kwenda, Stanley. 2009. *Q&A: Zimbabwe's Finance Minister, 'The Worst Job in the World'*, February 18. Inter Press Service News Agency. http://www.ipsnews.net/2009/02/qa-zimbabwe39s-finance-minister-lsquolquothe-worst-job-in-the-world3939/.

Matyszak, Derek. 2011. *Everything You Ever Wanted to Know (and Then Some) About Zimbabwe's Indigenisation and Economic Empowerment Legislation but (Quite Rightly) Were Too Afraid to Ask*. Harare: Research and Advocacy Unit.

———. 2014a. *Madness and Indigenisation: A History of Insanity in the Age of Lawlessness*. Harare: Research and Advocacy Unit.

———. 2014b. *Mugabe, Gono and the Rule of Law*. Harare: Research and Advocacy Unit.

MDC. 2012. *Resolutions of the MDC National Council*, April 12. Harare.

Muzondidya, James. 2013. The Opposition Dilemma in Zimbabwe: A Critical Review of the Politics of the Movement for Democratic Change Under the GPA Government Framework 2009–2012. In *The Hard Road to Reform – The Politics of Zimbabwe's Global Political Agreement*, ed. Brian Raftopolous, 39–70. Harare: Weaver Press.

Nehanda Internet News. 2012. Too Many Looters in Zimbabwe Government, September 30. http://nehandaradio.com/2012/09/30/too-many-looters-zimbabwe-governement/.

New Zimbabwe. 2012a. Biti Cuts Budget, Blames Diamonds, July 18. http://www.newzimbabwe.com/news-8531-Biti+cuts+budget+blames+diamonds/news.aspx.

———. 2012b. Reveal Source of US$ 20 Million, Mugabe Told, November 3. http://zimbabwesituation.com/old/nov5_2012.html#WXipzIWcEmz.

NewsDay Zimbabwe. 2012. Chance for Zanu Pf to Come Clean, December 7. https://www.newsday.co.zw/2012/12/07/chance-for-zanu-pf-to-come-clean/.

Office of the Prime Minister. 2012. *Statement on the Indigenization of Banks and Private Educational Institutions*, July 3. Harare: Press Release.

Partnership Africa Canada. 2010. *Diamonds and Clubs – The Militarized Control of Diamonds and Power in Zimbabwe*. Ottawa.

———. 2012. *Reap What You Sow: Greed and Corruption in Zimbabwe's Marange Diamond Fields*. Ottawa.

UNCTAD. 2012. *World Investment Report 2012*. New York/Geneva.

ZANU-PF. 2013. *Team ZANU-PF 2013*. Harare.

Zimbabwe Situation. 2014. ZCTF -Army General Booted Out of Save Valley Conservancy, May 22. http://www.zimbabwesituation.com/new/zimsit_zctf-army-general-booted-save-valley-conservancy/.

13

A Resurgent ZANU-PF

Rebuilding ZANU-PF Support and Rebooting the Rhetoric

With a view to projecting itself as the only natural party of choice amongst voters – and certainly the only choice of any right thinking 'patriotic' Zimbabwean – ZANU-PF had sought during the IG to both reinvigorate its ideology through the injection of new elements, and re-energise the public presentation of its position on a range of national issues. Its propagandists emphasised the party's unique combination of legitimacy derived from ZANU-PF's history of armed struggle and the independence it had won for the people, the social advances made under successive ZANU-PF governments, particularly in the areas of health and education, and above all the fundamental economic transformation wrought by the FTLRP which was couched in terms of the irreversible economic empowerment of the masses and the correction of historical wrongs. Where shortcomings were identified in Zimbabwe's post-independence trajectory, blame for this was deflected and attributed to external actors working in collusion with anti-patriotic elements within Zimbabwe who aimed to reverse the gains made since

M. Simpson, T. Hawkins, *The Primacy of Regime Survival*,
https://doi.org/10.1007/978-3-319-72520-8_13

Independence, overthrow ZANU-PF, and return Zimbabwe to a state of colonial subjugation.

ZANU-PF's 2013 election manifesto blended a powerful and heady combination of three main elements. Each aimed to rebuild the party's revolutionary credentials in the eyes of the population which its leadership believed had been negatively impacted by the artificial and enforced power-sharing arrangement of the IG, and also to delegitimise opposition parties by highlighting the role they had played (and would continue to play) in what were portrayed as anti-people and anti-Zimbabwe machinations conducted at the behest of the West.

The first pillar of its election platform was its undertaking to pursue final and irreversible economic empowerment based on the indigenisation policy referenced above. Not only was there an unequivocal commitment to pursue this policy to its logical conclusion for the benefit of all Zimbabweans – and this came to occupy centre stage in its manifesto – but election material also consistently put forward the case that only ZANU-PF was genuinely interested in delivering economic empowerment to the country's 'indigenous' Zimbabweans.

The second element was the manifesto's reaffirmation of a longstanding interpretation of the country's modern history (widely disseminated through history textbooks used in the country's schools), namely that ZANU-PF had played a unique and irreplaceable role in the country's liberation. It therefore possessed an incontrovertible right to guide Zimbabwe into the future given "the enduring and unforgettable fact that it is Zanu PF which liberated Zimbabwe after prosecuting a heroic armed struggle" (ZANU-PF 2013, 7). In addition, it was therefore the only natural home of all truly patriotic Zimbabweans since "Zanu PF is Zimbabwe's only Patriotic Front" (Ibid., 21), the clear inference being that the MDC formations were not patriotic.

Thirdly, the manifesto was replete with anti-Western and anti-opposition party rhetoric. The targets were Western powers who had imposed 'illegal sanctions', and provided support to opposition parties and a cabal of NGOs, all of whom worked together to bring about regime change while operating under the guise of their democratisation and human rights protection agendas, an unholy alliance of actors engaged in an anti-Zimbabwe plot. The manifesto built on a longstanding programme of propaganda carried by the state media which had cast such opposition parties as "stooges" of the West and "sell outs" of Zimbabwe's hard-won independence. ZANU-PF was thus engaged in a struggle against:

> the illegal and evil sanctions and the illegal regime change agenda sought by the founders and funders of reactionary political parties that do not have any programme of their own and which are essentially anti-people and pro-crisis not least because they have defined themselves as enemies of Zimbabwe's heroic liberation struggle (Ibid., 43).

The message was that ZANU-PF was the sole, best and last line of defence protecting the Zimbabwean people against attempts at re-colonisation and dispossession.

The manifesto also argued that ZANU-PF's decision to sign the Global Political Agreement (GPA) was not the result of external compulsion following its loss at the polls in 2008, but rather "a stroke of genius by the Party's President and First Secretary Cde Robert Mugabe" (ZANU-PF 2013, 60). The attribution of genius qualities to Mugabe derived from the fact that:

> The GPA has enabled Zanu PF to prove its leadership quality, political maturity and governance experience while it has also exposed the political immaturity, ideological bankruptcy, policy inexperience, corruption, sexual scandal[1] and the incapacity to govern of the MDC formations whose officials have used the GPA to show their true colours by abandoning the people in pursuit of selfish interests (Ibid., 61).

In addition to efforts to project ZANU-PF as true champion of the interests of the country's youth and war veterans, the party also sought to cast itself as the defender of the numerous new smallholders who had benefited from the FTLRP, seeking to convince them of the very real dangers of regime change which would be followed by the reversal of land reform as former owners repossessed their properties. Its election manifesto highlighted the role ZANU-PF had played during the COPAC negotiations in securing the inclusion of clauses guaranteeing the irreversibility of land reform, setting itself up as the party of choice for those who wanted to avoid future constitutional amendments on this issue, and a return to a pre-FTLRP situation. Beneficiaries were also promised new and more secure forms of title, and greater access to agricultural inputs through various support programmes.

The manifesto also granted pride of place to the country's security forces, and ZANU-PF sought to ensure their support by highlighting the fact that they were the offspring of the liberation struggle forces of ZANLA and ZIPRA. Members of the security sector were also reminded that they owed a debt of gratitude and continued loyalty to ZANU-PF, as the latter had helped ensure that the former were protected from external interference.

A ZANU-PF move to capture support amongst previously neglected segments of Zimbabwean society, and which went largely unnoticed at the time, was also detected by some analysts, and provided a good indication of the extent to which the party was single-mindedly seeking not only to rebuild its support amongst its traditional base, but also nurture new ones even if this meant compromises with economic operators which it had previously sought to control or eliminate. While the pre-2009 ZANU-PF regime had used an iron fist to secure full control of the diamond mines for its handpicked mining firms, and in the course of implementing this policy had used extensive violence against artisanal diamond miners, it now adopted a more nuanced approach towards small-scale gold miners. This was also a sector dominated by the youth, which as noted above was a segment of the electorate that ZANU-PF was actively seeking to woo given its importance in terms of potential votes. During the IG the ZANU-PF controlled Ministry of Mines thus went into reverse gear, and actively sought to support the country's growing number of artisanal miners engaged in gold mining by facilitating formalisation processes and registration of small mine claims, and setting up gold buyer centres where competitive prices would be paid.

Given that membership of the Zimbabwe Artisanal and Small-Scale Mining Council (ZASMC) stood at 25,000 registered miners, with those dependent on the sector either directly or indirectly as well as non-ZASMC miners likely representing many times a multiple of the number of registered miners, it was clear that cultivating this segment of the economy was likely to yield substantial electoral dividends for ZANU-PF.[2] It also helps to explain the inclusion in the party's 2013 election manifesto of a specific commitment to "Institute measures to legalise artisanal mining" (ZANU-PF 2013, 104).

MDC-T's Loss of Resonance

That such revitalised ZANU-PF propaganda gained purchase amongst diverse segments of the electorate was helped in no small measure by growing popular disillusionment with the MDC-T. During the IG, the state media had been quick to pick up and highlight every problem the main opposition party faced in order to undermine its credibility. Foremost amongst these was growing disquiet within the rank and file of the MDC-T that Tsvangirai, as well as many of the party's ministers and representatives in Parliament and at local government level, seemed to have taken to the benefits of office with unseemly relish, to the point where with a few notable exceptions it had become difficult to distinguish the luxurious ministerial homes, expensive cars and extended expenses paid international trips abroad of MDC-T notables from those enjoyed by their ZANU-PF counterparts. The common phenomenon of those fighting authoritarian regimes gradually taking on the characteristics of those they had opposed, and which in the case of Zimbabwe translated into the 'Zanufication' of the MDCs, appeared to have rapidly taken root during the IG.

Tsvangirai's apparent deference towards Mugabe, and willingness to accommodate ZANU-PF's concerns at every turn in order to avoid a collapse of the IG, and towards the end of the cohabitation arrangement his seeming acceptance of failure in the daily battle of wills within Cabinet on critical issues such as security sector reform, transitional justice, the conducting of a land audit, and need for greater transparency in terms of diamond revenues, all served to undermine his credibility in the eyes of many of his supporters. In contrast to the combative approach taken by some ministers from his party such as Mangoma and Biti, Tsvangirai's performance was in general less than impressive. Mugabe's wily efforts to gradually wear down the PM seemed to have borne fruit, with Tsvangirai eventually finding himself and his party bundled into elections at a time of ZANU-PF's choosing, and in an electoral landscape where objectively little had changed to suggest that it would be any more free or fair than in 2008, let alone that there was any greater likelihood that the results would be respected if they turned out to be prejudicial to ZANU-PF.

Coexistence with ZANU-PF at times seemed to have tipped over into cosiness (and overconfidence within the higher echelons of the MDC-T that the direction of travel was favourable to them, notwithstanding strong evidence to the contrary), and reached the point where Tsvangirai often appeared oblivious, or at worst indifferent, to the reality of ZANU-PF manoeuvres aimed at restoring its monopoly on power by side-lining the MDC-T at every opportunity.[3] At times it appeared the MDC-T's leader believed all that was required was to survive the IG, and ensure the new constitution helped level the electoral laying field so as to avoid a repeat of 2008 when his party's path to power had been blocked.

MDC-T signally failed to counter ZANU-PF's control of the powerful state media. The latter was used unashamedly by ZANU-PF propagandists to cast doubts over the performance of both MDCs during the IG, as well as to rewrite history and exonerate ZANU-PF from responsibility for the crisis decade. Such control also allowed ZANU-PF to claim that every improvement in the lives of ordinary Zimbabweans during the IG was in fact due either to its insistence that MDC-controlled ministries pursue specific policies which it approved of, or to its own visionary past policies, even if such gains were well known, at least amongst those with access to independent media sources, as due to the more recent efforts of MDC ministers. The deficient communications strategy of the MDC formations during the IG, and ZANU-PF's control of the state media and relentless output of its sophisticated propaganda machinery, allowed ZANU-PF to even claim credit for progress made in health, education, and macroeconomic stabilisation, all portfolios assigned to MDC ministers. Unsurprisingly, there was no coverage by the state media of the rebuilding of bridges with Western donors which had secured MDC ministers the necessary resources to initiate recovery in those sectors. To the extent that the reality of the crisis decade was acknowledged at all, control of state media also allowed ZANU-PF to continue to attribute the country's meltdown to 'illegal sanctions', again disassociating it from the consequences of its own former policies and actions.

As an example of the employment of this tactic, the extremely limited financial resources available to the MDC-T controlled Ministry of Housing and Social Amenities had resulted in little progress being made to address a national shelter deficit that had been accumulated over decades. This in turn enabled ZANU-PF to claim in its 2013 election manifesto that the country's severe housing shortages reflected MDC-T indifference to the plight of the people (the inference also being that such shortages were in no way related to the massive destruction of homes during Operation *Murambatsvina*, or years of ZANU-PF neglect of the need for more public investments in housing), with a central role again granted to the damaging effects of "illegal sanctions imposed on Zimbabwe by Western countries over the past 14 years" (ZANU-PF 2013, 27).

The same rationalisation was applied to the country's external debt burden. This was attributed not to previous reckless borrowing (and questionable lending by the IFIs), and the signal failure of successive ZANU-PF governments to service these debts, but rather to an onerous Rhodesian era debt Harare had inherited at Independence, the cost of government responses to successive droughts and most importantly and predictably the impact of recent 'illegal sanctions' as a result of which "Zimbabwe's debt burden multiplied over the last 14 years and the rest is history'"(Ibid., 48)

In a similar vein, as concerns the revival of education, and even though the ministry had been assigned to the MDC-M Minister David Coltart, the election manifesto claimed that the progress made in terms of the return of staff and reopening and reequipping of schools had little to do with his efforts. Rather it was a result of the fact that ZANU-PF had "ensured that the fundamental architecture of the country's internationally acclaimed system of education has remained intact…[and that] Zimbabwe's system of education is built on a profound and durable architecture enabled by ZANU-PF" (Ibid., 62–63).

Another argument pushed in ZANU-PF's elections propaganda was that the gains made during the IG were also tainted by their links to the regime change agenda of Western donors. So the latter's financing of the Trust Funds for Health and Education referenced in Chap. 10 was, in fact, aimed at the 'donorfication' of those sectors which had fallen under the control of the MDC formations. The hidden objective of the Western donors was to "uproot the architecture of education and health delivery built by Zanu PF since 1980 and widely acknowledged around the world as hallmarks of unparalleled success" (Ibid., 52).

Furthermore, in a clear attempt to counter MDC-T accusations of ZANU-PF's control over parallel revenue flows from diamonds and other sources, the flows of donor resources to Health and Education were also presented as sinister and lacking transparency. These donors have been "pouring funds into the two ministries through illegal parallel structures" and "outside government accountability structures" (Ibid., 51–52). In addition, in the same way that ZANU-PF was often accused of using its parallel revenue streams to secure support for regime maintenance, so the manifesto claimed that these donor funds were using education structures, "to transform them into political structures of opposition formations…for purposes of political mobilisation at the grassroots level" (Ibid., 52).

This recasting of the recent past also included the introduction of the multi-currency system in early 2009. Rather than resulting from belated recognition that the public had already abandoned the Zimbabwe dollar as a medium of exchange, and therefore forced on ZANU-PF at the tail end of the previous government, this was now packaged as a deliberate and foresighted decision by the then ZANU-PF Minister of Finance, and reflected a concern for the welfare of the people. According to the manifesto, the fact was that "Zanu PF had the strategic vision and ideologically stomached the use of Uncle Sam's currency to protect the people from the vagaries of hyperinflation" (Ibid., 62).

Overall, ZANU-PF's election manifesto stood in stark contrast to the MDC-T's not only in terms of length and detail,[4] but also the attractiveness and timeframes of policies presented, promising significant and immediate improvements in the welfare of all segments of the electorate. The magnitude of the wealth that would be "unlocked", and available for rapid distribution as a result of indigenisation and economic empowerment to those that supported ZANU-PF, was exhaustively detailed by source, amount and distribution mechanism.[5] The message was that a veritable cornucopia of goodies would become immediately available should ZANU-PF regain sole control of the reins of power, ranging from equity in indigenised companies to loans at preferential rates, in addition to packages of other enticing items such as agricultural inputs and scholarships available through various 'special Presidential initiatives'.

In a society in which radical dispossession by the state had become an accepted, if not deeply entrenched, route to individual wealth accumulation, and in which ZANU-PF had played the role of planner and enforcer of the necessary policies, its promise to take the next and final step in its indigenisation masterplan would have resonated deeply, and seen as credible, by an electorate with experience of the FTLRP and operations such as *Murambatsvina* and *Dzikisa Mutengo* amongst others. As the election manifesto itself joyously trumpeted "Team Zanu PF has something for everyone" (Ibid., 104).

In contrast, the MDC-T's manifesto committed the party to the immediate implementation (within the first 100 days of an MDC-T government) of the new constitutional provisions covering the key political and institutional reforms it had fought for. The proposed legislative programme for a new Parliament would cover areas ranging from security sector reform, the establishment of a National Peace and Reconciliation Commission, the repeal of oppressive legislation such as POSA and AIPPA, and strengthening of the Human Rights and Anti-Corruption Commissions.

However, when compared to ZANU-PF's promises of instant material gratification through yet another bout of wealth seizures and redistribution, the MDC-T's economic policy offerings promised less immediate gratification, focusing as they did on the harder, longer-term and more sustainable task of restoring output levels and employment growth, and emphasising the need to maintain macroeconomic stability. As the MDC-T's election manifesto stated: "The MDC economic pillar is based on the central idea that wealth creation is a solid foundation for sustainable distribution" (MDC-T 2013, 10). Featuring in the economic component of its election manifesto were items such as the need to review legislation to improve conditions for business and thereby attract FDI and raise the rate of domestic investment, and the creation of an environment conducive to job growth and the development of entrepreneurship. Additional commitments in the manifesto, specifically aimed at reducing Zimbabwe's fragility, included the establishment of a Sovereign Wealth Fund to ensure transparent management of the country's mineral resources,[6] facilitating the formalisation of informal enterprises, establishing the Land Commission as provided for in the new constitution and ensuring that land audits were conducted, and engaging the IFIs in order to secure new credit lines and a resolution of the external debt problem. These would, however, take time to yield results, putting MDC-T at a distinct disadvantage when compared to the immediate benefits on offer by ZANU-PF from wealth that could be immediately "unlocked" and distributed from indigenised companies once the revolutionary party was returned to power.[7]

The contrast was stark. If on the one hand the MDC-T promised to deliver a private sector-driven economy conducive to the acquisition by citizens of business skills and training which would in turn enable them to engage in the hard and long-term work of building and growing their own enterprises and increasing employment, ZANU-PF in exchange for support promised them existing enterprises and wealth, at no cost and immediately. And for those with any moral qualms about benefiting from such transfers ZANU-PF helpfully cast these in terms of a natural "God given" entitlement due to their beneficiary status as "indigenous Zimbabweans".

MDC-T's Estrangement From Allies

One consequence of the IG experience, and the drain on the limited human resources and experience of the MDC parties as they were forced to focus on daily and oftentimes bruising encounters with their ZANU-PF counterparts in Cabinet, was that Tsvangirai and his lieutenants gradually distanced themselves from their roots in both the independent trade union movement and vibrant CSO community. These two groups of actors had in the past provided his party with essential support in terms of votes, funding, organisational and mobilising skills, access to international networks as well as intellectual firepower.

The crisis years had taken a significant toll on the country's formally employed workforce. As a result of both deindustrialisation and migration, the latter had shrunk significantly and been overtaken numerically by those engaged in the informal sector, with inevitable consequences in terms of weakening of the country's unions, with the number of unionised workers falling from around 200,000 in 1990 to 162,000 in 2013 (Solidarity Peace Trust 2013, 19). Notwithstanding the undoubted benefits to workers of low inflation after the trauma of hyperinflation, the restoration of education and health services and improved supplies of basic goods that followed the entry of the MDC-T into government, the MDC-T controlled Ministry of Labour could subsequently do little to significantly improve wages and conditions for the urban working class given the fiscal stringency overseen by the MDC-T Ministry of Finance, low rates of investment, and slowing GDP growth rates registered after the initial rebound of 2009–2012.

In the case of public sector workers, and notwithstanding the welcome relief provided by the end of hyperinflation and the granting of hard currency wages to large numbers of teachers and health workers made possible through donor-funded schemes, subsequent wage freezes imposed by the Ministry of Finance, coupled with the abolition of price controls, gradually undermined support for the MDC-T from this significant segment of the country's workforce. And with no price to pay for the positions it took, ZANU-PF was then able to take the high ground as it called for salary increases for public sector workers, accusing the MDC-T of not having the interests of these workers at heart when such increases were not forthcoming.

In addition, early on during the IG, the Prime Minister had promised to deliver on a commitment in the GPA, namely to establish a National Economic Council with representation from the full range of economic and private sectors, academia and the labour unions. This body was to be tasked with the provision of advice to the IG government and formulation of economic policies and programmes. Like so many promised MDC-T initiatives, as a result of ZANU-PF resistance, it proved stillborn, further undermining the party's credibility in the eyes of key constituencies.

While not necessarily significant in terms of numbers of members and therefore votes, the country's CSOs had historically provided the MDC-T with vital support, not least those CSOs concerned with human rights issues. They had, at critical moments, furnished MDC-T leaders and activists with invaluable legal advice and assistance when harassed, arrested or imprisoned by the ZANU-PF regime, and also meticulously documented human rights violations and disseminated the evidence both domestically and internationally. However, MDC-T's seeming indifference or inability to make substantial progress during the IG on issues of transitional justice and accountability and security sector reform, most evident in the lack of any prosecutions of those responsible for the political violence of 2008, coupled with the alacrity with which its leadership and elected representatives seemed to have taken to the material benefits of office and reached an accommodation with ZANU-PF, led to a distinct cooling in relations between MDC-T and the country's main CSOs.

The most publicly strained of relations between the MDC-T and former non-state actor allies was that between the MDC-T and the NCA. The latter, it is worth recalling, had been one of the midwives of the MDC in the late 1990s. During the COPAC process, not only did the NCA take to accusing the MDC-T of neglecting its previous commitment to a 'people-driven' constitution-making process that was not led by political parties but rather by an independent Constitutional Commission, but also of engaging in closed door negotiations with ZANU-PF to arrive at what it characterised as a new 'politician-driven' constitution that primarily reflected the interests of political parties. Over the course of the COPAC process, the NCA's charges of MDC-T collusion with ZANU-PF became increasingly frequent and vociferous:

> we wish to tell the MDC-T to stop fooling Zimbabweans to support this scandalous draft which they crafted together with ZANU PF so that they enjoy the same powers. Instead their focus should be on dealing with internal problems which range from corruption, factionalism, waning popularity and not spending time attacking the NCA and its leadership for its principled stance on the drafting of a new charter for Zimbabwe (National Constitutional Assembly 2012).

The MDC-T regularly trumpeted the COPAC draft as one of its major achievements during the IG.[8] But the widely disseminated NCA critiques of the COPAC draft cast doubts as to whether MDC-T's triumphalism in regards to the new constitution, wherein it depicted itself as having successfully extracted concessions from ZANU-PF through the adoption of a tough and principled negotiating stance, was in fact deserved. More substantively, NCA criticisms also served to cast doubts over MDC-T's assertions that the new constitution represented a sea change for the country in terms of governance. The NCA argued, for example, that contrary to MDC-T claims that new constitutional provisions had weakened the Executive Presidency, very little had effectively changed.[9]

The NCA leader, Lovemore Madhuku, also strongly criticised the MDC-T leader for alleged failures during the IG, which in his opinion had led to a situation in which ZANU-PF now found itself in a more secure position from which to contest the upcoming elections:

> He allowed them to reach the next election without any reforms. The purpose of the inclusive government was to create a transitional arrangement at the end of which we would be able to have a stable country that can run free and fair elections. Tsvangirai spent the last three and a half years in an arrangement where he extracted no fundamental reforms (*Daily News* 2012).

The NCA was to subsequently call on its supporters to boycott the 2013 constitutional referendum.

In addition to weakened ties with organised labour and sections of the CSO community, it is important to note that the MDC-T also failed to build upon the inroads into ZANU-PF's key Shona rural support base it had made in the 2008 elections, most particularly amongst small-scale beneficiaries of land reform, and which proved so alarming to ZANU-PF. Not only did MDC-T activists continue to face obstacles in terms of accessing ZANU-PF's rural heartlands, but where they did succeed in establishing themselves the recent traumatic memories of the violence meted out by ZANU-PF supporters to MDC-T activists and voters in 2008 inevitably forced them to keep a low profile. ZANU-PF was also able to undermine MDC-T efforts to build support amongst small-scale land reform beneficiary farmers[10] by using the social control exercised by traditional leaders aligned to ZANU-PF to ensure the allegiance of community members. As noted in the previous chapter, through various special initiatives, ZANU-PF targeted its parallel resource flows in such a way as to maintain this large constituency of small-scale FTLRP beneficiaries, which it could rightly claim as its progeny, within the fold.

While revenue constraints meant the MDC-T Minister of Finance was only able to allocate minimal funds to support small-scale agriculture, this meant that the GMB, which fell within the purview of the ZANU-PF-controlled Ministry of Agriculture, was starved of resources and therefore could only offer low prices for the maize surpluses of farmers and few inputs, while agricultural infrastructure received negligible support. This enabled Mugabe's aforementioned Presidential Agricultural Input Scheme to step into the breach. In addition to ZANU-PF election manifesto promises to strengthen tenure security for all beneficiaries of the FTLRP, the party was thus able to claim that through the Presidential Scheme it was rescuing these farmers from what it characterised as a "Treasury [which] fell under the treacherous hands of a minister of finance whose hostility to the development of infrastructure, particularly in the sector of agriculture, knew no bounds" (ZANU-PF 2013, 85).

Warning Signs for the MDC-T

Growing ZANU-PF activism, and its single-minded focus on avoiding a repeat of the first round of the 2008 elections, converged with growing popular disenchantment with the MDC-T's performance during the IG, and soon translated into a marked fall in support for the latter, and a commensurate increase in support for the former. What had previously been anecdotal evidence that such shifts were taking place was given credence in 2012 when Freedom House[11] published the results of a public opinion survey, part of a series of surveys it had carried out since 2009 and the formation of the IG. A number of findings from the survey stood out.

Firstly, there were indications of a collapse in the public's trust in the MDC-T, accompanied by an increase in popular trust enjoyed by ZANU-PF. While in the 2010 survey 32 percent of respondents had stated that they trusted MDC-T 'a lot', by 2012 this percentage had fallen to 20 percent. In addition, and even more worrying for MDC-T given that as the "party of change" its electoral messaging had always stressed its transparency and honesty', the extent of popular disillusionment with the MDC-T can also be seen in the percentages of those who did not trust the MDC-T 'at all', which increased substantially from 9 percent to 25 percent. Equally significant was the fact that the responses of those who trusted ZANU-PF 'a lot' more than doubled from 16 percent to 34 percent, while those who trusted it 'not at all' fell from 34 percent to 24 percent between the two surveys (Freedom House 2012, 20).

The significant decline in approval ratings of MDC-T as a party was accompanied by falls in support for both Tsvangirai as party leader and MDC-T MPs. If 55 percent of respondents declared that they would have voted for an MDC-T Presidential candidate in 2009, and in 2010 38 percent would have voted for MDC-T parliamentary candidates, by 2012 these percentages had fallen to 19 percent and 20 percent respectively. In contrast, support for a ZANU-PF Presidential candidate had increased from 12 percent in 2009 to 31 percent in 2012, with similarly impressive growth in support for ZANU-PF parliamentary candidates from 17 percent in 2010 to 31 percent in 2012 (Ibid., 18).

Further analysis of the survey results provided additional insights into MDC-T's loss of credibility in the eyes of the electorate. While in the 2010 survey 52 percent of respondents attributed 'good' or 'very good' aspects of the IG to the MDC-T, by 2012 the credit given to the party as the main contributor to the IG's positive results had fallen to 15 percent. Furthermore, ZANU-PF's share of credit for the positive aspects of the IG's performance increased from 13 percent to 16 percent over the same period, a sure sign of the success of ZANU-PF's efforts mentioned above to redeem itself in the eyes of the electorate and claim credit for any IG driven improvements (Ibid., 31).

This bad news for MDC-T was compounded by additional data showing the even more marked (and for the MDC-T worrying), loss of support in the country's urban areas which were the party's traditional strongholds. While in the 2010 survey 50 percent of respondents in Harare, and 51 percent in Bulawayo declared their support for the MDC-T, by 2012 this had fallen to 17 percent and 29 percent respectively. This was accompanied by similar declines in support for the MDC-T in all of the other predominantly rural provinces. In addition, support for ZANU-PF in both Harare and Bulawayo increased significantly over the period (and in the case of Harare had overtaken support for MDC-T by 2012), with increases in support for ZANU-PF also registered in all of the country's other provinces (Ibid., 19).

The authors of the survey report were to draw a number of conclusions from the results which emphasised the MDC-T's loss of credibility:

> The years in power took their toll on the MDC-T. It was pressured to prove itself as a capable co-governing party, and often neglected to continuously nurture the political organisation. Leadership fatigue and battles, along with the MDC-T in office often being exposed as comparable-in-corruption to ZANU-PF helped complicate the MDC-T's early years in joint-but-dominated power. This dented its popular standing…There are indications that some MDC-T supporters may be moving away from seeing their party and its leaders as their unquestioned political saviour (Ibid., 10).

Initial MDC-T reactions to the survey results indicated a disturbing reluctance to face the facts and draw the necessary conclusions. There was a failure to recognise that profound damage had been done to its reputation amidst growing public perceptions that MDC-T representatives at central level had turned out to be no different from their ZANU-PF counterparts in terms of the priority they gave to the material benefits and prerogatives of office, added to the corruption exposed within the ranks of party members involved in urban local government (see Chap. 10), growing authoritarianism within the upper echelons of the party,[12] and most importantly a failure to do the necessary to recover ground lost to ZANU-PF. Frustration was often expressed by MDC-T supporters that they had been neglected and taken for granted by the party once it had entered the power-sharing arrangement, with their existence only recognised by the party leadership in the run-up to the 2013 referendum and elections.

The MDC-T's spokesman, however, denied that his party's support had fallen, and questioned the soundness of the Freedom House survey results on the grounds that it had been conducted "in an environment of fear and violence" (*Daily Telegraph* 2012).

ZANU-PF, however, was quick off the mark and latched onto the results, with one of its politburo members stating:

> Do they only believe these surveys if they are in their favour? Too bad because things speak for themselves on the ground. The MDC-T have

> proven to be a party too preoccupied with itself, they have spent four years in government fighting for positions, and not a single signature policy issue. On the other hand, Zanu PF has understood that to create jobs we need to indigenise the economy and people identify with that (*New Zimbabwe* 2012).

The above interpretation of ZANU-PF's favourable opinion survey results was to feature prominently in the party's 2013 election manifesto, with the party upbeat about its electoral prospects because:

> the party's Indigenisation and Empowerment Programme is synonymous with the goals of the people. These surveys which have been done by organisations that have nothing to do with Zanu PF and which have traditional links with the party's detractors have shown…that the support for President Mugabe and Zanu PF…is dramatically surging while the support for opposition formations with no policies to offer to uplift the livelihoods of the people is plummeting (ZANU-PF 2013, 107)

In the West, disappointment with the MDC-T was also clear. In a candid policy brief, the Directorate-General for External Policies of the European Parliament noted that in addition to the 'sexual adventures' of its leader, the reputation of the party has suffered from:

> reports of growing corruption and mismanagement within the MDC headquarters; and Tsvangirai's refusal to accept criticism of his increasingly centralised leadership. What is more, the MDC's participation in government…renders it increasingly difficult to argue that it could bring about a radical change for the better. Disenchanted with the party's inability to trigger decisive change, many young urbanites – previously the MDC's most devoted supporters – have stopped attending the party's once-overcrowded rallies (European Parliament 2013, 2).

The same report (from an institution that had in the recent past been extremely critical of the governance record of ZANU-PF and Mugabe, and instituted and maintained 'restrictive measures' against both senior members of the party, armed forces as well as business persons closely associated with ZANU-PF), also went on to conclude that one key lesson from the IG experience was that "Government turnover does not guarantee democratic change in Zimbabwe. ZANU-PF lacks democratic roots; but the MDC has, for its part, done little to prove its trustworthiness" (Ibid., 4).

Both domestic and external supporters would have also linked MDC-T's latest problems to an earlier development during its 2009 Congress following the establishment of the IG. In a move seen as uncomfortably reminiscent of ZANU-PF's manipulation of the country's constitution to allow Mugabe additional terms of office, and a sign of the 'Zanufication' of the MDC-T, the party's 2009 Congress participants were presented with a *fait accompli* amendment to the MDC-T party constitution, dropping a clause which had limited its President to two terms and which would have meant Tsvangirai had to step down in 2011 (*The Standard* 2009).

Arguments that the negative trends for MDC-T brought out by the Freedom House surveys had been statistical anomalies, as put forward by some party notables, were undermined by the results of another survey conducted in July 2012 by the Harare-based Mass Public Opinion Institute (MPOI). The margins of preference between the parties were significantly narrower in this survey than in the Freedom House exercise, with lower support expressed for ZANU-PF's leader and higher support for MDC-T's leader. However, while the same MPOI methodology applied in a May 2009 survey had yielded a 82 percent approval rating for performance for Tsvangirai and 24 percent for Mugabe, in July 2012 this had narrowed to 66 percent for Tsvangirai and 58 percent for Mugabe (Afrobarometer 2012, 5–6). One conclusion reached by MPOI analysts of these unfavourable results for MDC-T centred on shortcomings in terms of organisation and communication:

> While ZANU-PF seems to derive more benefit from recent government performance than it probably deserves, MDC-T seems to derive less. One reason may be that the former has paid more attention to grassroots organization and mass communication than the latter. While ZANU-PF has invested resources to rebuild its party machine and mobilise its political base, MDC-T has relied too heavily on a strategy of expecting political credit for improved service delivery (Ibid., 12).

Additional indications that ZANU-PF had successfully regrouped at local level during the IG were made available by the March 2013 constitutional referendum voting figures. With a turnout of 3.316 million voters, this was the largest in the country's history, and a clear sign that ZANU-PF had strengthened its mobilisation capacity at grassroots level and been able to bring out large numbers of its supporters to cast their ballots in favour of the new charter, most particularly in its heartland provinces of Mashonaland West, East and Central which registered the highest provincial level turnouts.[13] Compared to the 2008 elections, the turnout for the 2013 referendum in Mashonaland West saw an increase of 48.55 percent in the number of voters, in Mashonaland Central an increase of 45.51 percent, and in Mashonaland East an increase of 33.47 percent (Electoral Resource Centre 2013, 5). Significantly for the MDC-T, in its traditional stronghold provinces of Matabeleland North and South and Midlands, the increase in turnout was significantly lower at 14.46 percent, 17.13 percent and 17.39 percent respectively (Ibid., 5).

End of the Rebound and Continued Economic Fragility

While dollarization and price stability had been warmly welcomed by the majority of Zimbabweans in 2009, and the economic rebound of 2009–11 as measured by GDP growth had been significant with real GDP growth hitting 9.5 percent in 2010–11, by 2012 there were already concerns that this was beginning to peter out.[14] It was also evident that the rebound had not translated into significant improvements in formal employment figures. Losses incurred in formal non-farm employment in the aftermath of the FTLRP, which had fallen from just over 1,000,000 in the peak year of 1998, had still not been made up by 2012 and stood at 765,000. This represented a loss of some 240,000 jobs, with the largest losses in manufacturing (90,000), construction (60,000), and distribution including tourism at 25,000.[15]

Notwithstanding the best efforts of the MDC-T Minister of Finance, levels of economic fragility remained high and the pace of early progress proved not to be sustainable. The economy continued to be characterised by high levels of informality, with informal employment continuing to serve as an essential survivalist safety net for many Zimbabweans. Based on a 2011/12 welfare survey, out of the total estimated population of 11.7 million in 2011, 3.7 million Zimbabweans aged 10 years and over were employed in the informal sector. As their output was estimated to represent 14.2 percent of GDP, such high levels of informality continued to impact negatively on the already restricted government tax base (GOZ 2012, 100).

Post-GPA Zimbabwe also continued to show extremely high levels of poverty, with the same 2011/12 government welfare survey reporting a national household poverty incidence of 62.6 percent. Significantly – and undermining ZANU-PF's repeated claims of the impact of the FTLRP in terms of welfare improvements for rural households – 76.0 percent of all rural households were below the poverty line in 2011/12, with 76.4 percent of households in the country's resettlement areas where beneficiaries of land reform were located found to be in poverty. In addition, if as was often stated, one of the objectives of the FTLRP had been to improve livelihoods in communal areas through a process of decongestion, the even higher incidence of household poverty in communal areas at 79.4 percent clearly showed the limited impact of the programme in terms of poverty reduction criteria (Ibid., 74).

As highlighted in Chap. 10, the country continued to face an unresolved and worsening external debt problem. The IMF estimated that at end 2011 Zimbabwe's total external debt represented 113 percent of GDP. Further arrears had accumulated, which severely hampered access to new multilateral and bilateral loans, with total arrears amounting to US$6.34 billion at end 2011 (IMF 2012b, 2–3). In an all too familiar conclusion, the IMF stated that as a result Zimbabwe was "likely to remain in debt distress for the foreseeable future. The country's debt overhang remains a serious impediment to macroeconomic stability and sustainable growth and development" (Ibid., 8).

FDI, critically needed for the recovery of the economy, while registering an improvement over the negligible US$52 million for 2008, remained extremely low throughout the IG, and as observed in Chap. 12 was particularly poor when compared to the ability of Zimbabwe's regional neighbour to attract foreign investment. This performance in terms of FDI was in turn related to the poor business climate, which failed to register significant improvements. Amongst the contributing factors were high levels of corruption, and binding infrastructure bottlenecks, particularly in power and water supply, and which could not be addressed adequately during the IG given the resource constraints facing Treasury. To these might be added Zimbabwe's regulatory framework, an inheritance of decades of ZANU-PF economic dirigisme, and which together with the country's dismal track record in terms of respect for property rights and the provisions of bilateral investment treaties translated into an environment seen as extremely hostile to private sector operations.

Little was to change in terms of developing a business-friendly environment during the IG. The country continued to languish close to the bottom of the World Bank's Ease of Doing Business, rankings at 171st position out of a total of 183 countries (World Bank 2011, 138). In addition, the issue of indigenisation cast a significant pall over both potential domestic and foreign investors, with the IMF noting that "High country risk has maintained credit costs high, while political and policy uncertainty especially regarding the indigenization policy seems to have deterred long-term private investment inflows" (IMF 2012a, 26).

Despite the best efforts of the MDC-T Minister of Finance, as Zimbabwe entered its election year it was clear that he had made little headway in terms of securing the totality of revenues from diamond mining and sales, that most funds from this source remained outside his control, and that there was little he could do to reverse the situation. This subsector of the economy had, to all intents and purposes, become out of bounds to state institutions under his control, namely the Revenue Authority and the Treasury.

One consequence of failure to secure these resources, and a clear indication of continued economic fragility, was the fact that at end 2011 the country's international reserves were only marginally better than in 2008 when the country had less than a week's import cover (see Chap. 8). At end 2011, gross foreign reserves still represented less than ten days import cover (IMF 2012a, 5). This was in contrast to neighbouring South Africa with 4.7 months of import cover and Botswana at 15.9 months of reserves. Given that the recommended reserves for Zimbabwe were calculated at between 3.6 and 10 months of imports, vulnerability to external shocks of various kinds remained extremely high, with the country's reserves "much lower than the lower limit of the recommended range and... among the lowest among countries with similar exchange rate regimes" (Ibid., 52).

The reality of Zimbabwe's diamond operations was well known to the IFIs. While the IMF recommended in its 2012 evaluation that "The Government should follow through on its plans to enhance the revenue authority's capacity to monitor and assess the production and trade of diamonds", the agency was also clearly conversant with the resource curse in Zimbabwe, and went on to suggest that "Until transparency and the regulatory framework in the diamond sector are strengthened, it would be prudent to make sure the core budget can be financed without diamond revenue" (Ibid., 16–17).

The Delusions of Incumbency

Given the limited progress made in reforming Zimbabwe's extractive economic institutions and reducing state fragility, by early 2013 it was clear that the MDC-T could no longer rest on its laurels and assume that the macroeconomic stabilisation over which it had presided would still be a major vote winner. Yet four years after the ending of hyperinflation and the restoration of purchasing power of wages (even if at low levels for large segments of the population, especially those who remained below the poverty line), and improving the supply of goods and services and shaping a new constitution, in the higher echelons of the MDC-T there seemed to prevail a belief that these achievements were not only important but also sufficient conditions for it to be successful in the upcoming elections.

Another belief which seemed to hold sway within senior MDC-T circles was that all that was required for it to finally take office was to ensure that the next elections were as free and fair as possible. The expectation in 2013 was that ZANU-PF could be finally ousted by the opposition, even if the MDC remained divided as a result of failures to reunite the two MDC formations since their split in 2005, and despite supporters from both parties, as well as neutral observers, pointing out the dangers of splitting the opposition vote yet again as had happened in 2008.[16] A final push in 2013 was all that was required, with MDC-T leaders and supporters often referring to the moment which now presented itself as an opportunity to show Mugabe and ZANU-PF a "red card". Such views prevailed notwithstanding what was clear to many observers, namely a mostly unfinished GPA agenda, which given that the latter necessarily entailed the dismantling of ZANU-PF's parallel extractive political and economic structures had clearly not been accomplished.

As one international NGO was to observe in the run-up to the 2013 elections:

> Conditions for a free and fair vote do not exist. Confidence in the process and institutions is low. The voters roll is a shambles, security forces unreformed and the media grossly imbalanced. The electoral commission is underfunded and lacked time to prepare…The 31st July elections are to be held despite the failure of six years of SADC-facilitated negotiations to achieve significant reforms, including security sector realignment, fair media access and changes to laws inhibiting freedom of association and expression….[ZANU-PF] argues that the March 2013 constitution addresses these issues, but any chance for that document to make a practical difference was scuppered by the imposition of a date for the vote so early that implementing measures could not be ready in time (International Crisis Group 2013, 1–3).

The MDC-T clearly underestimated the extent to which, following its 2008 electoral debacle, ZANU-PF had successfully revived and strengthened its complex and sophisticated patronage networks, and through the finely calibrated inducement of actual or promised distribution of material goods had managed to tie significant segments of the population into a strengthened dependency on itself, with profound implications in terms of its electoral prospects. If ZANU-PF's election platform focused on the immediate provision of tangible goods to voters, and its manifesto went so far as to put specific figures to the wealth that would become available for redistribution through its indigenisation programme, MDC-T policies came across as more difficult to comprehend for many, and the material improvements promised less assured. In the aftermath of the 2013 elections, it became obvious that the MDC-T platform had not resonated as it had in 2008, and that as a result of growing detachment from its support base the party had failed to create and project an attractive set of policies that would appeal not only to the urbanised poor and middle class and those with jobs in the formal sector, but to Zimbabwe's impoverished rural masses.[17]

Prior to the 2013 elections, one foreign newspaper drew the necessary conclusions from the damage done to the MDC-T's reputation during the IG, and therefore its chances at the polls:

> The demise of authoritarianism in Zimbabwe will surely come. But there is little reason to think that the day is near, and even less to think that the opposition MDC is the party that will torpedo the current dictatorship. Today the party is more dysfunctional and commands less authority and support than ever before, and it shouldn't come as a surprise when it loses, even in a free and fair election (*The Guardian* 2013).

Notes

1. The 'sexual scandals' referred to Tsvangirai's relationship difficulties following the death of his wife in 2009. He was linked, *inter alia*, to a local businesswoman to whom he had to pay damages after he allegedly withdrew a promise to marry her, and pay maintenance to another woman with whom he had a young son, before eventually marrying another woman in September 2012 who was the daughter of a member of ZANU-PF's Central Committee. The state broadcaster took every opportunity to serialise the news on his turbulent relationships which had many Zimbabweans gripped, and served to raise doubts over his judgement and suitability as a national leader.
2. For a comprehensive treatment of the historical evolution of the mining sector in Zimbabwe from a political economy perspective see Mawowa 2013.
3. So, for example, in the course of a conference in Johannesburg in September 2010, Tsvangirai stated that Mugabe was "committed to this transition, once that transition is done he is committed to ensure that we have a peaceful election. That will restore his legacy as the founding

father of the nation as well as the liberator, rather than the villain he has come to be associated with" (*The Guardian* 2010).

4. ZANU-PF's 2013 manifesto was 108 pages long, whilst that of MDC-T stood at 30 pages.
5. So, for example, the manifesto drew attention to a figure of 1,138 earmarked foreign companies operating in 12 different sectors and valued at US$13.4 billion, with US$7.3 billion (51 percent of the value of the assets) thereby available for the economic empowerment of beneficiaries (ZANU-PF 2013, 83). The beneficiary mechanisms included Employee Empowerment Schemes (EES) which would ensure that equity was given to employees of indigenised companies, and Community Empowerment Schemes (CES) with communities benefiting from a share of royalties, profits and dividends from indigenised businesses operating in their areas.
6. Such a mechanism also featured in ZANU-PF's election manifesto and post-2013 economic plan, though some local wits were to characterise this as a 'Sovereign Slush Fund'.
7. To this might be added the complexity of some of the MDC-T's election commitments, which might be understood and appeal to an urbanised middle class and economics cognoscenti, but would not likely have been grasped by the vast majority of citizens despite the fact Zimbabwe continued to enjoy the highest literacy rate on the continent. So, for example, its commitment to promote a "social market economy", "Foster cluster based development" and "Reintegrate into regional and international value chains" (MDC-T 2013, 11–15).
8. Its 2013 election manifesto stated that "it was the MDC that fought hard and drove the constitution-making process" (MDC-T 2013, 2) and that the "MDC was the driving force in the formation and adoption of the constitution and is committed to its defence and full implementation" (Ibid., 27).
9. In a communique issued shortly before the referendum on the COPAC draft, the NCA complained that the constitution "leaves all power in the President, who is allowed to do what he/she wants." It noted that the President not only remained as the country's head of state, head of government and commander in chief, and notwithstanding the need to consult various bodies that to all intents and purposes the President's prerogatives remained effectively undiminished to appoint Ministers, Deputy Ministers, ambassadors, permanent secretaries, security chiefs,

judges, as well as members of various commissions. In addition, the NCA highlighted the absence of a provision guaranteeing the right to vote of the diaspora, and argued that the provisions governing decentralisation were weak while Presidential powers to dissolve the legislature remained essentially intact (National Constitutional Assembly 2013).

10. ZANU-PF's 2013 election manifesto put the total number of direct A1 beneficiaries from land reform at 162,750 (ZANU-PF 2013, 57).
11. An American NGO which advocates, researches and monitors the state of civil liberties and democracy around the world.
12. There was an increasing number of reports in the run-up to the 2013 elections that the party's central bodies were imposing their choice of candidates for local government and parliamentary representatives, and overturning the decisions of local MDC-T structures. Such impositions during the party's primaries were eventually to lead to a total of 28 candidates opting to run as independents in 2013, further splitting the anti-ZANU-PF vote.
13. As early as 2012 there were signs that ZANU-PF was engaged in a major recruitment drive for party members, and also seeking to increase the number of registered voters in its traditional strongholds.
14. In its 2012 Article IV consultation report the IMF was forecasting that GDP growth would fall to 5 percent for that year (IMF 2012a, 4).
15. These figures also help explain the weakened trade union movement referenced earlier, and its impact on the support base for the MDC-T in a context where employment was regularly reported as being as the single most pressing concern for Zimbabweans.
16. MDC-M was to suffer severe tribulations during the IG. Welshman Ncube, a leading light in the MDC-M team in the IG, and its Minister of Commerce and Industry, would eventually oust Mutambara from his position as leader of the smaller MDC faction, after which the MDC-M became known as MDC-N.
17. A few days prior to the 2013 elections, in a blatantly populist move to secure votes in urban areas, the ZANU-PF Minister for Local Government, Ignatius Chombo, issued instructions to local authorities to cancel the accumulated debts of urban households in terms of rentals, water and sewage and refuse collection payments (*New Zimbabwe* 2013).

References

Afrobarometer. 2012. *Voting Intentions in Zimbabwe: A Margin of Terror?*, Briefing Paper No. 103, August.

Daily News. 2012. Madhuku Ends MDC Relationship, November 29. Harare.

Daily Telegraph. 2012. Robert Mugabe's Zanu PF Has More Support Than Rival's Party, August 22. London.

Electoral Resource Centre. 2013. *Miracle Votes – An Analysis of the March 2013 Referendum*, March. Harare.

European Parliament. 2013. *Zimbabwe's 2013 General Elections: A Genuine Wind of Change?*, Quick Policy Insight. Directorate-General for External Policies, May 28.

Freedom House. 2012. *Change and 'New' Politics in Zimbabwe – Interim Report of a Nationwide Survey of Public Opinion in Zimbabwe: June–July 2012*, August 18. Washington, DC/New York.

GOZ. 2012. *Poverty Income Consumption and Expenditure Survey 2011/2012 Report*. Harare.

IMF. 2012a. *Zimbabwe – Staff Report for the 2012 Article IV Consultations*, IMF Country Report No. 12/279, September. Washington, DC.

———. 2012b. *Zimbabwe – Staff Report for the 2012 Article IV Consultation-Debt Sustainability Analysis*, September. Washington, DC.

International Crisis Group. 2013. *Zimbabwe's Elections: Mugabe's Last Stand*, Africa Briefing No. 95, July 29. Brussels.

Mawowa, Showers. 2013. *Political Economy of Crisis, Mining and Accumulation in Zimbabwe: Evidence from the Chegutu Mhondoro Area*, PhD Thesis. Durban: University of KwaZulu Natal.

MDC-T. 2013. *Election Manifesto 2013 – A New Zimbabwe – The Time Is Now!* Harare: MDC-T Information and Publicity Department.

National Constitutional Assembly. 2012. *NCA's Response to MDC-T*, November 22. Harare: Press Release.

———. 2013. *Take Charge: Vote NO in the Referendum*, February 5. Harare: Press Release.

New Zimbabwe. 2012. MDC-T Fury over Support Collapse Report, August 22. http://zimbabwesituation.com/old/aug24_2012.html#Z5.

———. 2013. Chombo Orders Debt Write-Offs Ahead of Polls, July 22. http://www.newzimbabwe.com/news-11794-Chombo+orders+urban+debt+write-off/news.aspx.

Solidarity Peace Trust. 2013. *The End of a Road: The 2013 Elections in Zimbabwe*, October. Johannesburg.

The Guardian. 2010. Morgan Tsvangirai Praises Mugabe 'the Hero', September 16. London.

———. 2013. Why Zimbabwean Voters Are Deserting Morgan Tsvangirai, April 23. London.

The Standard. 2009. MDC Amends Constitution to Suit Tsvangirai, October 8. https://www.thestandard.co.zw/2009/10/08/mdc-amends-constitution-to-suit-tsvangirai/.

World Bank. 2011. *Doing Business 2012: Doing Business in a More Transparent World*. Washington, DC: World Bank.

ZANU-PF. 2013. *Team ZANU-PF 2013*. Harare.

14

The Transitions That Weren't

ZANU-PF Triumphant

Contrary to the expectations of most external observers, and MDC-T supporters who had been told by their leaders they had ZANU-PF on the back foot and to dismiss the findings of the recent unfavourable opinion surveys as those surveyed had simply failed to express their real voting intentions due to fears based on memories of the violent reprisals by ZANU-PF in 2008, the results of the 31 July 2013 elections proved to be an overwhelming victory for Mugabe and ZANU-PF. It was also the sheer scale of that victory, with ZANU-PF swatting away the Opposition in a major rebound in its fortunes, which took many by surprise.

ZANU-PF went from being a minority party to enjoying a clear majority in the House of Assembly, increasing the number of its MPs to 160, and thus enjoying a large two-thirds majority (in fact, closer to a three quarters majority) in the lower chamber of 210 representatives. The size of its majority meant that it could ensure the passage of any amendments to the new constitution its leadership saw fit to introduce. It now had the means to remove any social, economic and political constitutional provisions which MDC-T had fought so hard to include in the hope that this

M. Simpson, T. Hawkins, *The Primacy of Regime Survival*,
https://doi.org/10.1007/978-3-319-72520-8_14

would help prevent a return to an unreformed, predatory and repressive ZANU-PF controlled state.

MDC-T's representation in the House of Assembly collapsed, falling from the 100 MPs elected in 2008 to 49 MPs in 2013. The smaller MDC-N grouping was wiped out in terms of representatives in the lower house.[1] Significantly, and in line with the opinion surveys referenced in the previous chapter which the MDC-T leadership had chosen to dismiss, ZANU-PF also managed to wrest a large number of urban seats from the MDC-T in Harare and Bulawayo. It made major inroads into the latter's strongholds in the Matabeleland provinces, regained lost ground in Manicaland, Midlands and Masvingo provinces, and secured almost total control of its rural heartlands (ZEC 2013, 62).

The results were equally stark in terms of the Presidential race. In a turnout which increased by close to 1 million voters compared to 2008, Mugabe won 60.6 percent of the vote compared to 43 percent in the first round of the 2008 elections. Tsvangirai's share of the vote fell from 48 percent in the first round of the 2008 elections to 33.7 percent. In 2013, the margin in favour of Mugabe was close to 940,000 votes (Ibid., 62).

Tsvangirai sought to have the results overturned through the Constitutional Court. Given that the new constitution had only been approved in March 2013, with Mugabe signing it into law in May 2013, it was now clear that the country had gone into elections in July 2013 under a new constitution, but with key institutions unreformed, and therefore still staffed by Mugabe appointees such as the Chief Justice, as likely intended by ZANU-PF. Tsvangirai was eventually compelled to withdraw his legal challenge when another MDC-T attempt through the Constitutional Court, seeking to compel ZEC to release material MDC-T judged to be vital evidence for its case, failed.[2]

There were numerous allegations of irregularities, though comprehensive reports that analysed the evidence were only to emerge later. Irregularities ranged from disenfranchisement of large numbers of voters, particularly in urban areas, whose names did not appear on the roll in polling stations and who were thus turned away on election day, ZEC's failure to hand over electoral rolls to parties (which would have enabled inspection and verification by candidates, parties and voters themselves) until two days before the poll, concerns over the large number of surplus ballot papers that were printed and their possible misuse, and reports of traditional leaders (most of whom aligned to ZANU-PF) frogmarching villagers to polling stations. However, MDC-T efforts to challenge the results were eventually to fail as it was unable to gather and present the necessary evidence in time.[3]

Over and above the by now almost ritualised allegations of electoral fraud, few analysts made the effort to gain a deeper understanding of how ZANU-PF had regained its hold over voters, particularly in the country's rural areas. One notable exception was an analyst who drew upon his own experiences and observations from the 2013 elections. While highlighting the importance of the 'fear factor' in the countryside as an explanatory variable in both the ruling party's continued grip on the rural population, and the challenges faced by the Opposition in 2013 to reach those areas as they had done, at least partially, in 2008, he also argues that the problem is deeper and more complex than at first sight. The oppressive omnipresence of the ruling party, and the extent to which it had succeeded in creating a party-state that penetrated down to the local level, led to a situation whereby "District and Provincial Offices are also ZANU PF spaces [and] Chiefs, Headmen and Village Heads switch [between] their formal and ZANU roles with seamless ease". This in turn means that the "structures of the state and the structures of the party have seamless interaction [and significantly] to the rural voter, ZANU PF is the state and the state is ZANU PF – there is literally no difference." (Magaisa 2017).

In addition, watching over the activities of rural inhabitants are:

> traditional leaders…police, intelligence and military, civil servants in administrative structures and ZANU PF political officers [who together exercise] disciplinary power whenever rural citizens do not conform to the rules…the voter is constantly labouring under the belief that he is being watched [and so] behaves in a manner that he believes is expected of him by the central authority. (Ibid.)

Furthermore, any state-provided assistance to these areas is given in the name of the ruling party, and "villagers who are associated with the opposition parties are excluded [which for] most villagers who rely upon agriculture [is] quite literally a matter of life or death" (Ibid.). Extreme scarcity and dependence on the state for agricultural inputs and food aid (this constituting as argued by the present authors an objective that was intentionally pursued by the regime), the insecurity of livelihoods arising from precarious tenure arrangements, and physical insecurity given experiences of the punishing state violence regularly meted out to dissidents, all converge and create an enforced loyalty that supports regime perpetuation. As the same observer astutely noted the "technologies of power employed to affect elections stretch over a longer period of time, well before and well after the observers have come and gone" (Ibid.). Such insights speak again to the strength of extractive political and economic institutions globally, derived from their mutual reinforcement as identified by Acemoglu and Robinson, with profound implications for the longer-term prospects of overhauling the extractive party-state in Zimbabwe.

In a clear sign of disappointment with the Opposition, Western support for MDC-T's attempts to challenge the 2013 results could best be described as lukewarm. While Washington, London and the EU expressed concerns over the alleged irregularities, there was little they were prepared to do beyond stating their reservations, committing to monitor the situation, and maintaining sanctions against ZANU-PF notables. Their adoption of a more hard-line stance was also handicapped by the clear endorsement given to both the electoral process and results by African organisations. To this might be added a degree of exasperation in the West that once again the MDC-T had been outmanoeuvred by ZANU-PF, bundled into an election when it was clear that the necessary preconditions for a free and fair process were lacking as had happened in 2005 and 2008, yet somehow hoping that the results in 2013 would be any different.

The relatively clean bill of health for the elections provided by SADC and the AU – which the reports of their election observer missions judged to have been "free, peaceful and generally credible" in the case of SADC, and in the case of the AU a process characterised as "a generally peaceful campaign" as well as "free and credible" – effectively closed off the possibility of regional and continental mediation of the kind called for by Tsvangirai in 2008 that had led to the GPA. ZANU-PF's claim that both the process and results were credible was helped in no small measure by the fact that close to 20,000 monitors had been present in the country (of whom nearly half were domestic observers), while Tsvangirai had failed to level the playing field and reverse ZANU-PF's entrenched position not to invite election observer teams from countries which it judged hostile to itself. African governments, and particularly those in Southern Africa, felt finally able to wash their hands of the Zimbabwe question which had proved a thorn in their side and source of tensions with the West for so many years.

In mid-August 2013 Mugabe was to return to Harare in triumphalist mode from a SADC summit where he had been elected Deputy Chairman of the organisation, and warmly congratulated for his victory by his Southern African colleagues.[4] He was sworn in for his seventh term as President of Zimbabwe on 22 August 2013, presenting both domestic and foreign opponents, as he had done after the second round of the 2008 elections, with yet another *fait accompli*.

In his inaugural address, Mugabe claimed that "Except for a few Western dishonest countries, our elections have been hailed as peaceful, free, fair and credible" (Mugabe 2013a). Furthermore, the election results were taken as definitive proof of popular approval of ZANU-PF's past policies, as well as the path it intended to take the country down as detailed in its election manifesto. In his address, Mugabe argued that the revolutionary party had the popular mandate to take the next step in its long-term strategy:

> much remains to be done before we assume full sovereignty...Yes, we regained control over our land and our people are happy...But our dominion goes beyond land. It extends to all those resources found in and on our territory including those lying beneath our land, principally minerals...we are aware that people of ill-will have cast aspersions on our hallowed policy of indigenisation and economic empowerment...Well, it is a set policy, our chosen path to full sovereignty. (Mugabe 2013a)

A combative and self-assured Mugabe, flushed with confidence as a result of the elections and the approval of his fellow Africans, was also on display at the 68th Session of the UN General Assembly. Targeting his *bête noire* of Western sanctions which, in time tested fashion, he linked to the land reform programme and imperialist designs of the West, Mugabe argued that sanctions had failed to achieve their objective:

> In the eyes of our people, the sanctions constitute a form of hostility and violence against them for the simple crime of undertaking the land reform programme by which land was put in the hands of the then majority landless Zimbabweans....Our small and peaceful country is threatened daily by covetous and bigoted big powers whose hunger for domination and control of other nations and their resources knows no bounds...If these sanctions were intended to effect regime change, well, the results of the recent national elections have clearly shown you what they can do. (Mugabe 2013b)

The MDC-T: Things Fall Apart

In the aftermath of the elections, there were soon increasing calls from within the senior ranks of the MDC-T for the removal of Tsvangirai as party leader. This was hardly surprising given that he had led the party to its third Presidential electoral defeat in a row, though the speed with which splits within the party surfaced was an indication of older and deep fault lines. Anti-Tsvangirai protagonists were subsequently to claim that in addition to concerns regarding his alleged growing authoritarianism, they had also advised him, unsuccessfully, to ensure the completion of the IG agenda as a precondition for the holding of elections, and to boycott the poll if progress had not been made on critical issues.

Reflecting on the results, some MDC-T notables were also to concede that they had simply been outsmarted by Mugabe during the four and a half years of the IG, and failed to be pro-active and demand a more genuine sharing of power. One senior MDC-T figure, Gordon Moyo, who had been Minister of State Enterprises and Parastatals in the IG, was to argue that with the exception of a few of the ministries that had been allocated to the MDC-T, most were irrelevant and that "It is only Finance, Health, Labour, Energy and Water Ministries that we had and the rest were like departments. We were there to make up the numbers. We were conned" (*NewsDay* 2014c).

Returned to the wilderness of opposition politics after the interlude of the IG, the MDC-T fell upon itself in mutual recrimination for its failure, yet again, to dislodge ZANU-PF. Roy Bennett, the combative MDC-T treasurer who had been imprisoned and unable to take up his post as Deputy Minister of Agriculture (see Chap. 9), and was then forced into exile in South Africa, was to fire one of the opening shots, calling for Tsvangirai to step down and allow the party to find a new leader (*Business Day* 2013). Post-election blues rapidly degenerated into a vicious internecine struggle between various factions centred around personalities rather than any clear policy differences. This was all too similar to ZANU-PF's internal politics and factionalism which had often reared its head around the succession issue, but with Tsvangirai lacking Mugabe's capacity to hold his party together and deal effectively with dissent.

By early 2014 the squabbles had descended into farce, with former ministers Biti and Mangoma seeking to have Tsvangirai called before a party disciplinary committee in order to expel him from the party, and Tsvangirai responding by securing the expulsion of both Mangoma and Biti. The latter two figures then went on to form a new party, MDC-Renewal, with both MDC factions subsequently quarrelling over their respective share of party assets. Sekai Holland, who had been a Co-Minister for National Healing, Reconciliation and Integration in the IG, and a founding member of the MDC in 1999, originally headed up MDC-Renewal. She, however, would eventually resign from her position as a result of growing tensions between Biti and Mangoma over leadership of the new party, with the latter in turn leaving it to establish his own party, the Renewal Democrats of Zimbabwe.

Chickens also came home to roost in terms of the MDC-T's estrangement from its CSO allies during the IG. In September 2013 the NCA decided to formally transform itself from a constitutional lobby group into a political party, further dividing opposition forces.

Violence between supporters of one or another MDC figure broke out on a number of occasions, as well as violence directed at the key notables themselves. Mangoma was assaulted in February 2014 by youths claiming loyalty to Tsvangirai following a letter from Mangoma to Tsvangirai calling for him to resign. In a subsequent interview with a local newspaper, Mangoma was to make clear his views on the need to secure

Tsvangirai's removal because of his failure to ensure that the necessary reforms were carried out during the IG:

> If you zero in on the issue of reforms, as espoused by the GPA, and the issues that were forwarded for further negotiation or implementation, it is clear that our leadership was found wanting…For me leadership renewal is the only way to save this party and ensure victory in 2018 [the next scheduled elections]. (*Daily News* 2014a)

Tendai Biti's home was firebombed before his formal split from the MDC-T, though it was unclear whether by Tsvangirai supporters or agents from ZANU-PF's well-oiled dirty tricks department aimed at sowing further discord within the MDC-T (*Nehanda Radio* 2014). Prior to the establishment of his MDC-Renewal party, Biti shared his views on what he saw as the underlying weaknesses afflicting the MDC and the country:

> The other problem is because Zimbabwe has been under dictators since 1891 [the year that Mashonaland and Matabeleland were declared British Protectorates]...what has changed is the colour of the dictator's skin… Zimbabwe has not known other value systems other than Zanu PF, Ian Smith and the repressive colonial state…It is easy for people to behave, think and talk like Zanu PF. Put in simple terms Zanu PF has normalised the abnormal…The aim should not only be to remove Zanu PF but the culture of Zanu PF, to de-Zanuise the Zimbabwean state and institutions'. (*Zimbabwe Independent* 2014b)

Recourse to heavy-handed tactics by supporters of the various MDC factions was all too redolent of the intolerance and violence that had been one of the primary drivers of the original split within the MDC in 2005, and only served to further discredit the party in the eyes of most observers. Dirty laundry was washed in public, while the state-controlled media had a field day providing detailed and sensationalist coverage of every twist and turn, accusation and counter-accusation in the divorce proceedings, with ZANU-PF able to stand back and revel not only in its restored monopoly hold on power, but also in the self-destruction of the party which had once constituted the only serious threat to the survival of the regime over which it presided.

The Return to Economic Regression

The large turnout of its supporters in the 2013 elections meant ZANU-PF now had to deliver on its election promises and meet the heightened expectations it had nurtured, namely that another term in office would transform Zimbabwe into the promised land of milk and honey, with the country taking the final steps to 'full sovereignty' through implementation of its indigenisation policy. In October 2013, in time honoured fashion and once back in sole control of the country, the new ZANU-PF government launched with much aplomb yet another economic turnaround strategy to be added to an already extensive list of past programmes, all of which had signally failed to revive the economy.

The latest in the series was entitled the Zimbabwe Agenda for Sustainable Socio-Economic Transformation (Zim Asset), and was to run from 2013 to 2018. In the President's foreword in the document, Mugabe stated that "Zim Asset was crafted to achieve sustainable development and social equity anchored on indigenization, empowerment and employment creation which will be largely propelled by the judicious exploitation of the country's abundant human and natural resources" (GOZ 2013, 6).

As ambitious as all previous plans, amongst the document's targets were that "During the plan period, the economy is projected to grow by an average of 7.3%…by 3.4% in 2013 and 6.2% in 2014 and continue an upward growth trajectory to 9.9% by 2018" (Ibid., 27). In terms of sectoral growth projections, manufacturing output would register an annual 9.5 percent growth by 2018, agriculture would reach 12.5 percent, mining and quarrying 12.6 percent, and finance and insurance 10.3 percent (Ibid., 28).

In what at least represented an improvement on earlier economic strategies in which detail was usually conspicuous by its absence, Zim Asset contained an exhaustive list of proposed programmatic and project level interventions and projected outputs, all laid out in an extensive and detailed set of results matrices which ran close to 80 pages. Furthermore, and again in stark contrast to earlier documents, Zim Asset emphasised the importance of results management, an implementation structure, and the need for monitoring and evaluation of progress.

Yet true to form, the necessary fine detail was still lacking in terms of where exactly the funds to support the long list of ambitious interventions were to come from, as well as costings. As with earlier strategic documents, these aspects were largely sidestepped. No reference was made to the total costs of either the overall plan or individual sectoral interventions.

Funding for the plan was expected to come, with broad brush strokes, from a long wish list of sources:

> tax and non-tax revenue, leveraging resources, Sovereign Wealth Fund, issuance of bonds, accelerated implementation of Public Private Partnerships, securitization of remittances, re-engagement with the international and multilateral finance institutions, and other financing options, focusing on Brazil, Russia, India, China and South Africa (BRICS). (Ibid., 11)

On funding, the plan showed signs of collective amnesia and apparent economic illiteracy, evident when the above list of sources is viewed against the backdrop of ZANU-PF's track record of economic management. Under successive ZANU-PF governments, tax and non-tax revenues had collapsed as the economy shrank and the Reserve Bank engaged in expansionary monetary policies to support its 'quasi fiscal' activities which would eventually translate into hyperinflation, while the deterioration in Zimbabwe's credit ratings made the issuing of bonds problematic and extremely costly given the risk premium attached. State-Business Relations (or more precisely state-independent private sector relations), had deteriorated throughout ZANU-PF's long tenure in office, making substantial Public Private Partnerships (PPPs) of the size needed to deal with the country's tremendous infrastructure backlog unlikely. Deep-rooted diaspora mistrust of financial institutions given past Reserve Bank efforts to capture their remittances (added to resentment against ZANU-PF felt by many in the diaspora that the ruling party had taken a hard line during negotiations on the new constitution against extending the franchise to Zimbabweans outside the country), made any increase in the volume of remittances through the formal financial sector an equally dubious proposition. Most importantly, Harare's continued unwillingness to deal with the issue of its debt arrears to bilateral and multilateral lenders, as well as to commit to reforms in the context of a joint World Bank/IMF Staff Monitored Programme as a precondition for a resumption of loans, also cut off at the pass the possibility of new loans from these institutions, a point that had over the years been emphasised *ad nauseam* by the IFIs.[5]

It is only in light of such an apparently tenuous grasp on the reality of the challenges facing the country that it is possible to understand statements in Zim Asset such as that "The Government will mobilise funding from domestic resources, which are in abundance and ready for full exploitation and utilisation" (Ibid., 48). The latter was a clear denial of the fiscally constrained position the country found itself in, and the historical reasons for this. It also increased the likelihood that funding for Zim Asset was only going to be secured through another round of state-sponsored dispossessions.

Where the plan also remained firmly embedded in the past was in its ritualistic attribution of all past economic regression to external sanctions:

> Zimbabwe experienced a deteriorating economic and social environment since 2000 that was caused by illegal sanctions imposed by the Western countries. This resulted in a deep economic and social crisis characterised by a hyperinflationary environment, industrial capacity utilisation below 10% and an overall cumulative Gross Domestic Product (GDP) decline of 50% by 2008. (Ibid., 17)

The effects of the FTLRP on agricultural production and its devastating impact on other sectors of the economy, the collapse of investor confidence as a result of the state's failure to protect private property rights or honour bilateral investment protection agreements, the country's compromised judicial system and erosion of the rule of law, the destruction of livelihoods in the informal sector, implementation of price control initiatives backed by coercion and the monetary and fiscal policies pursued during the crisis decade, the haemorrhaging of essential human capital in the context of mass migration amidst an increasingly repressive and adverse political and economic environment, the 'privatization' by the ruling party of the country's diamond wealth, the high levels of corruption over which the party presided, and the failure to honour its foreign debt servicing obligations to the IFIs and Western donors, were all developments studiously ignored in Zim Asset. On the basis of a reading of the document and its diagnosis of the problems the country faced, it was clear that ZANU-PF had no intention of dismantling the extractive economic institutions and processes over which it exercised monopoly control, from which it benefited, and upon which it depended for its survival.

Never missing an opportunity to sell the party's worldview and pay tribute to the security forces (even if very incongruous in an economic development plan), Zim Asset highlighted the important roles they were to play in safeguarding the promised gains in terms of growth and development:

> Although the country is enjoying peace and tranquillity, the country continues to face the threats of interference, subversion and economic sabotage, In view of this, the security and defence forces will continue to safeguard the country's hard won Independence and maintain peace and security and guarantee Zimbabwe's sovereignty and territorial integrity, economic growth and prosperity. (Ibid., 25)

Further evidence that little had changed in the ruling party's mind set, and in particular its attitude to dispossession as a tool of economic policy, was soon to be provided by May 2014 in the form of renewed land invasions of the few commercial farms remaining in white hands, estimated by then to number less than 150, with further loss of output and the displacement of farm workers. Following reports that Mugabe had allegedly called for the dispossession of the remaining white commercial farmers at his 91st birthday celebrations in March 2015, and which was taken as official blessing and encouragement for such actions, there was yet another wave of farm invasions in 2015 (*Zimbabwe Independent* 2015).

By May 2014, the IMF was warning that:

> The economic rebound experienced since 2009 has ended, with economic growth decelerating in 2013. The external position is vulnerable…The baseline scenario is marked by sluggish growth in 2014 and over the medium term, with risks clearly to the downside in the near term. Key risks

> to the outlook include lower than programmed tax collections, policy slippages, financial sector stress and global commodity prices. Zimbabwe faces these risks with very thin buffers. (IMF 2014, 1)

In a by now tedious repetition of numerous past policy recommendations, which with very few alterations might be found in any set of BWI prescriptions for Zimbabwe dating back to the 1990s and 2000s, the IMF noted that:

> Zimbabwe faces medium-term challenges, and a vigorous reform programme is needed to put the country on a sustainable, inclusive growth path…To attract much-needed FDI and access affordable funding, the authorities need to improve the business environment…Zimbabwe's debt situation remains a serious impediment to external sustainability and economic development. (Ibid., 1)

The full extent of the adverse environment in which businesses continued to operate, and low levels of FDI, domestic investment and growth rates, were again captured by the World Bank in its 2016 'Doing Business' profile for Zimbabwe. This showed that on the composite index, out of the 186 countries covered by the survey, Zimbabwe ranked in 155th position, compared to neighbouring economies such as South Africa in 73rd position, and Botswana in 72nd position (World Bank 2016, 8).

Of particular significance in terms of the negative impact on entrepreneurship and market formation of Zimbabwe's adverse regulatory environment was its dismal ranking in one of the eleven areas examined in the World Bank survey, namely the ease of 'starting a business'.[6] On this indicator Zimbabwe ranked 182nd position out of 189 economies worldwide (Ibid., 19), a clear reflection of the ruling party's unchanging hostility to the independent private sector and market-driven economics, and its selective application of regulations within the context of patronage considerations to reward party supporters and deny them to anyone else.

The World Bank report also threw light on the nature and extent of the adverse conditions facing the private sector in the post-IG era in terms of contract enforcement. The latter was a critical constraint given it reflected, amongst other considerations, the efficiency and effectiveness of the court system in terms of commercial disputes, and more specifically the extent to which the courts protected and enforced the contractually determined rights and obligations of parties. On this variable Zimbabwe ranked in 166th position worldwide in 2016, compared to South Africa in 119th position and Botswana in 128th (Ibid., 79).

In sharp contrast to copious references to the Indigenisation and Economic Empowerment policy, Zim Asset's 80 pages of action matrices contained a single line reference to the need to "Improve the country's 'doing business/investment environment'", with no further details provided as to which specific bottlenecks would be tackled, by whom, when and how (GOZ 2013, 117). There was also a noticeable absence of concrete proposals to improve the competitiveness of the economy. Such lacunae indicated both the minor role that the private sector was expected to play in the achievement of Zim Asset objectives, and the state-centric dirigisme which continued to dominate ZANU-PF's economic thinking. Given the World Bank rankings, it was also left to the reader to square the circle in terms of reconciling the prevailing adverse business environment with the stated strategic objective of "the growing of a robust economy that is highly competitive in the region and the rest of Africa" (Ibid., 33).

In an all too familiar reprise of the rapid loss of credibility of past plans, no sooner had the growth targets in Zim Asset been released they were overtaken by the economy's actual performance. As against a Zim Asset target of 6.1 percent growth for 2014, real GDP growth fell from 5.3 percent in 2013 to 2.8 percent in 2014, and then further to 1.4 percent in 2015 as against the Zim Asset target of 6.4 percent, while the IMF estimated growth at only 0.7 percent for 2016 as opposed to the planned target of 6.5 percent (IMF 2017a, 12). The "robust economy" referenced in the plan, and which was projected to deliver annual GDP growth of 9.9 percent by 2018, was once again, as it had during the crisis decade, moving in the opposite direction. In a further indication of the downturn, total investment as a percentage of GDP, which had improved from a low of 15 percent in 2009 at the beginning of the IG to 23.9 percent by 2010, was estimated to have fallen back to 13 percent by 2014, with a downward trend projected for the remainder of Zim Asset's lifespan.

A heavy dose of reality was meted out to the new ZANU-PF Minister of Finance, veteran ZANU-PF stalwart Chinamasa, as he sought with a growing sense of urgency to find external funding to support Zim Asset, and this in a context in which dollarization had removed the government's capacity to simply print money as in the past to meet funding needs, and where borrowing on both domestic and international markets had high costs given the risk premium associated with loans to the Zimbabwean government. After being reminded, yet again, by the BWIs in the course of a visit to Washington in October 2013, of the preconditions that Zimbabwe would have to meet for debt forgiveness and new concessional loans, he was also to return empty-handed from a visit to China in January 2014, a country specifically touted in Zim Asset as a source of funding for the plan (*Zimbabwe Independent* 2014a).[7]

Brazil, another developing economic giant referenced as a source of funding for Zim Asset, was likewise to disappoint Zimbabwe, with the Ambassador in Harare pointedly stating that:

> As a rule Brazil does not give support to sovereign nations and we don't give hand-outs either. Usually, we find synergies and business opportunities where we can work with people on various projects. Zimbabwe is a rich country and does not need donations but [rather] investments…but there is need for clarity on the country's economic policies. (*Daily News* 2014d)

Solidarity within the Global South clearly had its limits, and Zimbabwe's indigenisation policy was acting as a deterrent to FDI, even from those developing economies which ZANU-PF assumed might be more sympathetic to its objectives. The position conveyed by the Brazilian ambassador might well have been expressed by the representative of any Western government concerned about Zimbabwe's investment climate, the unpredictability of its policies, and its track record on loan repayments and guarantees on the protection of property rights.

Additional signs of a return to the past included rolling power outages which began to hit the country at the beginning of 2014. These resulted from longstanding maintenance backlogs which the IG had been unable to address in any substantive manner, and failure to expand the country's power generation capacity, as well as the government's decision in the early days of the new administration to cancel outstanding debts owed to the power utility company.[8] The blackouts hit all sectors of the economy, leading to falls in output and increased lay-offs, with the ZCTU reporting that 75 companies failed to reopen in the New Year after the end of year holiday season of 2013 (*NewsDay* 2014b). By March 2014 the CZI was reporting that capacity utilisation in manufacturing had fallen back again to below 40 percent, with its head opining that the sector was in the "intensive care unit" (*Daily News* 2014b).

In January 2014, the Zimbabwe Revenue Authority (ZIMRA) reported that Treasury had missed its revenue target for 2013 by 8 percent, with total collections for the year amounting to US$3.4 billion as against a target of US$3.64 billion, and against a budget presented by the new Minister of Finance costed at US$4.1 billion. The impact of further company closures was a significant contributor to the shortfall in revenue collected from corporate tax, at US$401 million as opposed to a target of US$457 million (*NewsDay* 2014a).

Such revenue shortfalls needed to be seen not only against the backdrop of the limited resources available to meet the country's enormous recovery priorities, but also the poor levels of financial accountability within the public sector manifested even during the IG. In an audit report for the financial year 2011, the Auditor-General had noted that at least US$140 million disbursed simply could not be accounted for by a range of Government ministries, including those headed by the both MDCs (*Financial Gazette* 2014).[9]

As the Government scrambled to find the money to meet its growing wage bill, by the first quarter of 2014 delays in the payment of salaries of public sector workers had once again became a regular occurrence.[10] Amidst this, a scandal erupted surrounding the salaries of senior executives within the state company and parastatal sector, which as with many other reform issues had seen little progress during the IG. Dubbed by the media 'Salarygate', revelations showed the full extent to which these bodies had come to be treated as sinecures to be milked by those appointed by ZANU-PF, with minimal concern for performance.

The scandal was triggered by reports that the CEO of the Premier Service Medical Aid Society, an outfit providing medical insurance for public sector workers, was earning an estimated total salary package of at least US$250,000 a month, with even the state's mouthpiece getting in on the act and expressing (or at least feigning) outrage (*The Herald* 2014). Subsequent media investigations revealed that similar packages were being enjoyed by, amongst others, the heads of ZIMRA, the Zimbabwe Electricity Supply Authority (ZESA), and the Zimbabwe Broadcasting Corporation (ZBC).

Further insights into the extent of mismanagement of public funds in state enterprises and parastatals were revealed in a detailed report produced by the Auditor-General in 2015. Amongst the litany of breaches of corporate governance standards, the report noted, *inter alia* that:

> Some entities did not have declaration of interest registers while in some cases board members were not declaring their interest before meetings…A number of entities were paying board fees and management salaries and benefits which were not authorised. For example, EMA [the Environmental Management Agency] whose board passed a resolution to increase its own fees without the parent Ministry approval…ZMDC [Zimbabwe Mining Development Corporation] which gave non-executive directors a total of 2,940 litres of fuel and holiday allowances of US$27,450 each without the parent Ministry's approval. (Office of the Auditor-General 2015, ii–iii)

To this might be added evidence of ghost employees on payroll, with the number of employees exceeded those authorised in staffing tables. There was also evidence of expenditures with no acknowledgement of receipt by beneficiaries, unauthorised payments,[11] widespread non-compliance with procurement regulations, and the non-servicing of domestic and foreign loans with resulting accumulation of significant arrears.[12] The extent of lack of accountability, and the high levels of insolvency within the sector, can be gauged from the report's findings. This showed that as of end-year 2014 the country's public entities owed the revenue authority a staggering total of close to US$450 million (Ibid., 62).[13] In addition, there was the drain on the public purse of their perennial loss-making operations with, for example, the Civil Aviation Authority of Zimbabwe (CAAZ) incurring net losses of close to US$23.6 million in 2012 and nearly US$14.8 million in 2013 (Ibid., 2), while the National Railways of Zimbabwe (NRZ) incurred a net loss of US$49.1

million in 2013 and US$31.6 million in 2014 contributing to a cumulative loss of US$235.5 million since it began operations (Ibid., 108).

Obert Gutu, a former MDC-T Senator who during the IG had publicly raised concerns over the destination of revenue from the country's diamond sales (see Chap. 12) argued that:

> The root cause of the Salarygate scandal is the near dysfunctional and incorrigibly corrupt system of misgovernance in most, if not all parastatals and other state-owned corporations. The systems in these organizations have over the years been allowed to degenerate and rot beyond redemption. (*Bulawayo24* 2014)

In a clear sign of the dire straits in which the new ZANU-PF Government found itself given the limited resources at its disposal on the one hand, and economic growth and employment targets it had committed to in Zim Asset on the other, in an unprecedented move the Minister of Industry resorted to appealing to the private sector for help to achieve the plan's objectives. The Minister was reported as candidly stating (or more correctly understating) – even if the diagnosis was a highly selective one which shifted the problem from the erroneous policies themselves to a capacity constraint – that:

> As we all know, the country has got policies that fall short in the implementation department. I am appealing to the private sector to help government in the implementation of these policies to speed up economic development. (*Daily News* 2014c)

If the country's industrial sector was repeating its dismal performance during the crisis decade, agriculture was not far behind. Under Joseph Made – a ZANU-PF Minister who had occupied the post on a number of previous occasions, and developed a reputation for announcing bumper harvests on an annual basis when the sector's direction of travel was very much in the opposite direction whilst blaming all slippages on 'illegal sanctions' – the sector's performance soon made Zim Asset's stated objective of creating "a self-sufficient and food surplus economy and see Zimbabwe re-emerge as the 'Basket of Southern Africa'" (GOZ 2013, 50) so much pie in the sky.

In terms of maize, the country's staple food crop, the familiar stories of late or non-delivery of inputs to small-scale farmers by the GMB, poor transport and storage facilities and delayed payments to farmers for maize deliveries, were to recur again soon after the new government took office.[14] Faced with shortfalls, the Ministry of Agriculture reverted to its default dirigiste form and distrust of independent operators, and in early 2014 reversed a policy adopted during the IG to grant private traders licenses to import staple grains and thereby fill the gaps left by the GMB's historic inability to meet national needs.

As noted in Chap. 5, tobacco output saw significant growth during the IG, with many small-scale beneficiaries of the FTLRP switching from maize production to this cash crop, and their performance being widely trumpeted as a vindication of land reform by ZANU-PF. Between 2011/12 and 2014/15 the number of tobacco growers increased from 52,000 to around 92,000, while output nearly quadrupled from 58 million kg in 2010 to 216 million kg in 2014. Thereafter, however, the boom proved to be short lived. Output began to fall, dropping to 199 million kg in 2015, with a further fall to 170 million kg predicted for 2016 (*Zimbabwe Independent* 2016a).

Some small-scale farmers began to abandon tobacco as a result of increasingly erratic rainfall patterns (with most heavily dependent on rain given their reduced use of mechanised irrigation), and poor support from the still debilitated public agricultural extension services. In addition they complained of the low prices offered by buyers at auction, with buyers countering with claims of poor quality of the crop produced by many small growers that were not members of private contract farming schemes which provided timely inputs, extension services and quality control.

Small-scale tobacco growers also faced continued funding constraints. This resulted from reluctance on the part of banks to extend credit given their continued poor security of tenure and collateral – 'ownership' being based on a mixture of customary tenure arrangements, offer letters which formalised occupation and use but which could be easily reversed by the Government, 99-year leases which granted extensive rights and powers to the state and few to the lessee, and often no documentation at all. To this might be added persistently low levels of surveying, demarcation and registration of plots (which necessarily also required, as a precondition, a comprehensive land audit which ZANU-PF notables had fought off at every opportunity). Land dispossession by the state remained a constant threat, even for those with freehold title, and if any reminder of the tenuous state of property rights in Zimbabwe and the ruling party's hostility to free markets and desire to exercise control over the economy was needed, many banks still held as loan collateral the title deeds of former commercial farms which had been taken over and apportioned to the new small-scale FTLRP beneficiary tobacco growers.

The Frayed Social Contract: Corruption, Rule of Law and Privileging the Securocrats

Sensitive to objections levelled against its indigenisation policy, foremost amongst which that it simply constituted another attempt at looting by the country's elites, ZANU-PF's 2013 election manifesto had gone to great lengths to counter such criticisms and reassure voters that proceeds from the programme would redound to the benefit of ordinary Zimbabweans. It specifically stated, for example, that "the Indigenisation and Economic Empowerment programme will not favour or benefit the political elite or the well-connected at the expense of the ordinary Zimbabweans" (ZANU-PF 2013, 81).

It did not take long for those who had taken such reassurances to heart to be disappointed. Prior to the 2013 elections, Saviour Kasukuwere, the ZANU-PF Minister for Youth Development, Indigenisation and Empowerment during the IG, had secured extensive media coverage of what was portrayed as a major development, namely news that some of the mining companies operating in the Chiadzwa/Marange fields had supposedly pledged US$50 million to the local Community Empowerment Scheme. This was held up as a shining example of both his own ability to secure the compliance of mining companies with national policy, and an indication of future largesse to come from indigenisation.

By March 2014, however, officials of the Marange Community Ownership Scheme Trust were complaining that they had seen little of the money, and mining company representatives were in turn denying that they had made any such pledges of specific sums, and confirmed that this was the case when invited to testify before the relevant Parliamentary subcommittee. There were reports that Kasukuwere had, in fact, used a dud cheque to create a false impression of progress on indigenising the mining sector during a ceremony at which Mugabe was the guest of honour to launch the Trust. The destination of those funds, which according to some companies had actually been disbursed to benefit the relevant communities, remained unknown.[15]

Lack of public trust in state institutions, the failure of successive ZANU-PF governments to fight corruption, weak accountability mechanisms and shortcomings in terms of the rule of law, all reappeared in heightened form in the post-IG era, and faithfully reflected the key features of a fragile state detailed in Chap. 2. An already frayed social contract was furthered weakened by a deepened sense of alienation from a state controlled by a party, civil service and members of the security forces which continued to be seen as predatory, unpredictable and unprofessional. Post-IG data on governance variables showed that Zimbabwe was, once again, sliding backwards after the new government had taken office.

For example, Transparency International's 2015 survey of perceptions of corruption in SSA showed that 80 percent of those interviewed in Zimbabwe thought the new government was doing badly in terms of fighting corruption, the third highest figure for SSA (Transparency International 2015, 11), while 48 percent stated that corruption had increased 'a lot' over the previous year (Ibid., 37). More fine-grained survey data also revealed the extent of lack of trust in the integrity of state institutions and its agents. Seen collectively as the country's most powerful group of actors, 30 percent believed the President to be corrupt, 38 percent believed this to be true of MPs, with 41 percent characterising government officials as corrupt. In terms of those providing services, 42 percent of those surveyed held local councillors to be corrupt, while the figure for perceived corruption within the police force was 58 percent, 46 percent for tax officials and 29 percent for judges and magistrates (Ibid., 36).

If in the post-IG Zimbabwe the country's judiciary continued to be held in low regard by the general public, this reflected the insidious weakening of the rule of law over decades of ZANU-PF rule which the IG had done little to reverse. While the relevant provisions in the new constitution held some promise in terms of restoring the independence of the judiciary and court system from the Executive, and the professionalism of its members, implementation of these had not taken place before the 2013 elections, amongst the consequences being MDC-T's aforementioned failure to challenge the results in an unreformed Constitutional Court composed of Mugabe appointees.

In a clear sign of the ruling party's intentions to roll back gains made during the IG in terms of reforming Zimbabwe's extractive political institutions, the new constitution was once again subjected to modifications in the course of 2017, and therefore only four years after coming into effect, so as to buttress the regime and recentralise power in the Presidency. In a major blow to efforts to improve prospects for an independent judiciary which the Opposition had thought it had secured through the inclusion of important clauses in the new constitution, by using its required two thirds majority in the National Assembly ZANU-PF passed the first constitutional amendment in July 2017 (*The Herald* 2017a). This restored to the President the right to directly appoint the country's Chief Justice, Deputy Chief Justice and Judge President of the High Court without the need, as had been required under Section 180 of the 2013 Constitution, for the Judicial Services Commission to advertise posts, invite nominations from the public, conduct public interviews of candidates, and then submit shortlists to the President for consideration (see Chap. 11). To all intents and purposes this meant that the appointment of these three key members of the judicial arm became, as in the past, directly subject to the control of the President. Removing any doubts as to its implications for an independent judiciary, while the Amendment retained the requirement for the President to consult with the Judicial Services Commission in regards to these three appointments (with past form during the IG as to what was understood by the Office of the President as 'consultations' providing few grounds for optimism), it also "declared that the decision of the President as to such appointments shall be final" (Constitution of Zimbabwe Amendment (No.1) Bill 2017 – 6 (1) (3)).

Against the backdrop of such developments, one measure of the public's continuing mistrust of state institutions and sorry state of the rule of law in post-IG Zimbabwe was provided by data generated by the World Justice Project (WJP).[16] In the context of its work to assess the state of the rule of law on a global basis, the WJP focused on practice, i.e. the extent to which countries actually adhered to the rule of law and applied the law in practice, rather than focusing on legal frameworks and justice institutions. The WJP included Zimbabwe for the first time in its 2012–13 Rule of Law Index report, with the data collected and analysed while the IG was still in office (WJP 2012–13).

Of the eight factors used to measure the rule of law in the 97 countries covered, Zimbabwe stood in 96th position globally in terms of the 'Limited Government Powers' indicator, and in last position out of the 18 SSA countries included in the survey in terms of that indicator, and on the 'Open Government' factor it stood in 97th position and also last in the SSA rankings.[17] (WJP 2012–13, 156). By the time of WJP's 2015 report, Zimbabwe's post-IG performance was to show no improvement. With a larger sample of 102 countries, Zimbabwe's aggregate score for all eight factors placed it in 100th position globally in terms of the rule of law, just above Afghanistan and Venezuela (WJP 2015, 20).

In another sure sign that ZANU-PF was back in full control of the state apparatus, and intended to use it to again serve regime interests and reward its supporters, the process of militarisation of state institutions was also speeded up, with demonstrations of loyalty to ZANU-PF and a background in the liberation struggle trumping all other criteria in appointments to state bodies. Notwithstanding the severe fiscal constraints faced by the new government, after the 2013 elections the war veterans were rewarded with a completely new ministry, the Ministry of Welfare Services for War Veterans, War Collaborators, Former Political Detainees and Restrictees. All the latter groups occupied elevated positions in ZANU-PF's official liberation struggle historiography, and had featured prominently in the party's 2013 election manifesto. The new ministry looking after their welfare was to be headed by a Brigadier-General as Permanent Secretary, and assisted by three Directors, two of whom also Brigadier-Generals and the other a Major-General.

The renewed militarisation of state institutions went beyond veteran affairs – where a case might have plausibly been made that a military background was an essential requirement for a managerial role in the new ministry – and extended to a range of other ministries. In addition to the appointments made by Mugabe to the newly created ministry, in April 2015 a Brigadier-General was appointed as Principal Director in the

Ministry of Finance and Economic Development, an Air Commodore made Principal Director in the Ministry of Higher and Tertiary Education, Science and Technology Development, whilst another Brigadier-General took on the position of Principal Director in the Ministry of Youth Development, Indigenisation and Empowerment (*The Herald* 2015).

The Return to a Humanitarian Emergency

Even the absence of the high levels of political violence seen during the crisis decade could not compensate for the diminishing prospects that the recovery of growth rates achieved during the IG would be sustained by the new ZANU-PF government. There were persistent rumours that the government was planning to reintroduce the Zimbabwe dollar and dust off the printing machines as a way of solving its fiscal constraints, and that it would also soon embark on another round of asset seizures in order to lubricate the machinery of patronage and keep its support base satisfied.

By early 2014 there were also reports that Zimbabweans were, once again, running for the door. Evidence for this included a doubling in the number of passport applications (to six hundred a day) received by the Registrar-General's Office in the first quarter of 2014 compared to the same period the previous year, with police having to be called in to control the queues, and the Registrar-General reporting to a Parliamentary Committee that his staff were overwhelmed (*New Zimbabwe* 2014). Needless to say, such passport applicants were made up of those willing to follow the legal route to join the Diaspora, with an unknown number of others simply prepared to illegally jump across the borders with Botswana and South Africa as had been the case throughout the crisis decade, and even to brave increasingly frequent and deadly outbreaks of anti-immigrant xenophobia in the latter.

There was also growing evidence that household vulnerability to external shocks was rising again (particularly amongst poor households), and that Zimbabwe was reverting to a humanitarian emergency. Rather than the "food surplus economy" promised in Zim Asset, and despite the Agricultural Minister's repeated assurances of yet another bumper year for agriculture, three successive years of poor maize harvests in 2013, 2014 and 2015 in a context in which the government's own welfare survey of 2011/12 had revealed extremely high levels of household poverty – rapidly translated into heightened levels of household food insecurity and hunger.

A combination of protracted drought and crop failures, debilitated food reserves, low incomes, depleted assets and rising food prices, coupled with the knock-on effects of reduced demand for agricultural labour as the hectarage cultivated fell, meant that while in 2012/13 the number of people at risk of food insecurity according to UN estimates had stood at 1.67 million, by 2013/14 this had risen to 2.2 million (UN-OCHA 2014, 3). Following another poor harvest in 2014/2015 which saw a decline in cereal output of 46 percent compared to the previous year, the price of the country staple, maize, rose 38 percent (UN-OCHA 2016a, 9).

By early 2016 UN data showed the full extent of the deterioration, with 2.8 million Zimbabweans food insecure and in need of food aid (Ibid., 5), while an estimated 2.1 percent of children were suffering from Severe Acute Malnutrition (SAM) (Ibid., 16). There was evidence of the widespread adoption of negative coping strategies by households, which included the skipping of meals, the distressed sale of assets (in particular livestock) in order to purchase food items, and falls in school attendance that could be attributed to the withdrawal of children from school to help with household income generation, and the switching of household expenditure on schooling to food purchases.

The situation was only to deteriorate, further belying the optimistic claims in Zim Asset of Zimbabwe's return to the status of a bread basket. By October 2016, based on a Vulnerability Assessment, the UN reported that around 4.1 million people (around 42 percent of the rural population) would require some form of food assistance by the first quarter of 2017 which it noted was "the highest since 2009." Furthermore, it noted that malnutrition indicators had also deteriorated, with 15 districts with a SAM rate of more than 5 percent, which was "unprecedented in Zimbabwe" (UN-OCHA 2016b).

The new constitution's Bill of Rights had detailed the state's duties to ensure citizens had access to decent food, shelter and health. Against a backdrop of widening hunger and rapid deterioration in the quality of safe water and sanitation provisioning which made a mockery of these constitutional obligations, and in a clear sign of a return to the nadir of the earlier crisis years, Zimbabwe was hit by a fatal outbreak of typhoid in 2014. This was followed by another cholera epidemic in early 2015, though lessons learned from the 2008 outbreak meant that this time around the epidemic was quickly contained.

Highlighting the country's growing fragility under the new ZANU-PF government, the UN's 2016 humanitarian report drew attention to the fact that the drivers of the humanitarian crisis went far beyond simply poor rainfall and its impact on food production:

> the country's fiscal space remains constrained due to subdued economic activity…Companies continue to close down and unemployment has reduced real incomes, and put many basic commodities and services beyond the reach of much of the population in both urban and rural areas. Infrastructure is deteriorating and services such as water and waste disposal are struggling to cope with increased urban populations. Arguably and more worrying, however, is the government's limited financial reserves, the lack of any prospect of imminent economic recovery, and the depressed financial support from key international players. (UN-OCHA 2016a, 7)

Regime Priorities Amidst Growing Fragility

Following the improvements of the IG era, after 2013 the *de facto* 'sovereignty gap' referenced in Chap. 2 rapidly began to widen again. While ZANU-PF propaganda showed the party continuing to focus its efforts, with the assistance of its heroic security forces, on ensuring the defeat of both foreign and domestic enemies who sought to overthrow the regime and return black Zimbabweans to colonial subjugation, the Zimbabwean state was again failing to fulfil a set of fundamental domestic obligations to its own citizens. The economy was moribund, with economic policies weakening already debilitated markets. Unemployment and poverty rates were again on the rise, with Zimbabweans again leaving the country in large numbers. The state was once more failing to provide essential infrastructure and public services, properly manage public finances and assets such as those held by state enterprises and parastatals, and service its debts. The key priority, once ZANU-PF had re-established its monopoly on the levers of economic policy, seemed to be to ensure that resources were once again flowing, and as soon as possible, in accordance with regime maintenance objectives.

After it regained control over the Ministry of Finance and the RBZ and therefore the printing presses, the worst fears of Zimbabweans concerning a return to the insanity of the crisis years were confirmed when in May 2016, for the first time since the abolition of the Zimbabwe dollar in 2009, the Reserve Bank announced plans to resume the printing of *de facto* local bank notes in the form of Bond Notes to solve its 'cash crisis', namely the lack of US dollars. Significantly, and in a clear sign of a full-blown return to the standard ZANU-PF style of governance, Mugabe used his prerogatives under the Presidential Powers (Temporary Measures) Act to sign into law the required statutory instrument amending the RBZ Act while completely sidelining Parliament, thus providing the legal framework for the issuing of bond notes. Whilst retaining the existing multi-currency system, the RBZ argued (all evidence to the contrary) that these non-convertible bond notes did not represent a return to a local currency. They were pegged at parity with the US dollar, their 'value' being announced with pride by the President. Within a few months after their release in November 2016, they were already trading at a discount of between 5 percent and 7 percent against the US dollar (IMF 2017a, 10).

The liquidity crisis was due to poor export receipts arising from both declining global commodity prices and weak export competitiveness of the manufacturing and agriculture sectors, with merchandise exports falling from US$3.99 billion in 2012 to an estimated US$3.7 billion in 2016. In addition there was negligible FDI, which fell from US$351 million in 2012 to a projected US$132 million in 2017 (Ibid., 22), and stagnant (in US dollar terms) diaspora remittances through formal channels. The fall in the latter is partly attributable to a drop in the value of the South African Rand against the US dollar (South Africa being a major source of Zimbabwe Diaspora remittances), but also a preference on the part of remitters to continue to use informal channels and steer clear of the local banking system. Such stagnation in the level of remittances had taken place despite the RBZ's renewed efforts to, once again, encourage the channelling of remittances through formal channels by providing a percentage bonus in the form of bond notes of the value of the funds sent.

The search for unorthodox responses to the liquidity crisis, and the deterioration in the country's external position, were given increased urgency as hopes were dashed that a solution to the external debt problems had finally been found leading to debt forgiveness and access to new loans on concessional terms. In the wake of the so-called 'Lima Agreement' of October 2015 – concluded during the IMF/World Bank meeting in Peru and which set out terms for re-engagement spearheaded by the repayment of around \$1.8 billion in arrears that Zimbabwe then owed the IMF, World Bank and African Development Bank – Zimbabwe finally settled its arrears to the IMF's PRGF in October 2016 by drawing down on remnants of its 2009 SDR allocation from the IMF (see Chap. 10). Replacing the ZAADDS debt management strategy of 2012 referenced in Chap. 10, in late 2015 Harare developed a new framework (GOZ 2015).

However, the proposals put forward by Finance Minister Chinamasa to fund clearance of arrears to the World Bank and African Development Bank, through the contracting of additional loans from bilateral creditors and syndicated loans from foreign banks, did not gain traction amongst the IFIs. As a result of the failure to resolve arrears with other official creditors, and continued lack of progress with implementation of fiscal adjustments and structural reforms aimed at ensuring debt sustainability, expectations that the country would find lasting solutions to its arrears problem, and thereby regain access to funding from both bilaterals and multilaterals, proved misplaced. This would not have been a surprise to seasoned observers of Zimbabwe's economics, for whom the prospects of such measures ever being introduced by the ruling party were minimal, as amongst the structural reforms still judged to be outstanding were "measures to increase transparency in the mining sector, support property rights, and reduce fears of expropriation" (IMF 2017a, 6), and which necessarily implied an overhaul of the foundational *modus operandi* of the extractive economic institutions over which ZANU-PF presided.

By the end of 2016 Zimbabwe's total external debt had risen from US$7.25 billion in 2013, representing 47.6 percent of GDP, to US$9.35 billion and 58.0 percent of GDP, of which US$7.23 billion was Public and Publicly Guaranteed (PPG) debt and the remainder private sector debt. In an indication of the extent of arrears accumulation, of the US$7.23 billion PPG debt, US$5.01 billion was arrears against outstanding principal of US$2.21 billion (IMF 2017b, 5). If its external debt to GDP ratio was significantly lower that it had been at the height of the country's economic meltdown in 2008, due to positive growth rates between 2009 and 2013 under the IG which had seen GDP (in current US dollars) rise from a historic low of US$4.41 billion to US$14.05 billion, the IMF nevertheless pointed out that Zimbabwe was still very much in debt distress, with its PPG external debt representing 168.8 percent of exports and 192.3 percent of government revenue in 2016 (Ibid., 10).

As a solution to the external debt problem remained elusive and foreign currency dried up, this drove renewed dirigisme. Economic extraction was soon back in full force. Daily withdrawal limits were re-imposed on bank accounts (with clients obliged to accept a mixture of US dollars and bond notes), exporters were again compelled to partially or totally surrender their foreign exchange earnings and accept bond notes and electronic balances in exchange, and an amalgam of import and currency controls and higher protective import tariffs were put in place. In addition to bond notes, and in an effort to plug its ever increasing budget deficit which soared from US$80 million in 2012 under Tendai Biti's programme of fiscal restraint to US$1.46 billion by 2016 (Ibid., 23), and revelling in its re-established monetary and fiscal independence, the government took with relish to the issuing of Treasury Bills which to all intents and purposes were treated by the Ministry of Finance as another 'quasi-currency'. Government also benefitted from an overdraft facility from the RBZ of US$961 million, with the RBZ in turn borrowing from commercial banks; in a replay of the emergency plugging of holes that characterised fiscal and monetary policy during the crisis decade, given that the RBZ could not honour its loan repayments to them it then authorised commercial banks to introduce the aforementioned withdrawal limits on accounts (World Bank 2017, 1).

Over a period of only four years, domestic debt rose from US$287 million in 2012 to an estimated US$4 billion in 2016, representing close to 25 percent of GDP (IMF 2017a, 21). One effect of this renewed domestic borrowing by Government, and another aspect of increased state intervention in the economy after the IG, was that lending to the private sector was crowded out. If in 2012 annual growth in credit to the private sector stood at 27.1 percent, by 2017 this was projected to have moved into negative territory, shrinking by 10 percent (Ibid., 21). By 2017, government borrowing, accounting for almost half total domestic credit, was a serious threat to banking sector stability, because lending to the state was heavily concentrated in a handful of domestic banks. Because domestic debt is denominated in US dollars, its explosive growth since 2012 was tantamount to a 64 percent increase in the state's US dollar exposure, taking the total to almost $15 billion, or 90 percent of GDP.

A new burst of dirigisme was also evident in the Reserve Bank's return to quasi-fiscal activities, with a new Governor providing information in his Mid-Term Monetary Policy Statement of August 2017 on the extent of the Central Bank's engagement in what he described as "supply-side funding initiatives" (RBZ 2017, 6). So, for example, regarding the period January–June 2017, the public were informed that through its 'Supplementary Funding' operations, the RBZ used the US$886 million received under its Foreign Exchange Management System to pay, *inter alia,* US$193 million for fuel imports, US$41.6 million for fertiliser, US$31.6 million on machinery and spares, US$60.2 million on grain and wheat, US$2.3 million on vehicles and US$3.4 million on agricultural equipment (Ibid., 15).

Unsurprisingly given its past role as lender of last resort to the regime and its quasi-fiscal interventions during the crisis decade to purchase support for the ruling party and provide opportunities for personal enrichment, suspicions were raised that RBZ resources were once again being allocated, with eyes firmly fixed on the 2018 elections, to meet regime survival needs and fulfil electoral promises made in 2013 of "something for everyone". In terms of beneficiaries, the Policy Statement made only a passing reference the "business linkages fund…women empowerment fund, youth empowerment fund, horticulture support facility" (Ibid., 6) all under the aegis of ZANU-PF controlled state institutions, providing further opportunities, as in the past, to secure the political loyalty of recipients and opportunities for some personal enrichment.[18]

The same imperatives also seemed to underpin the launch of a new agricultural support scheme in 2016. The 'Specialised Maize and Production and Import Substitution Programme', more commonly known as the Command Agriculture Programme, was spearheaded by Vice-President Emmerson Mnangagwa. The latter was a long-standing Mugabe loyalist, widely seen as Mugabe's 'enforcer' who enjoyed strong liberation struggle credentials and links to the security forces and war veterans, and who had, amongst other positions, been Minister of State Security in the 1980s and Minister of Defence between 2009 and 2013. Together with new funding for the Presidential Inputs Scheme which targeted small farmers, both these initiatives were clearly designed with an eye to the forthcoming elections, and in the case of Command Agriculture to Mnangagwa's own Presidential ambitions.

As details of the Command agriculture programme emerged, it became increasingly redolent of the various support programmes of the former Governor of the Reserve Bank, such as the costly and ill-fated Agriculture Mechanisation Programme. Aimed at 2,000 individual farmers who would each commit to plant 200 hectares under maize, with a minimum total target of 2 million tonnes of maize, the hectarage conditionality of the Command Agriculture Programme meant that beneficiaries would necessarily be the larger A2 farmers, many key pillars of the regime made up of members of Government and Parliament, the judiciary, senior commanders of the security forces and civil service who had secured large holdings from former white commercial farms during the FTLRP. Each farmer was to receive inputs to the value of US$250,000, in exchange for which they were to commit to deliver 1,000 tonnes of maize to the GMB, and allowed to retain any surplus. They were additionally assisted by the GMB adopting a fixed buying price for 2016 of US$390/tonne, twice that of the prevailing international price (IMF 2017a, b, 13), which would mean rapid repayment of their debt, as well as opening up significant opportunities for arbitrage. Even assuming the recovery rates on the loans would be better than the negligible rates seen under the various RBZ support schemes of the 2000s, the programme in effect represented a significant transfer of resources to politically important beneficiaries, with the state incurring further debt as Treasury Bills were issued to raise the necessary funding (*Financial Gazette* 2017), and this notwithstanding initial claims that this was going to be a fully private sector-driven initiative.

There were reports that Command Agriculture, like so many aspects of Zimbabwe's economic life, was also being militarised, with senior officers deployed to oversee its implementation and soldiers used to ensure that farmers did not hold on to their harvests. In a further sign that ZANU-PF's style of economic management was firmly back in place, despite government's announcements that the programme meant the country could expect a 'bumper harvest' and thereby fulfil pledges contained both in its 2013 election manifesto and Zim Asset to recover the country's 'bread basket' status, by July 2017 only a fraction of the forecast 2.1 million tonnes of maize had been delivered to the GMB (*Daily News* 2017a).

Fiscal profligacy with a view to the upcoming elections, with little thought given to its longer-term consequences, was also clearly the driver behind the decision to award another key constituency, the War Veterans, with increased payments in August 2017. In a disconcerting repetition of one of the key events which had triggered the onset of Zimbabwe's crisis in 1997, namely the unbudgeted pay out of allowances to war veterans (see Chap. 4), and in the face of growing complaints from the latter that they were still not benefiting from their wartime sacrifices, the new ministry charged with their welfare announced plans to more than double the payments they had extracted from Mugabe in 1997 (*Sunday News* 2017).

In a clear indication of the extent of elite detachment from the deteriorating living conditions facing ordinary Zimbabweans, after the 2013 elections ZANU-PF's attention soon turned inwards, consumed as was so often the case by the question of the succession to Mugabe to the exclusion of more pressing national issues. There was increasingly vicious infighting as Mugabe's wife sought to obtain a senior position within the party, clearly conscious of her own vulnerability and that of her family members, and the possible threat to the riches she had managed to amass when Mugabe eventually died.[19] Her efforts were seen in some quarters as an attempt to ensure a dynastic succession, as well as an indication of the extent to which the country had come to be viewed by the Mugabes as private property.[20]

She successfully secured election to the powerful position of head of ZANU-PF's Women's League in 2014, with the support of a group of 'Young Turks' within ZANU-PF such as Saviour Kasukuwere which came to be known as Generation 40 (G-40), a reference to the average age of the aspirants, while also enjoying the backing of the party's youth wing. This post, in turn, entitled her to a place on the Politburo. En route she struck an alliance with Mnangagwa to ensure the downfall of a rival claimant to the succession, Vice-President Joice Mujuru, who was accused of plotting against Mugabe (*Reuters* 2014). Mujuru was subsequently expelled from ZANU-PF, together with a number of other senior figures who supported her, with Mnangagwa then elevated to the post of Vice-President.

This, however, turned out to be only a temporary marriage of convenience between Grace Mugabe and Mnangagwa. The latter's supporters coalesced into a group known as 'Team Lacoste', a reference to his nickname of 'Crocodile' and the crocodile motif used by the fashion label. Made up of a group of older ZANU-PF figures, many with strong liberation struggle credentials, this faction included senior figures within the country's army, air force, and intelligence services, as well as the leadership of the 'war veterans'. As tensions between the two factions grew, and both Grace Mugabe and Mnangagwa fell out publicly as they made their intentions to succeed Mugabe clear, and with the G-40 group launching increasingly vitriolic attacks on Mnangagwa and his backers within the defence establishment, senior figures within the defence forces voiced their deepening concerns that factionalism was tearing ZANU-PF apart and that the G-40 group was not showing the necessary respect due to the 'old guard' and their liberation credentials (*Zimbabwe Independent* 2016b). As attacks on Mnangagwa increased, it also became clear to Team Lacoste and its military backers that either Mugabe's ability to manage factionalism within the ruling party had been severely compromised as a result of his advanced age, or more significantly for them that he was supportive of his wife's ambitions and those of the G-40 and their plans to side-line the old guard.

As growing numbers of Zimbabweans struggled to put food on the table, and as the promised milk and honey featured in the ruling party's 2013 election manifesto and Zim Asset proved to be yet another chimera, all spare bandwidth within the ruling party not taken up by the internecine struggles, and efforts to secure more assets for patronage purposes, was directed towards ensuring that Mugabe's birthdays were celebrated in a manner befitting the longstanding leader of the ruling revolutionary party, and the country's Head of State and Commander-in-Chief.[21] Against the backdrop of a rapid return to the economic malaise and increasing state fragility of the crisis decade, Mugabe at the age of ninety-one was able at ZANU-PF's annual conference in December 2015 to secure the unanimous endorsement of the party to run for re-election in 2018.

Regime Consolidation: The Old Guard Reasserts Control

Pressure on Mnangagwa and his supporters escalated in the course of October 2017, with a key figure within the G-40 faction, Saviour Kasukuwere and now Minister of Local Government and ZANU-PF political commissar, conducting a purge of Mnangagwa's provincial support base (*NewsDay* 2017b). The writing on the wall in terms of the ascendancy of the G-40 faction also became clearer when Mnangagwa made a presentation to Cabinet on his 'Command Agriculture' initiative in which, as noted above, the military were extensively involved and which many saw as a personal project aimed at strengthening his support base amongst beneficiaries; his request for additional funding was rejected by Cabinet in a decision-making process led by ministers aligned to G-40 (*Zimbabwe Independent* 2017a).

By early November 2017, Grace Mugabe felt sufficiently emboldened and confident of her husband's support to call for Mnangagwa and his supporters to be forcefully dealt with on the grounds of fomenting factionalism and plotting against the President, reportedly stating not only that purges of Team Lacoste members from the ruling party would take place, but also that further punitive measures were to follow. In addition, she announced she was ready to take on the role of Vice-President (*NewsDay* 2017c). On 6th November 2017 Mnangagwa was ousted from his position as Vice-President, and on 8th November a Politburo decision was taken to expel him from the party, according to the party's spokesperson "at the request of the women and youth leagues" aligned to Grace Mugabe (*New Zimbabwe* 2017). Mnangagwa fled the country, and issued statements from South Africa that he would return to overthrow the Mugabes, with elements within ZANU-PF aligned to the Grace Mugabe faction calling for him to be arrested and prosecuted for corruption, a development that would have been taken note of by his supporters within the ruling party and the military elite (*Daily News* 2017b).

Corporatist interests began to make themselves felt as a result of the gradual unravelling of the historically strong compact between Mugabe and the securocrats. With the rise of Grace Mugabe and the G-40, the securocrats had increasingly felt they could no longer rely on these mutually supportive ties, previously viewed as inviolable. Amidst progressively tighter national budgets they came to see that the unspoken principle of privileged and generous allocations to the defence forces they had come to rely on, notwithstanding other pressing national priorities, was no longer sacrosanct. So, for example, in the midst of the growing pressures on Mnangagwa whom they saw as their champion in the corridors of power, commanders in the ZNA expressed dismay that their 2018 budget submission of US$965 million had been slashed to a US$77 million allocation (*The Standard* 2017). The Air Force was also subjected to budget cuts, and its commanders drew the necessary conclusions as regards the intentions of the new Finance Minister appointed in October 2017, Ignatius Chombo, who was known to be a key member of the G-40 group and who had replaced Chinamasa who was linked to Mnangagwa's faction (*NewsDay* 2017d).

In terms of the private economic interests of senior commanders who had benefitted from years of ruling party largesse in the form of farms and agricultural machinery and inputs, privileged access to foreign exchange, sinecures in the parastatal sector and stakes in the mining sector, it also gradually became clear that the rise of the G-40 constituted a threat to their wealth. In a context of increasingly constrained resources, there were few guarantees that with the G-40 in control the latter might not launch another round of spoliation in order to reward its support base, this time with them as targets. If any evidence was required that this was a real possibility, proof positive was provided by news that a police unit had been set up to investigate Mnangagwa's alleged crimes. In addition to murder, the unit's brief included the looting of companies in ZANU-PF's business empire and crimes associated with his mining interests (*Zimbabwe Independent* 2017b).

On 13th November, General Chiwenga in his capacity as Commander of the ZDF called a press conference. In an indication of the extent to which Mugabe's nurturing and elevation of the defence forces to the position of *primus inter pares* amongst Zimbabwe's state institutions, and first and last line of defence for the ruling party, had been internalised by the military elite, Chiwenga, flanked by the heads of the ZNA and Zimbabwe Air Force, stated that the defence forces "remain the major stockholders in respect to the gains of the liberation struggle" and that when "these gains are threatened we are obliged to take corrective measures". Referencing the new Constitution, and liberally interpreting Section 212 which detailed the functions of the defence forces – while also studiously ignoring Section 213 according to which only the Head of State as Commander in Chief of the Defence Forces had the power to authorise the mobilisation of the Defence Forces – Chiwenga warned that if the ongoing purges within ZANU-PF "targeting members associated with our liberation history" and "reckless utterances denigrating the military" were not halted, they "would not hesitate to step in" to deal with the "machinations of counter revolutionaries who have infiltrated the party [and] who were set on returning our country to foreign domination" (*The Zimbabwean* 2017a).

In a serious misreading of the concerns of the military establishment, on 14th November the G-40 aligned leader of ZANU-PF's Youth League read out a statement, another "reckless utterance" which Chiwenga the day before had specifically demanded not be permitted. Confirming the current dominance of the G-40 which now clearly enjoyed Mugabe's blessing, Chiwenga was warned that the ZANU-PF's youth wing would not allow "any individual military man [to] interfere with the leader of the party and legitimately voted President of this country Cde Robert Gabriel Mugabe" And further confirming suspicions that another round of dispossession might take place under the leadership of the G-40, and that this time the axe might fall on the military elite, the youth leader went on to state that:

> As Commander of the Defence Forces Cde Chiwenga, we await a full report on the whereabouts of the 15 billion dollars as the army never accounted for the [diamond] revenue after extraction…He cannot benefit from his own mischief and misdeeds in that together with former Minister of Defence Cde Dambudzo Mnangagwa, they dismally failed in the stewardship of revenue streams that flowed from diamond concessions allocated to the Defence Forces…A day will come when those responsible will have to account to the people. (*The Herald* 2017b)

Further provocation took place on 14th November, when the spokesman for the ruling party issued a statement in which Chiwenga's comments were characterised as "treasonable conduct on his part as this was meant to incite insurrection and violent challenge to the constitutional order" (*The Herald* 2017c).

Thereafter the ZDF moved quickly, and in the early hours of 15th November military vehicles and troops moved into Harare. They took control of the state broadcaster, ZANU-PF headquarters and Parliament, and restricted the Mugabe family to their private residence in an operation which the military – aware of possible opprobrium from the AU and SADC given their proscriptions on military coups – insisted was not a coup but simply a mission targeting "criminals" surrounding Mugabe.

The next day negotiations between Mugabe and senior military figures led by Chiwenga began, with reports that despite offers from the armed forces to grant him an honourable exit Mugabe was proving stubborn and refusing to resign. On the 16th November *The Herald*, clearly now changed from mouthpiece of the G-40 into that of Mnangagwa and the military establishment, editorialised that the military intervention would help in "rekindling the revolutionary spirit which has made Zanu-PF a household name in Zimbabwe and beyond…which was unfortunately being soiled by those who should be helping the President in his duties" (*The Herald* 2017d).

Against the backdrop of reports that Mnangagwa was planning to return to Zimbabwe, on 19th November the Central Committee of ZANU-PF met and voted to "recall" Mugabe as President and First Secretary of the party. Mnangagwa's previous expulsion was nullified, and he was elected party leader and selected as the party's presidential candidate for the upcoming 2018 elections, while Grace Mugabe and other G-40 heavy weights such as Saviour Kasukuwere and Ignatius Chombo were ejected from the party. The body also resolved that if Mugabe did not resign as Head of State and Government by midday on 20th November, ZANU-PF's Parliamentary Chief Whip was instructed to initiate impeachment proceedings. Faced with the threat of being ignominiously impeached as President of the Republic of Zimbabwe by a Parliament which he had fought so hard to ensure was dominated by ZANU-PF, Mugabe eventually tendered his resignation on 21st November 2017.

The next day ZANU-PF nominated Mnangagwa to replace Mugabe as President of the Republic, and on 24th November 2017 he was sworn in. Amidst calls for a new inclusive interim government to be established to oversee reforms prior to elections set for 2018, coupled with advice that a new government might need some new faces in order to reengage with the West (and in an early indication of the triumphalist mind-set within the new dominant ZANU-PF faction), a key member of the Mnangagwa group reportedly responded that "we were correcting our own mess, we have the majority in Parliament, we can expel the President alone and we are the ruling party, so where does a coalition come in?" (*The Zimbabwean* 2017b).

Notes

1. A single Independent candidate picked up the remaining House of Assembly seat.
2. The Constitutional Court upheld the results, and confirmed Mugabe as the winner of the Presidential race.
3. ZESN, with over 7,000 observers deployed, produced a report, but this was only released on 13th September 2013 (ZESN 2013).
4. As was so often the case with the issue of Zimbabwe, the sole voice of dissent within SADC circles was Botswana, which argued to no avail that evidence of electoral irregularities was sufficiently compelling to merit an independent audit of the results.

5. One of the last actions taken by Tendai Biti as Minister of Finance had been to negotiate an SMP with the BWIs in June 2013. This allowed the IMF to provide Zimbabwe with technical assistance for the first time since the 'declaration of non-cooperation' by the IMF's Executive Board in 2002 (see Chap. 8). Partly because of that year's elections, little progress was made in implementing the policies set out in the SMP. The new ZANU-PF government was to express a commitment to seeing through the policies and reforms in the SMP initiated by the previous IG. The IMF agreed to extend the SMP, which was renewed until mid-2014. Despite this, key targets were missed including measures to ensure diamond revenue transparency, new mining legislation, recapitalisation of the central bank and a reduction in the public sector wage bill as a proportion of government spending.
6. The report reiterated the fundamental importance of this area, noting that "Where governments make registration easier, more entrepreneurs start businesses in the formal sector, creating more good jobs and generating more revenue for the government" (World Bank 2016, 17). For Zimbabwe, given its fiscal constraints, as well as the key funding assumptions of Zim Asset namely that the plan would be partly funded from tax and non-tax revenues, this variable took on even greater importance.
7. Zimbabwe's 'Look East' policy, and the supportive role Beijing had played internationally as a 'friend' of Zimbabwe in international fora such as the UN Security Council, was also strained. In the course of meetings between Chinese and Zimbabwean officials on the side-lines of the World Economic Forum meeting in Switzerland that year, the latter informed the Zimbabweans of their concerns that Harare was in arrears in terms of repayment of Chinese loans, though the objectives, amounts and conditions were not publicised given the secrecy surrounding the loans (*AFRIK NEWS* 2010). Beijing was to issue an even sterner warning to Zimbabwe in January 2016 when Harare moved to seize all diamond mining claims in the context of its indigenisation policy, negatively affecting two Chinese companies. Beijing called upon the Zimbabwean government to respect the China-Zimbabwe Bilateral Investment Promotion and Protection Agreement signed in 1996, thus finding itself in illustrious company, even if in a crowded field, of numerous other countries who had tried to enforce their respective BIPPAs with Harare (*Daily News* 2016).

8. In a further sign that 'something for nothing' remained the order of the day as far as economic policy was concerned, and a reminder of the role state companies played in the system of largesse distribution, Zim Asset contained a commitment to cancel US$80 million of debt owed by farmers to the state power company, and which would only further weaken its financial position and capacity to operate (GOZ 2013, 38). In October 2013 the power utility was instructed to cancel the debts it was owed by consumers, both households and farmers, amounting to an estimated US$170 million. 'Something for everyone', one of the slogans used in the ruling party's 2013 election manifesto, was clearly being zealously implemented, with little thought given to the longer-term consequences for the company's operations.
9. It was noteworthy that the report also referenced the failure of Tsvangirai's Office of the Prime Minister to account for expenditures to the tune of US$15 million (*Financial Gazette* 2014).
10. Little progress was made in terms of reducing the public sector wage bill notwithstanding the flushing out of large numbers of 'ghost workers' during the IG (see Chap. 10). Fulfilling its electoral commitment to improve the wages of public sector workers, the new government had granted wage increases such that the IMF estimated that total employment costs would represent 79 percent of projected revenue for 2014 (IMF 2014, 12).
11. In the case of the Zimbabwe National Road Administration (ZINARA), payments unsupported by authorised payment vouchers amounted to US$4.15 million (Office of the Auditor-General 2015, 45).
12. In the case of the Civil Aviation Authority of Zimbabwe (CAAZ), these debts amounted to US$242 million (Ibid., 3).
13. A particularly strong 'Adverse Opinion' was reserved for the ZMDC, in which the opacity of its operations was highlighted, with the Auditor-General concluding that "the Group financial statements do not give a true and fair view of the financial position of the Zimbabwe Mining Development Corporation and its subsidiaries as at 31 December 2014" (Office of the Auditor General 2015, 137). The report would have been of particular interest to those who during the IG had raised concerns, including the then MDC-T Finance Minister, regarding the amounts Treasury was receiving from diamond operations and specifically the operations of Anjin, the private Chinese mining company operating in Chiadzwa/Marange diamond areas (see Chap. 12). Under a joint venture with

ZMDC, Anjin was supposed to pay a resource depletion fee of 3 percent of its gross revenue to the ZMDC. This had amounted to only US$3.24 million for 2013. The Auditor–General noted in the report that she had been "unable to obtain sufficient appropriate audit evidence on the completeness and accuracy of the 3% share of revenue as no financial information was availed from Anjin Investments (Private) Limited" (Ibid., 135). Further evidence that the ZMDC had become a body operating outside the country's regulatory framework, included the fact that while its organisational structure had 108 approved positions, the actual staff number on the payroll was 133 (Ibid., 153), it had failed to pay taxes and income taxes amounting to US$5.25 million, and had not remitted employer and employee contributions to pension funds (Ibid., 146).

14. In the course of his 2014 budget presentation, the new Finance Minister disclosed that maize output for the 2013 season had fallen to just under 800,000 tonnes, down from 968,000 tonnes in 2012. This against a national requirement of around 2 million tonnes, with needs having to be met through imports and donor-funded emergency food assistance.
15. There were reports that the US$30 million actually raised from the country's corporate sector prior to the 2013 elections, and earmarked for a range of community trusts, was used to oil ZANU-PF's elections machinery (*Zimbabwe Independent* 2014c).
16. The WJP is an initiative of the American Bar Association, launched in 2006 and based in Washington, D.C. The project's focus is on assessing "a nation's adherence to the rule of law from the bottom up, that is, from the perspective of ordinary people who are directly affected by the degree of rule of law in their societies" (WJP 2012–13, 7).
17. The eight factors covered in the WJP surveys are: 1. Limited Government Powers (which included sub-factors such as extent to which government powers were limited by the legislature and the judiciary, and government officials were sanctioned for misconduct); 2. Absence of corruption (in the legislative, executive and judicial branches of government as well as in the police and military); 3. Order and Security (with sub-factors such as the extent to which civil conflict is effectively limited); 4. Fundamental Rights (sub-factors including due process of the law, and freedom of opinion, expression, assembly and association); 5. Open Government (including the degree to which official information is available); 6. Regulatory Enforcement (covering sub-factors such as extent to which Government Regulations were applied without improper influence and

properly enforced, and the Government does not expropriate without adequate compensation); 7. Civil Justice (with sub-factors such as the access of people to affordable civil justice, the extent to which it is effectively enforced, and free of corruption and undue government interference). 8. Criminal Justice (including the effectiveness of the criminal investigation system, and the extent to which the criminal justice system is free of corruption and improper government influence).

18. Regarding the Youth Fund, just three months prior to the Monetary Policy Statement, the Parliament Portfolio Committee on Youth Development, Indigenization and Economic Empowerment conducted an inquiry into the Fund's operations, concluding that US$40 million could not be accounted for, and that 95 percent of projects for which funds were disbursed were either non-existent or had collapsed (*NewsDay* 2017a).
19. Known amongst Zimbabwe's wits as 'DisGrace', 'Grasping Grace' or the 'First Shopper', following her 1996 marriage to the President, First Lady Grace Mugabe rapidly acquired a reputation for ostentatious living and acquisitiveness, the former through her foreign shopping trips and mansions she was reported to have built around the country, and the latter through her seizure of a number of white-owned commercial farms during the FTLRP. In an effort to build credibility within ZANU-PF, in 2014 she secured a PhD in Sociology from the University of Zimbabwe (of which her husband was Chancellor). The academic qualification was achieved in record time a few months after registering for the programme, (though the subsequent efforts of investigative journalists to track down a copy of the doctoral thesis in the university libraries proved fruitless). Streets around the country were soon being renamed in honour of Dr. Grace Mugabe.
20. Further evidence of the country being turned into a family business was provided by the appointment of Mugabe's nephew to the post of Minister of Youth, Indigenisation and Economic Empowerment in the new Cabinet.
21. The costs of these celebrations were regularly estimated at over US$1 million a time, with wildlife, including elephants, being shot to feed the tens of thousands of invited guests, and private companies being 'encouraged' to make financial contributions to support the festivities.

References

AFRIK NEWS. 2010. China Warns Zimbabwe: We Are Not 'Friends', February 22.

Bulawayo24. 2014. Salarygate – Zimbabweans Sold a Dummy, March 28. http://bulawayo24.com/index-id-opinion-sc-columnist-byo-45082.html.

Business Day. 2013. Bennett Wants Tsvangirai to Quit as MDC-T Leader, September 11. Harare

Daily News. 2014a. Leadership Renewal Only Way to Save MDC, February 24. Harare

———. 2014b. Zimbabwe Government Clueless, as Economy Burns, March 21. Harare

———. 2014c. Zimbabwe Government Appeals to the Private Sector, April 1. Harare

———. 2014d. Brazil Rules Out ZimAsset Funding, May 20. Harare

———. 2016. China Warns Zimbabwe over Mine Grabs, March 1. Harare

———. 2017a. Command Agriculture: Govt Ropes in Soldiers, August 22. Harare

———. 2017b. Probe, Arrest Mnangagwa, November 10. Harare

Financial Gazette. 2014. Zimbabwe Government Fails to Account for US$140 Million, March 27. Harare

———. 2017. US$50m Bond for Command Agriculture, July15. Harare

GOZ. 2013. *Zimbabwe Agenda for Sustainable Socio-Economic Transformation (Zim Asset) 'Towards an Empowered Society and a Growing Economy' October 2013–December 2018.* Harare.

———. 2015. *Strategies for Clearing External Debt Arrears and the Supportive Economic Reform Agenda*, September. Harare.

IMF. 2014. *Zimbabwe – Staff Report for the Article IV Consultation-Press Release; Staff Report; and Statement by the Executive Director for Zimbabwe*, IMF Country Report No. 14/202, July. Washington, DC.

———. 2017a. *Zimbabwe – Staff Report for the Article IV Consultations – Press Release; Staff Report; and Statement by the Executive Director for Zimbabwe*, IMF Country Report No. 17/197, July. Washington, DC.

———. 2017b. *Zimbabwe – Staff Report for the Article IV Consultations-Debt Sustainability Analysis*, June16. Washington, DC.

Magaisa, Alex. 2017. *Big Saturday Read: Battle for Hearts and Minds of Rural Zimbabwe*, June 10. https://www.bigsr.co.uk/single-post/2017/06/10/Big-Saturday-Read-Battle-for-hearts-and-minds-inrural-Zimbabwe.

Mugabe, R.G. 2013a. *Transcript – Mugabe's Inauguration Speech 22 August 2013.* http://www.zimbabwesituation.com/news/transcript-mugabes-inauguration-speech-22-august-2013/.

———. 2013b. *Mugabe's 2013 UN Speech – Full Transcript 26 August 2013.* http://www.zimbabwesituation.com/news/mugabes-2013-un-speech-full-transcript/.

Nehanda Radio. 2014. Tendai Biti's Harare Home Petrol Bombed, Again, February 25. http://nehandaradio.com/2014/02/25/bitis-harare-home-petrol-bombed.

New Zimbabwe. 2014. Fresh Waves Flee Worsening Economy, March 22.

———. 2017. Mnangagwa Fired from Zanu PF, November 8.

NewsDay. 2014a. Zimra Warns of Company Closures, January 24.

———. 2014b. Zimbabwe Records 75 Company Closures, over 9,000 Jobs Losses, February 21.

———. 2014c. Former MDC-T Ministers Were in Government to Make Up Numbers, March 15.

———. 2017a. Youth Disillusioned as Empowerment Fund Is Looted, July 8.

———. 2017b. Mnangagwa Allies Cry Foul, October 30.

———. 2017c. Mnangagwa Out-Grace, November 6.

———. 2017d. Airforce Bemoans Low Budgetary Allocation, November 15.

Office of the Auditor General. 2015. *Report of the Auditor-General, 2015*. Harare.

Parliament of Zimbabwe. *Constitution of Zimbabwe Amendment (No.1) Bill 2017*. Harare.

RBZ. 2017. *Mid-Term Monetary Policy Statement*, August 2. Harare.

Reuters. 2014. Zimbabwe's Mugabe Fires Deputy, Seven Ministers, December 9. https://www.reuters.com/article/us-zimbabwe-mujuru-idUSKBN0JN0P420141209.

Sunday News. 2017. War Vets to Earn $500 Per Month, August 20. Harare.

The Herald. 2014. PSMAS Shock Salary Schedule, January 23. Harare.

———. 2015. President Appoints Permanent Secretaries, April 16. Harare.

———. 2017a. Amendment Bill Passed-Zanu-PF Flexes Majority Muscle-President Set to Appoint Judges, July 26. Harare.

———. 2017b. In Defence of the Revolution, People's Rights, November 15. Harare.

———. 2017c. Zanu-PF Unfazed by Chiwenga…Raps Him for Treasonous Statements…Reaffirms Primacy of Politics over Gun, November 15. Harare.

———. 2017d. EDITORIAL COMMENT: Custodians Returning Revolution to Source. Harare.
The Standard. 2017. General Warns of Security 'Threat', November 12. Harare.
The Zimbabwean. 2017a. WATCH: BREAKING: Zimbabwe Army Chief Warns Mugabe's Party After VP Sacked, November 15. http://www.zimbabwesituation.com/news/watch-breaking-zimbabwe-army-chief-warns-mugabes-party-after-vp-sacked.
———. 2017b. Zimbabwe: Choosing Between the Devil and Lucifer, November 23. Harare.
Transparency International. 2015. *People and Corruption: Africa Survey 2015*. Berlin.
UN-OCHA. 2014. *Humanitarian Bulletin: Southern Africa*, No. 14, February. New York: UN-Office for the Coordination of Humanitarian Affairs.
———. 2016a. *Humanitarian Needs Overview 2016 – Zimbabwe*, March. New York: UN-Office for the Coordination of Humanitarian Affairs.
———. 2016b. *Zimbabwe Country Profile*, October. https://www.unocha.org/legacy/southern-and-eastern-africa/country-profiles/zimbabwe.
WJP. 2013. *Rule of Law Index Report 2012–2013*. Washington, DC: World Justice Project.
———. 2015. *Rule of Law Index 2015*. Washington, DC: World Justice Project.
World Bank. 2016. *Doing Business 2016: Measuring Regulatory Quality and Efficiency-Economy Profile Zimbabwe*. Washington, DC.
———. 2017. *Macro Poverty Outlook for Zimbabwe*, April. Washington, DC.
ZANU-PF. 2013. *Team ZANU-PF 2013*. Harare.
ZEC. 2013. *Harmonised Elections Report 2013*. Harare.
ZESN. 2013. *Advance Harmonised Election Report 2013*. Harare: Zimbabwe Elections Support Network.
Zimbabwe Independent. 2014a. No Chinese Money for Desperate Chinamasa, January 24. Harare.
———. 2014b. Democracy Must Not Be a Mere Slogan, February 21. Harare.
———. 2014c. Wadyajena, Kasukuwere War Opens Can of Worms, August 14. Harare.
———. 2015. Gov't Farm Invasion Threats Spark Anxiety, March 13. Harare.
———. 2016a. Tobacco Farmers Languish in Poverty, April 8. Harare
———. 2016b. Army Resistance Shocks Mugabe, April 29. Harare.
———. 2017a. Cabinet Rejects Mnangagwa Proposal, November 3. Harare.
———. 2017b. Ousted VP Faces Arrest, November 10. Harare.

Index[1]

[1] Note: Page numbers followed by 'n' refer to notes.

M. Simpson, T. Hawkins, *The Primacy of Regime Survival*,
https://doi.org/10.1007/978-3-319-72520-8

D

E

The manufacturer's authorised representative in the EU is Springer Nature Customer Service Centre GmbH, Europaplatz 3, 69115 Heidelberg, Germany. If you have any concerns regarding our products, please contact ProductSafety@springernature.com

Printed and bound by CPI Group (UK) Ltd, Croydon, CR0 4YY
30/09/2026
02225597-0011